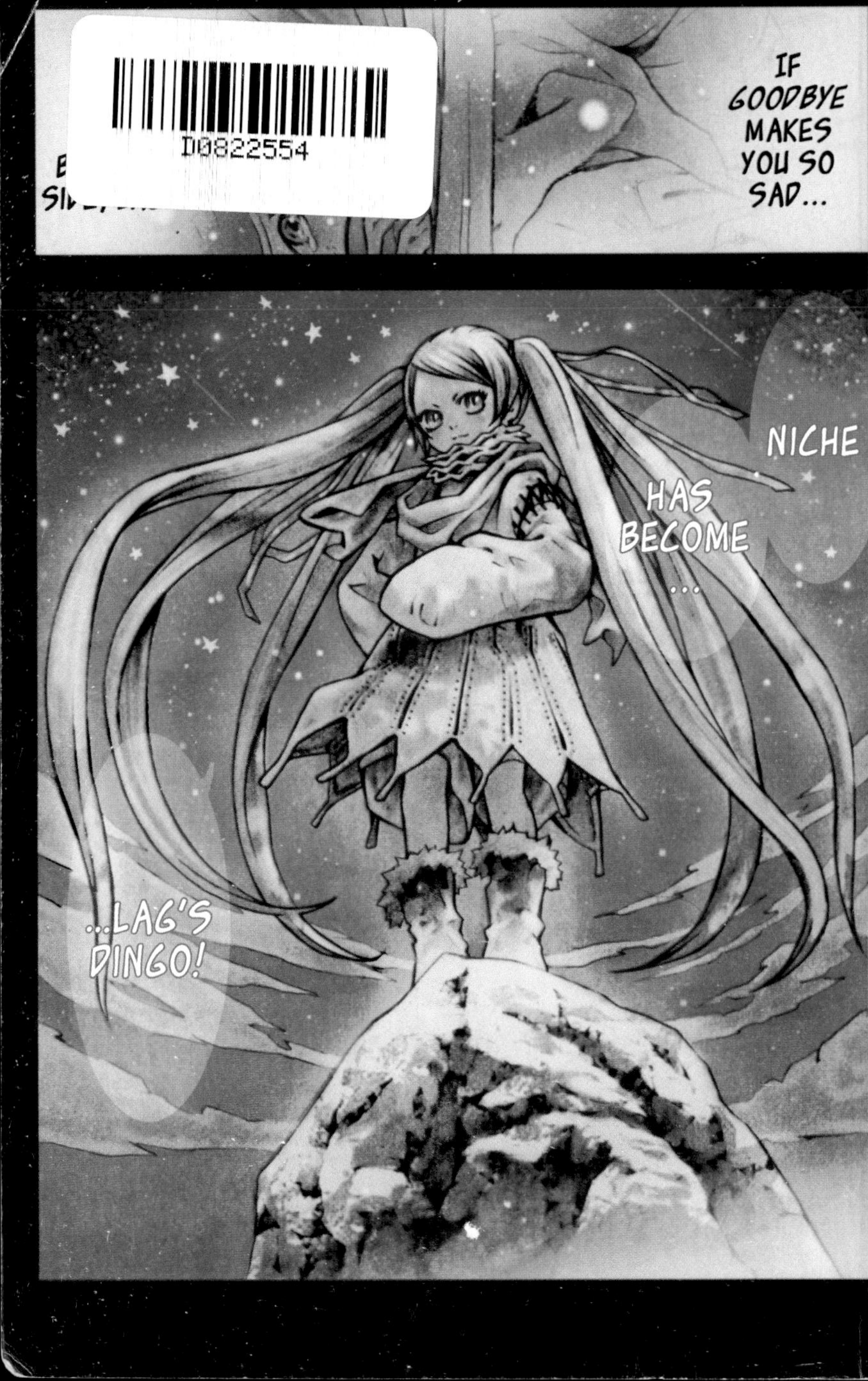
IF GOODBYE MAKES YOU SO SAD...
NICHE
HAS BECOME ...
...LAG'S DINGO!

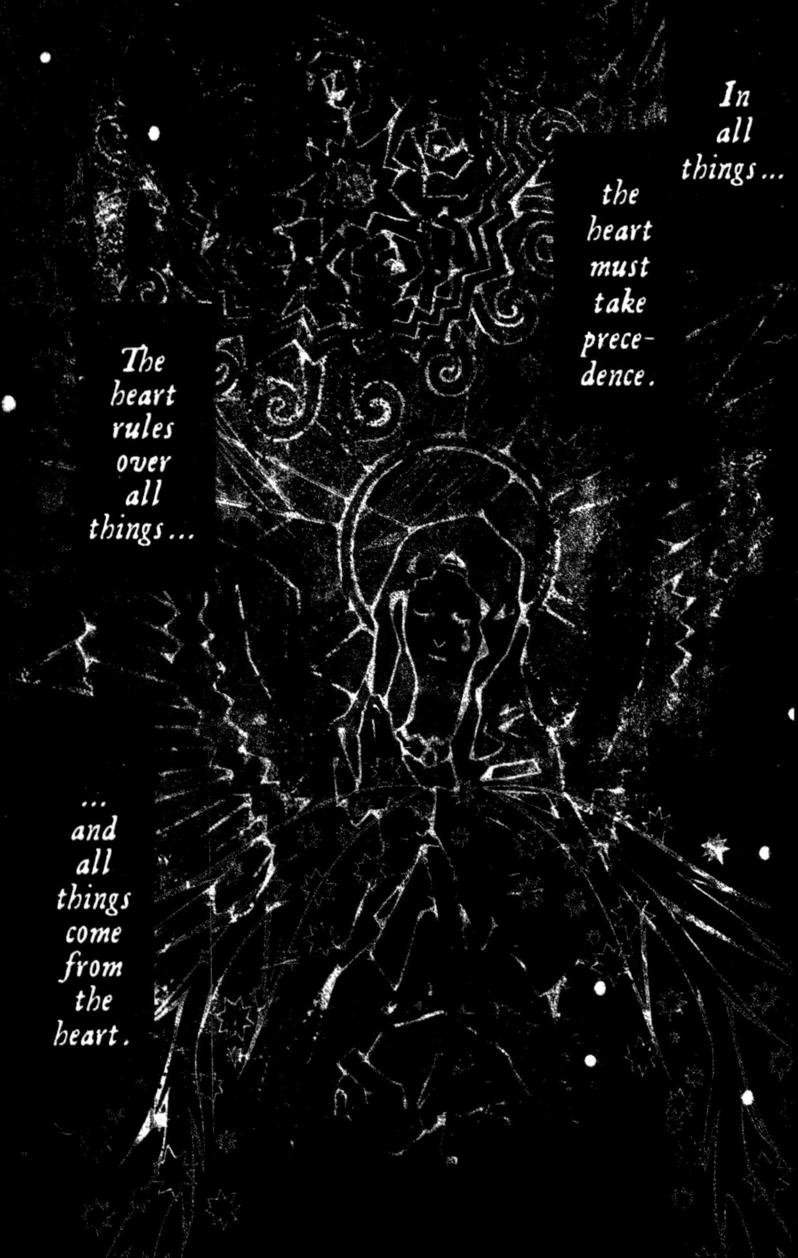
In all things...
the heart must take precedence.
The heart rules over all things...
... and all things come from the heart.

–THE SCRIPTURES OF AMBERGROUND, 1st verse

Tegami Bachi

LETTER · BEE

VOLUME 2

THE LETTER TO JIGGY PEPPER

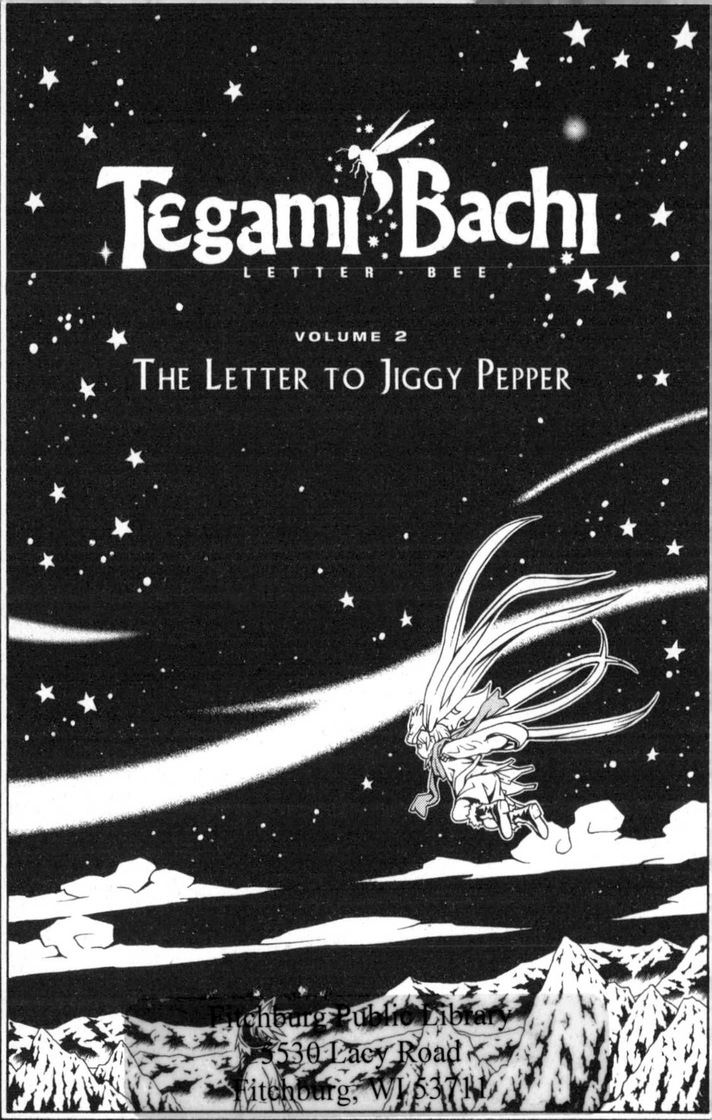

STORY AND ART BY
HIROYUKI ASADA

This is a country known as Amberground, where night never ends.

Its capital, Akatsuki, is illuminated by a man-made sun. The farther one strays from the capital, the weaker the light. The Yuusari region is cast in twilight; the Yodaka region survives only on pale moonlight.

Letter Bee Gauche Suede and young Lag Seeing meet in Yodaka—a postal worker and the "letter" he must deliver.

Gauche is the sole support for his young, wheelchair-bound sister, and Lag has been marked for delivery to an unfamiliar place after his mother is abducted by strange men. Each begins the journey burdened with his own sadness, but as they endure the rain and fog and fight off the gigantic metal insects known as Gaichuu, they forge a strong bond of friendship. At their journey's end, they go their separate ways: Gauche is promoted to Akatsuki, where he can earn the money to cure his sister. Lag determines to become a Letter Bee like Gauche.

Five years later, Lag sets out for Yuusari to take the Letter Bee exam. On the way, he finds a strange young girl in a niche at the train station, marked for delivery with inadequate postage. Lag names her Niche and offers to deliver her. However, the recipient turns out to be the owner of a freakshow that plans on exhibiting Niche as the "Child of Maka." Lag rushes to save her, but Niche has already escaped to the forest, where she encounters a Gaichuu. In the nick of time, Lag arrives and destroys the Gaichuu, winning Niche's trust. And so Lag continues his journey with Niche as his trusty dingo.

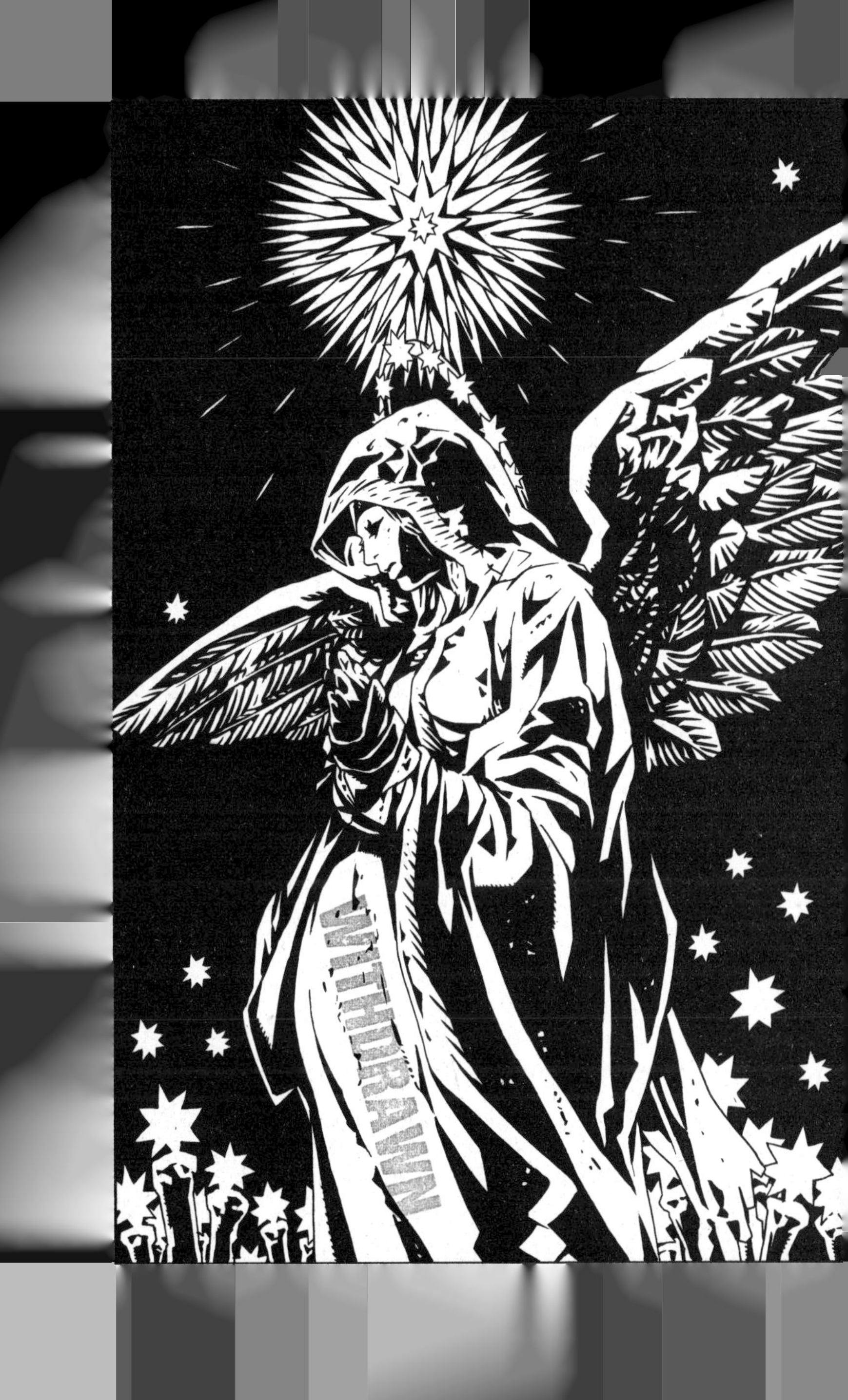

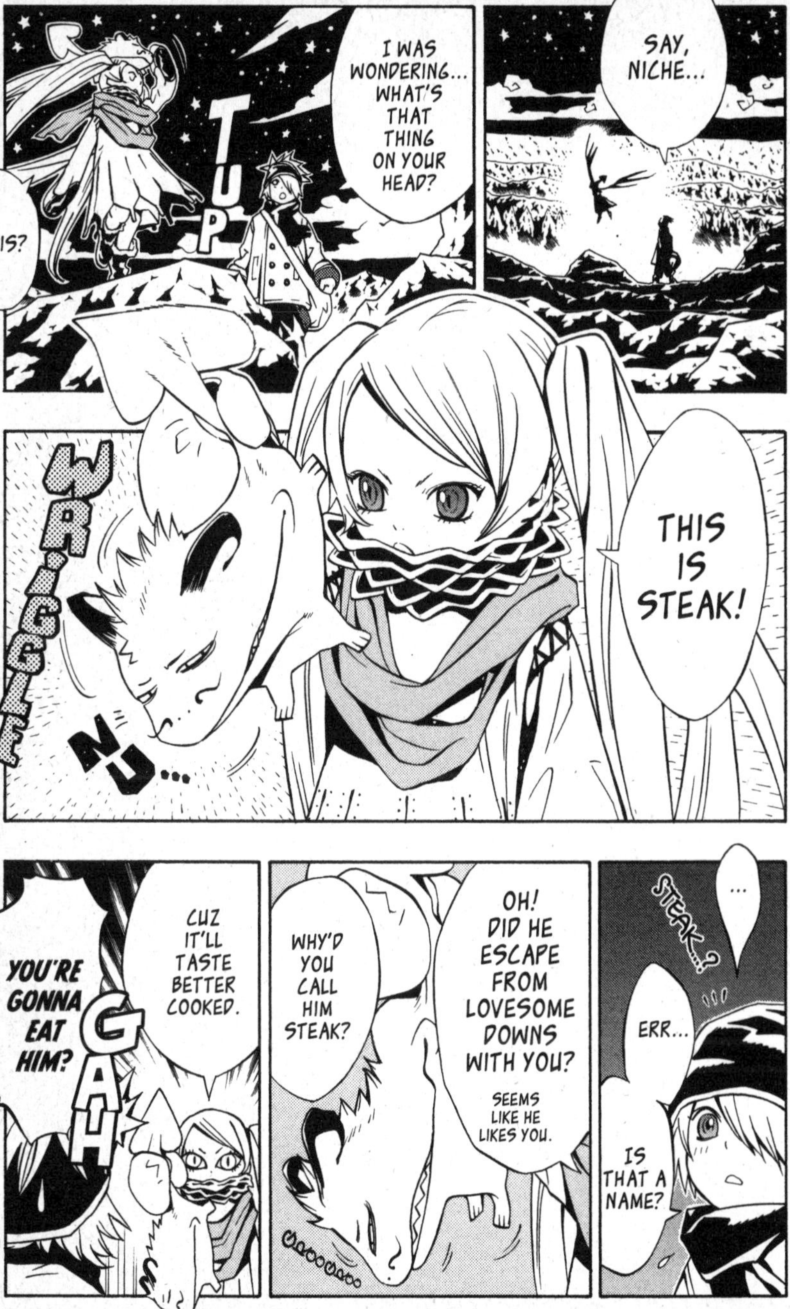
SAY, NICHE...
I WAS WONDERING... WHAT'S THAT THING ON YOUR HEAD?
TUP
THIS?
THIS IS STEAK!
WRIGGLE
NU...
STEAK...?
...
ERR...
IS THAT A NAME?
OH! DID HE ESCAPE FROM LOVESOME DOWNS WITH YOU?
SEEMS LIKE HE LIKES YOU.
WHY'D YOU CALL HIM STEAK?
CUZ IT'LL TASTE BETTER COOKED.
YOU'RE GONNA EAT HIM?
GAH

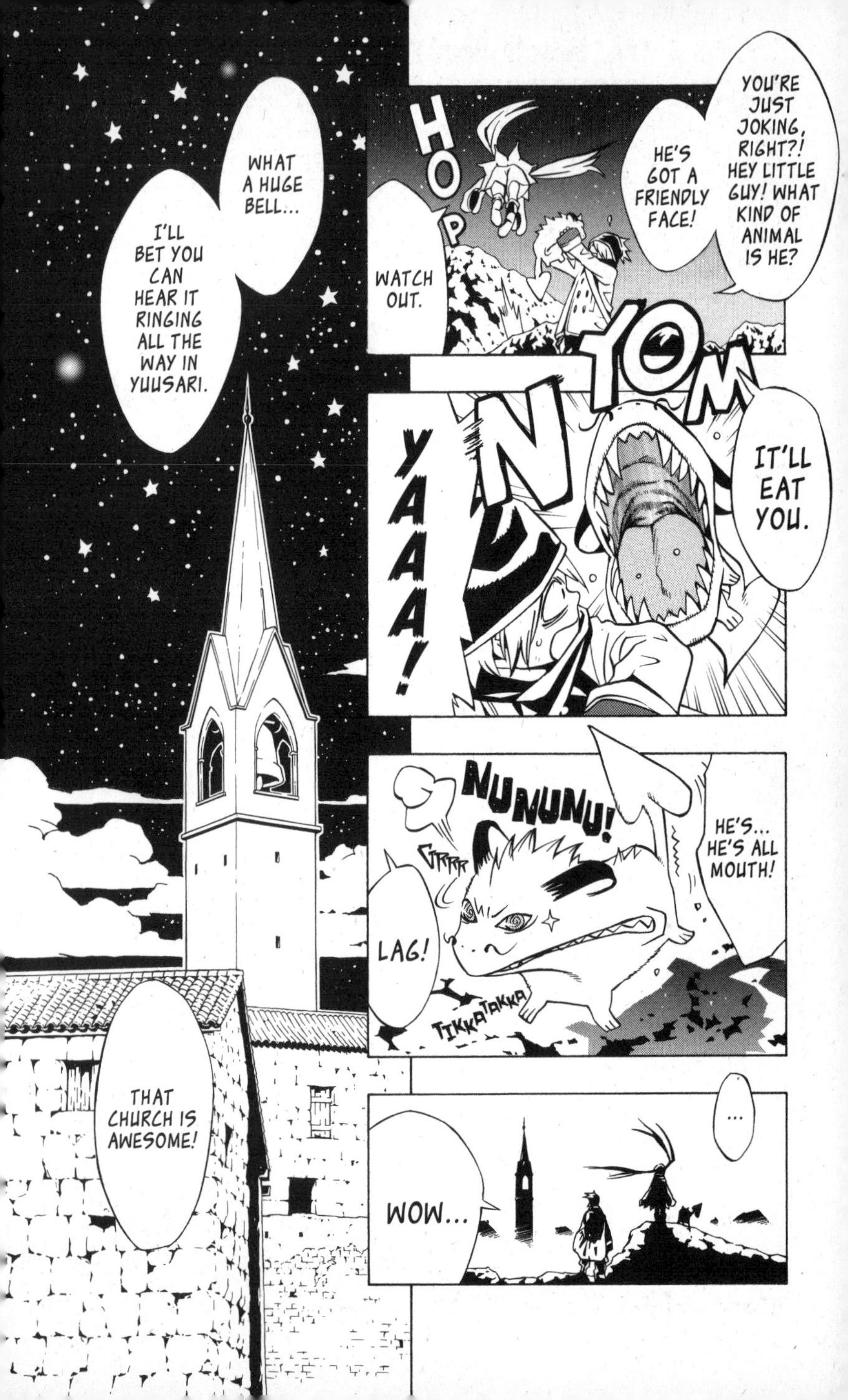
YOU'RE JUST JOKING, RIGHT?! HEY LITTLE GUY! WHAT KIND OF ANIMAL IS HE?
HE'S GOT A FRIENDLY FACE!
HOP
WATCH OUT.
YOM
N
IT'LL EAT YOU.
YAAAA!
HE'S... HE'S ALL MOUTH!
NUNUNU!
GRRRR
LAG!
TIKKATAKKA
...
WOW...
WHAT A HUGE BELL...
I'LL BET YOU CAN HEAR IT RINGING ALL THE WAY IN YUUSARI.
THAT CHURCH IS AWESOME!

Chapter 3: The Letter to Jiggy Pepper, Part One

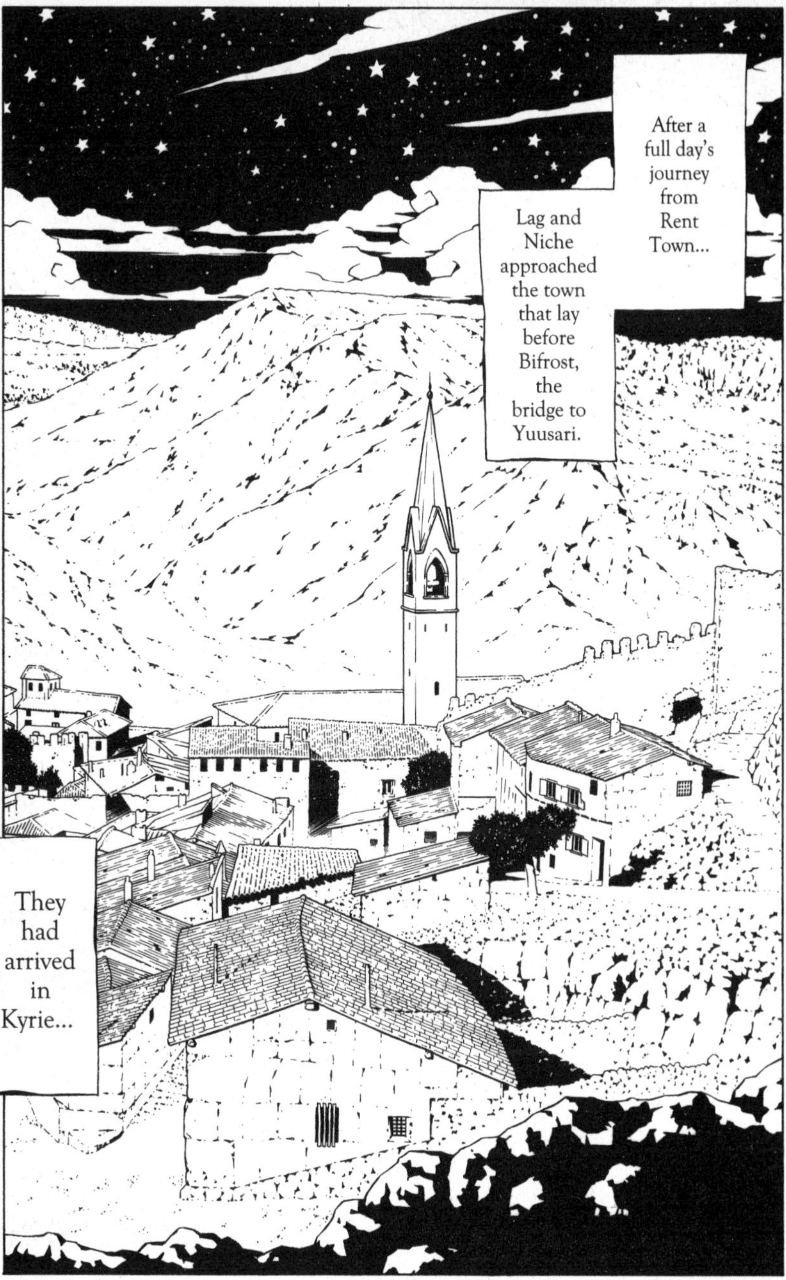
After a full day's journey from Rent Town...
Lag and Niche approached the town that lay before Bifrost, the bridge to Yuusari.
They had arrived in Kyrie...

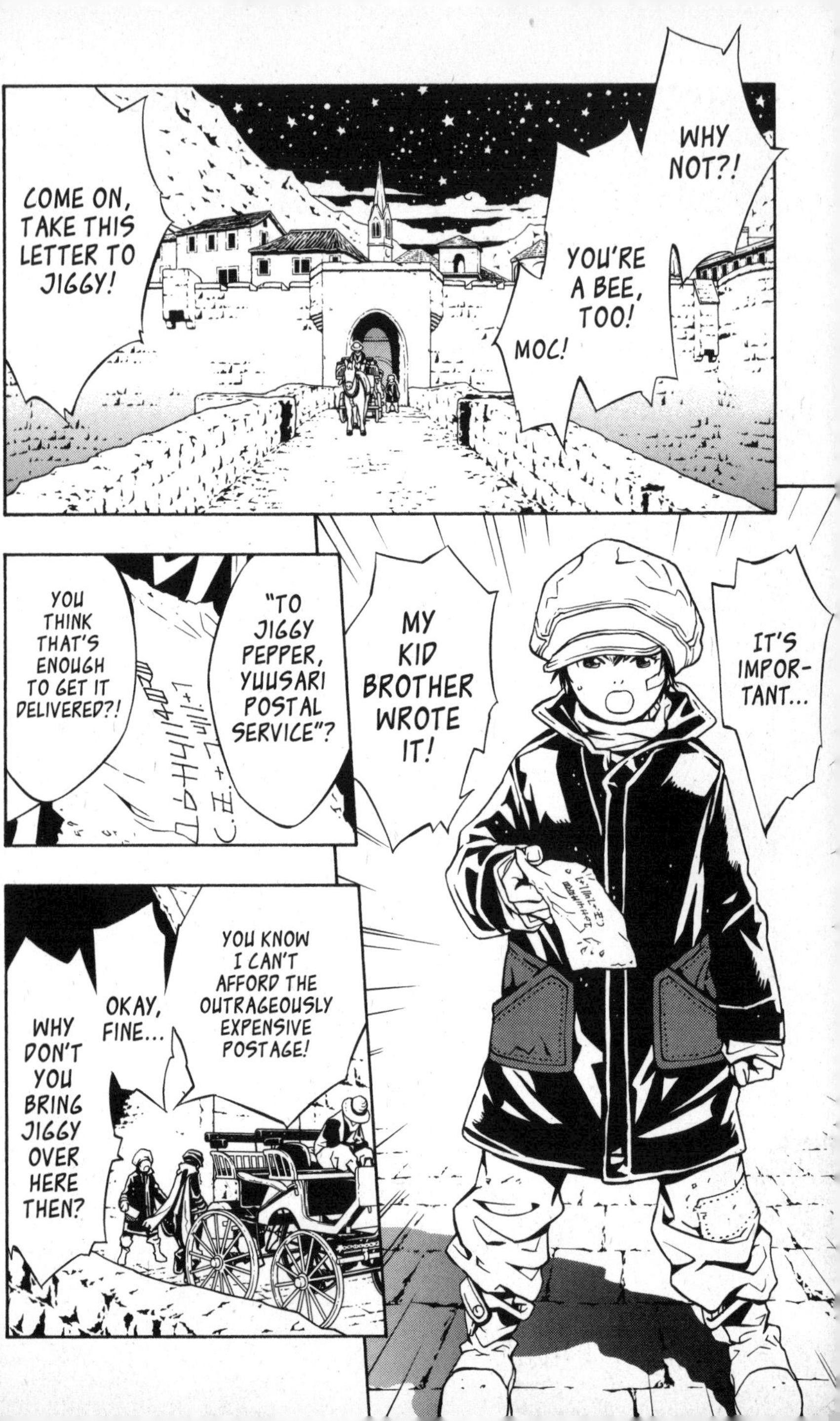
WHY NOT?!
YOU'RE A BEE, TOO!
MOC!
COME ON, TAKE THIS LETTER TO JIGGY!
IT'S IMPOR-TANT...
MY KID BROTHER WROTE IT!
"TO JIGGY PEPPER, YUUSARI POSTAL SERVICE"?
YOU THINK THAT'S ENOUGH TO GET IT DELIVERED?!
YOU KNOW I CAN'T AFFORD THE OUTRAGEOUSLY EXPENSIVE POSTAGE!
OKAY, FINE...
WHY DON'T YOU BRING JIGGY OVER HERE THEN?

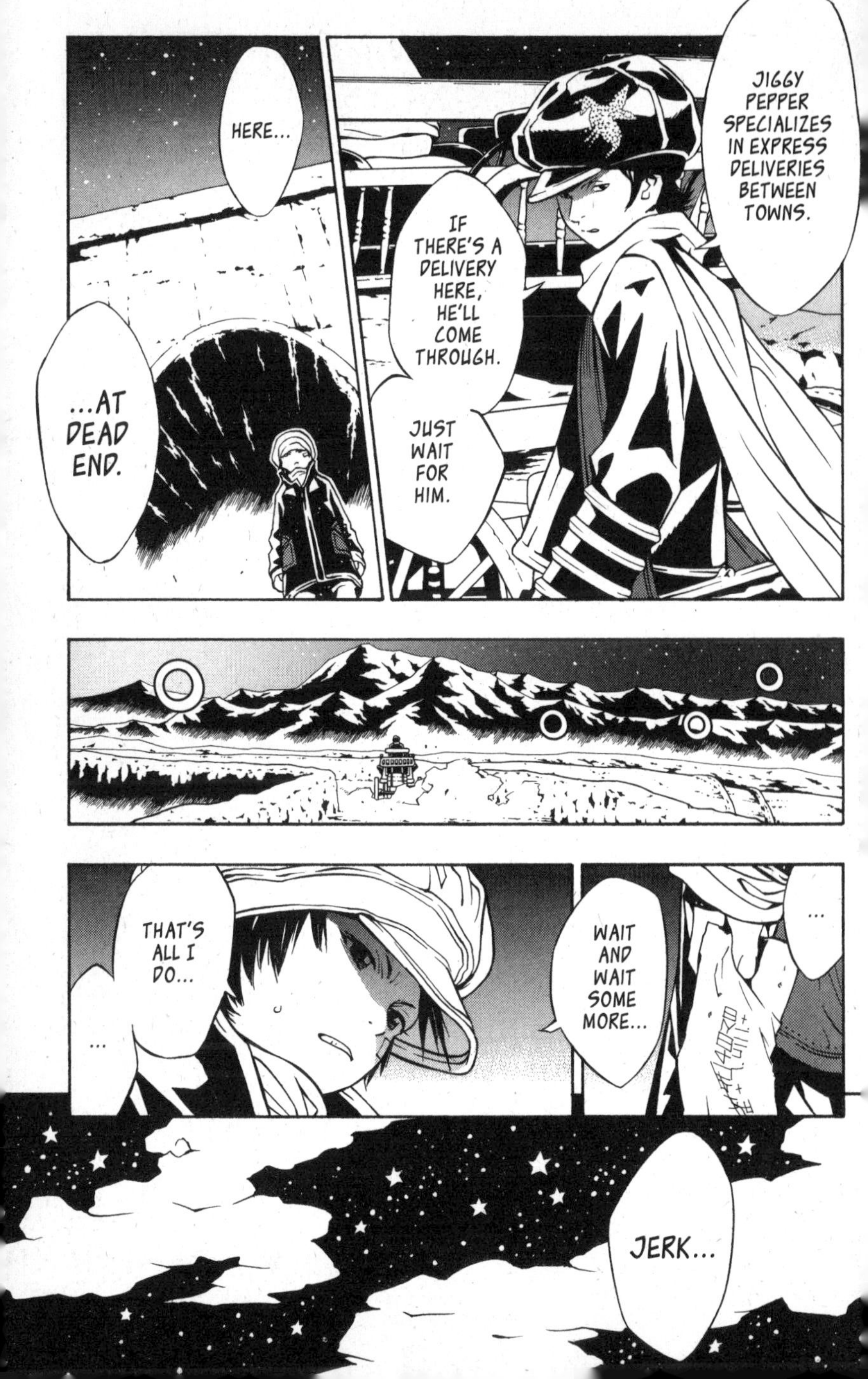
JIGGY PEPPER SPECIALIZES IN EXPRESS DELIVERIES BETWEEN TOWNS.
IF THERE'S A DELIVERY HERE, HE'LL COME THROUGH.
JUST WAIT FOR HIM.
HERE...
...AT DEAD END.
...
WAIT AND WAIT SOME MORE...
THAT'S ALL I DO...
...
JERK...

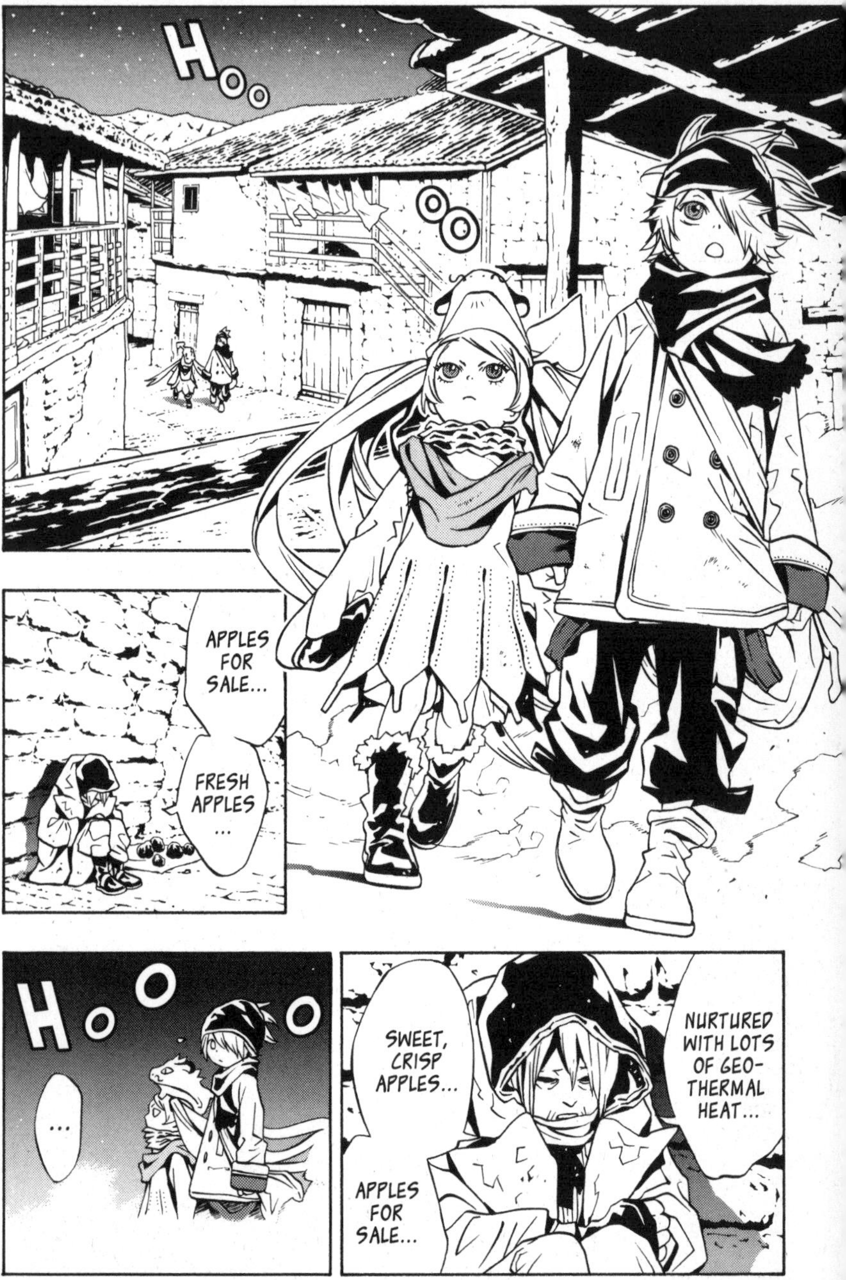
HOOOO
APPLES FOR SALE...
FRESH APPLES...
NURTURED WITH LOTS OF GEO-THERMAL HEAT...
SWEET, CRISP APPLES...
APPLES FOR SALE...
HOOO
...

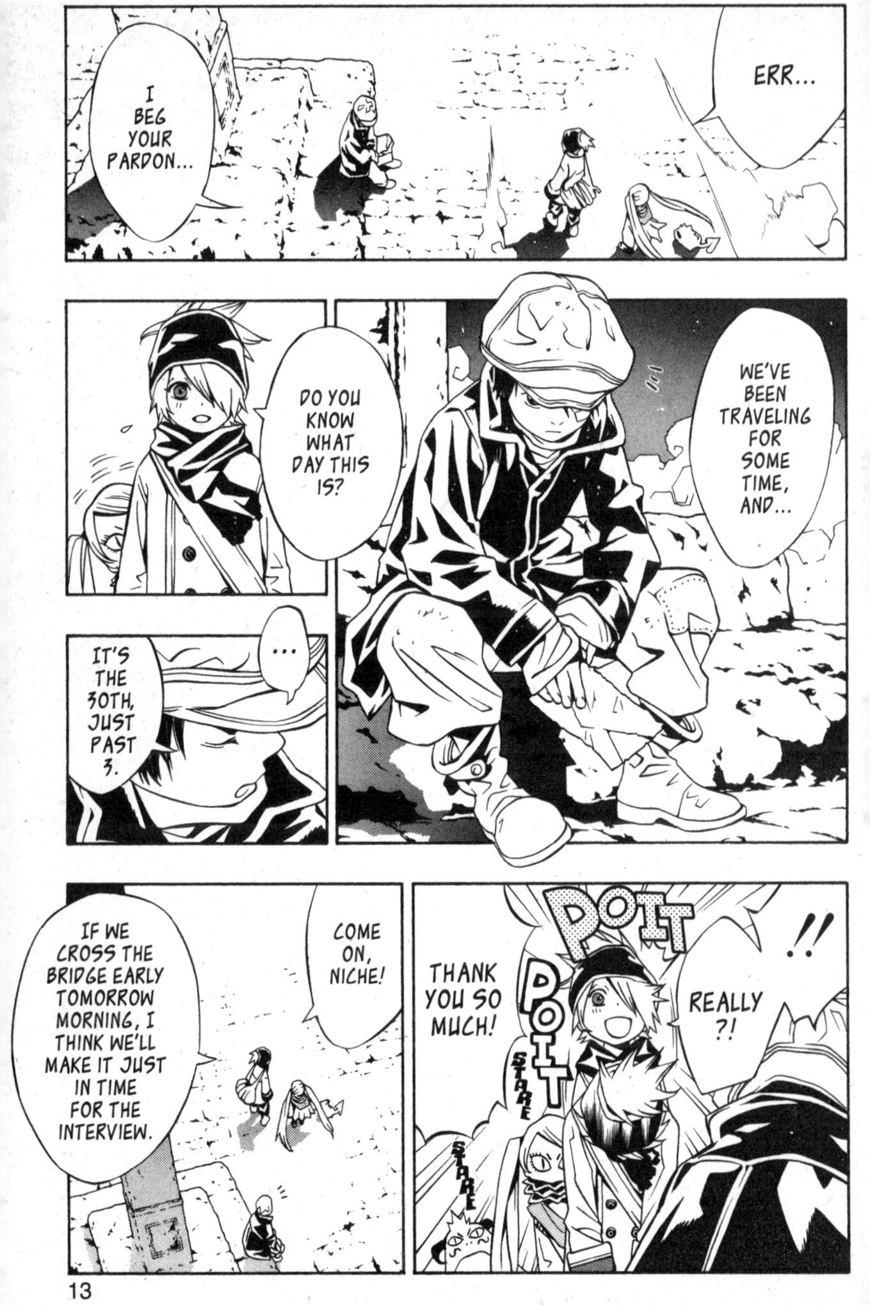
ERR...
I BEG YOUR PARDON...
WE'VE BEEN TRAVELING FOR SOME TIME, AND...
DO YOU KNOW WHAT DAY THIS IS?
...
IT'S THE 30TH, JUST PAST 3.
!!
REALLY?!
POIT
POIT
THANK YOU SO MUCH!
STARE
STARE
COME ON, NICHE!
IF WE CROSS THE BRIDGE EARLY TOMORROW MORNING, I THINK WE'LL MAKE IT JUST IN TIME FOR THE INTERVIEW.

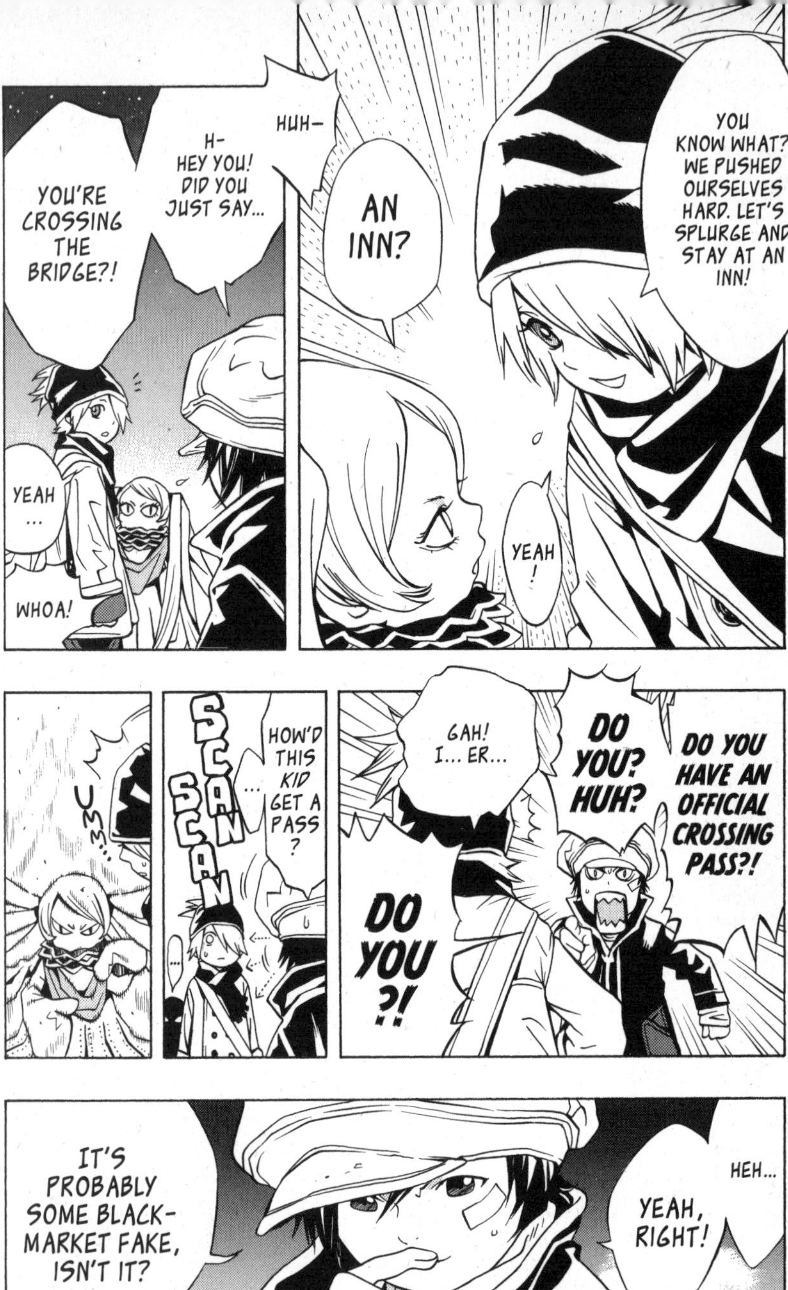

YOU KNOW WHAT? WE PUSHED OURSELVES HARD. LET'S SPLURGE AND STAY AT AN INN!
AN INN?
YEAH!
HUH—
H- HEY YOU! DID YOU JUST SAY...
YOU'RE CROSSING THE BRIDGE?!
YEAH ...
WHOA!
DO YOU HAVE AN OFFICIAL CROSSING PASS?!
DO YOU? HUH?
GAH! I... ER...
DO YOU ?!
HOW'D THIS KID GET A PASS?
SCAN SCAN
...
...
UMM...
HEH...
YEAH, RIGHT!
IT'S PROBABLY SOME BLACK-MARKET FAKE, ISN'T IT?

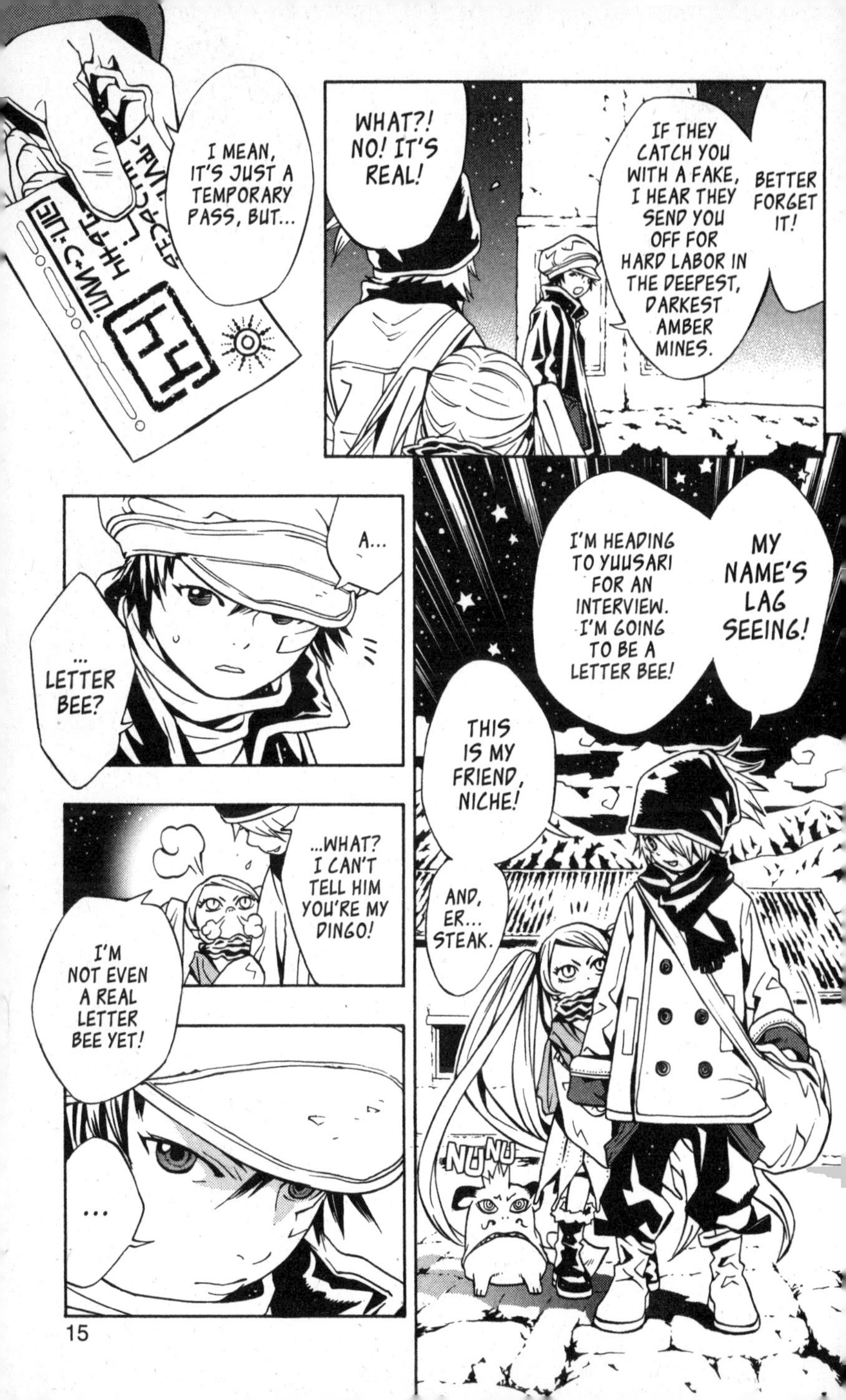
BETTER FORGET IT!
IF THEY CATCH YOU WITH A FAKE, I HEAR THEY SEND YOU OFF FOR HARD LABOR IN THE DEEPEST, DARKEST AMBER MINES.
WHAT?! NO! IT'S REAL!
I MEAN, IT'S JUST A TEMPORARY PASS, BUT...
MY NAME'S LAG SEEING!
I'M HEADING TO YUUSARI FOR AN INTERVIEW. I'M GOING TO BE A LETTER BEE!
THIS IS MY FRIEND, NICHE!
AND, ER... STEAK.
NU NU
A...
... LETTER BEE?
...WHAT? I CAN'T TELL HIM YOU'RE MY DINGO!
I'M NOT EVEN A REAL LETTER BEE YET!
...

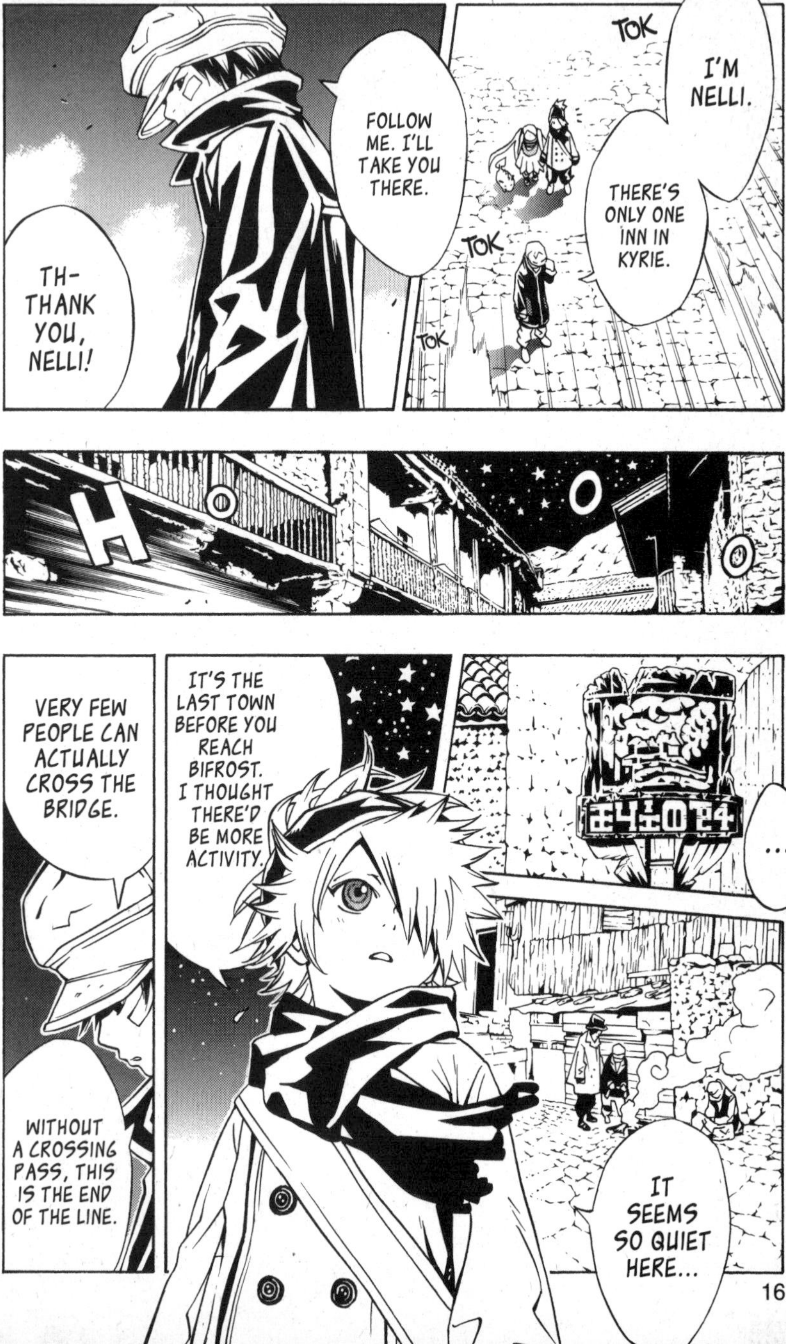
TOK
I'M NELLI.
THERE'S ONLY ONE INN IN KYRIE.
TOK
TOK
FOLLOW ME. I'LL TAKE YOU THERE.
TH- THANK YOU, NELLI!
...
IT SEEMS SO QUIET HERE...
IT'S THE LAST TOWN BEFORE YOU REACH BIFROST. I THOUGHT THERE'D BE MORE ACTIVITY.
VERY FEW PEOPLE CAN ACTUALLY CROSS THE BRIDGE.
WITHOUT A CROSSING PASS, THIS IS THE END OF THE LINE.

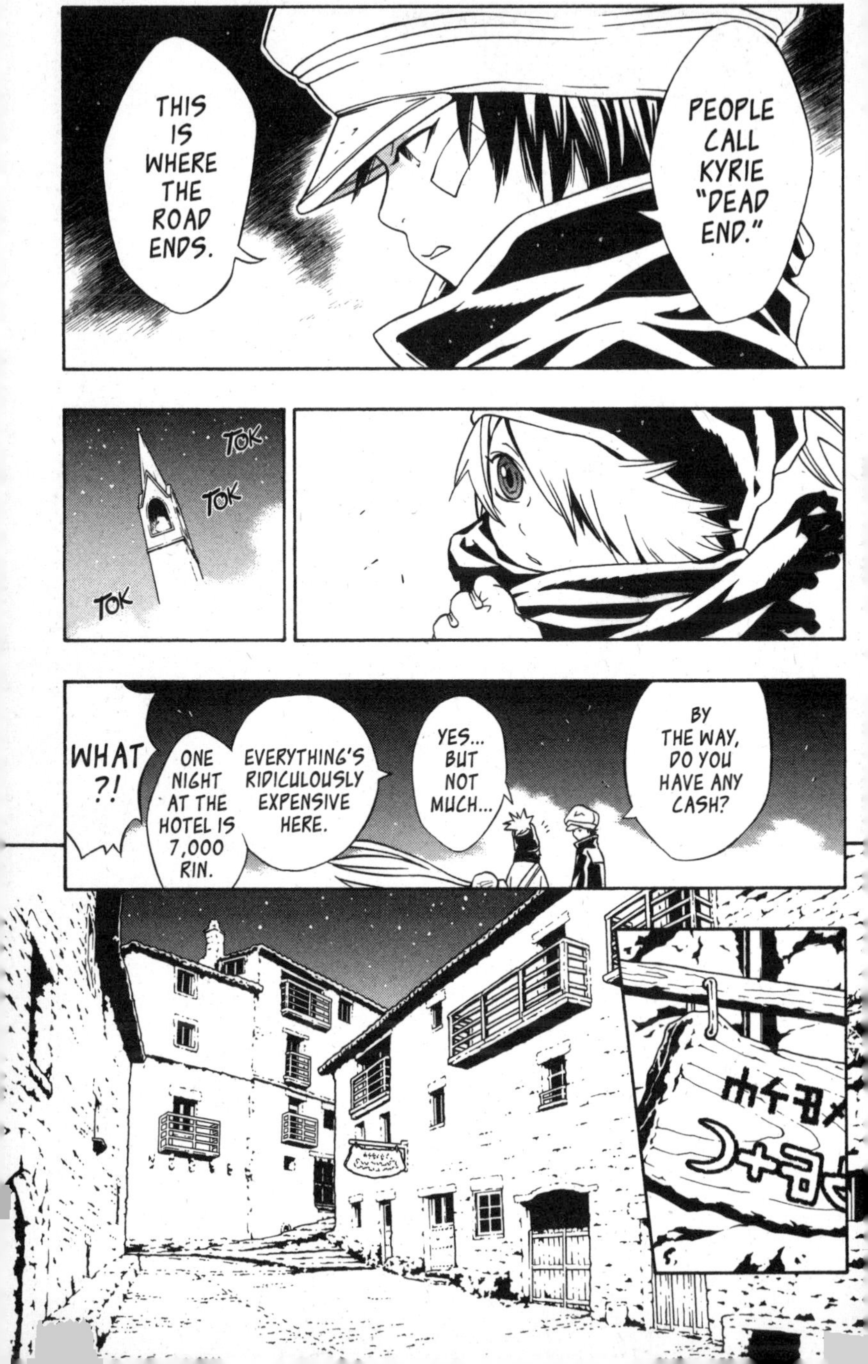
PEOPLE CALL KYRIE "DEAD END."
THIS IS WHERE THE ROAD ENDS.
TOK
TOK
TOK
BY THE WAY, DO YOU HAVE ANY CASH?
YES... BUT NOT MUCH...
EVERYTHING'S RIDICULOUSLY EXPENSIVE HERE.
ONE NIGHT AT THE HOTEL IS 7,000 RIN.
WHAT?!

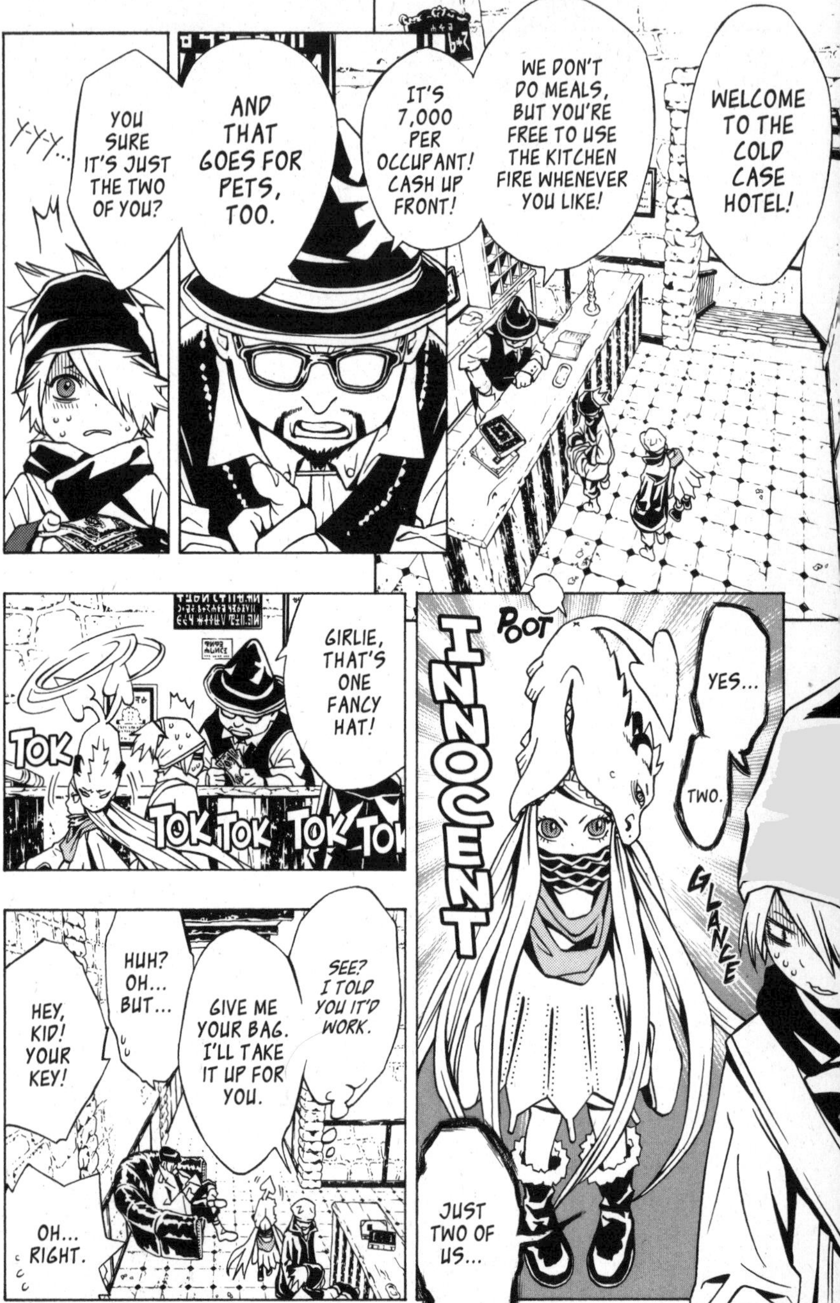
WELCOME TO THE COLD CASE HOTEL!
WE DON'T DO MEALS, BUT YOU'RE FREE TO USE THE KITCHEN FIRE WHENEVER YOU LIKE!
IT'S 7,000 PER OCCUPANT! CASH UP FRONT!
AND THAT GOES FOR PETS, TOO.
Y-Y-Y...
YOU SURE IT'S JUST THE TWO OF YOU?
YES...
TWO.
POOT
INNOCENT
GLANCE
JUST TWO OF US...
GIRLIE, THAT'S ONE FANCY HAT!
TOK
TOK TOK TOK TOK
SEE? I TOLD YOU IT'D WORK.
GIVE ME YOUR BAG. I'LL TAKE IT UP FOR YOU.
HUH? OH... BUT...
HEY, KID! YOUR KEY!
OH... RIGHT.

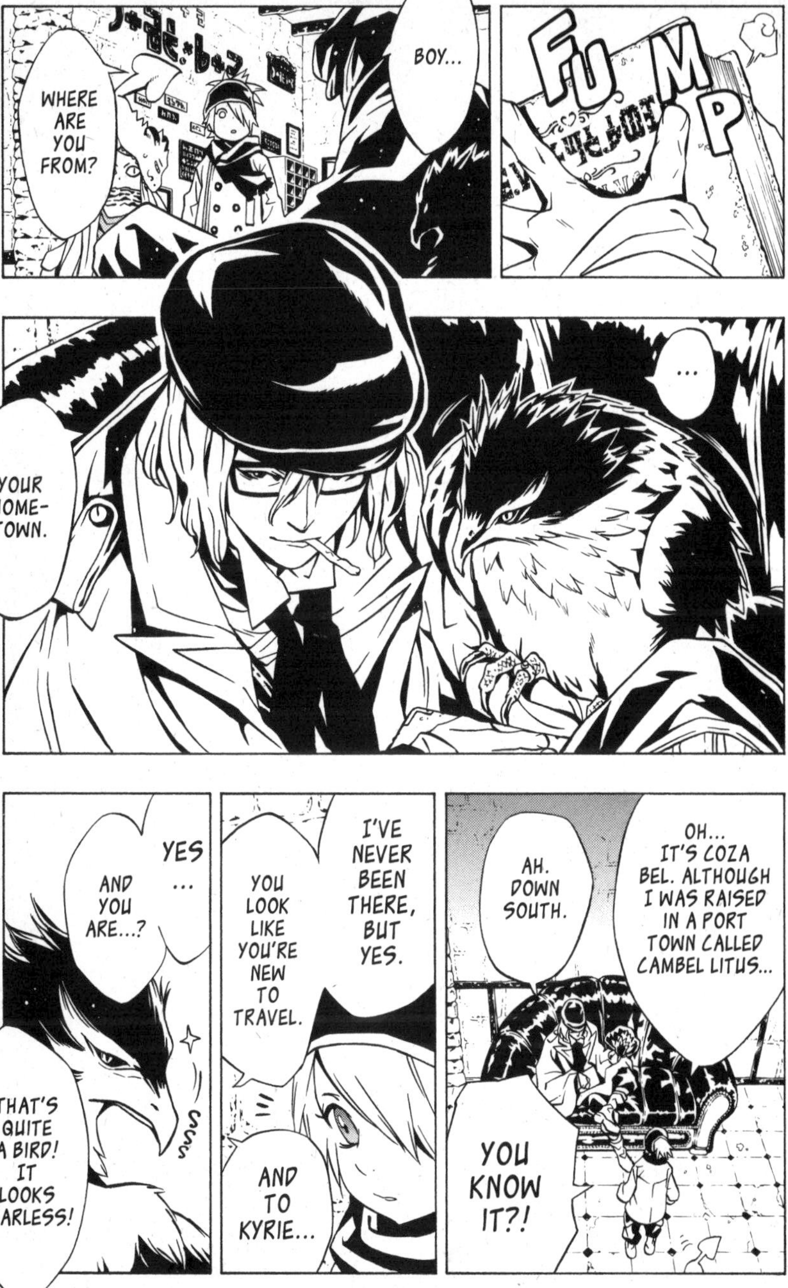
FUMP
BOY...
WHERE ARE YOU FROM?
...
YOUR HOME-TOWN.
OH... IT'S COZA BEL. ALTHOUGH I WAS RAISED IN A PORT TOWN CALLED CAMBEL LITUS...
AH. DOWN SOUTH.
YOU KNOW IT?!
I'VE NEVER BEEN THERE, BUT YES.
YOU LOOK LIKE YOU'RE NEW TO TRAVEL.
AND TO KYRIE...
YES ...
AND YOU ARE...?
THAT'S QUITE A BIRD! IT LOOKS FEARLESS!

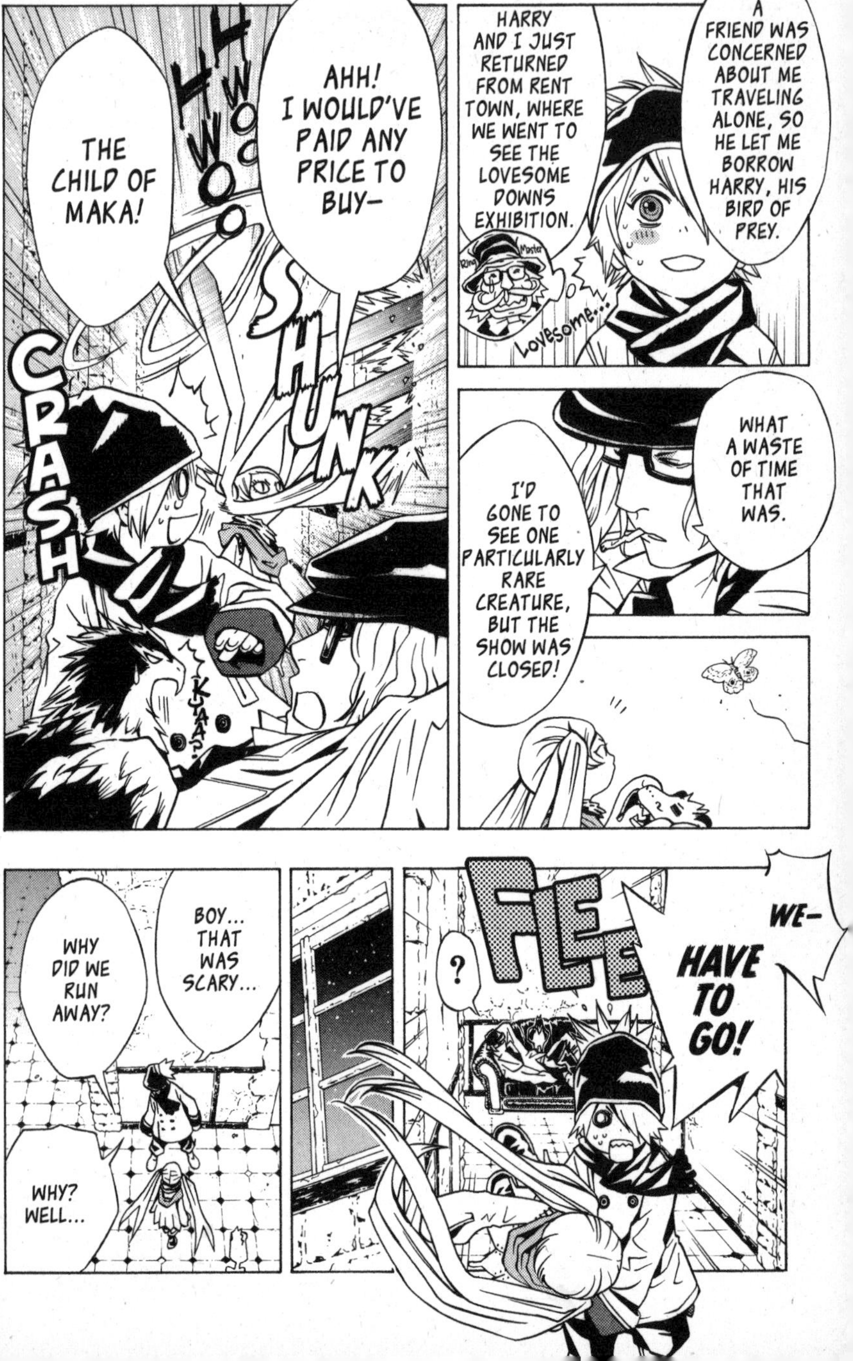
A FRIEND WAS CONCERNED ABOUT ME TRAVELING ALONE, SO HE LET ME BORROW HARRY, HIS BIRD OF PREY.
HARRY AND I JUST RETURNED FROM RENT TOWN, WHERE WE WENT TO SEE THE LOVESOME DOWNS EXHIBITION.
Ring Master
Lovesome...
WHAT A WASTE OF TIME THAT WAS.
I'D GONE TO SEE ONE PARTICULARLY RARE CREATURE, BUT THE SHOW WAS CLOSED!
AHH! I WOULD'VE PAID ANY PRICE TO BUY–
SHUNK
THE CHILD OF MAKA!
CRASH
KYAA?
WE–
HAVE TO GO!
FLEE
?
BOY... THAT WAS SCARY...
WHY DID WE RUN AWAY?
WHY? WELL...

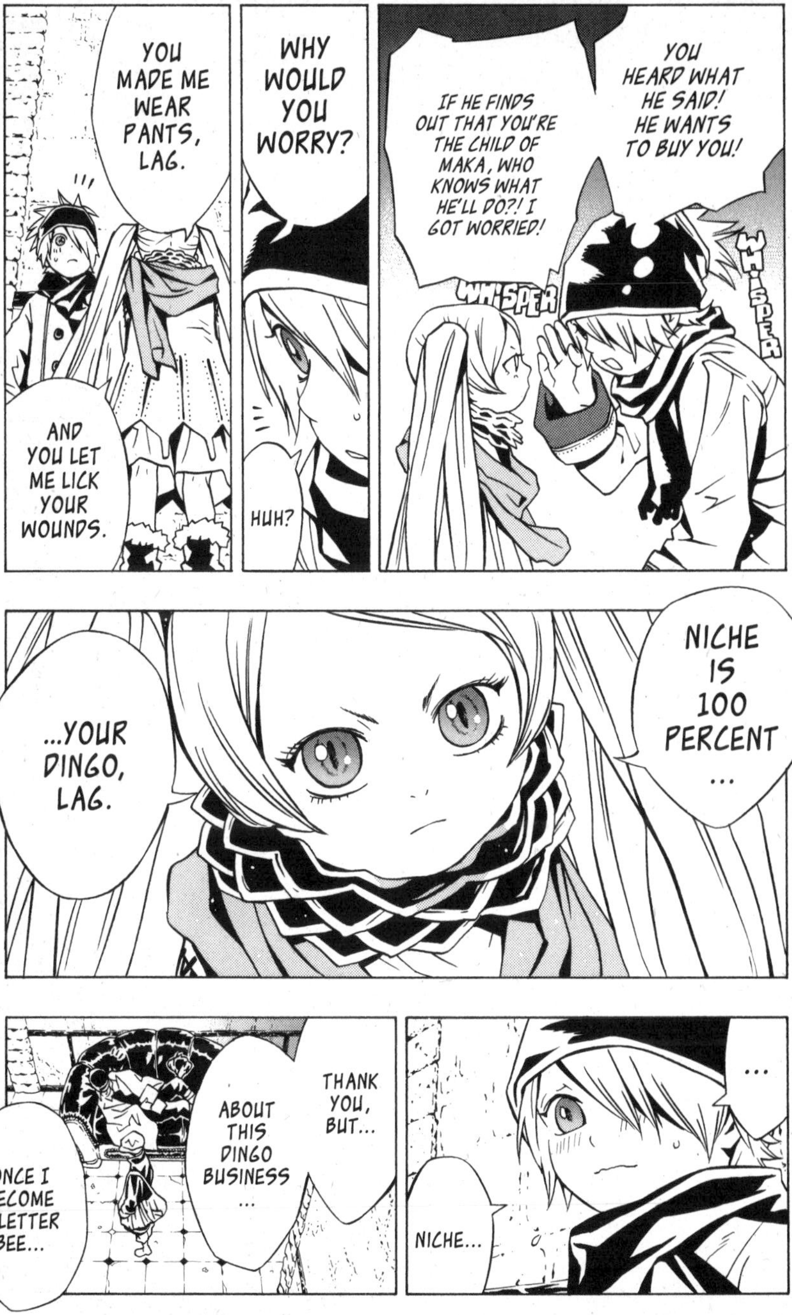
YOU HEARD WHAT HE SAID! HE WANTS TO BUY YOU!
WHISPER
IF HE FINDS OUT THAT YOU'RE THE CHILD OF MAKA, WHO KNOWS WHAT HE'LL DO?! I GOT WORRIED!
WHISPER
WHY WOULD YOU WORRY?
HUH?
YOU MADE ME WEAR PANTS, LAG.
AND YOU LET ME LICK YOUR WOUNDS.
NICHE IS 100 PERCENT...
...YOUR DINGO, LAG.
...
NICHE...
THANK YOU, BUT...
ABOUT THIS DINGO BUSINESS...
ONCE I BECOME A LETTER BEE...

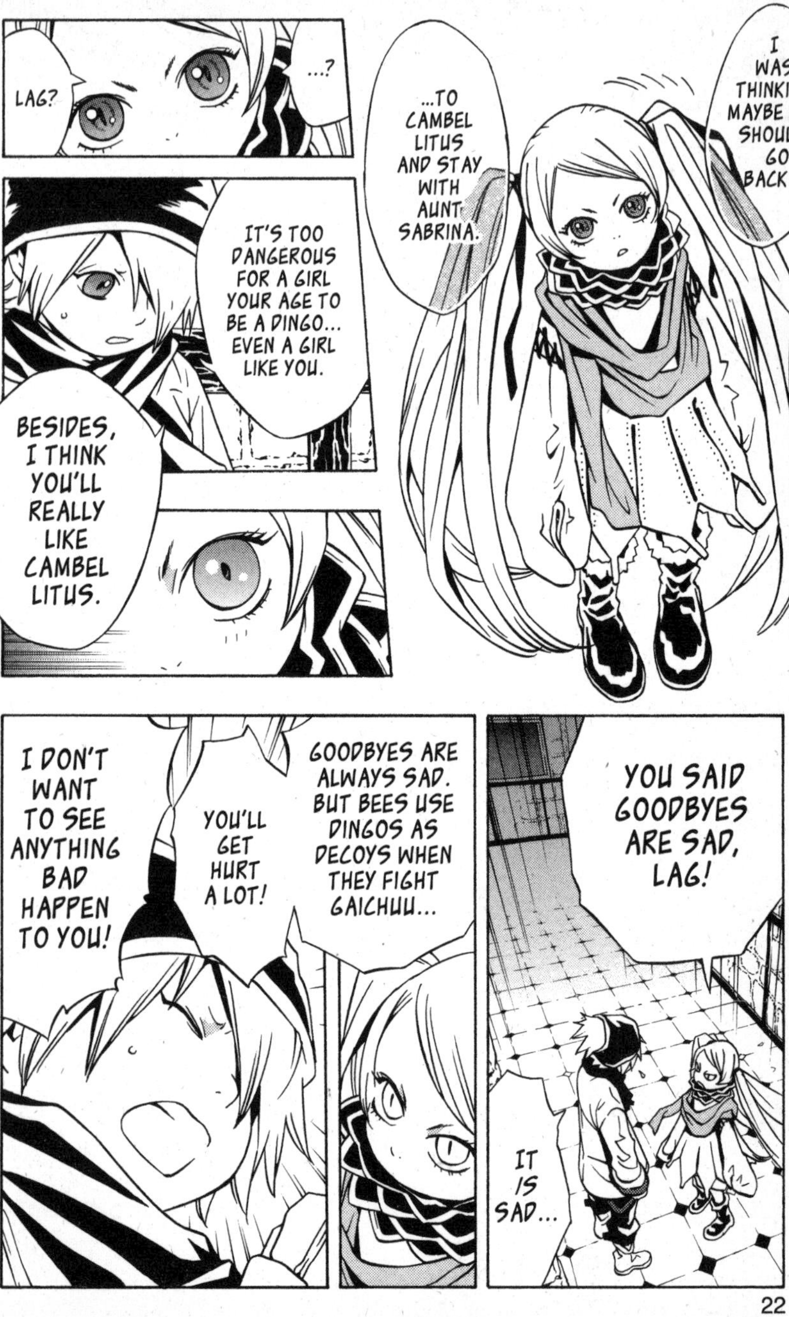
I WAS THINKING MAYBE YOU SHOULD GO BACK...
...TO CAMBEL LITUS AND STAY WITH AUNT SABRINA.
...?
LAG?
IT'S TOO DANGEROUS FOR A GIRL YOUR AGE TO BE A DINGO... EVEN A GIRL LIKE YOU.
BESIDES, I THINK YOU'LL REALLY LIKE CAMBEL LITUS.
YOU SAID GOODBYES ARE SAD, LAG!
IT IS SAD...
GOODBYES ARE ALWAYS SAD. BUT BEES USE DINGOS AS DECOYS WHEN THEY FIGHT GAICHUU...
YOU'LL GET HURT A LOT!
I DON'T WANT TO SEE ANYTHING BAD HAPPEN TO YOU!

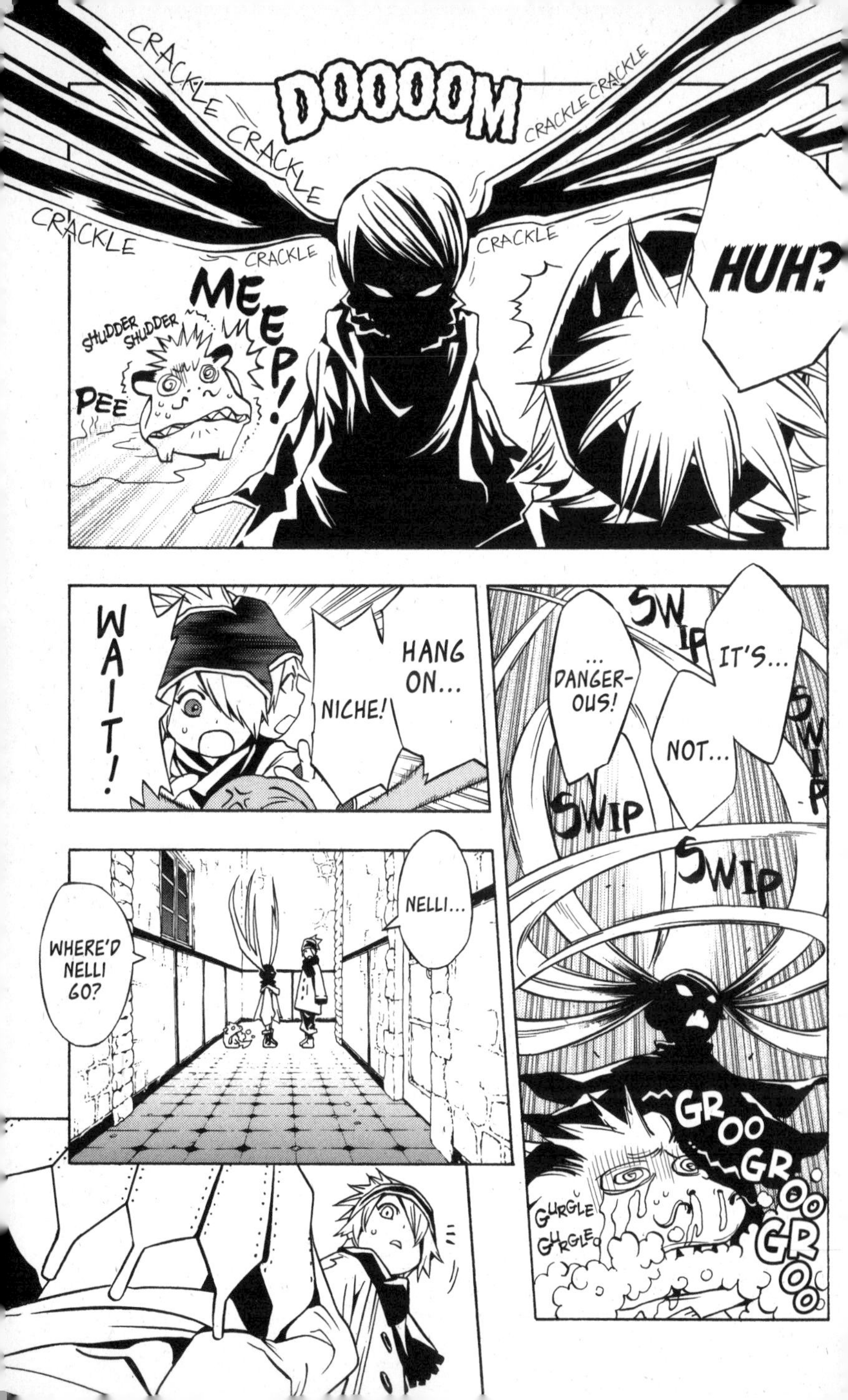
CRACKLE CRACKLE
HUH?
DOOOOM
CRACKLE
CRACKLE
CRACKLE
CRACKLE
CRACKLE
MEEP!
SHUDDER SHUDDER
PEE
IT'S...
NOT...
...DANGER-OUS!
SWIP
SWIP
SWIP
SWIP
GROO GROO GROO
GURGLE GURGLE
HANG ON...
NICHE!
WAIT!
NELLI...
WHERE'D NELLI GO?

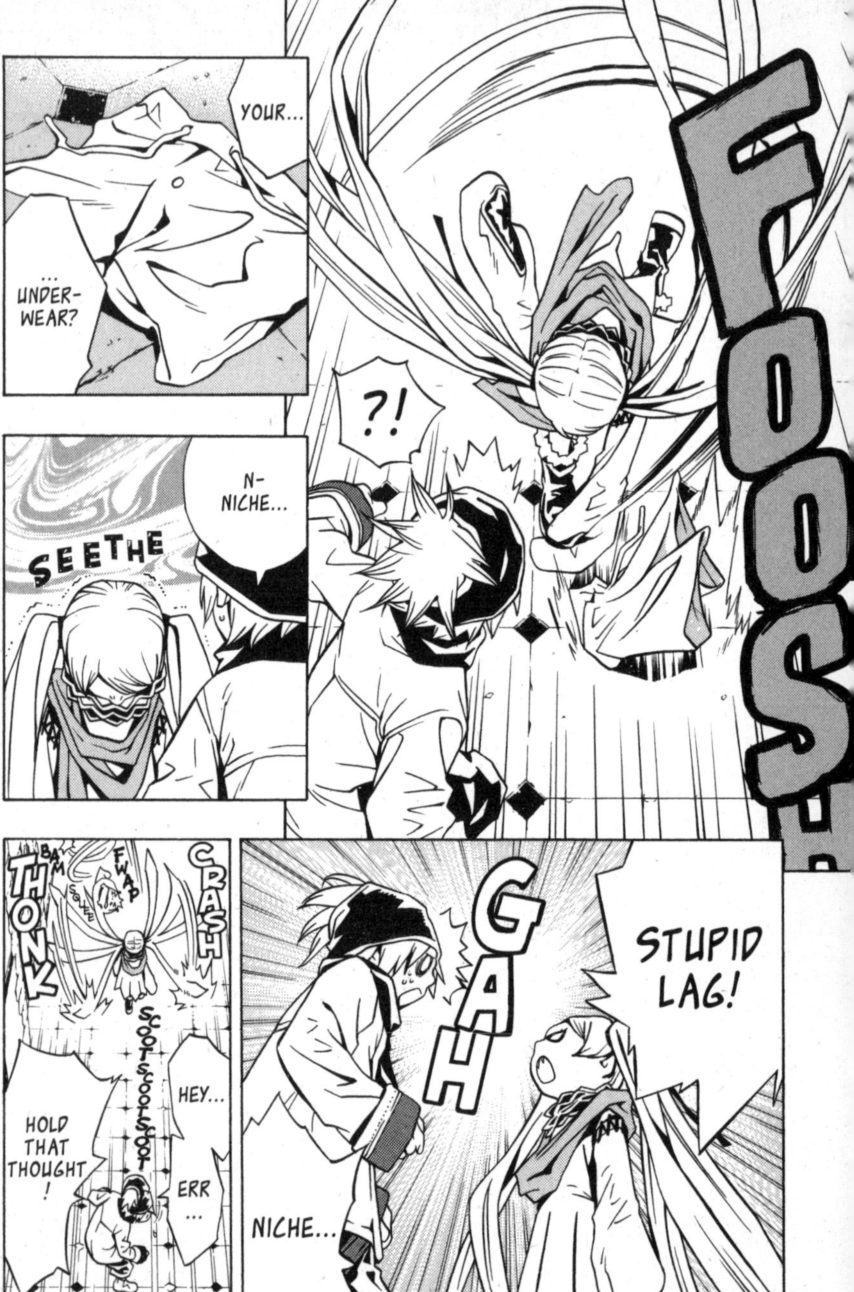

FOOSH
?!
YOUR...
... UNDERWEAR?
N-NICHE...
SEETHE
GAAH
STUPID LAG!
NICHE...
CRASH
FWAP
BAM
SQUEEE
THONK
SCOOT SCOOT SCOOT
HEY...
ERR ...
HOLD THAT THOUGHT!

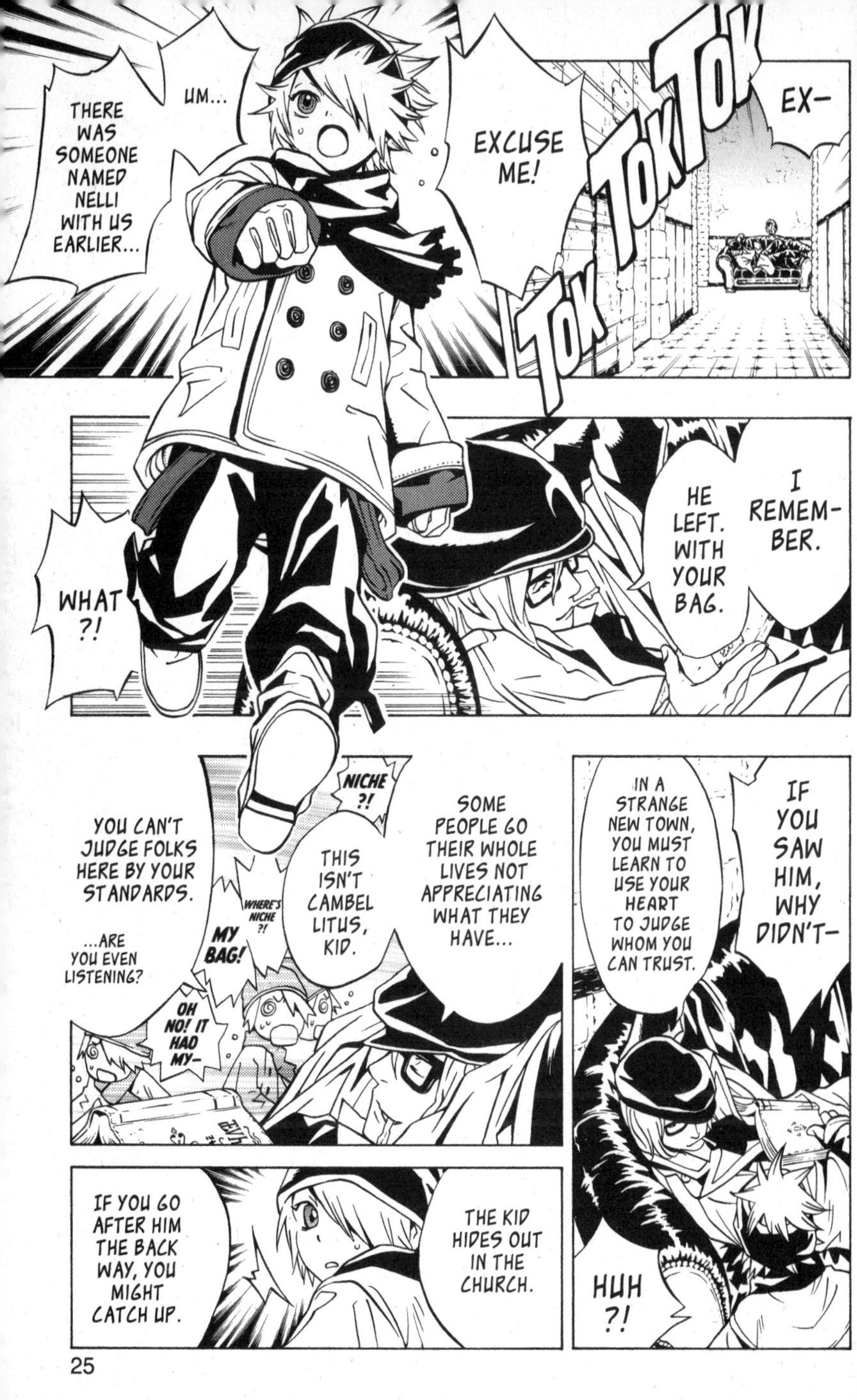
EX—
TOK TOK TOK
EXCUSE ME!
UM...
THERE WAS SOMEONE NAMED NELLI WITH US EARLIER...
I REMEMBER.
HE LEFT. WITH YOUR BAG.
WHAT?!
IF YOU SAW HIM, WHY DIDN'T—
IN A STRANGE NEW TOWN, YOU MUST LEARN TO USE YOUR HEART TO JUDGE WHOM YOU CAN TRUST.
HUH?!
SOME PEOPLE GO THEIR WHOLE LIVES NOT APPRECIATING WHAT THEY HAVE...
THIS ISN'T CAMBEL LITUS, KID.
NICHE?!
WHERE'S NICHE?!
MY BAG!
OH NO! IT HAD MY—
YOU CAN'T JUDGE FOLKS HERE BY YOUR STANDARDS.
...ARE YOU EVEN LISTENING?
THE KID HIDES OUT IN THE CHURCH.
IF YOU GO AFTER HIM THE BACK WAY, YOU MIGHT CATCH UP.

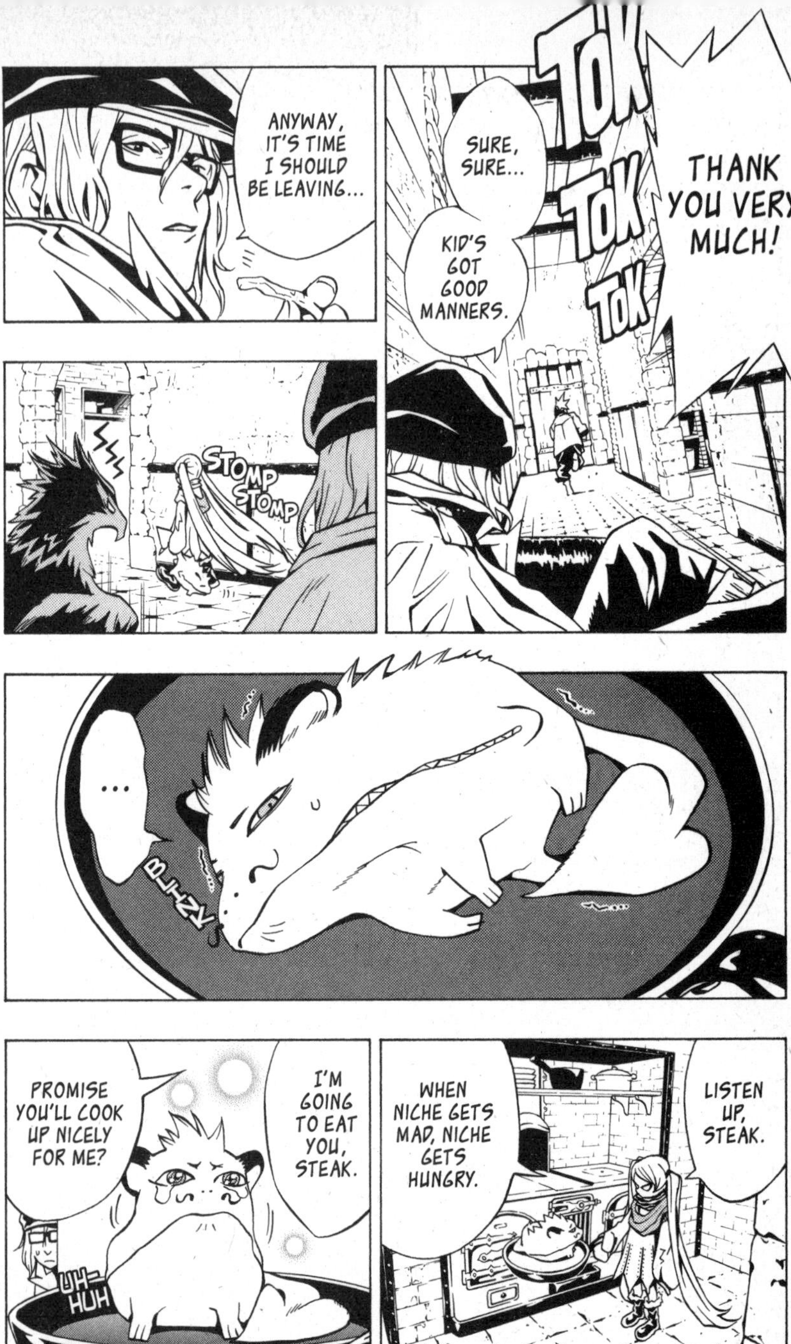
TOK TOK TOK
THANK YOU VERY MUCH!
SURE, SURE...
KID'S GOT GOOD MANNERS.
ANYWAY, IT'S TIME I SHOULD BE LEAVING...
STOMP STOMP
...
LISTEN UP, STEAK.
WHEN NICHE GETS MAD, NICHE GETS HUNGRY.
I'M GOING TO EAT YOU, STEAK.
PROMISE YOU'LL COOK UP NICELY FOR ME?
UH-HUH

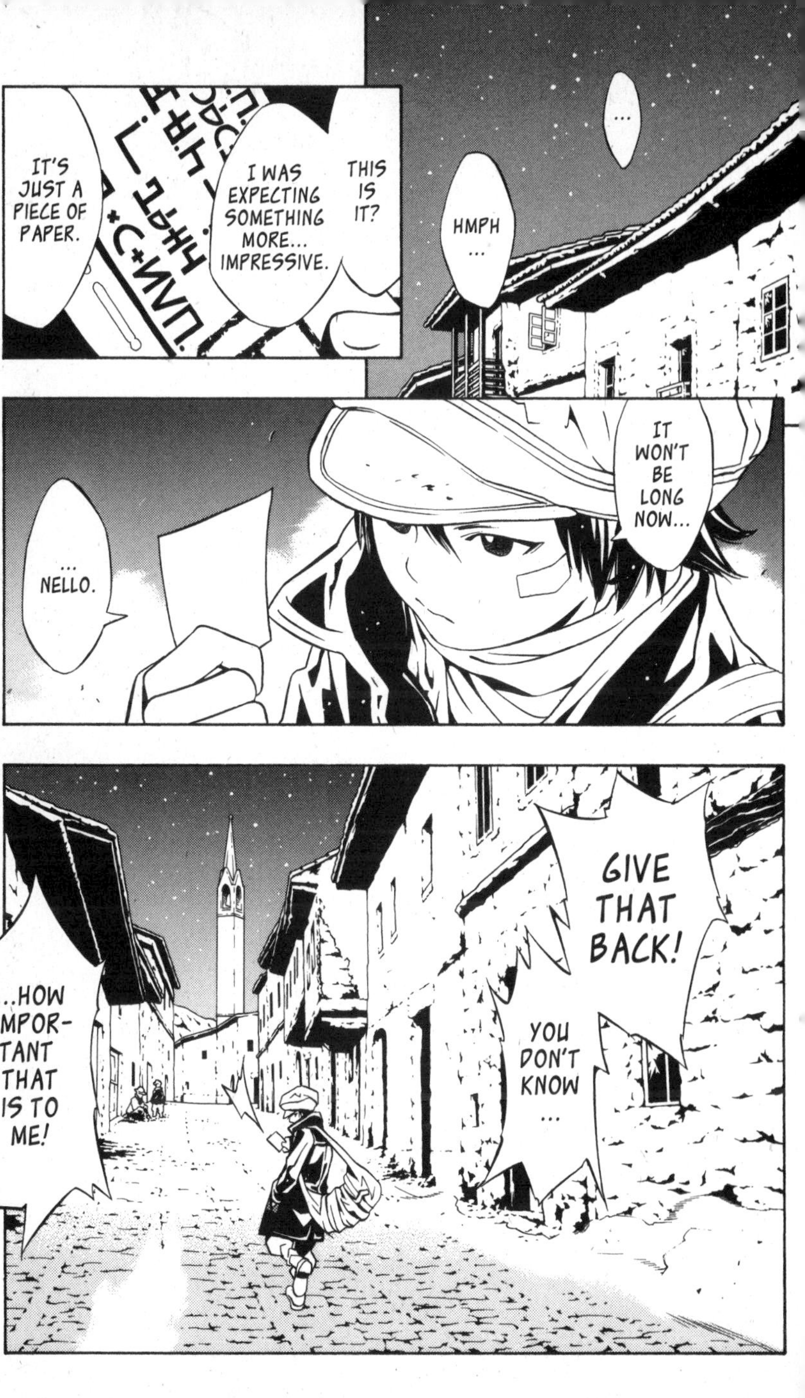
...
HMPH ...
THIS IS IT?
I WAS EXPECTING SOMETHING MORE... IMPRESSIVE.
IT'S JUST A PIECE OF PAPER.
IT WON'T BE LONG NOW...
... NELLO.
GIVE THAT BACK!
YOU DON'T KNOW ...
...HOW IMPOR-TANT THAT IS TO ME!

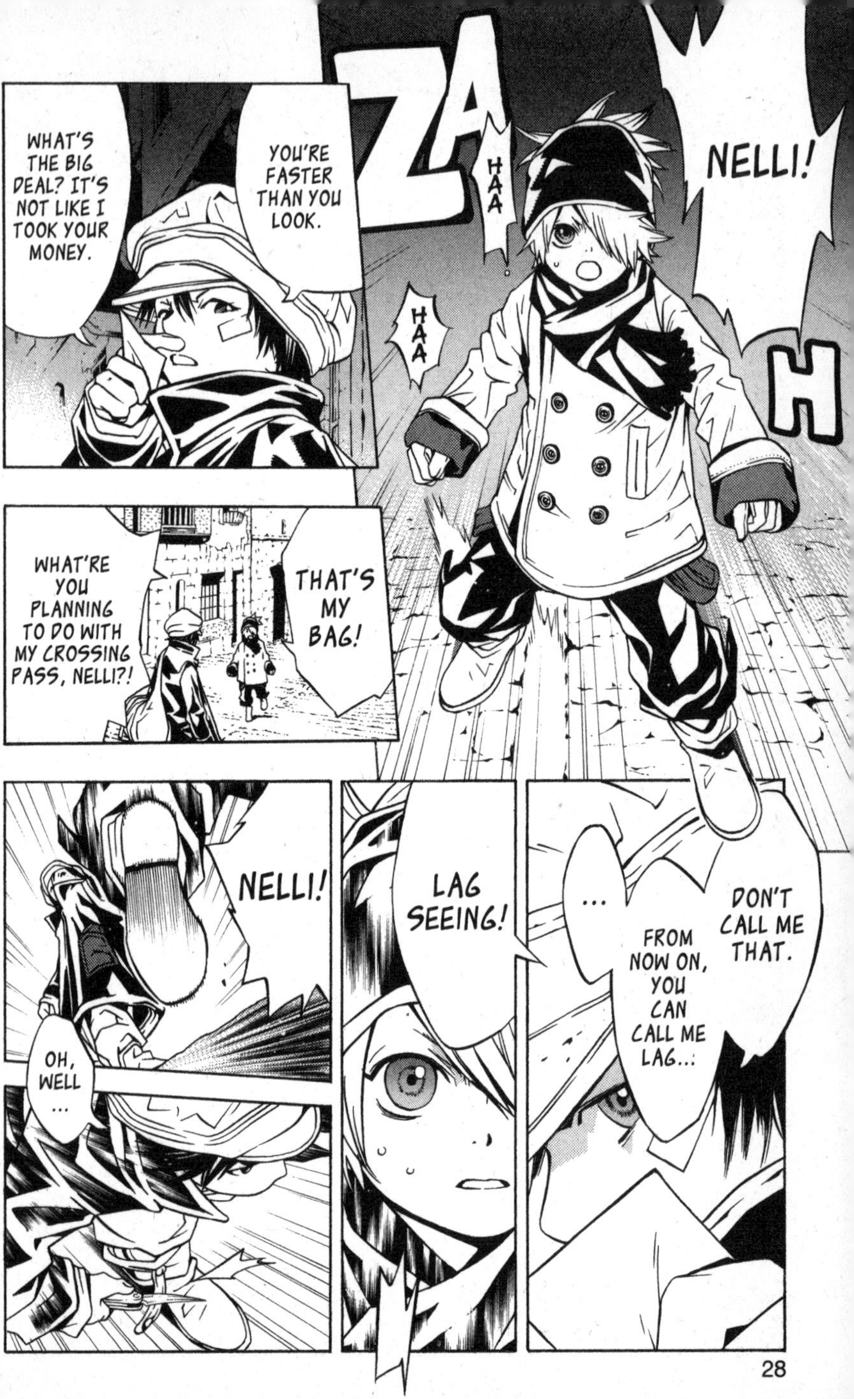
ZAWH
NELLI!
HAA
HAA
YOU'RE FASTER THAN YOU LOOK.
WHAT'S THE BIG DEAL? IT'S NOT LIKE I TOOK YOUR MONEY.
THAT'S MY BAG!
WHAT'RE YOU PLANNING TO DO WITH MY CROSSING PASS, NELLI?!
...
DON'T CALL ME THAT.
FROM NOW ON, YOU CAN CALL ME LAG...:
LAG SEEING!
NELLI!
OH, WELL ...

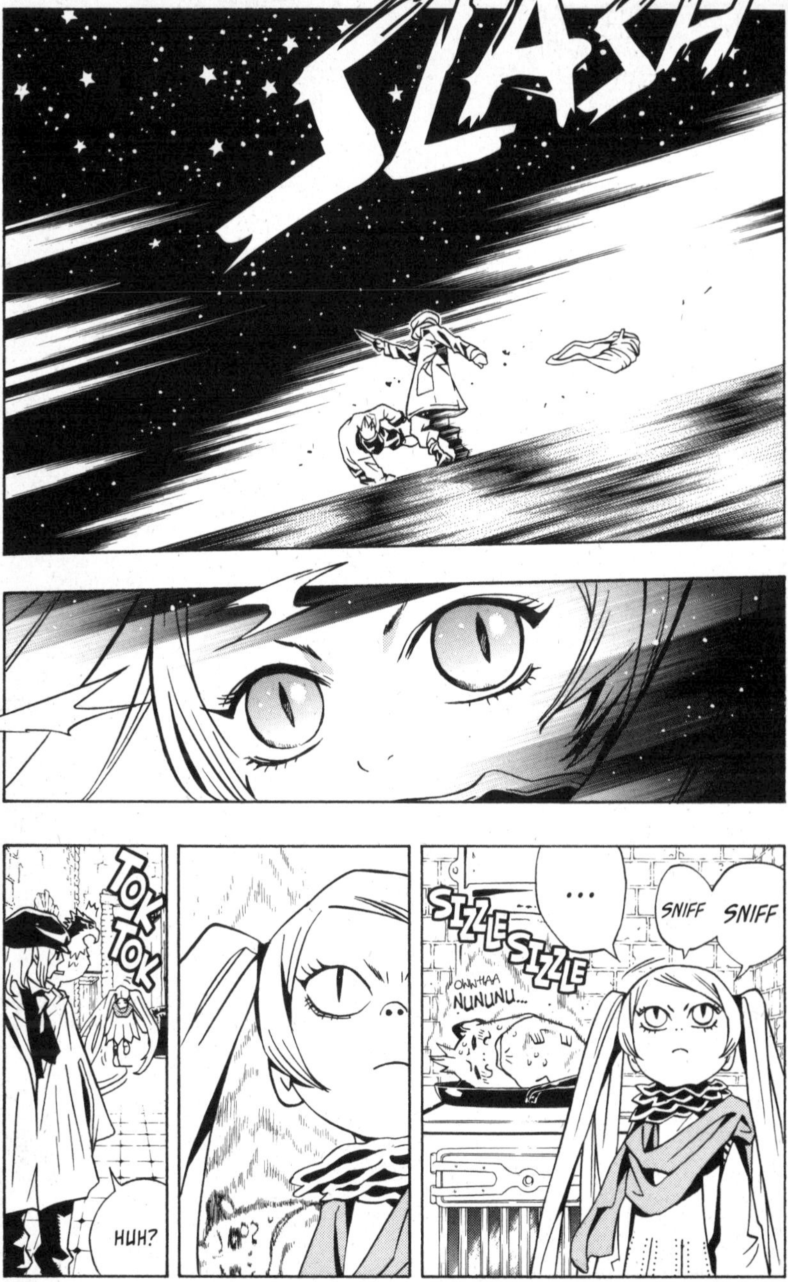
SLASH
SNIFF SNIFF
...
SIZZLE SIZZLE
OWHAA NUNUNU...
TOK TOK
HUH?

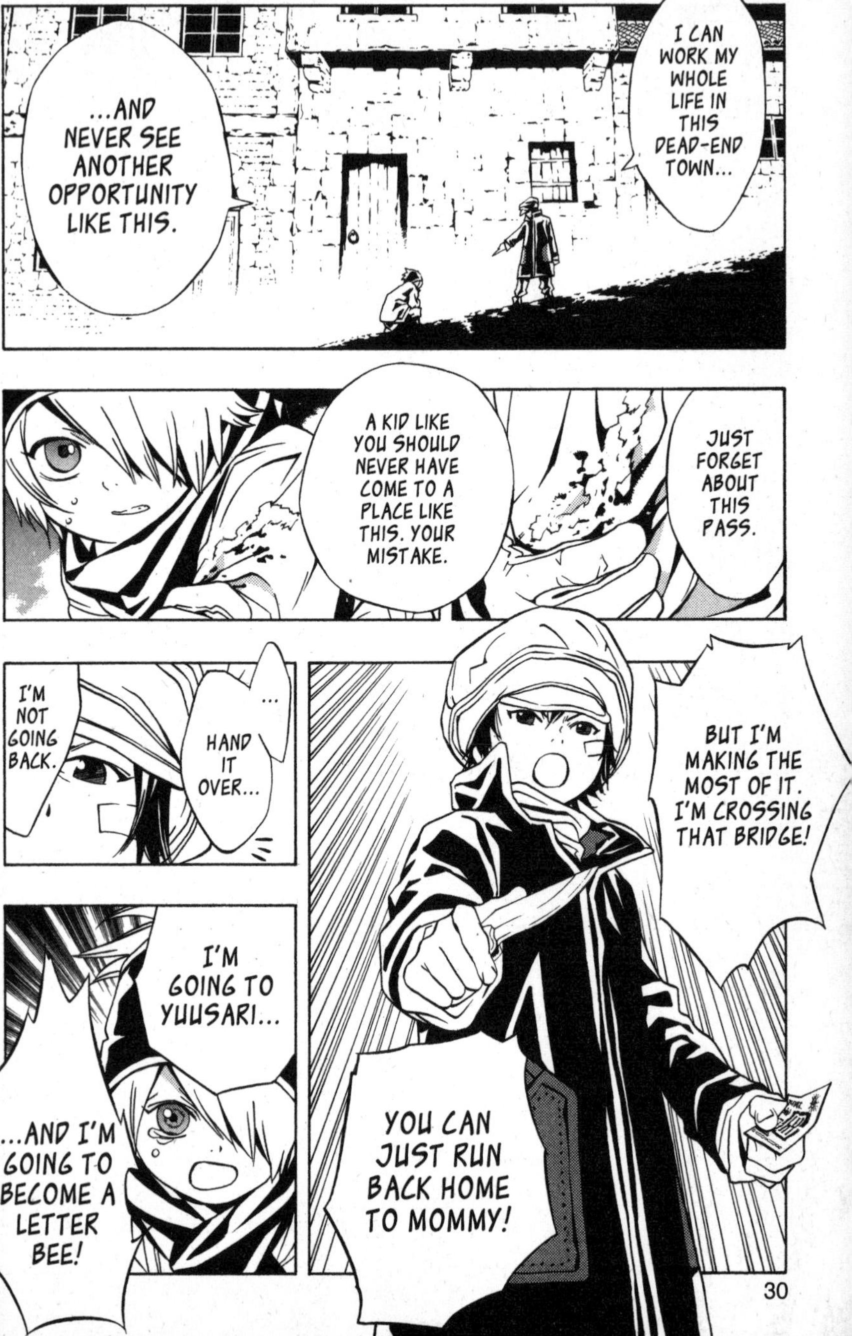
I CAN WORK MY WHOLE LIFE IN THIS DEAD-END TOWN...
...AND NEVER SEE ANOTHER OPPORTUNITY LIKE THIS.
JUST FORGET ABOUT THIS PASS.
A KID LIKE YOU SHOULD NEVER HAVE COME TO A PLACE LIKE THIS. YOUR MISTAKE.
BUT I'M MAKING THE MOST OF IT. I'M CROSSING THAT BRIDGE!
YOU CAN JUST RUN BACK HOME TO MOMMY!
...
HAND IT OVER...
I'M NOT GOING BACK.
I'M GOING TO YUUSARI...
...AND I'M GOING TO BECOME A LETTER BEE!

...
HEH...
DO YOU EVEN KNOW WHAT A LETTER BEE IS?
TAKE A LOOK AT THIS, LAG.
YOU SEE THIS TATTERED OLD LETTER?
MY KID BROTHER, NELLO, WROTE IT WHEN HE WAS SICK.
HE WAS IN A LOT OF PAIN WHEN HE WROTE THIS— PRACTICALLY ON HIS DEATHBED.
MY BROTHER POURED HIS HEART INTO THIS LETTER. TWO YEARS LATER, IT'S STILL UNDELIVERED.
BEES DON'T CARE ABOUT PEOPLE LIKE US WHO CAN'T AFFORD THEIR FEES. NOW DO YOU GET IT?
THOSE LETTER BEES?
THEY'VE ALL SOLD THEIR HEART TO THE GOVERN-MENT!

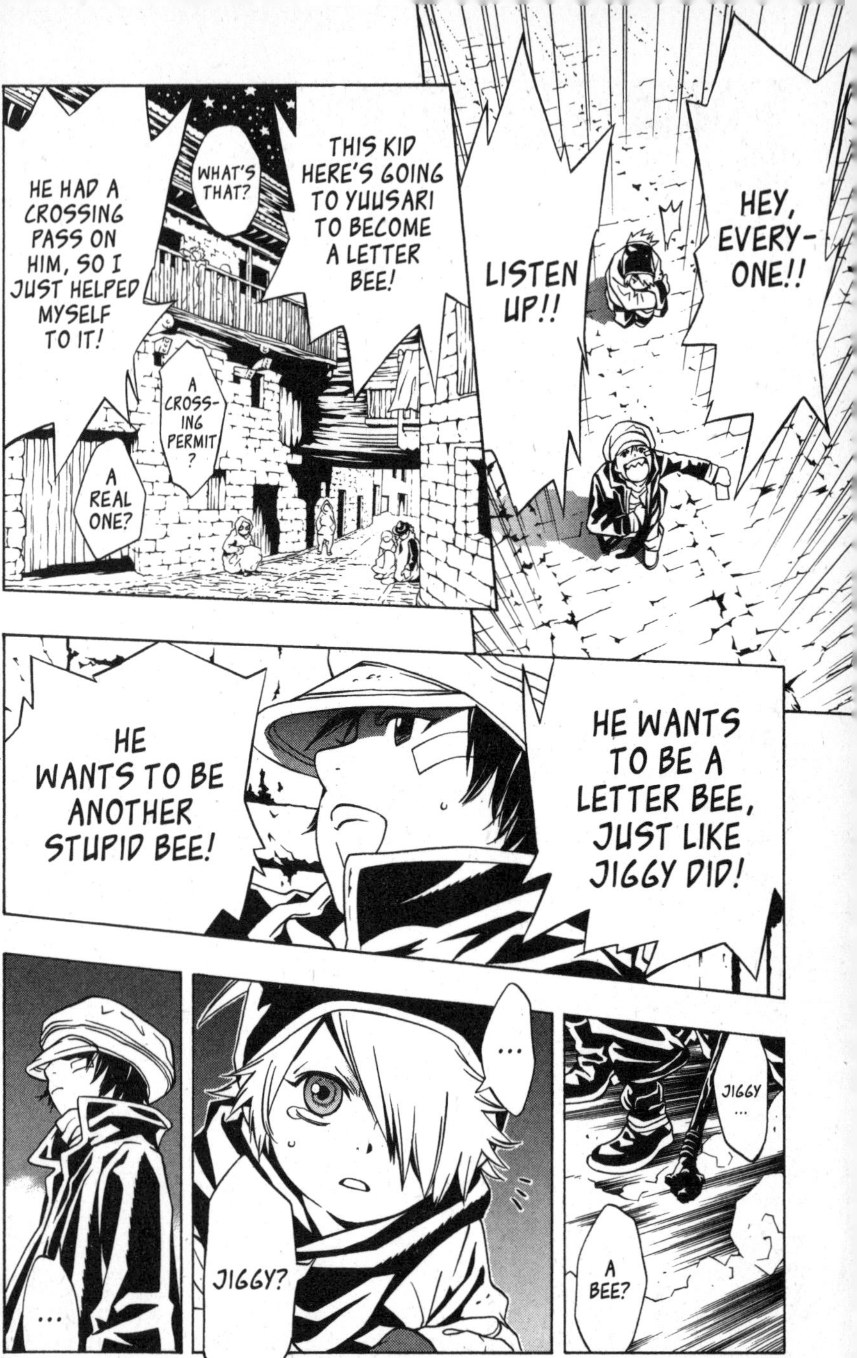
HEY, EVERY-ONE!!
LISTEN UP!!
THIS KID HERE'S GOING TO YUUSARI TO BECOME A LETTER BEE!
WHAT'S THAT?
HE HAD A CROSSING PASS ON HIM, SO I JUST HELPED MYSELF TO IT!
A CROSS-ING PERMIT?
A REAL ONE?
HE WANTS TO BE A LETTER BEE, JUST LIKE JIGGY DID!
HE WANTS TO BE ANOTHER STUPID BEE!
JIGGY ...
A BEE?
...
JIGGY?
...

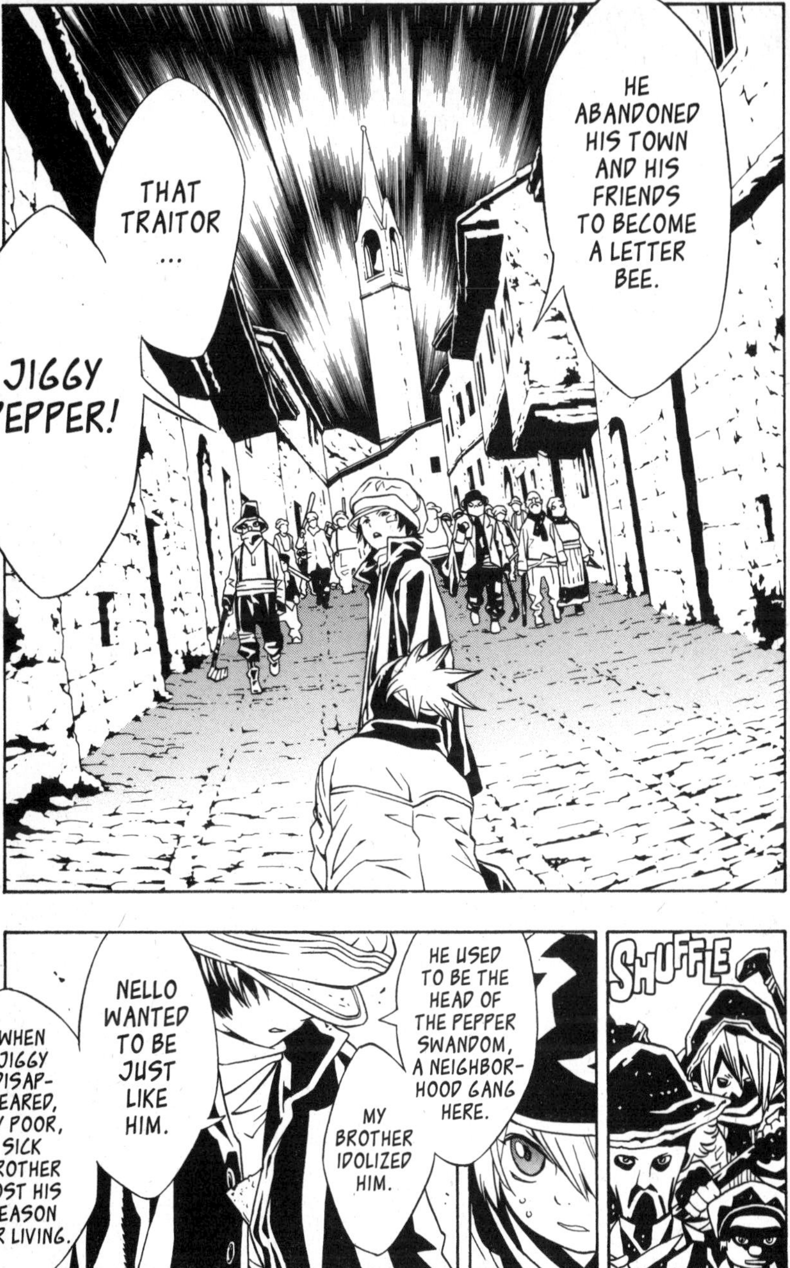
HE ABANDONED HIS TOWN AND HIS FRIENDS TO BECOME A LETTER BEE.
THAT TRAITOR ...
JIGGY PEPPER!
SHUFFLE
HE USED TO BE THE HEAD OF THE PEPPER SWANDOM, A NEIGHBORHOOD GANG HERE.
MY BROTHER IDOLIZED HIM.
NELLO WANTED TO BE JUST LIKE HIM.
WHEN JIGGY DISAPPEARED, MY POOR, SICK BROTHER LOST HIS REASON FOR LIVING.

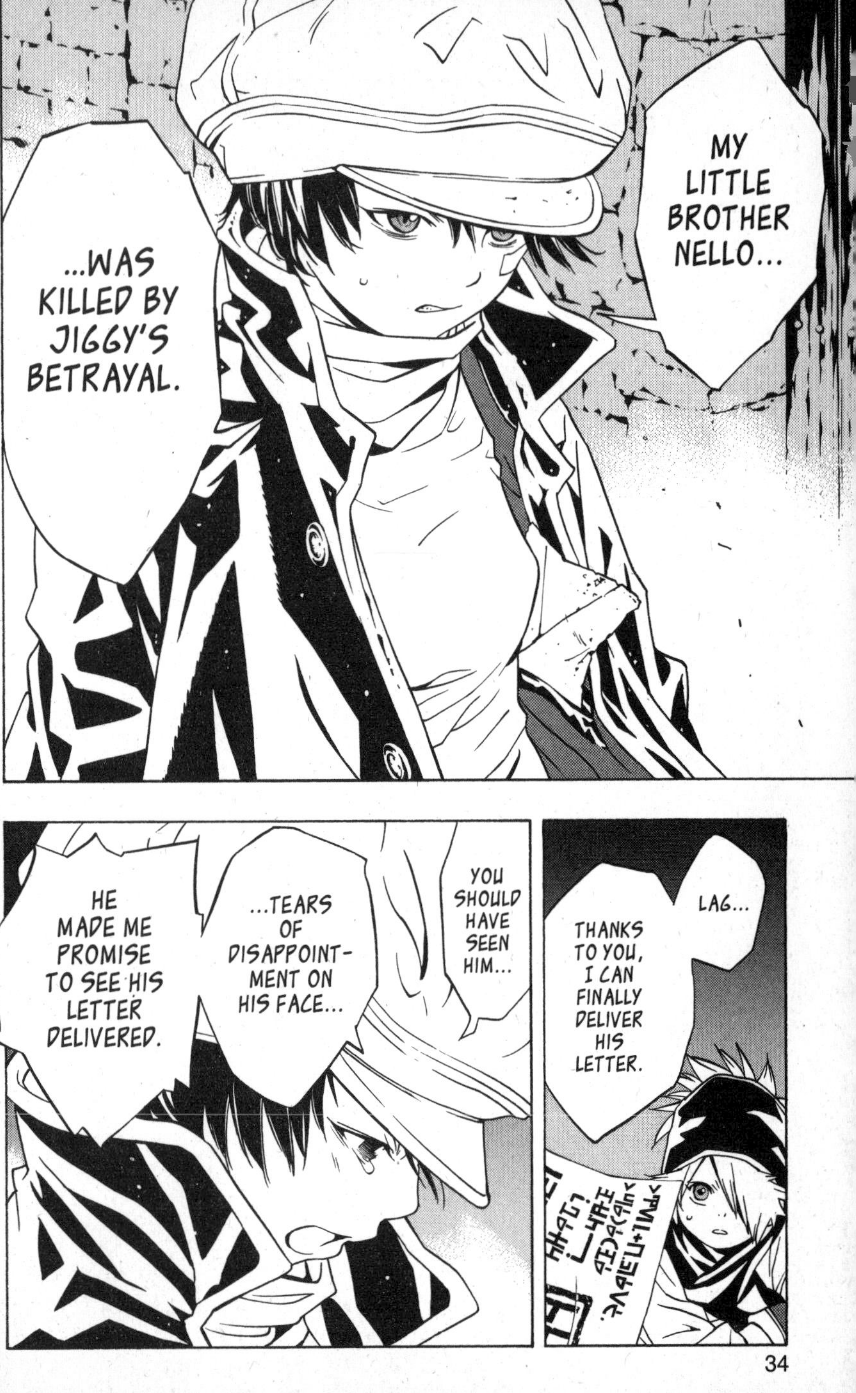
MY LITTLE BROTHER NELLO...
...WAS KILLED BY JIGGY'S BETRAYAL.
LAG...
THANKS TO YOU, I CAN FINALLY DELIVER HIS LETTER.
YOU SHOULD HAVE SEEN HIM...
...TEARS OF DISAPPOINT-MENT ON HIS FACE...
HE MADE ME PROMISE TO SEE HIS LETTER DELIVERED.

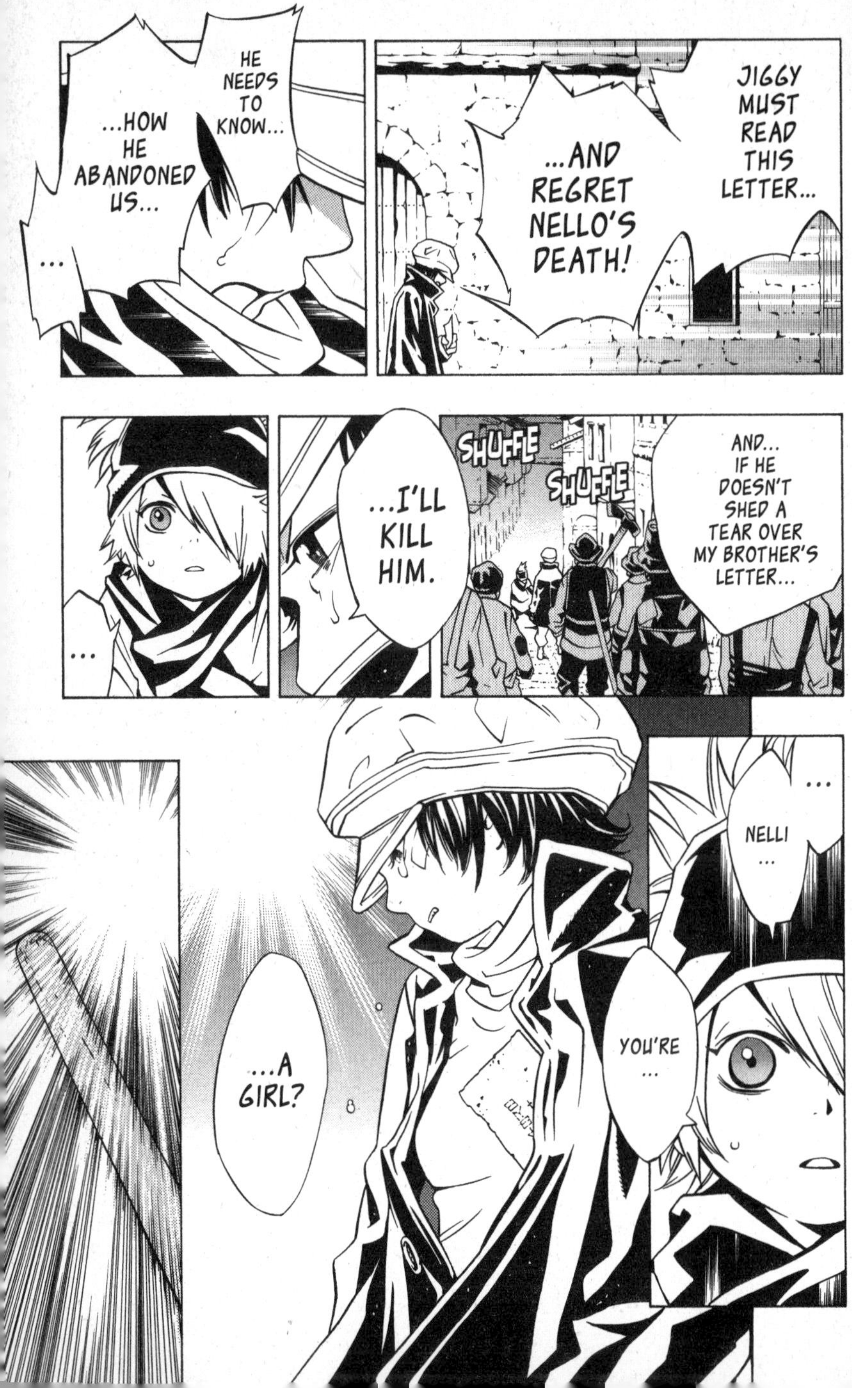
JIGGY MUST READ THIS LETTER...
...AND REGRET NELLO'S DEATH!
HE NEEDS TO KNOW...
...HOW HE ABANDONED US...
...
AND... IF HE DOESN'T SHED A TEAR OVER MY BROTHER'S LETTER...
SHUFFLE
SHUFFLE
...I'LL KILL HIM.
...
...
NELLI...
YOU'RE...
...A GIRL?

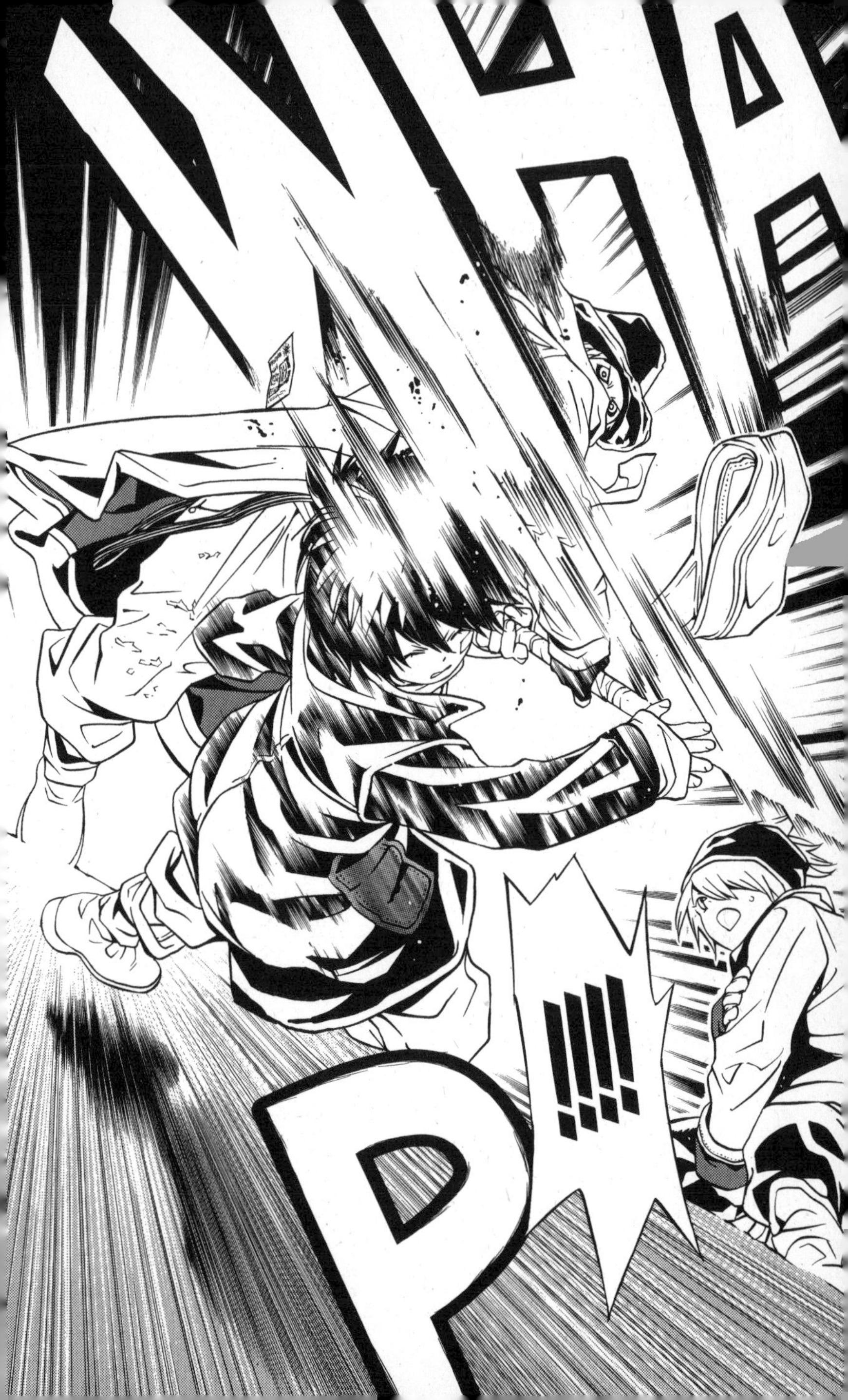
WHAP!!!!!

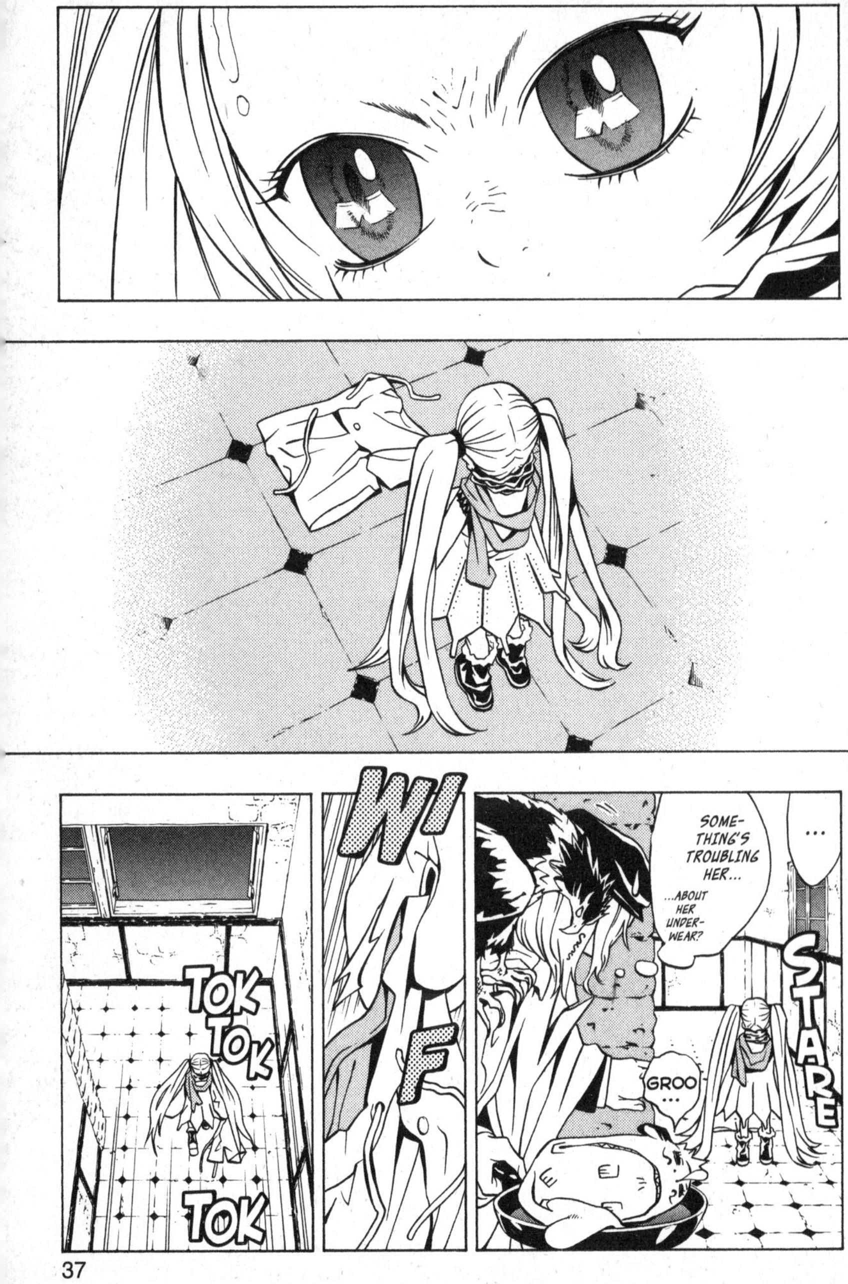
...
SOME-THING'S TROUBLING HER...
...ABOUT HER UNDER-WEAR?
STARE
GROO...
WIF
TOK TOK
TOK

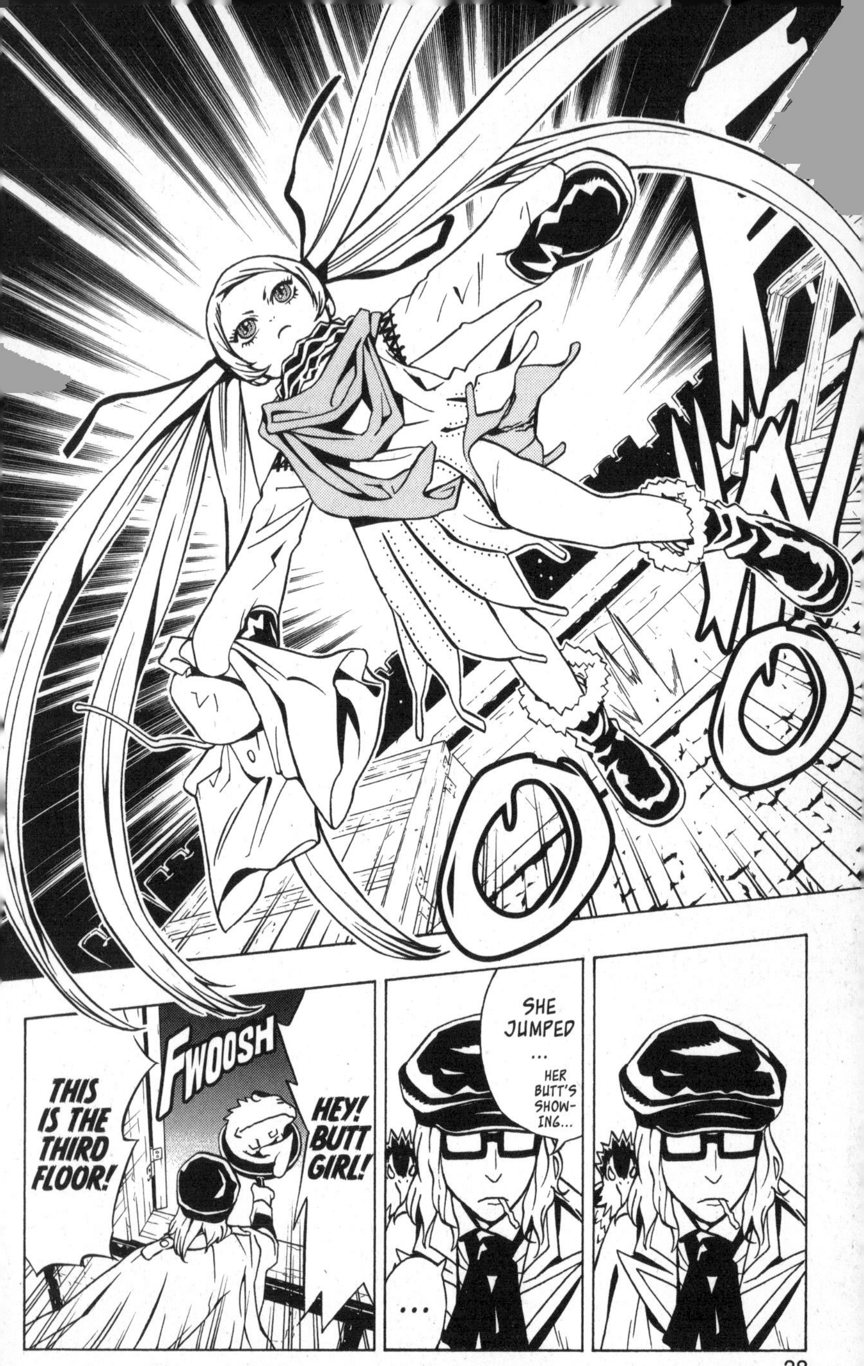
SHE JUMPED ... HER BUTT'S SHOWING...
...
HEY! BUTT GIRL!
FWOOSH
THIS IS THE THIRD FLOOR!

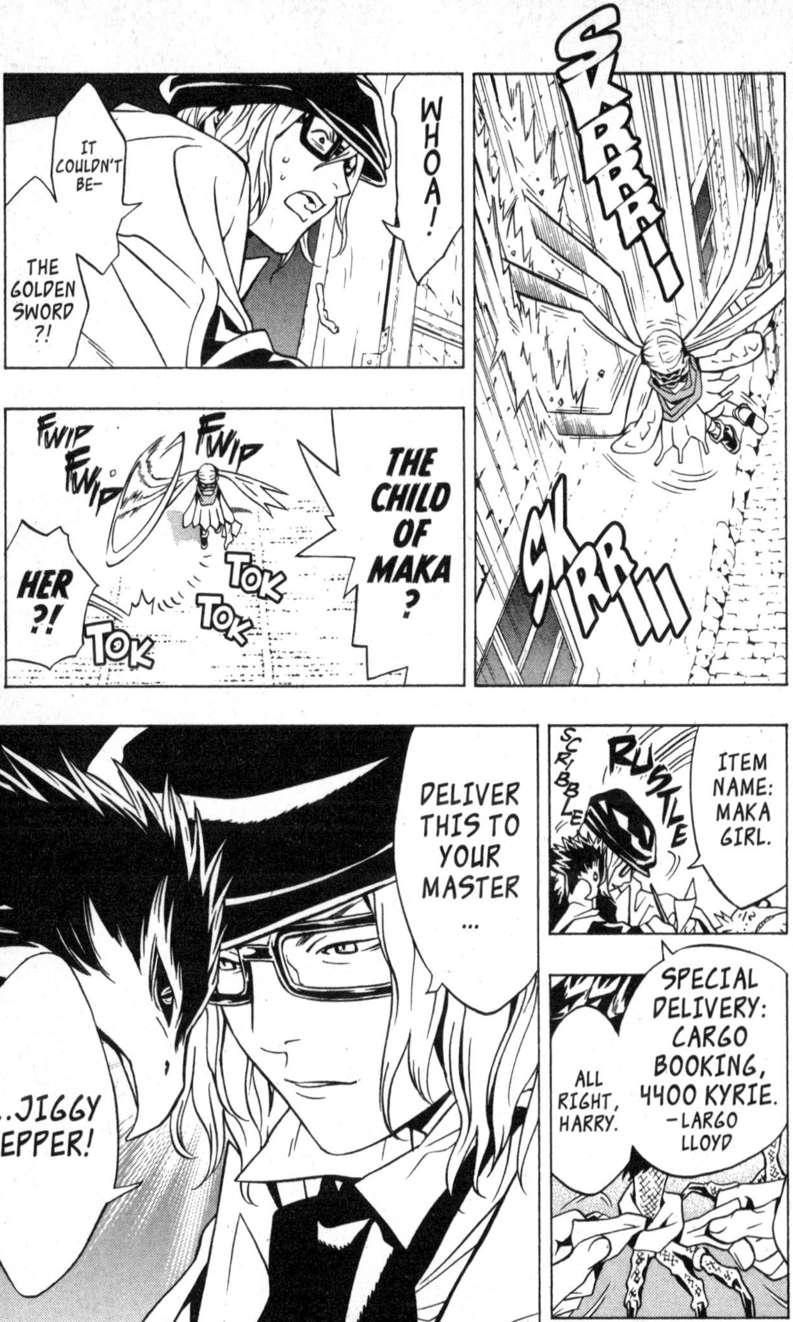
SKRRRR!!
SKRR!!!
WHOA!
IT COULDN'T BE—
THE GOLDEN SWORD ?!
THE CHILD OF MAKA ?
FWIP
FWIP
FWIP
TOK
TOK
TOK
HER ?!
ITEM NAME: MAKA GIRL.
RUSTLE
SCRIBBLE
SPECIAL DELIVERY: CARGO BOOKING, 4400 KYRIE. —LARGO LLOYD
ALL RIGHT, HARRY.
DELIVER THIS TO YOUR MASTER ...
...JIGGY PEPPER!

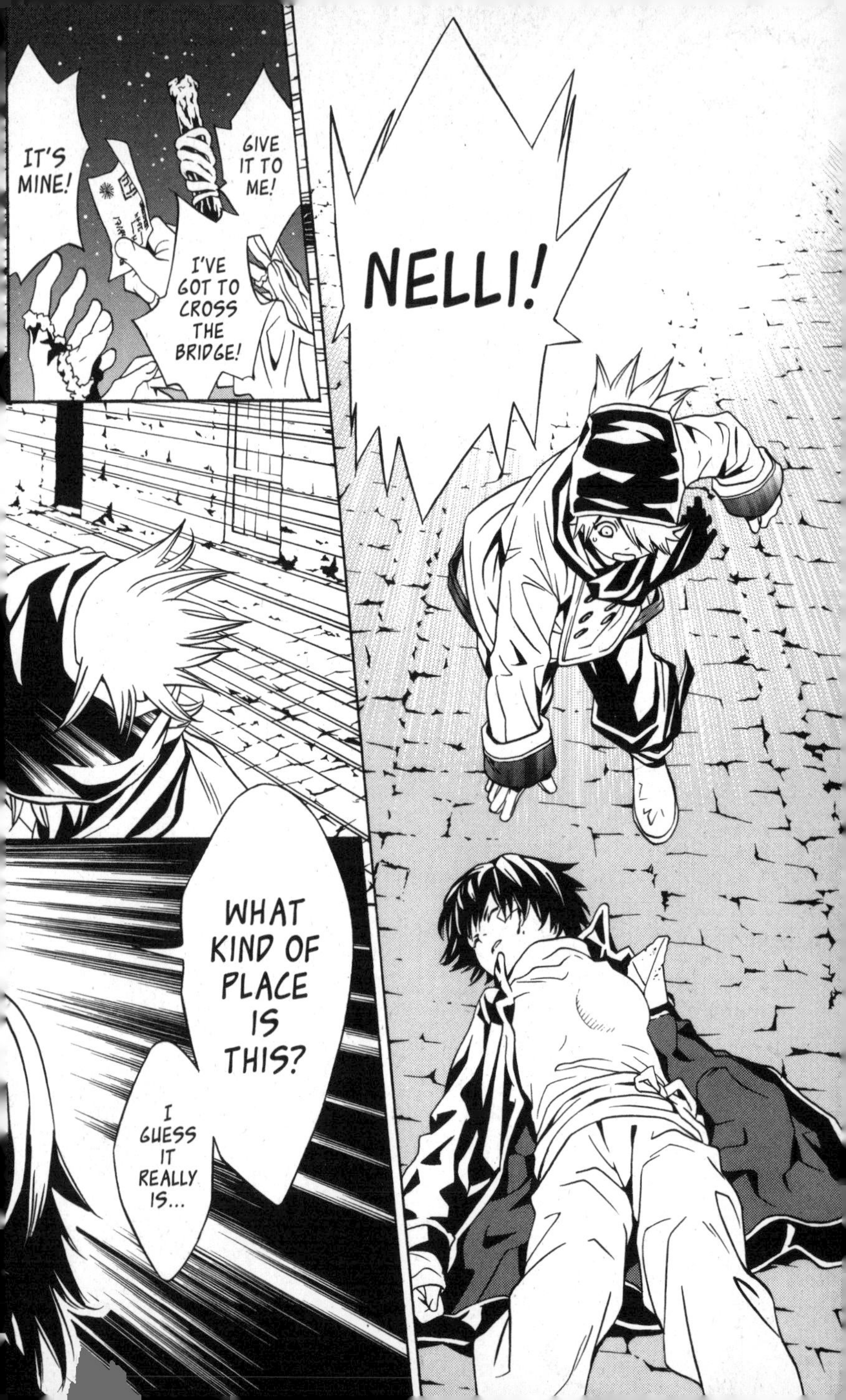
NELLI!
GIVE IT TO ME!
I'VE GOT TO CROSS THE BRIDGE!
IT'S MINE!
WHAT KIND OF PLACE IS THIS?
I GUESS IT REALLY IS...

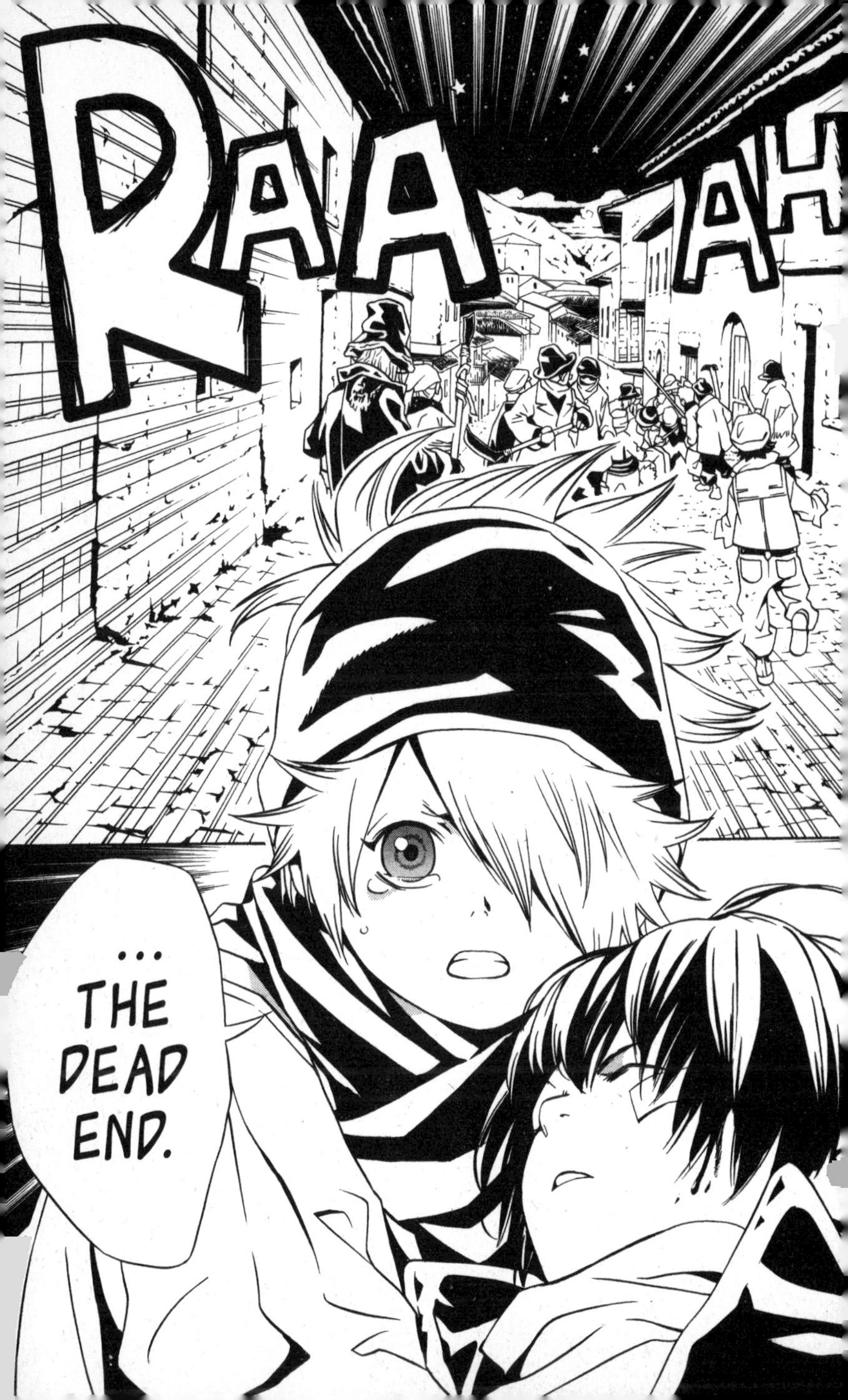
RAAAAH
... THE DEAD END.

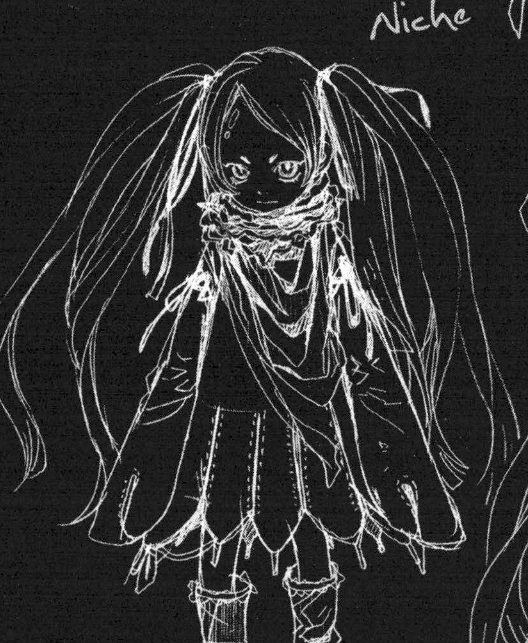
Niche

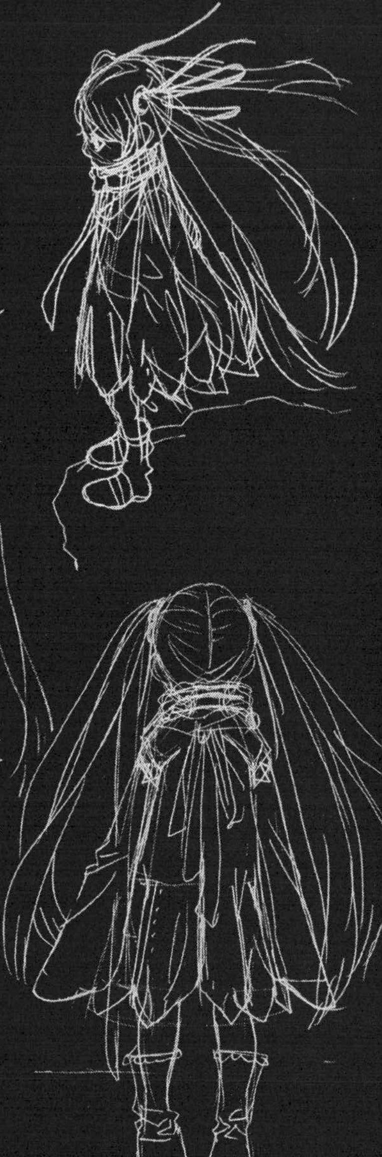

Niche ニッチ

In Western architecture, a hollow where the statue of the Virgin Mary or flowers are placed. It means "crevice" or "narrow space."

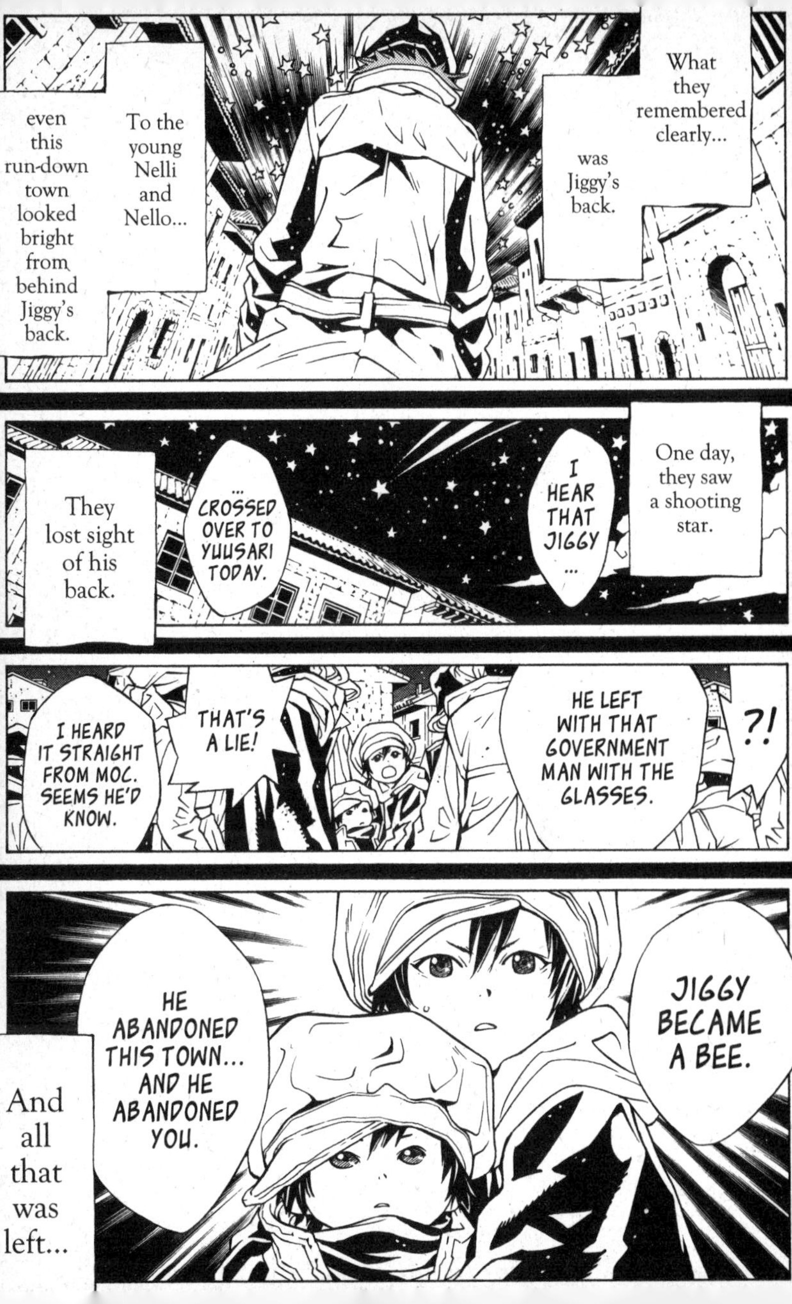
What they remembered clearly...
was Jiggy's back.
To the young Nelli and Nello...
even this run-down town looked bright from behind Jiggy's back.
One day, they saw a shooting star.
I HEAR THAT JIGGY...
...CROSSED OVER TO YUUSARI TODAY.
They lost sight of his back.
?!
HE LEFT WITH THAT GOVERNMENT MAN WITH THE GLASSES.
THAT'S A LIE!
I HEARD IT STRAIGHT FROM MOC. SEEMS HE'D KNOW.
JIGGY BECAME A BEE.
HE ABANDONED THIS TOWN... AND HE ABANDONED YOU.
And all that was left...

Chapter 4: The Letter to Jiggy Pepper, Part Two

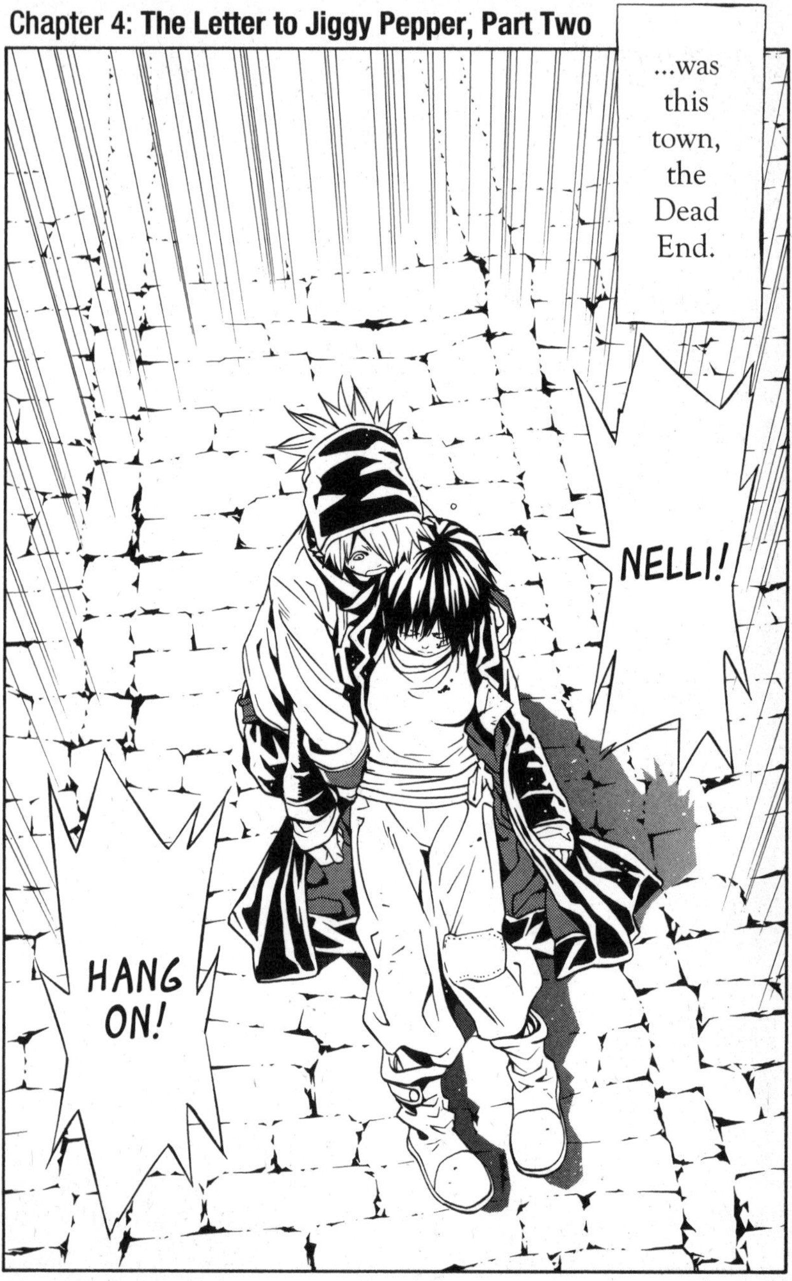
...was this town, the Dead End.
NELLI!
HANG ON!

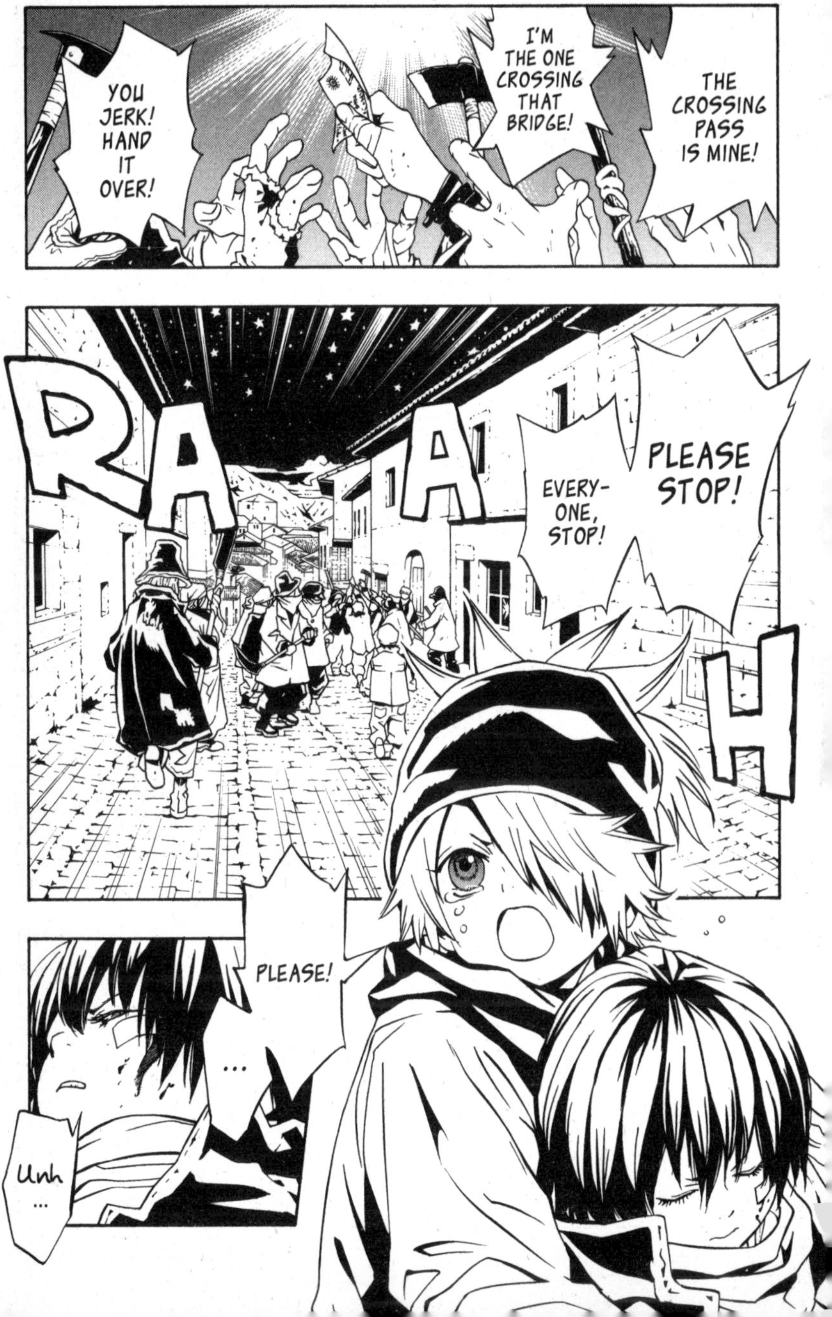
THE CROSSING PASS IS MINE!
I'M THE ONE CROSSING THAT BRIDGE!
YOU JERK! HAND IT OVER!
RAAH
PLEASE STOP!
EVERY-ONE, STOP!
PLEASE!
...
Unh ...

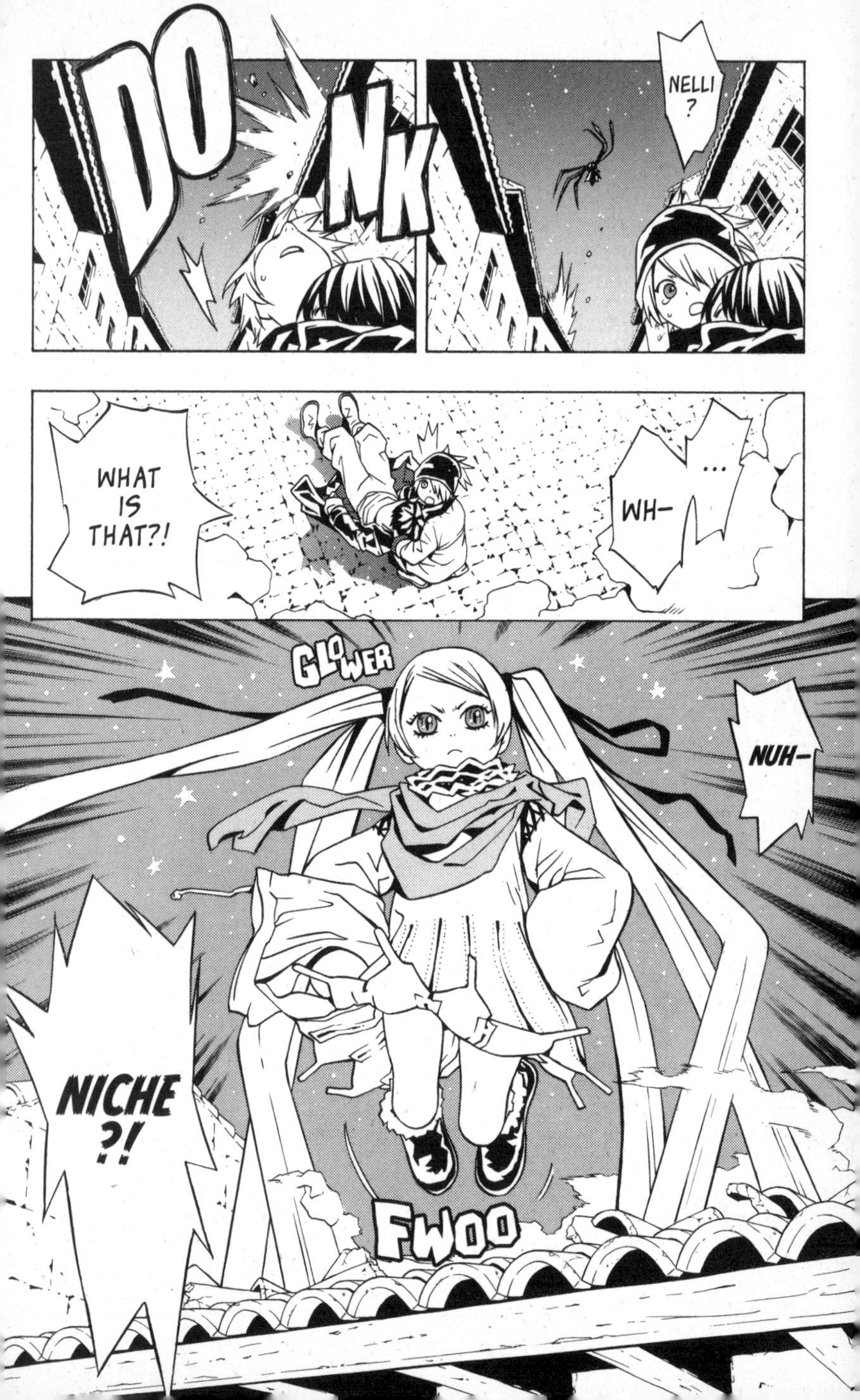

NELLI?
DONK
... WH-
WHAT IS THAT?!
NUH-
GLOWER
NICHE?!
FWOO

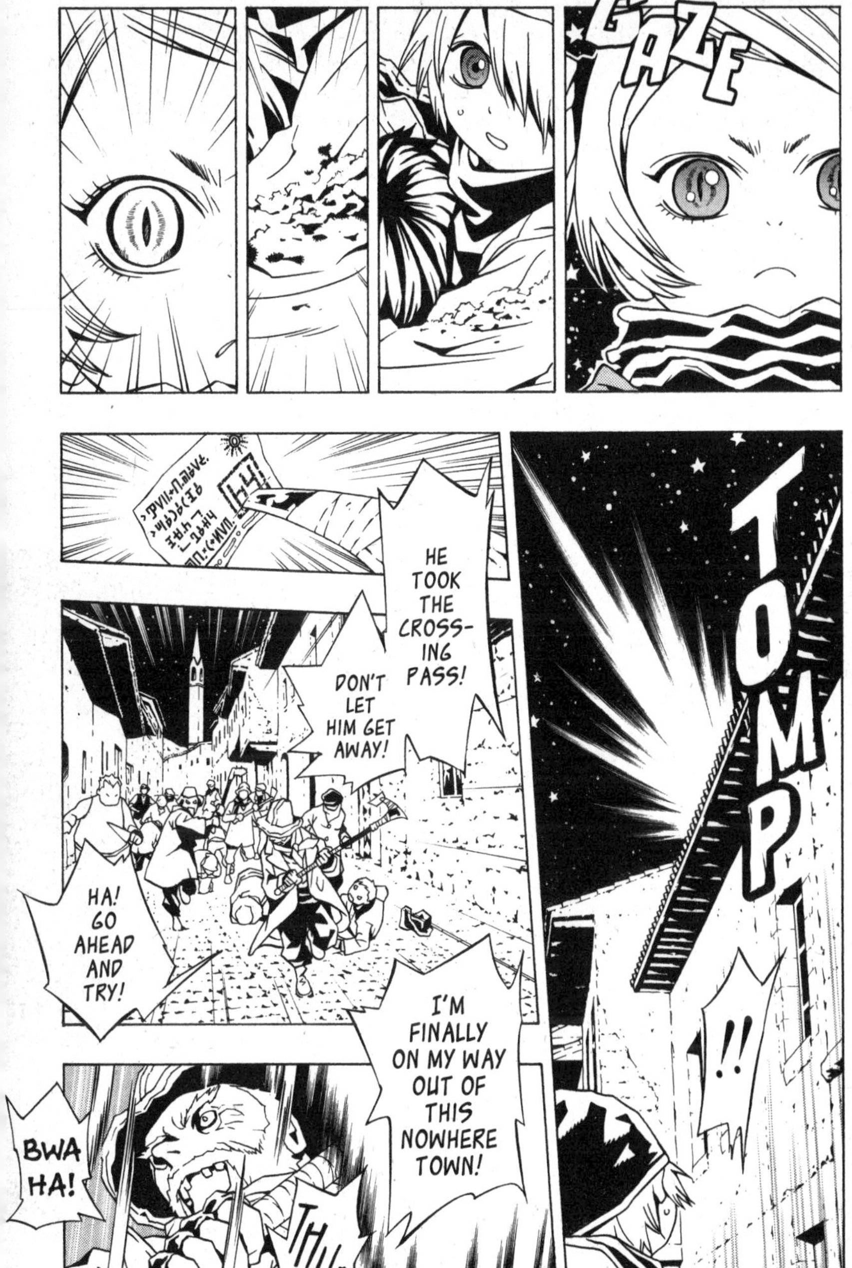
GAZE
TOMP
!!
HE TOOK THE CROSS-ING PASS!
DON'T LET HIM GET AWAY!
HA! GO AHEAD AND TRY!
I'M FINALLY ON MY WAY OUT OF THIS NOWHERE TOWN!
BWA HA!
THUD

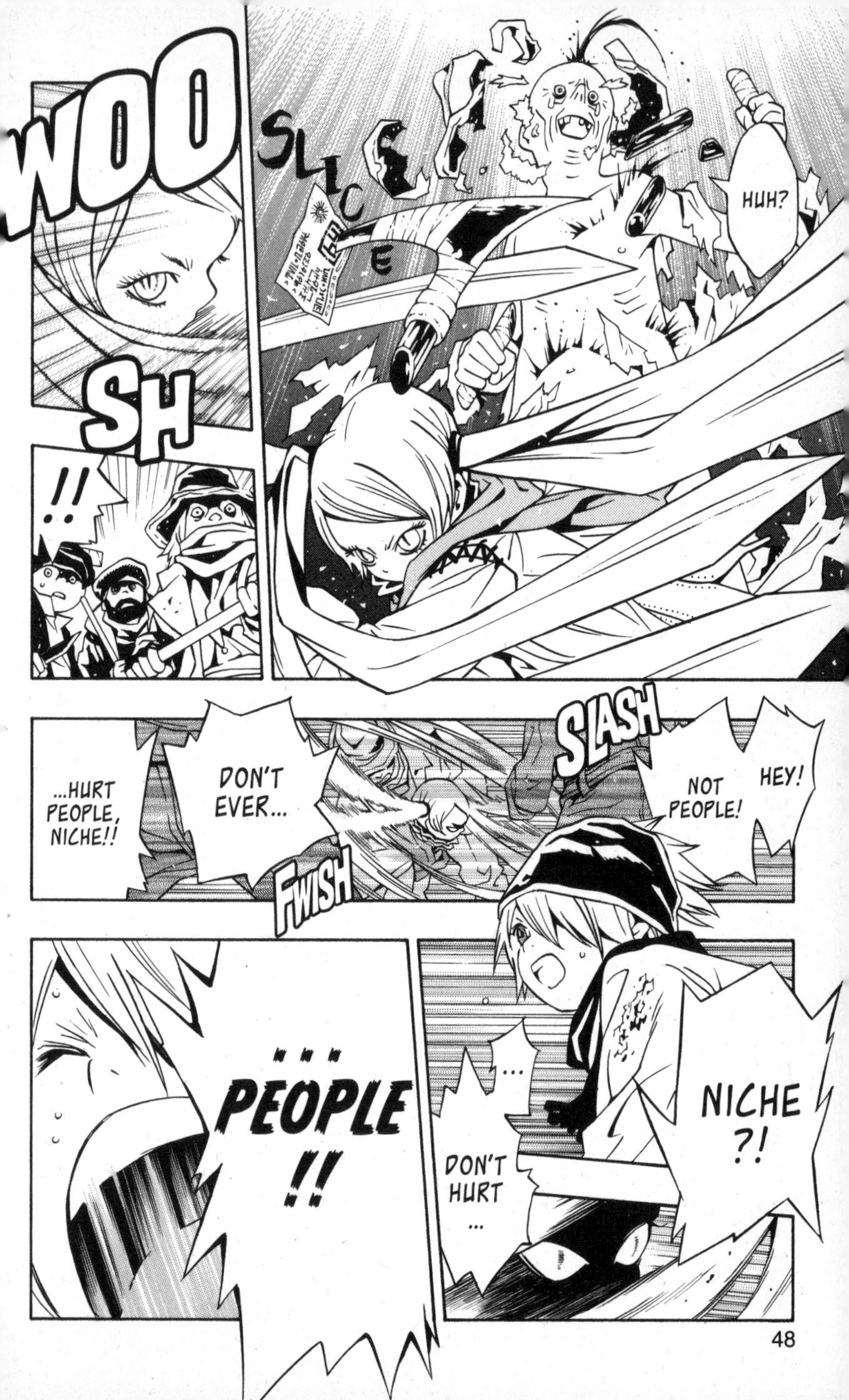
SLICE
HUH?
WOO
SH
!!
HEY!
NOT PEOPLE!
SLASH
FWISH
DON'T EVER...
...HURT PEOPLE, NICHE!!
NICHE ?!
...
DON'T HURT ...
...PEOPLE !!

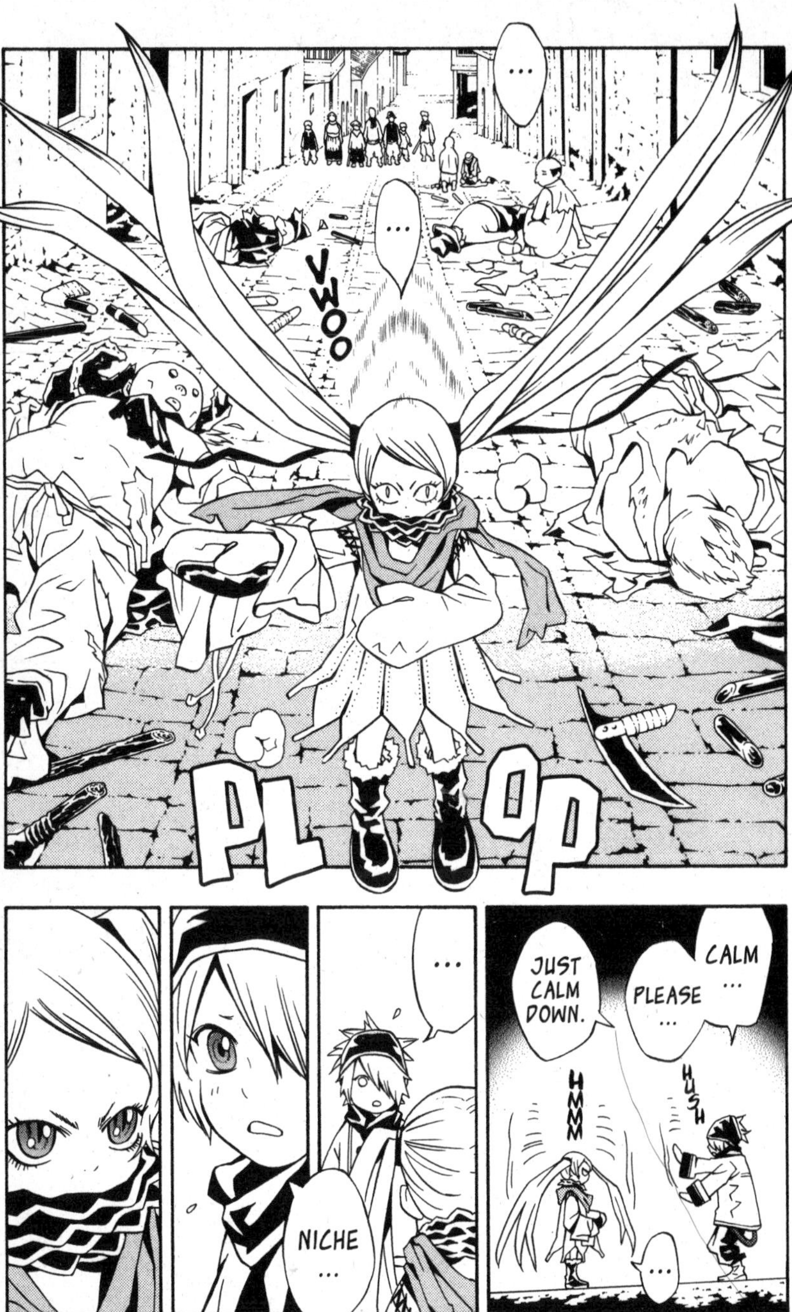
...
...
VWOO
PLOP
CALM ...
PLEASE ...
JUST CALM DOWN.
HUSH
HMMM
...
...
NICHE ...

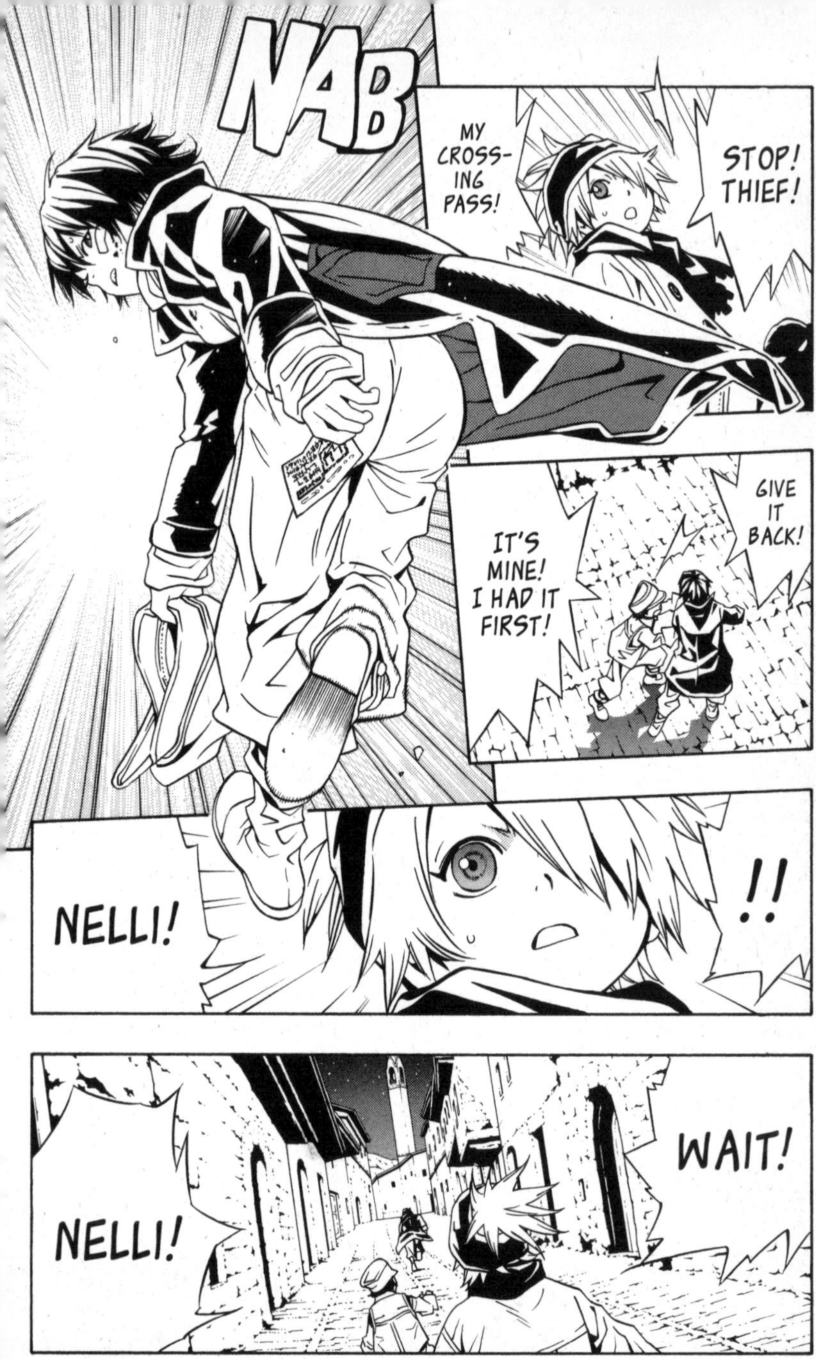
STOP! THIEF!
MY CROSSING-PASS!
GIVE IT BACK!
IT'S MINE! I HAD IT FIRST!
NAB
!!
NELLI!
WAIT!
NELLI!

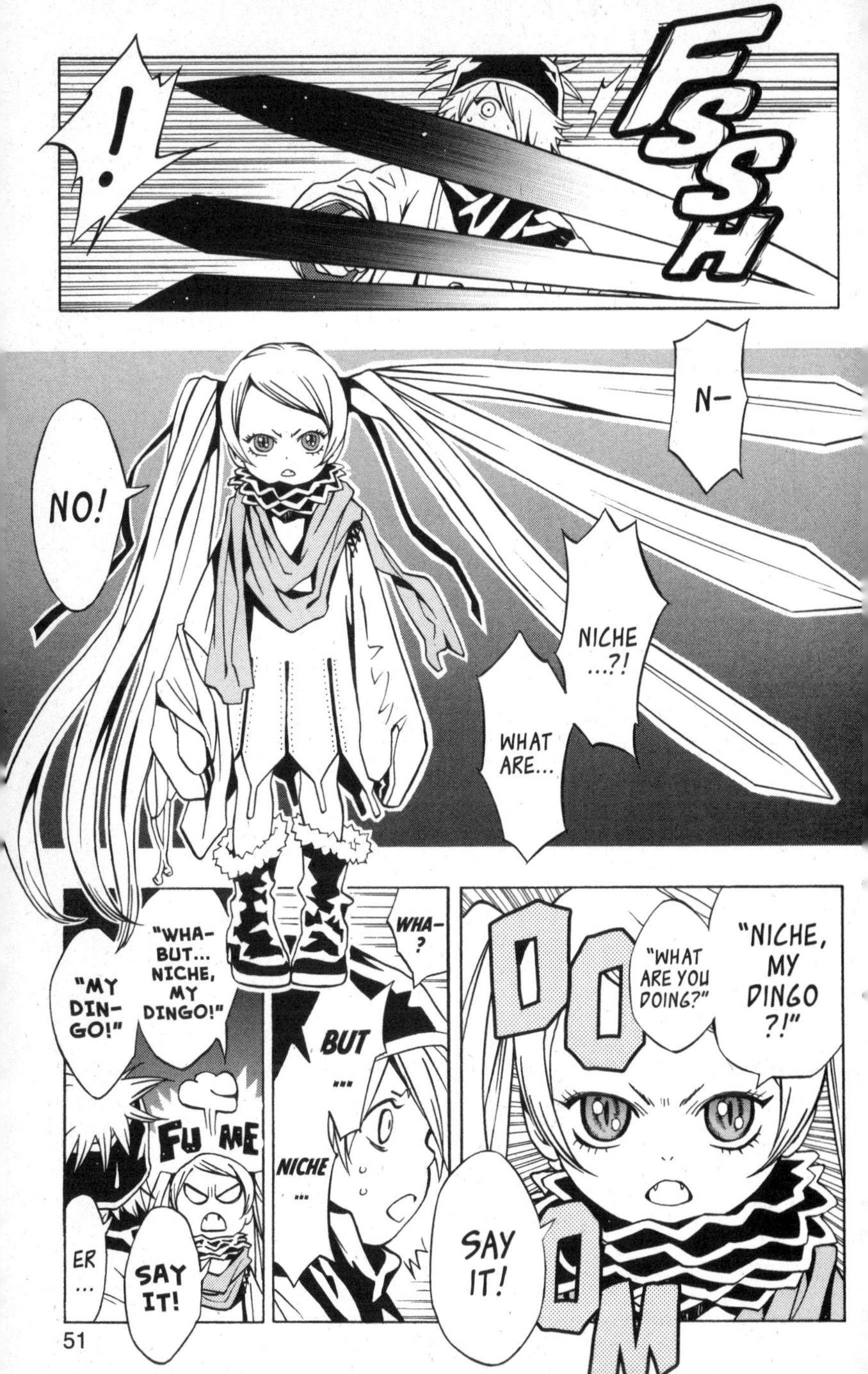
FSSH
!
N–
NICHE ...?!
WHAT ARE...
NO!
"NICHE, MY DINGO ?!"
"WHAT ARE YOU DOING?"
DOOM
SAY IT!
WHA- ?
BUT ...
NICHE ...
"WHA- BUT... NICHE, MY DINGO!"
"MY DIN- GO!"
FUME
ER ...
SAY IT!

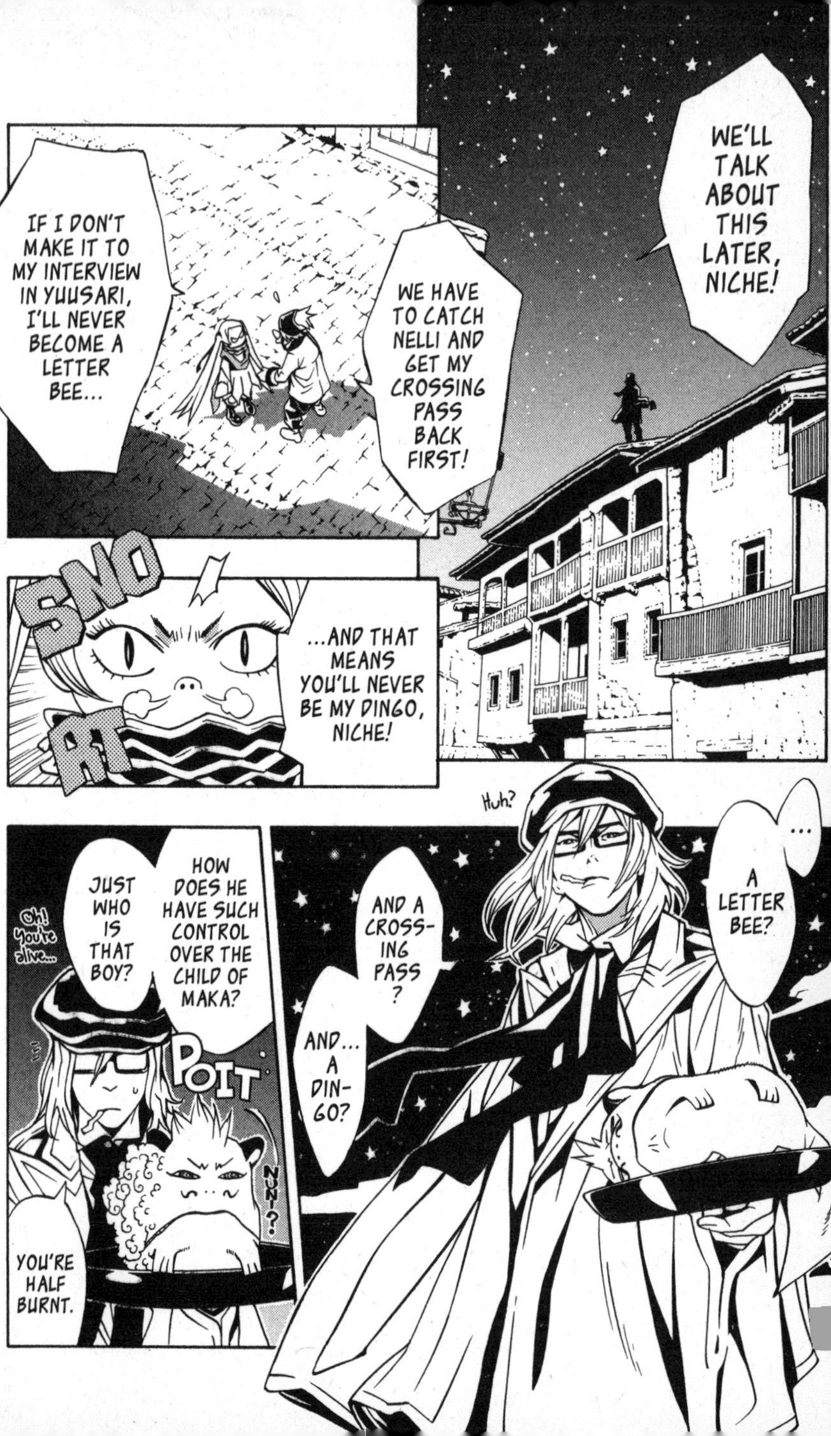
WE'LL TALK ABOUT THIS LATER, NICHE!
WE HAVE TO CATCH NELLI AND GET MY CROSSING PASS BACK FIRST!
IF I DON'T MAKE IT TO MY INTERVIEW IN YUUSARI, I'LL NEVER BECOME A LETTER BEE...
...AND THAT MEANS YOU'LL NEVER BE MY DINGO, NICHE!
SNOAT
Huh?
... A LETTER BEE?
AND A CROSSING PASS?
AND... A DINGO?
HOW DOES HE HAVE SUCH CONTROL OVER THE CHILD OF MAKA?
JUST WHO IS THAT BOY?
Oh! You're alive...
POIT
NUNI?
YOU'RE HALF BURNT.

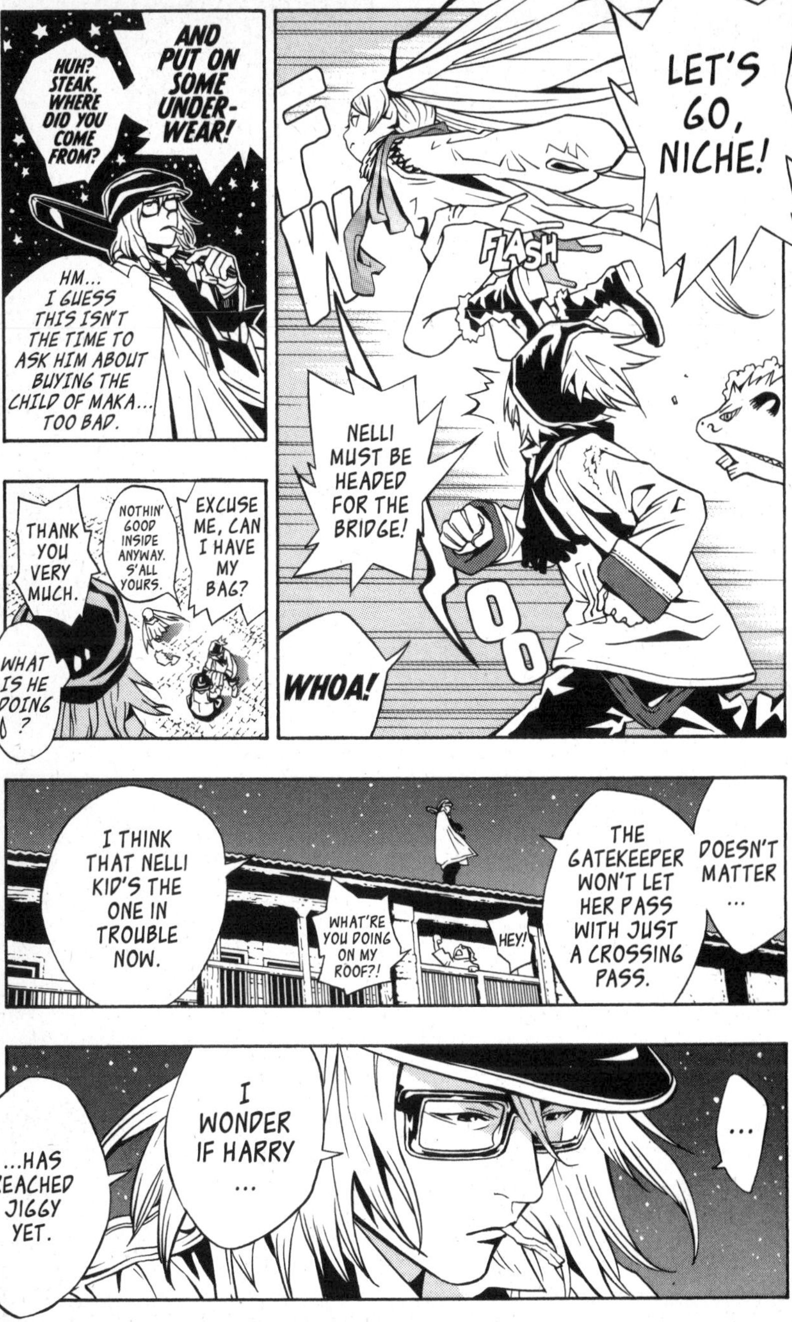
LET'S GO, NICHE!
FLASH
NELLI MUST BE HEADED FOR THE BRIDGE!
WHOA!
AND PUT ON SOME UNDER-WEAR!
HUH? STEAK, WHERE DID YOU COME FROM?
HM... I GUESS THIS ISN'T THE TIME TO ASK HIM ABOUT BUYING THE CHILD OF MAKA... TOO BAD.
EXCUSE ME, CAN I HAVE MY BAG?
NOTHIN' GOOD INSIDE ANYWAY. S'ALL YOURS.
THANK YOU VERY MUCH.
WHAT IS HE DOING?
DOESN'T MATTER...
THE GATEKEEPER WON'T LET HER PASS WITH JUST A CROSSING PASS.
HEY!
WHAT'RE YOU DOING ON MY ROOF?!
I THINK THAT NELLI KID'S THE ONE IN TROUBLE NOW.
...
I WONDER IF HARRY...
...HAS REACHED JIGGY YET.

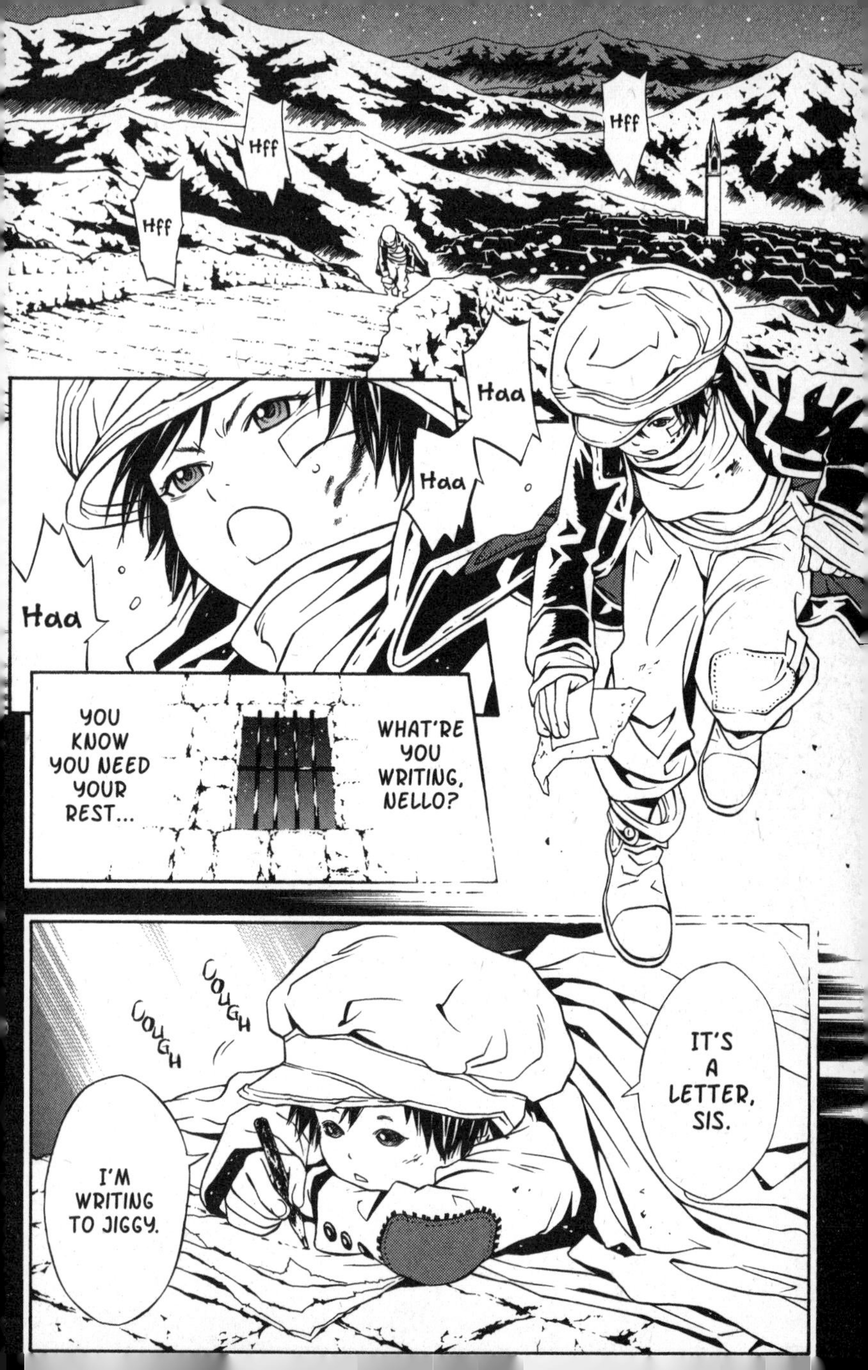
Hff
Hff
Hff
Haa
Haa
Haa
WHAT'RE YOU WRITING, NELLO?
YOU KNOW YOU NEED YOUR REST...
IT'S A LETTER, SIS.
COUGH
COUGH
I'M WRITING TO JIGGY.

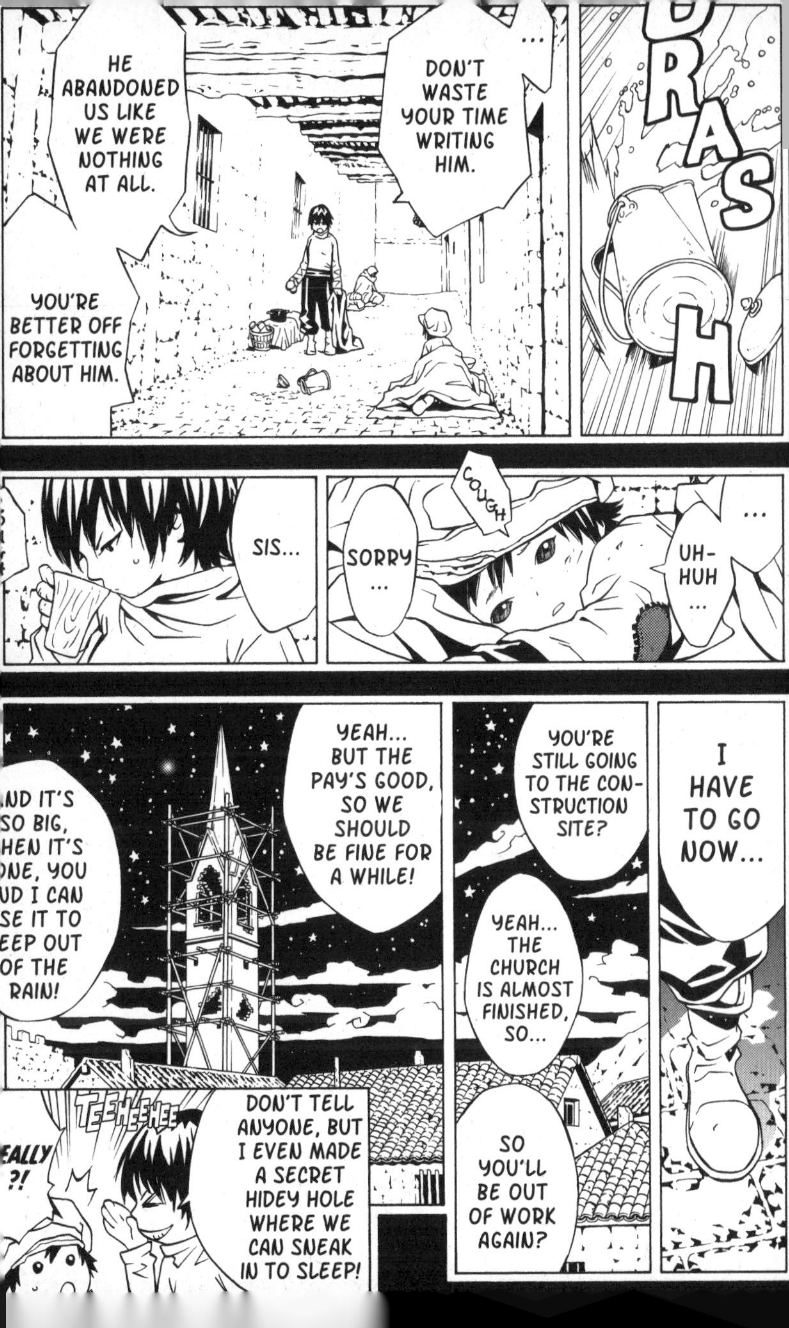
DRASH
...
DON'T WASTE YOUR TIME WRITING HIM.
HE ABANDONED US LIKE WE WERE NOTHING AT ALL.
YOU'RE BETTER OFF FORGETTING ABOUT HIM.
...
UH-HUH ...
COUGH
SORRY ...
SIS...
I HAVE TO GO NOW...
YOU'RE STILL GOING TO THE CONSTRUCTION SITE?
YEAH... THE CHURCH IS ALMOST FINISHED, SO...
SO YOU'LL BE OUT OF WORK AGAIN?
YEAH... BUT THE PAY'S GOOD, SO WE SHOULD BE FINE FOR A WHILE!
ND IT'S SO BIG, HEN IT'S ONE, YOU ND I CAN SE IT TO EEP OUT OF THE RAIN!
TEEHEEHEE
DON'T TELL ANYONE, BUT I EVEN MADE A SECRET HIDEY HOLE WHERE WE CAN SNEAK IN TO SLEEP!
EALLY ?!

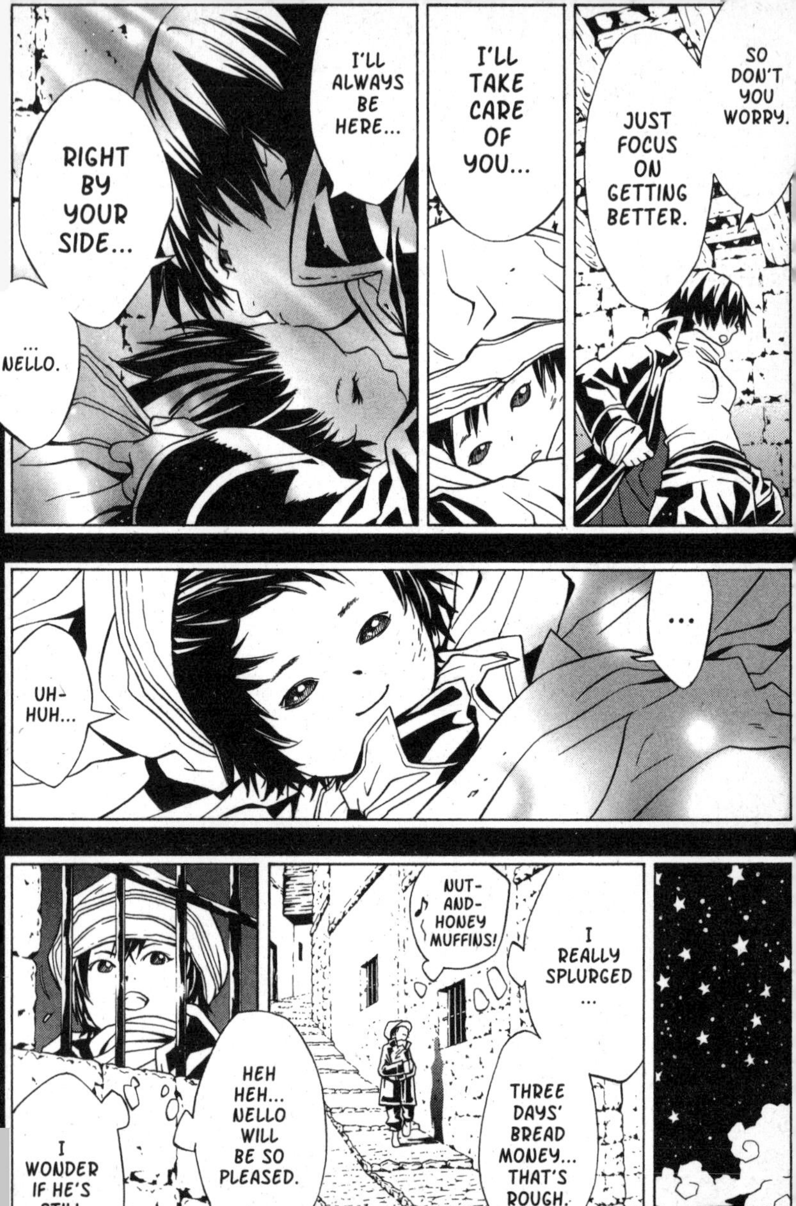
SO DON'T YOU WORRY.
JUST FOCUS ON GETTING BETTER.
I'LL TAKE CARE OF YOU...
I'LL ALWAYS BE HERE...
RIGHT BY YOUR SIDE...
...NELLO.
...
UH-HUH...
NUT-AND-HONEY MUFFINS!
I REALLY SPLURGED...
THREE DAYS' BREAD MONEY... THAT'S ROUGH.
HEH HEH... NELLO WILL BE SO PLEASED.
I WONDER IF HE'S STILL UP...

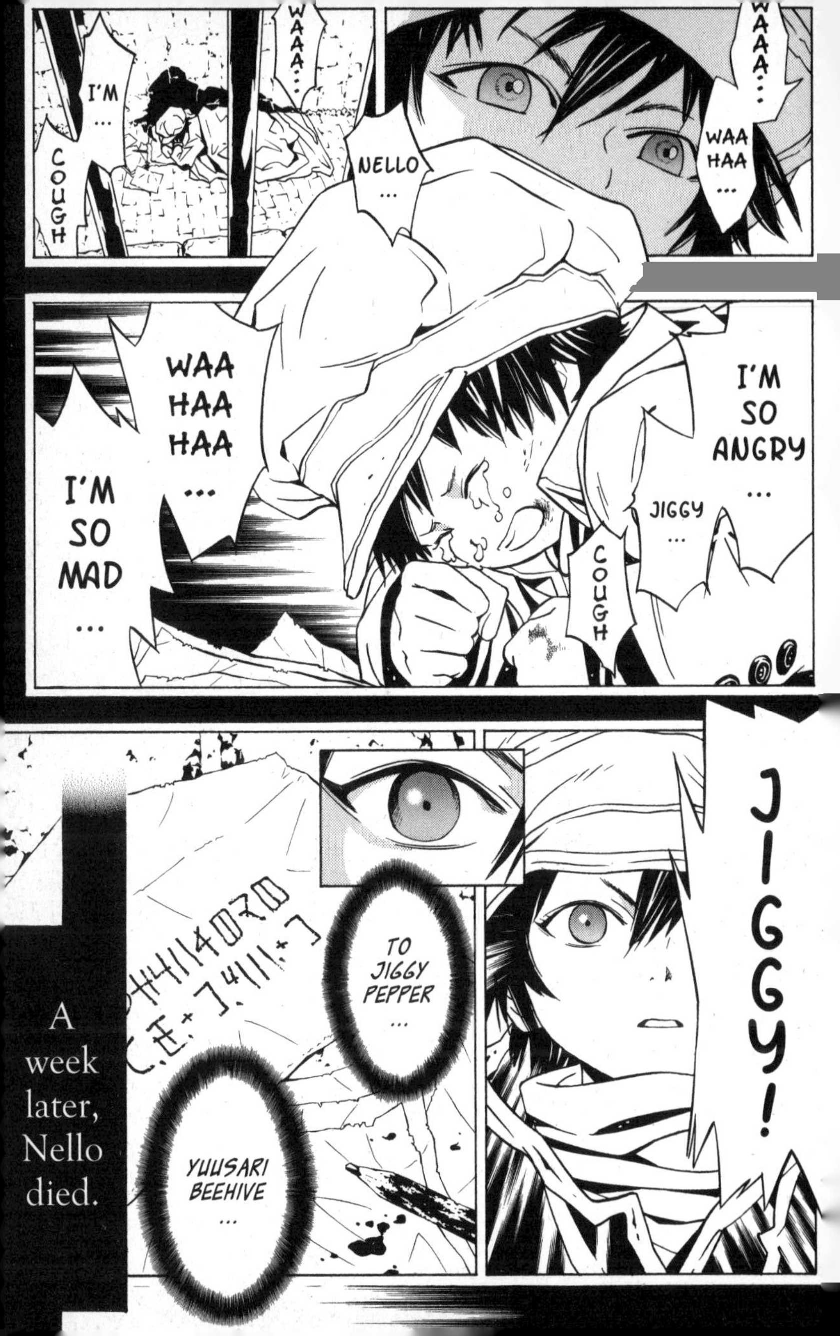
WAAA...
WAA HAA ...
NELLO ...
WAAA...
I'M ...
COUGH
I'M SO ANGRY ...
JIGGY ...
COUGH
WAA HAA HAA ...
I'M SO MAD ...
JIGGY!
TO JIGGY PEPPER ...
YUUSARI BEEHIVE ...
A week later, Nello died.

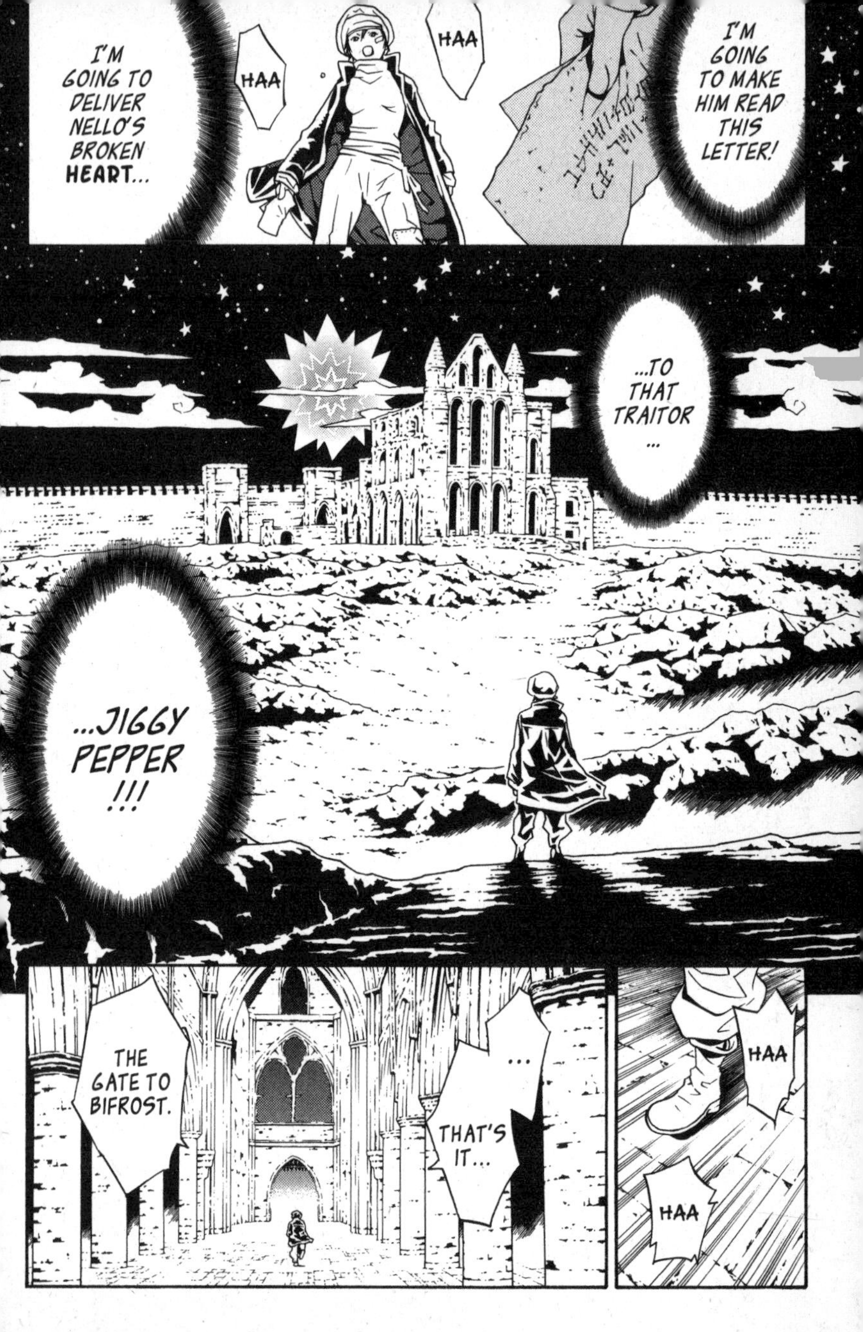
I'M GOING TO MAKE HIM READ THIS LETTER!
HAA
HAA
I'M GOING TO DELIVER NELLO'S BROKEN HEART...
...TO THAT TRAITOR...
...JIGGY PEPPER!!!
HAA
HAA
...
THAT'S IT...
THE GATE TO BIFROST.

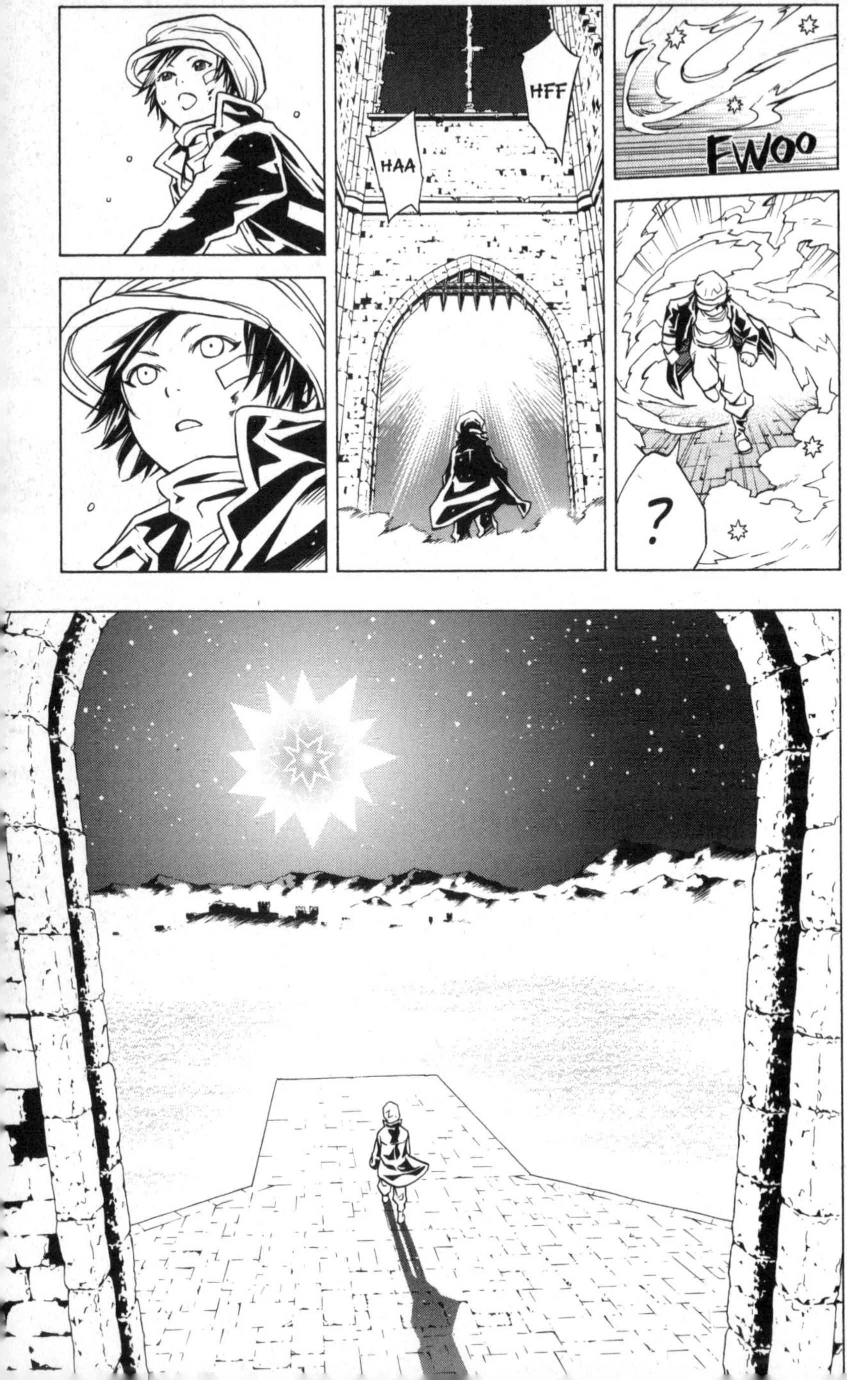
FWOO
?
HFF
HAA

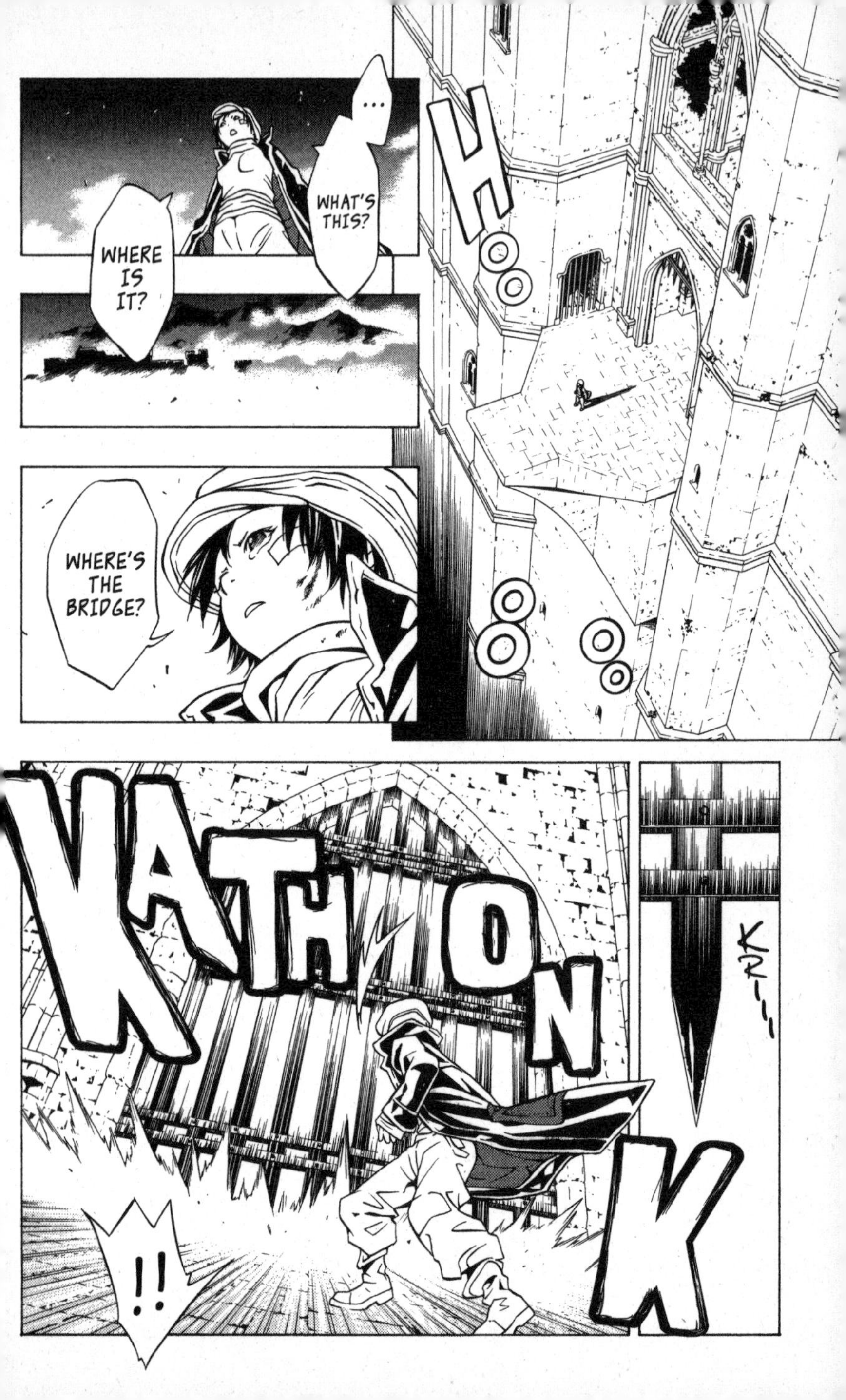
HOOOOO
...
WHAT'S THIS?
WHERE IS IT?
WHERE'S THE BRIDGE?
KRIII
KATHOONK
!!

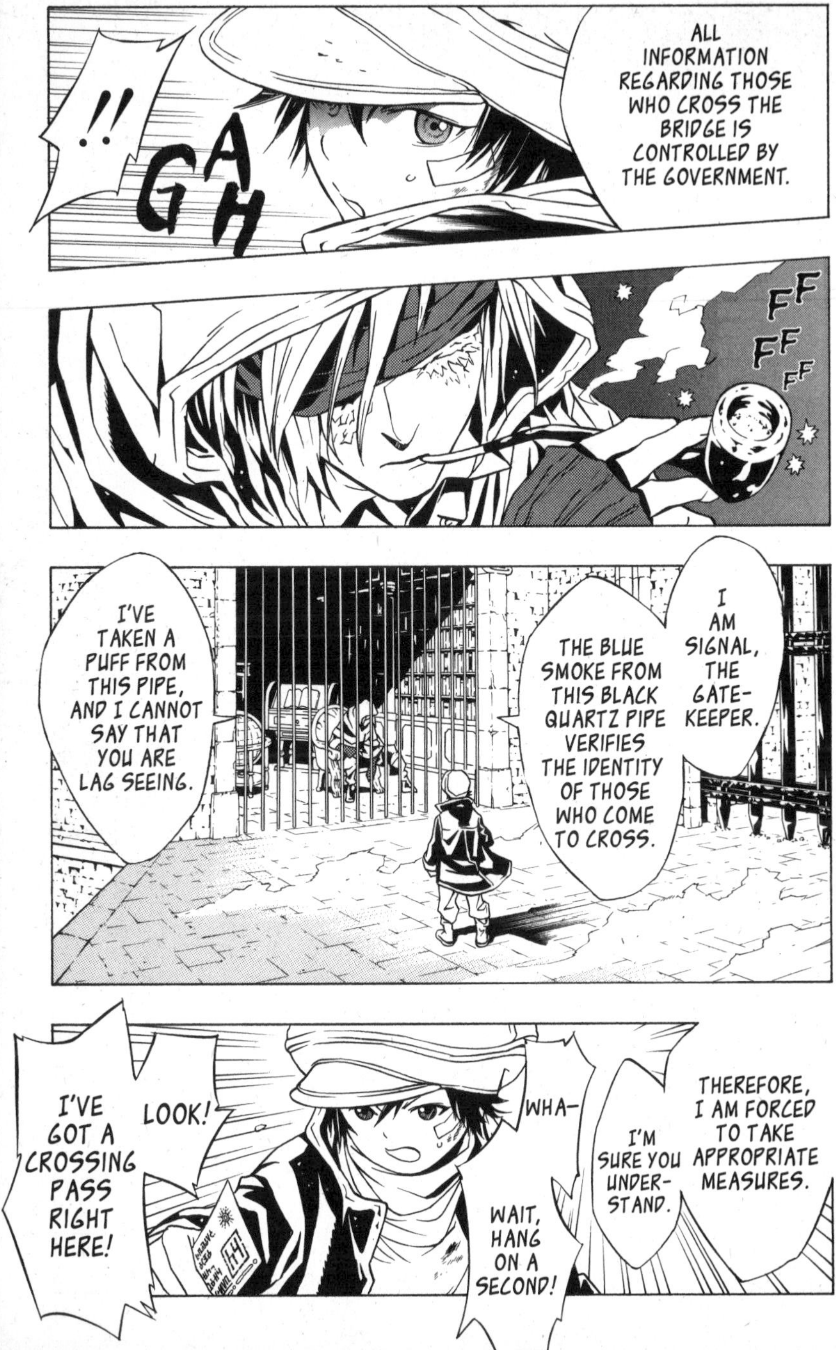

ALL INFORMATION REGARDING THOSE WHO CROSS THE BRIDGE IS CONTROLLED BY THE GOVERNMENT.
!!
GAH
FF FF FF
I AM SIGNAL, THE GATE-KEEPER.
THE BLUE SMOKE FROM THIS BLACK QUARTZ PIPE VERIFIES THE IDENTITY OF THOSE WHO COME TO CROSS.
I'VE TAKEN A PUFF FROM THIS PIPE, AND I CANNOT SAY THAT YOU ARE LAG SEEING.
THEREFORE, I AM FORCED TO TAKE APPROPRIATE MEASURES.
I'M SURE YOU UNDER-STAND.
WHA-
WAIT, HANG ON A SECOND!
LOOK!
I'VE GOT A CROSSING PASS RIGHT HERE!

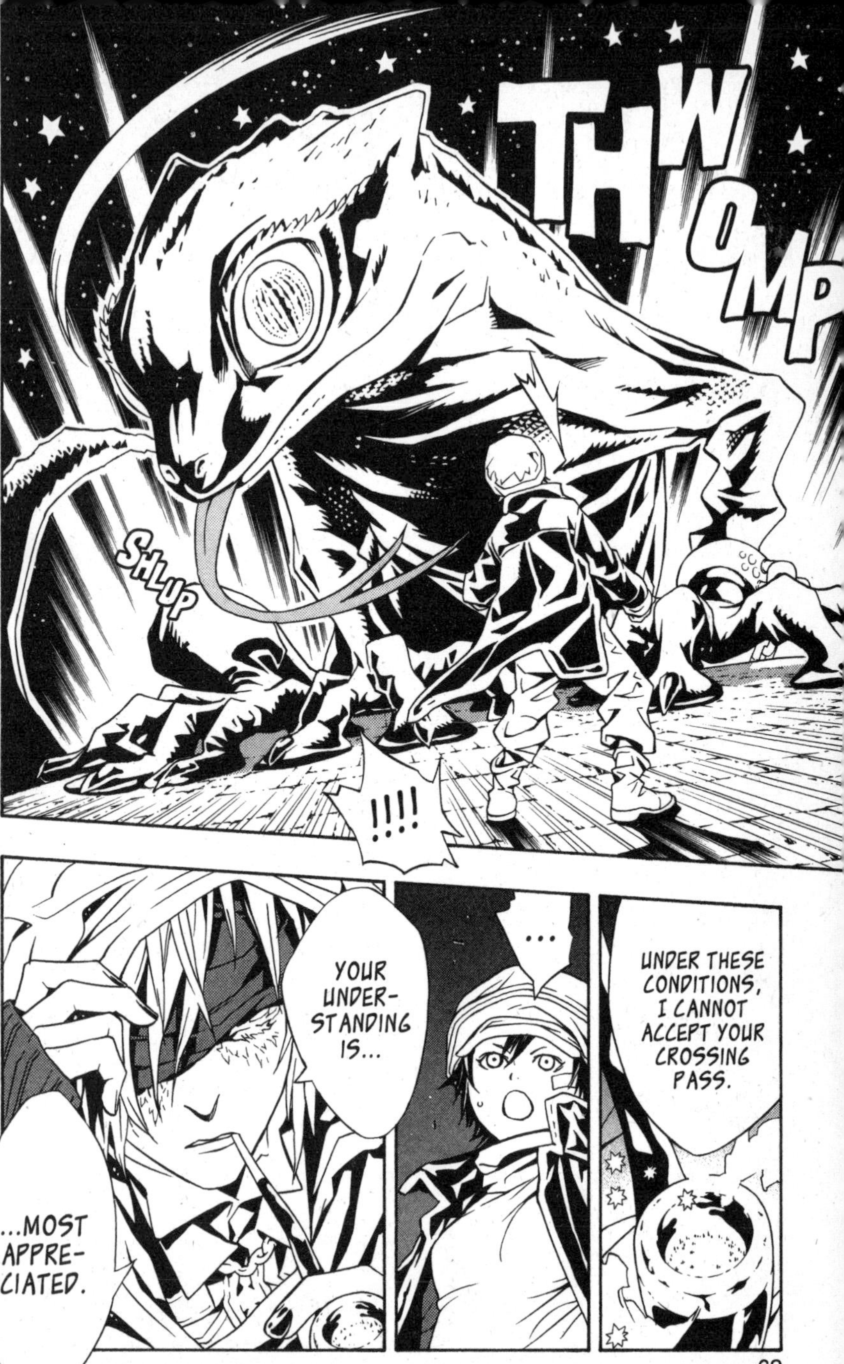
THWOMP
SHLUP
!!!!
UNDER THESE CONDITIONS, I CANNOT ACCEPT YOUR CROSSING PASS.
...
YOUR UNDER-STANDING IS...
...MOST APPRECIATED.

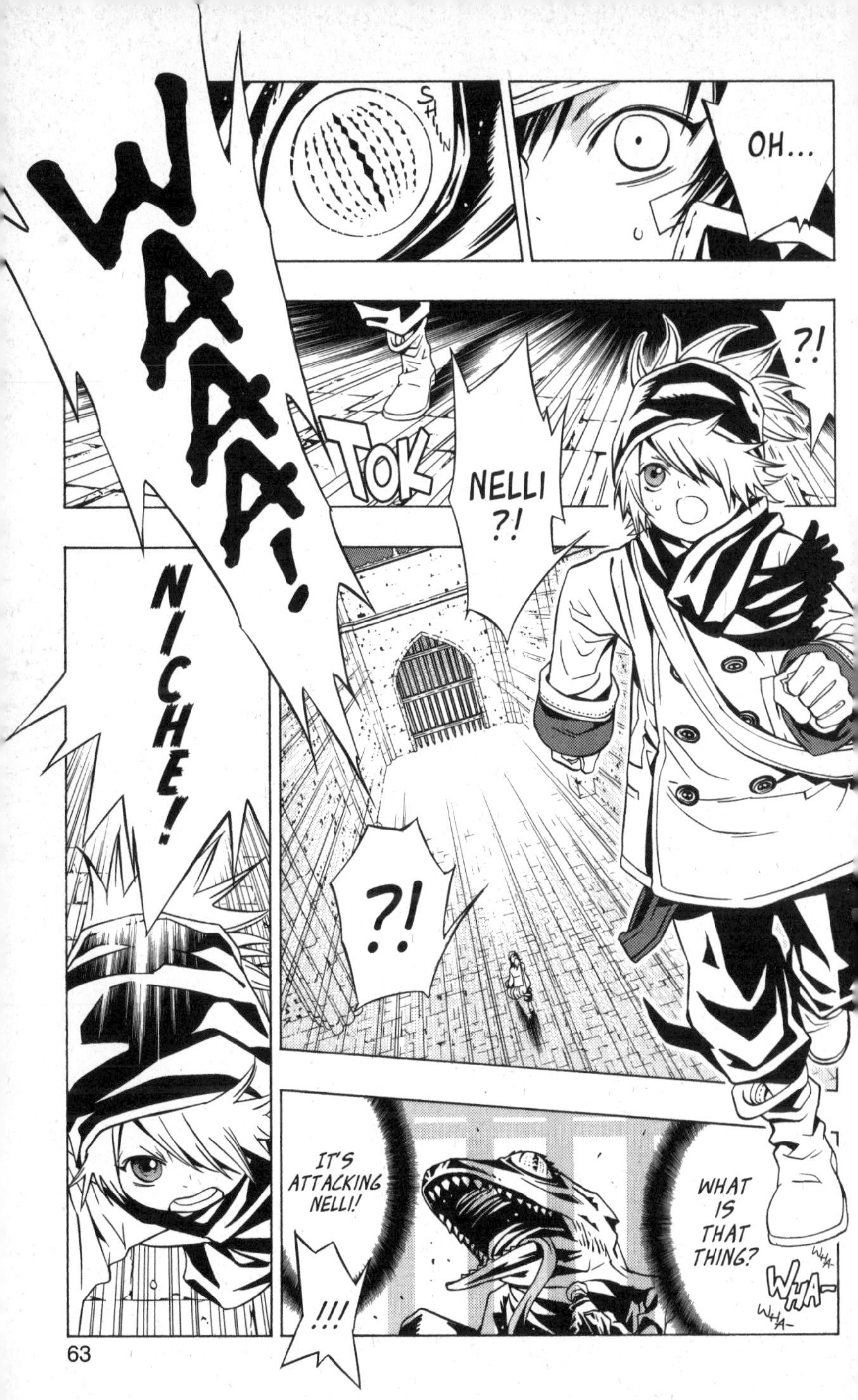
OH...
SHIIN
?!
NELLI ?!
TOK
?!
WHAT IS THAT THING?
WHA- WHA- WHA-
IT'S ATTACKING NELLI!
!!!
WAAA!!
NICHE!!

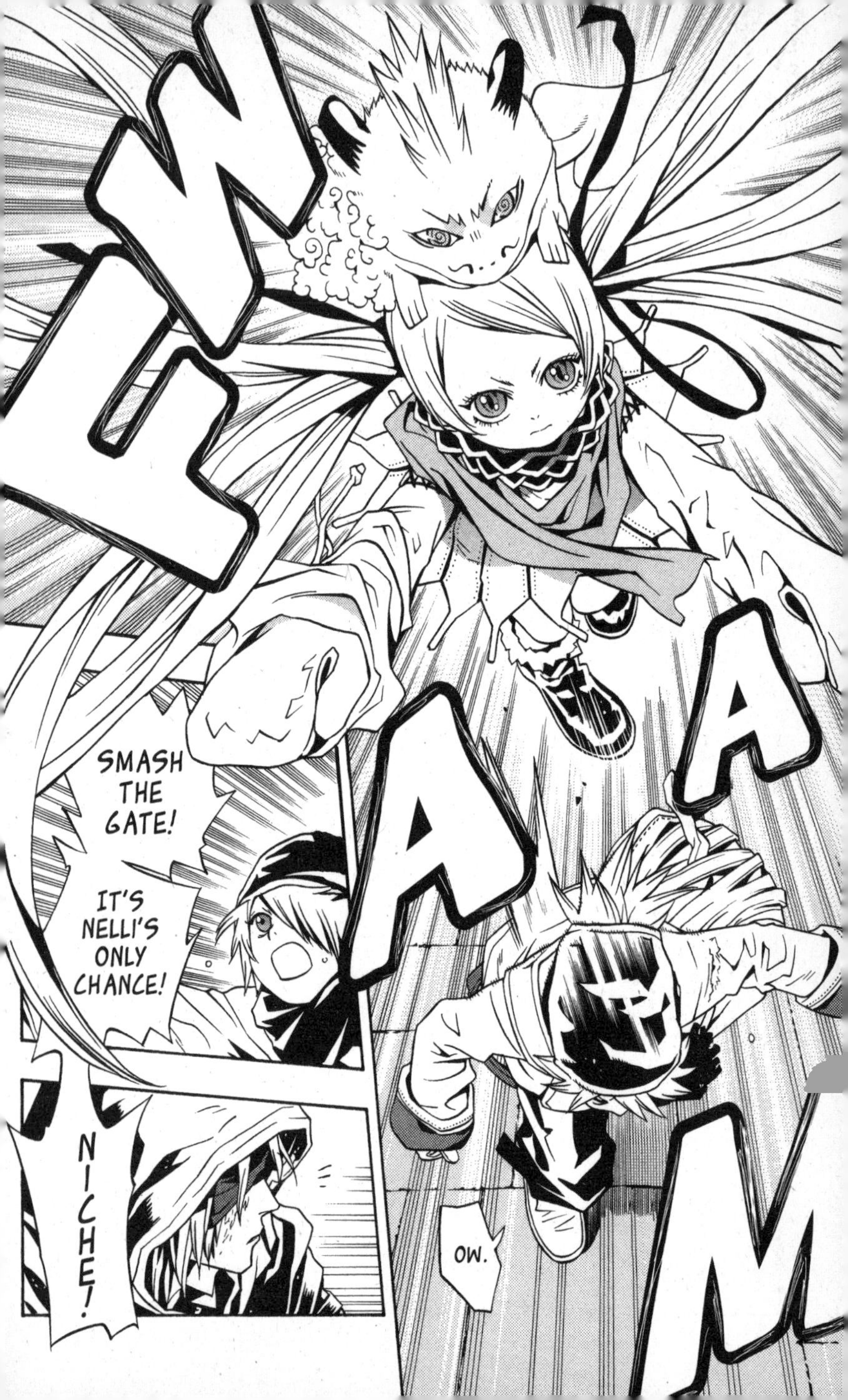
SMASH THE GATE!
IT'S NELLI'S ONLY CHANCE!
OW.
NICHE!

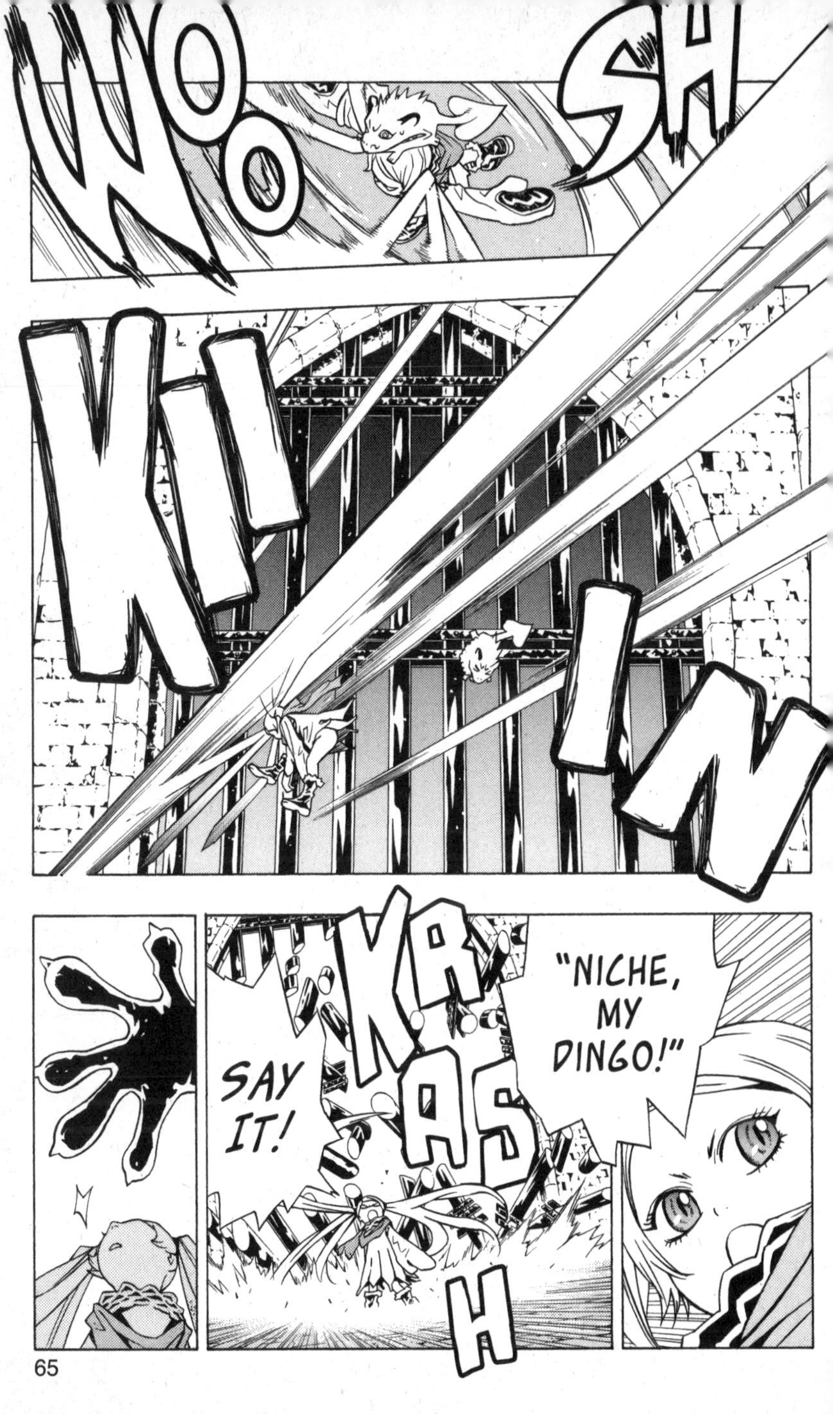
WOOSH
KIIIN
"NICHE, MY DINGO!"
KRASH
SAY IT!

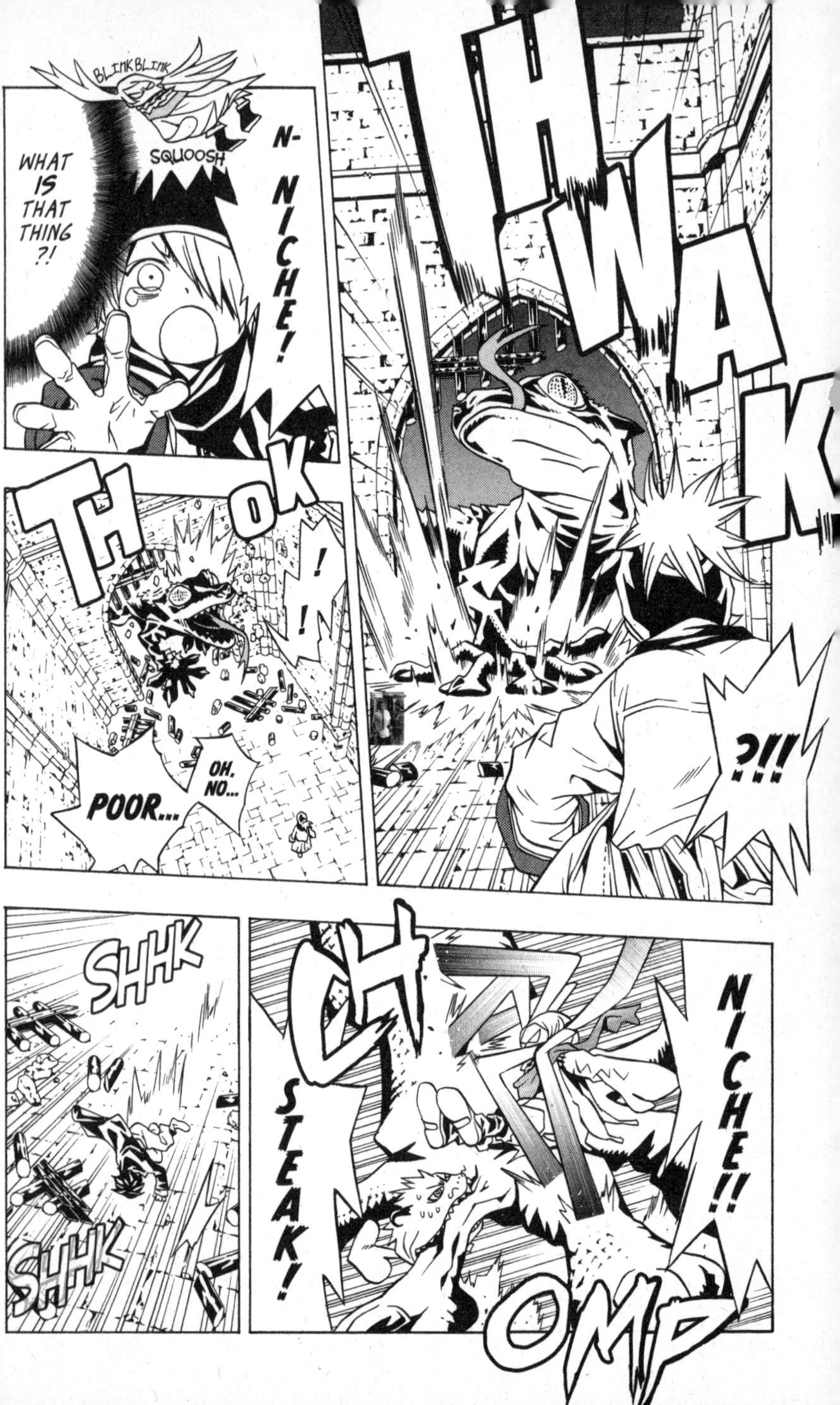
THWAK
?!!
BLINK BLINK
SQUOOSH
N-NICHE!
WHAT IS THAT THING?!
THOK!!
OH, NO...
POOR...
CH
OMP
NICHE!!
STEAK!
SHHK
SHHK

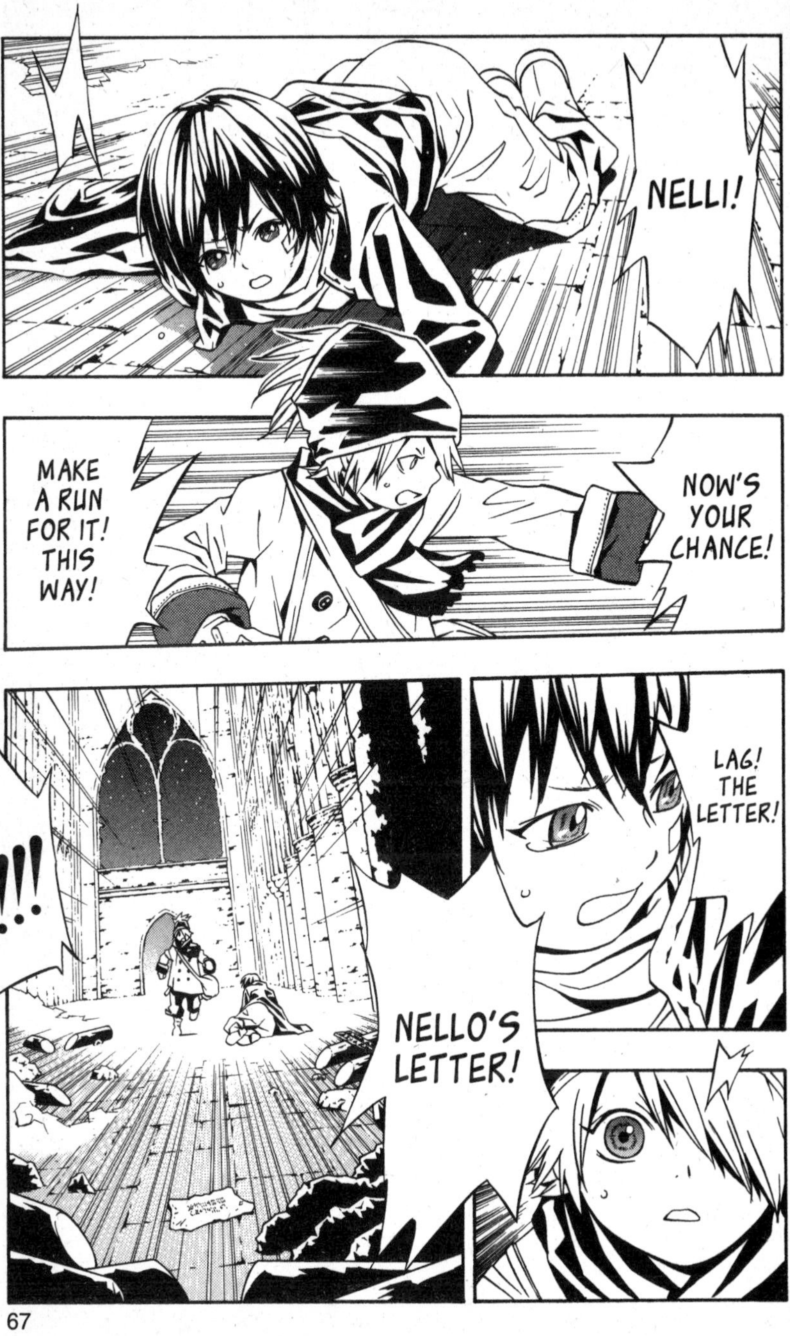
NELLI!
NOW'S YOUR CHANCE!
MAKE A RUN FOR IT! THIS WAY!
LAG! THE LETTER!
NELLO'S LETTER!
!!!

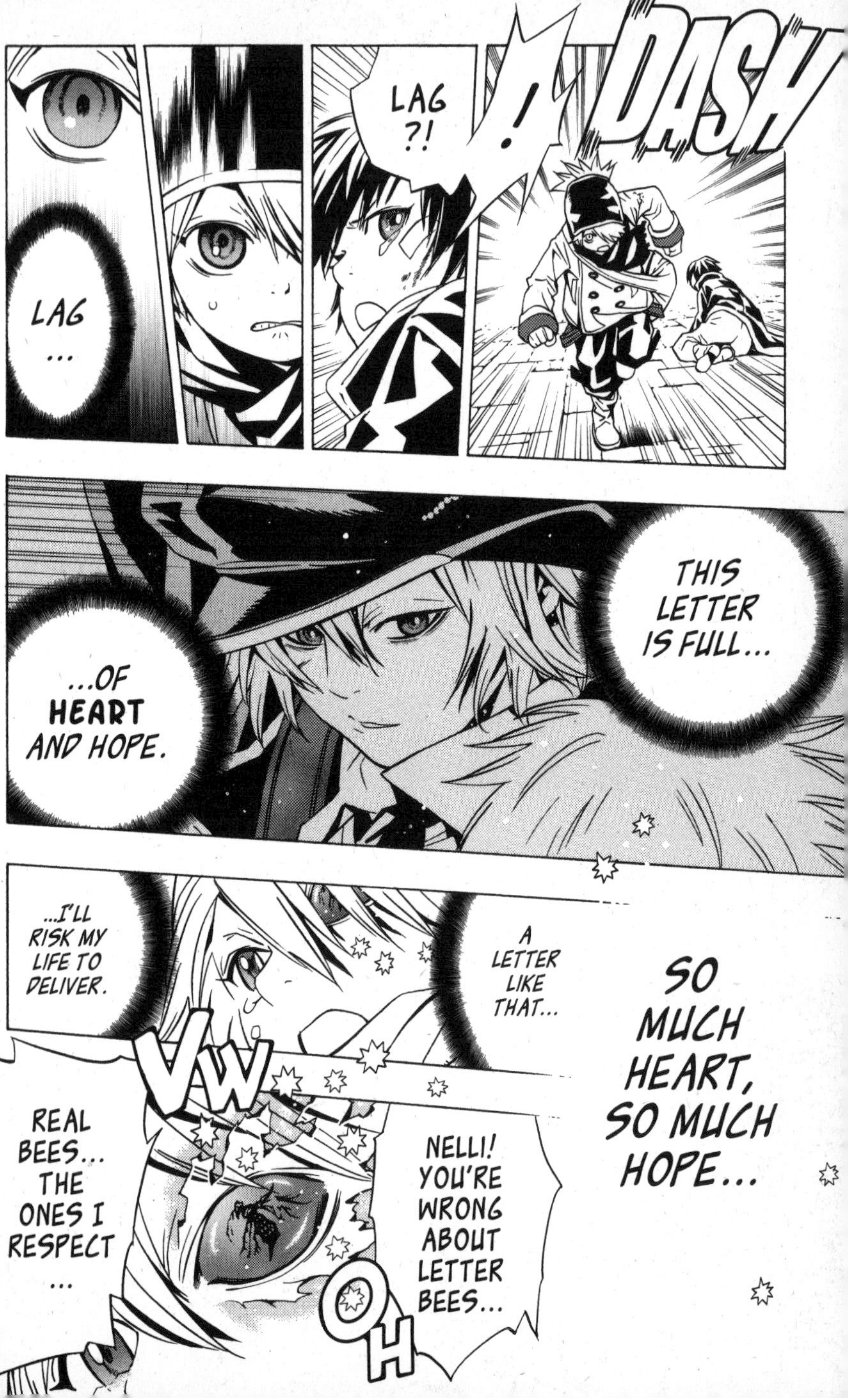
DASH
!
LAG ?!
LAG ...
THIS LETTER IS FULL...
...OF HEART AND HOPE.
SO MUCH HEART, SO MUCH HOPE...
A LETTER LIKE THAT...
...I'LL RISK MY LIFE TO DELIVER.
VW
NELLI! YOU'RE WRONG ABOUT LETTER BEES...
OH
REAL BEES... THE ONES I RESPECT ...

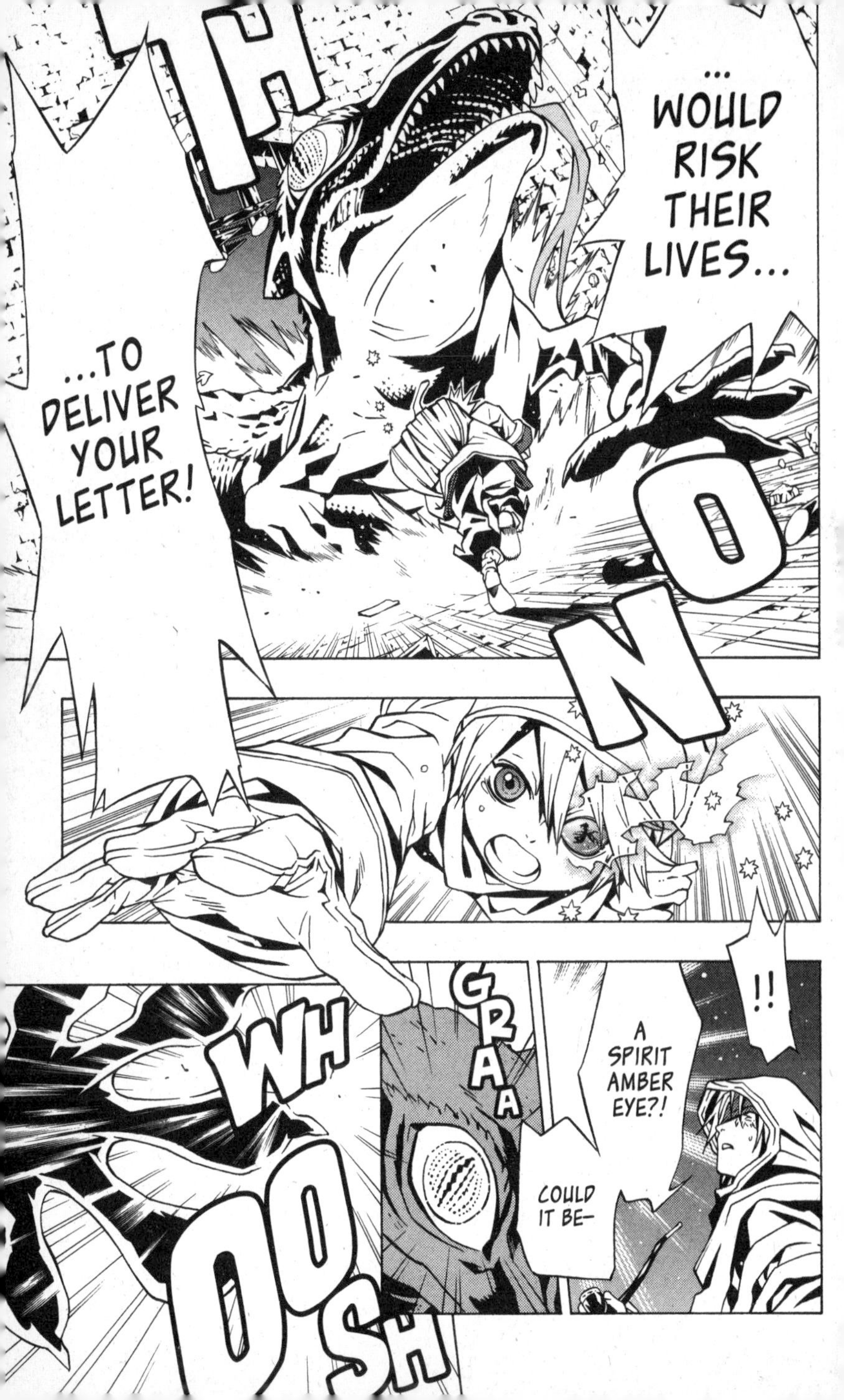

H
...WOULD RISK THEIR LIVES...
...TO DELIVER YOUR LETTER!
NO
!!
A SPIRIT AMBER EYE?!
COULD IT BE—
GRAAA
WHOOSH

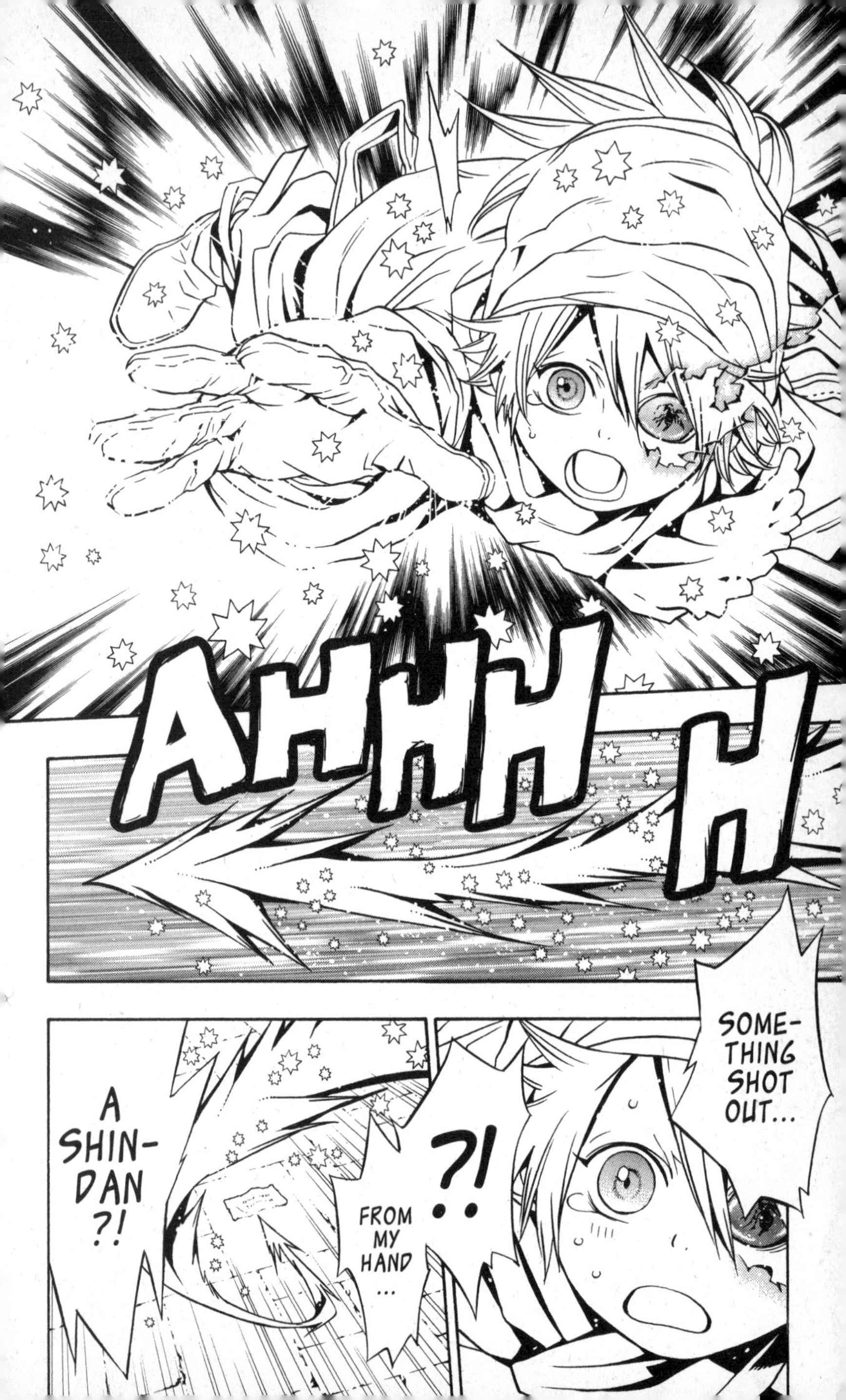
AHHH H
SOME-THING SHOT OUT...
?!
FROM MY HAND ...
A SHIN-DAN ?!

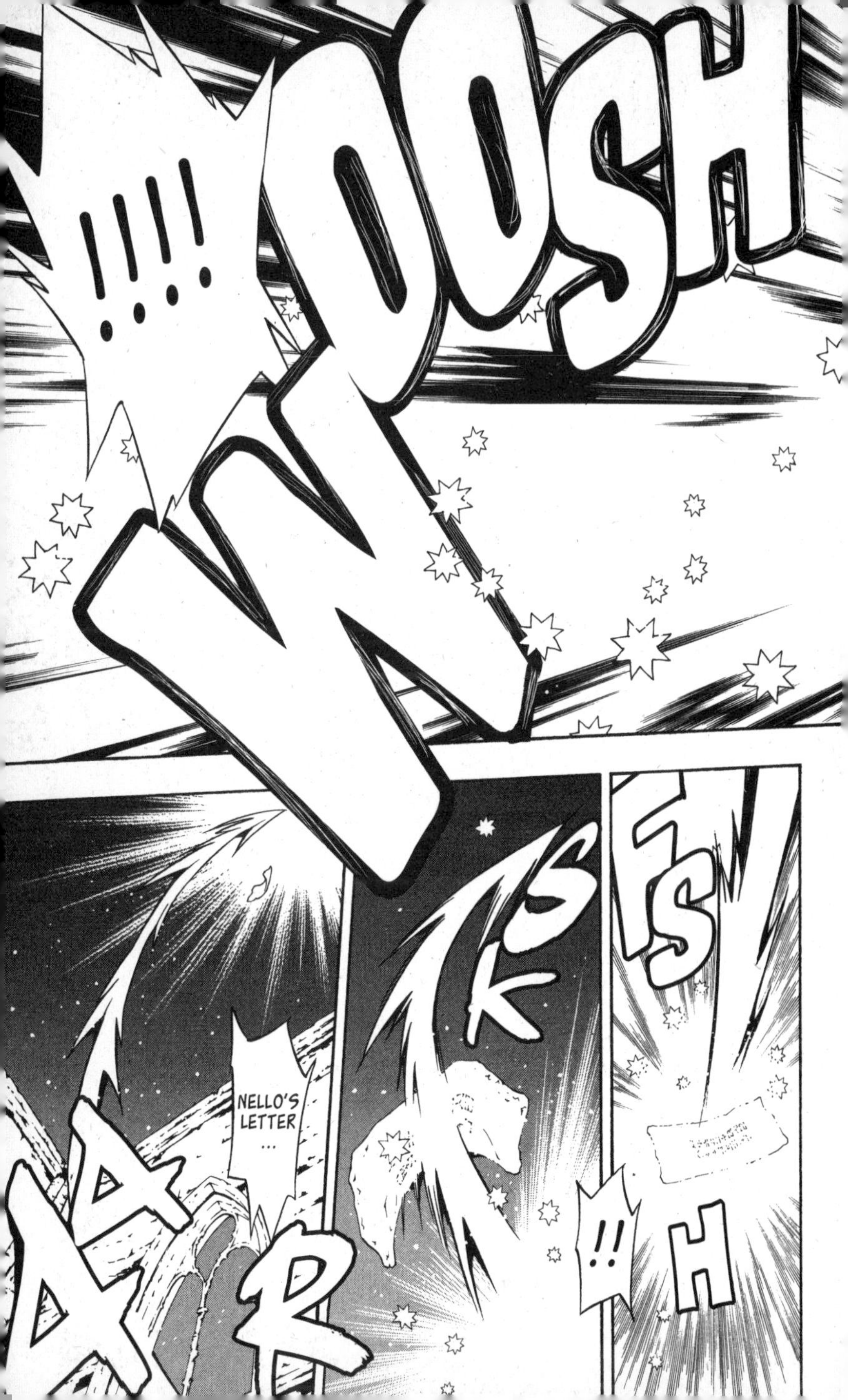
WOOSH
!!!!
NELLO'S LETTER ...
!!

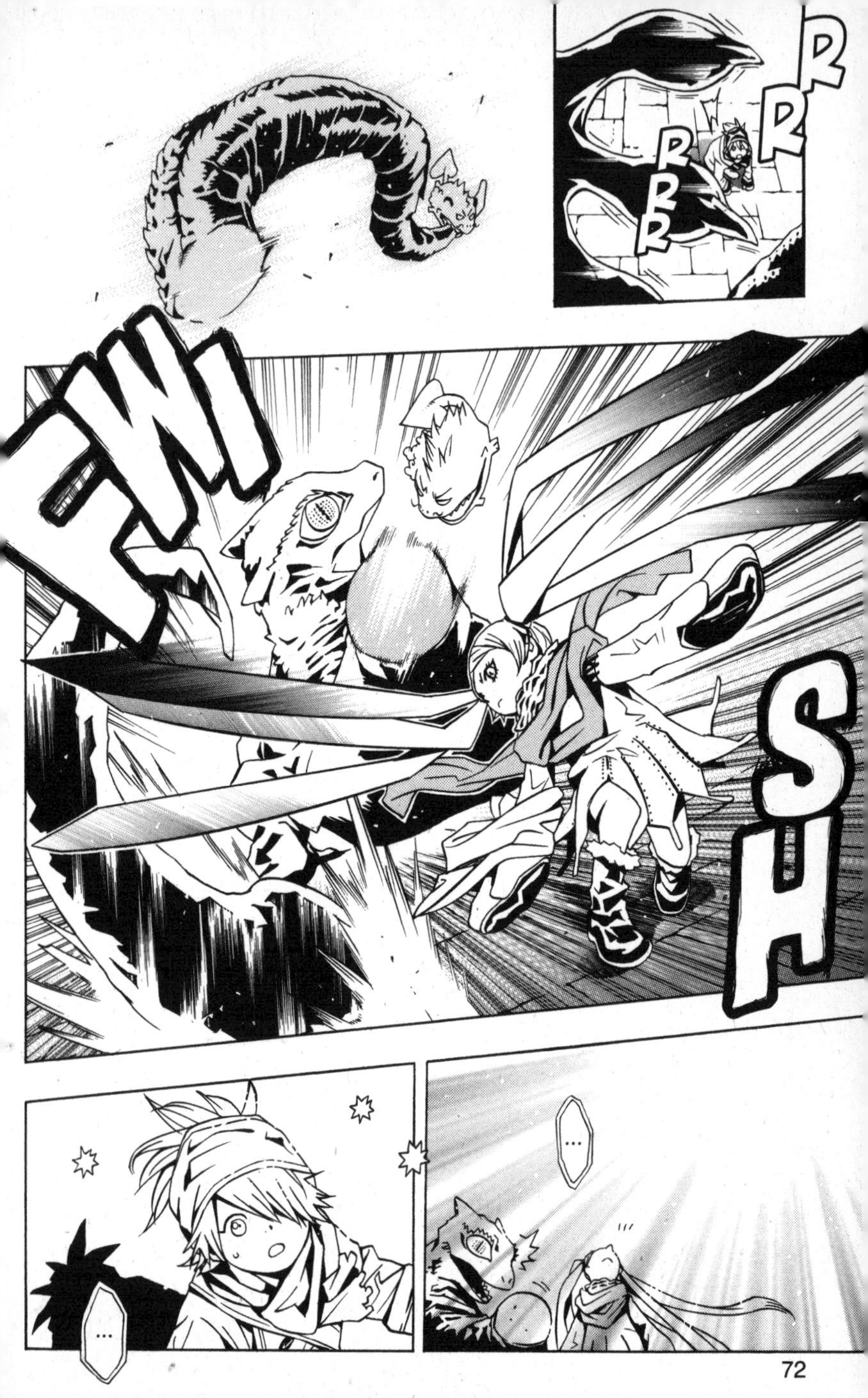
RRRRR
FWI
SH
...
...

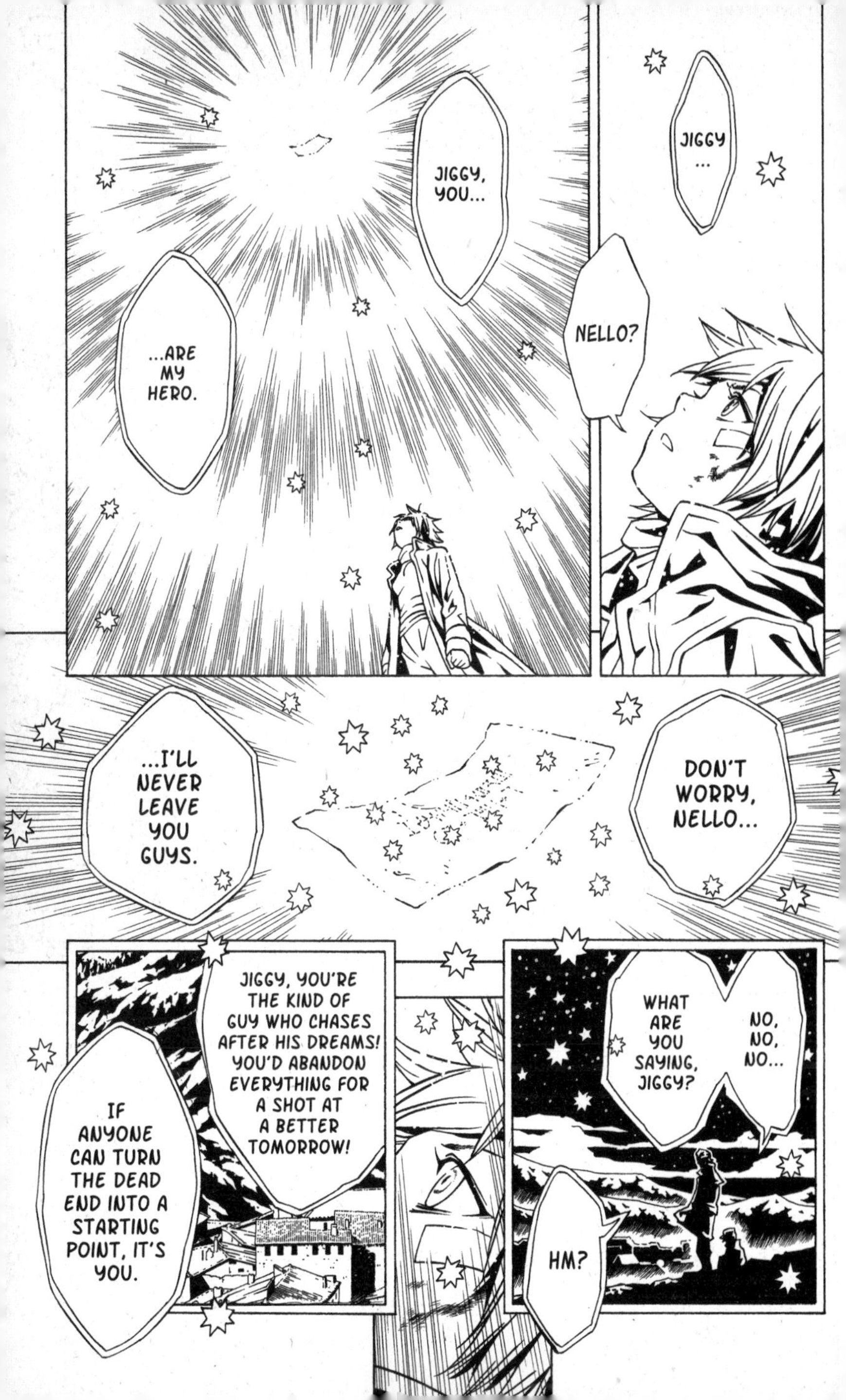
JIGGY ...
NELLO?
JIGGY, YOU...
...ARE MY HERO.
DON'T WORRY, NELLO...
...I'LL NEVER LEAVE YOU GUYS.
NO, NO, NO...
WHAT ARE YOU SAYING, JIGGY?
HM?
JIGGY, YOU'RE THE KIND OF GUY WHO CHASES AFTER HIS DREAMS! YOU'D ABANDON EVERYTHING FOR A SHOT AT A BETTER TOMORROW!
IF ANYONE CAN TURN THE DEAD END INTO A STARTING POINT, IT'S YOU.

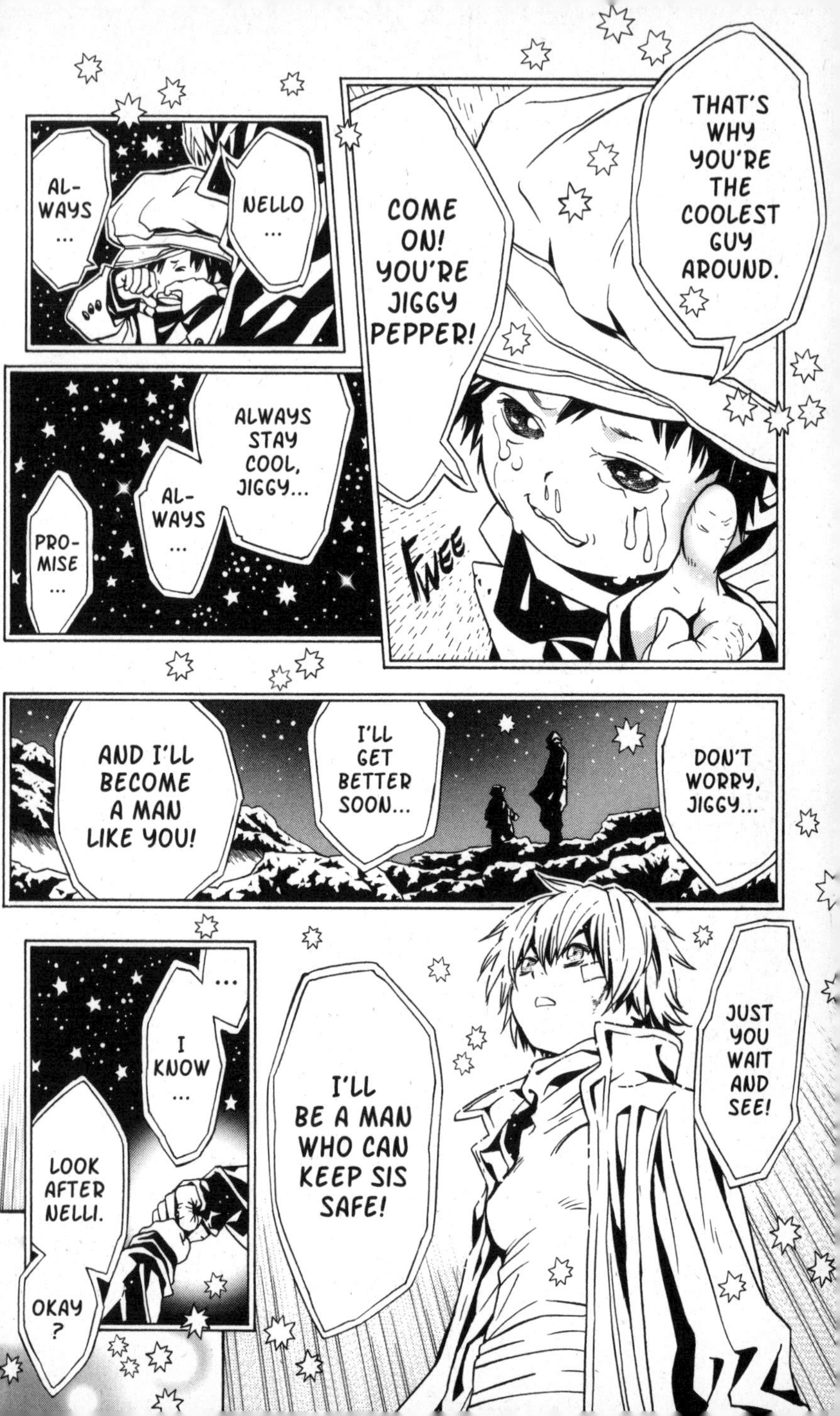
THAT'S WHY YOU'RE THE COOLEST GUY AROUND.
COME ON! YOU'RE JIGGY PEPPER!
FWEE
NELLO...
AL-WAYS...
ALWAYS STAY COOL, JIGGY...
AL-WAYS...
PRO-MISE...
DON'T WORRY, JIGGY...
I'LL GET BETTER SOON...
AND I'LL BECOME A MAN LIKE YOU!
JUST YOU WAIT AND SEE!
I'LL BE A MAN WHO CAN KEEP SIS SAFE!
...
I KNOW...
LOOK AFTER NELLI.
OKAY?

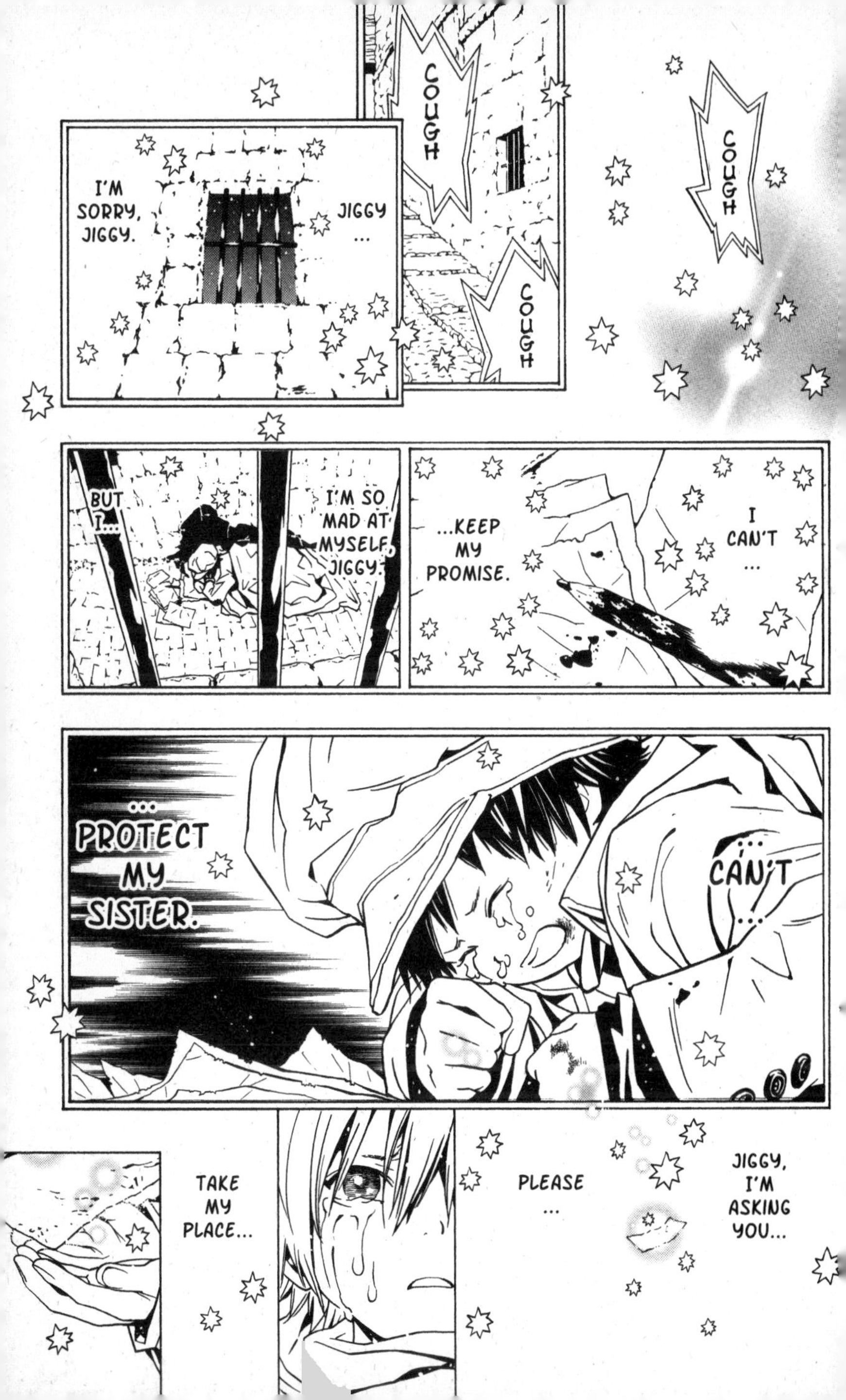
COUGH
COUGH
COUGH
JIGGY ...
I'M SORRY, JIGGY.
I CAN'T ...
...KEEP MY PROMISE.
I'M SO MAD AT MYSELF, JIGGY.
BUT I...
...CAN'T ...
...PROTECT MY SISTER.
JIGGY, I'M ASKING YOU...
PLEASE ...
TAKE MY PLACE...

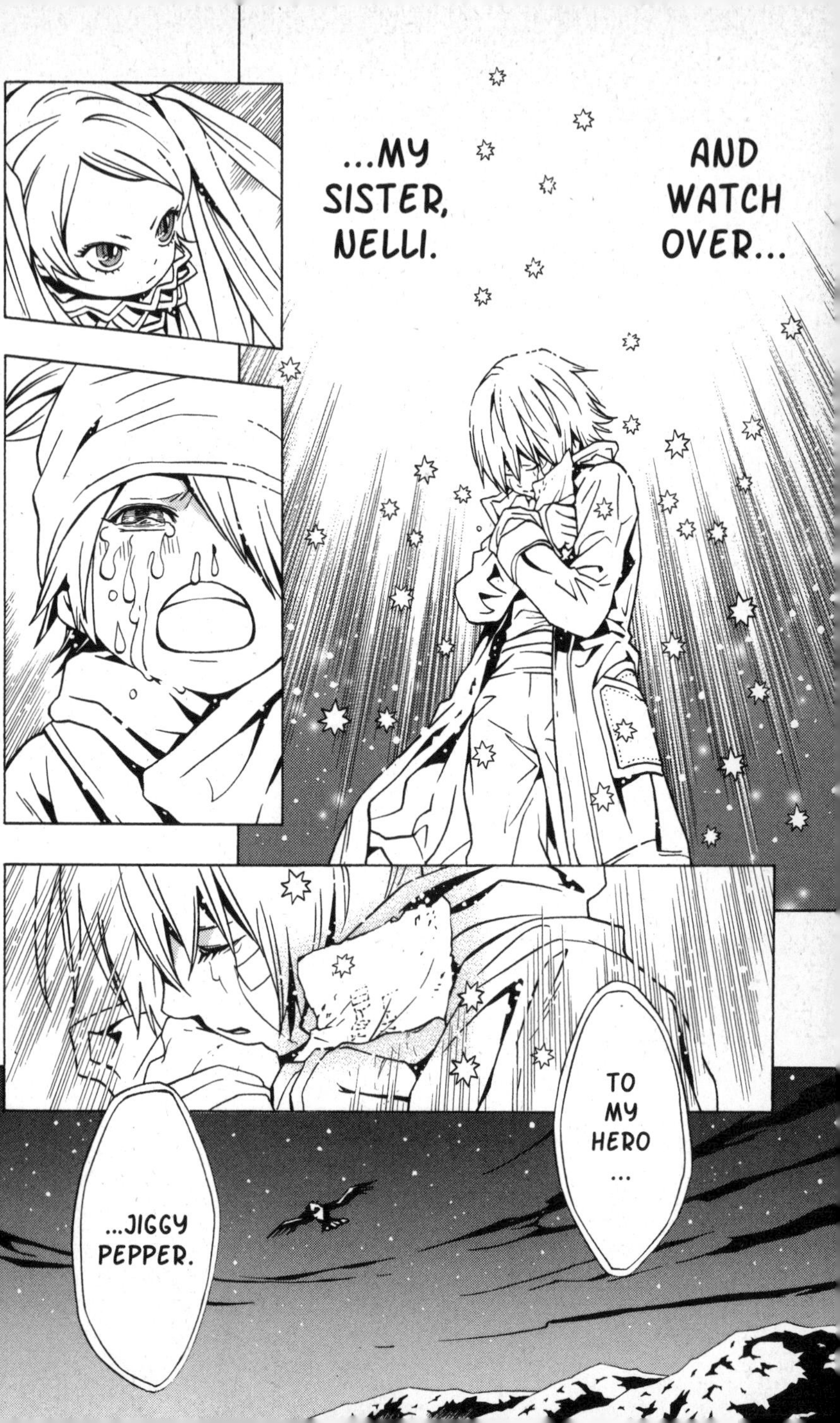
AND WATCH OVER...
...MY SISTER, NELLI.
TO MY HERO ...
...JIGGY PEPPER.

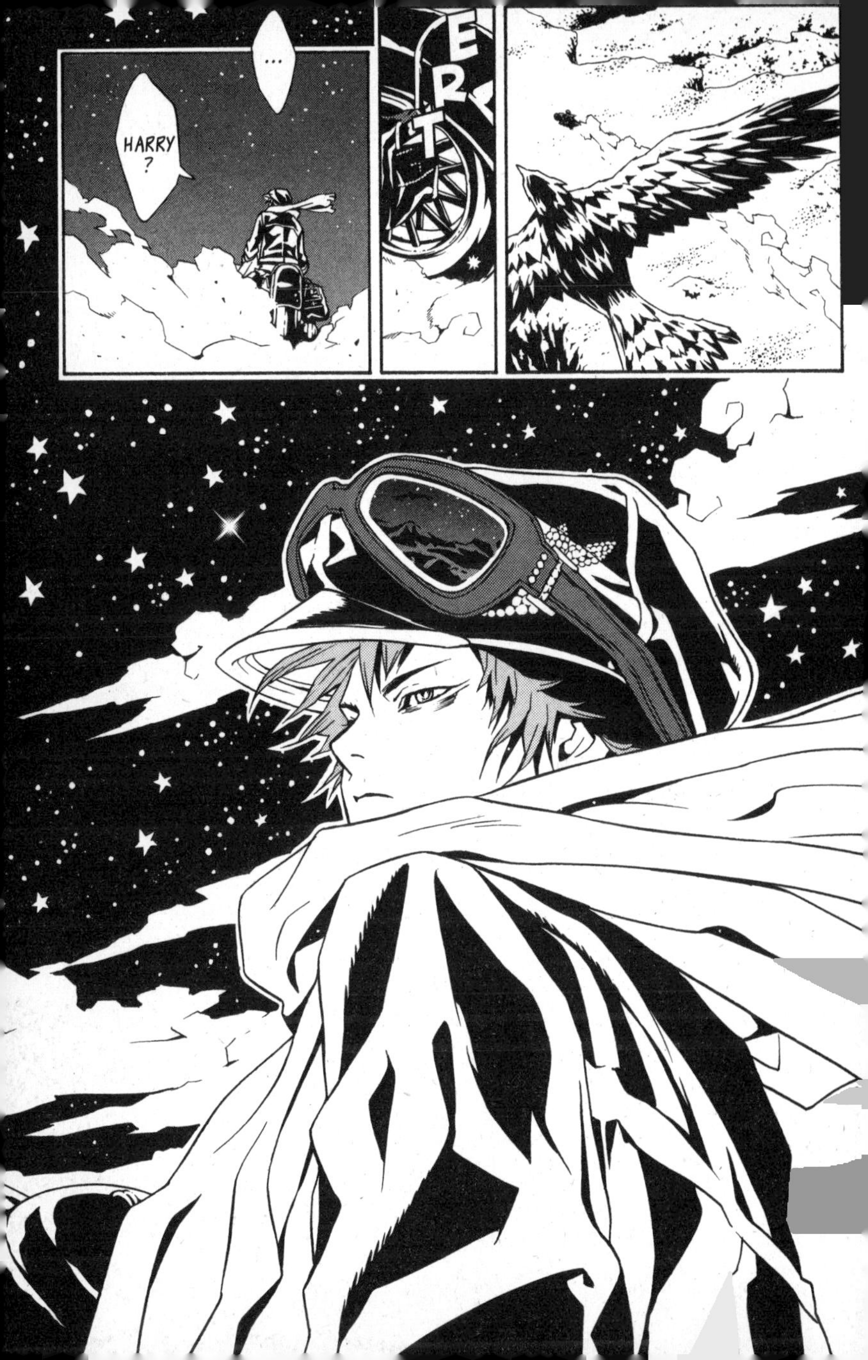

ERT
...
HARRY?

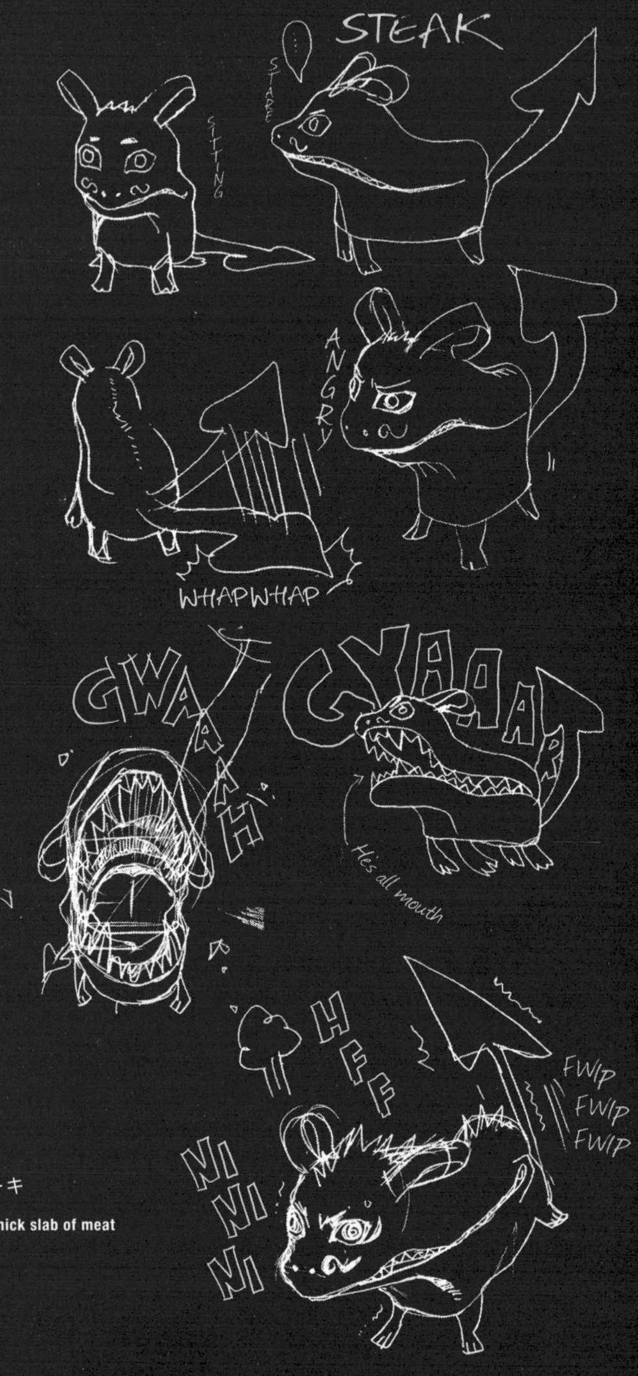

STEAK
...
STARE
SITTING
ANGRY
WHAPWHAP
GYAAAA
GWAAAH
He's all mouth
HFF
FWIP
FWIP
FWIP
NI NI NI

Steak ステーキ

A dish in which a thick slab of meat or fish is grilled.

Chapter 5: The Letter to Jiggy Pepper, Part 3

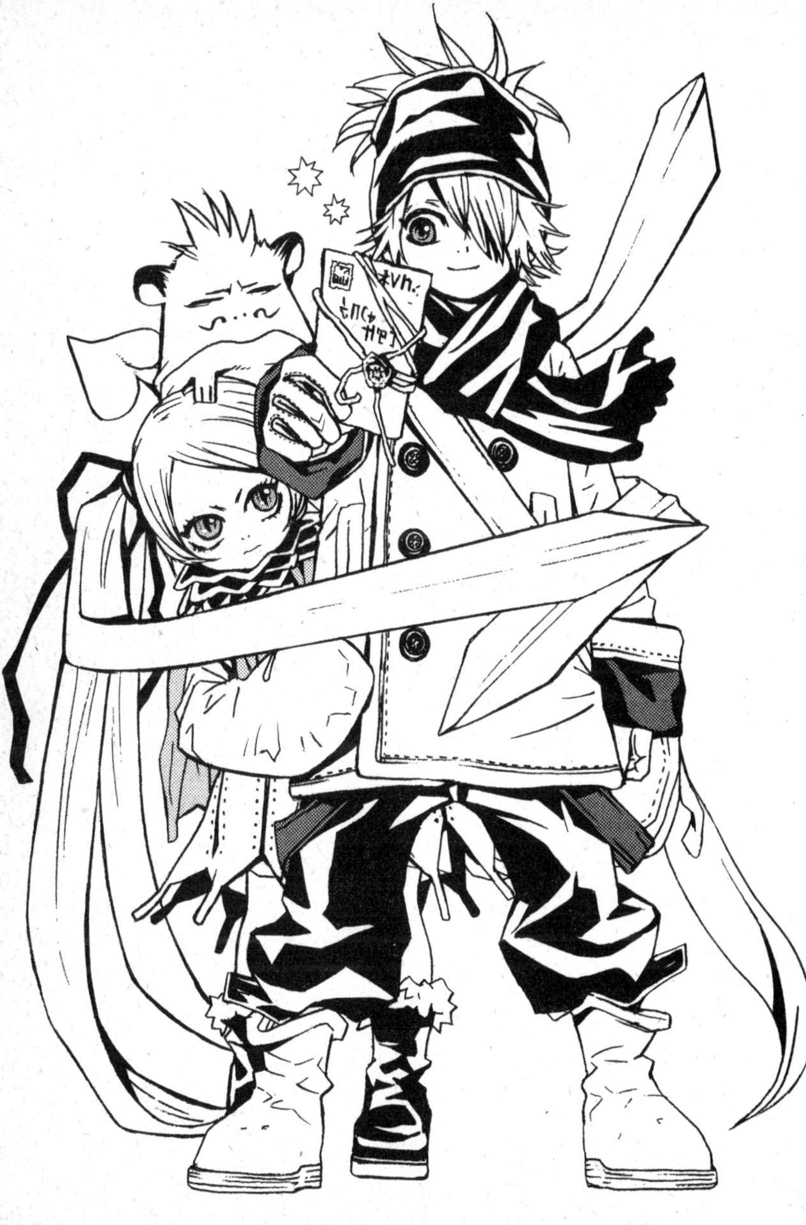

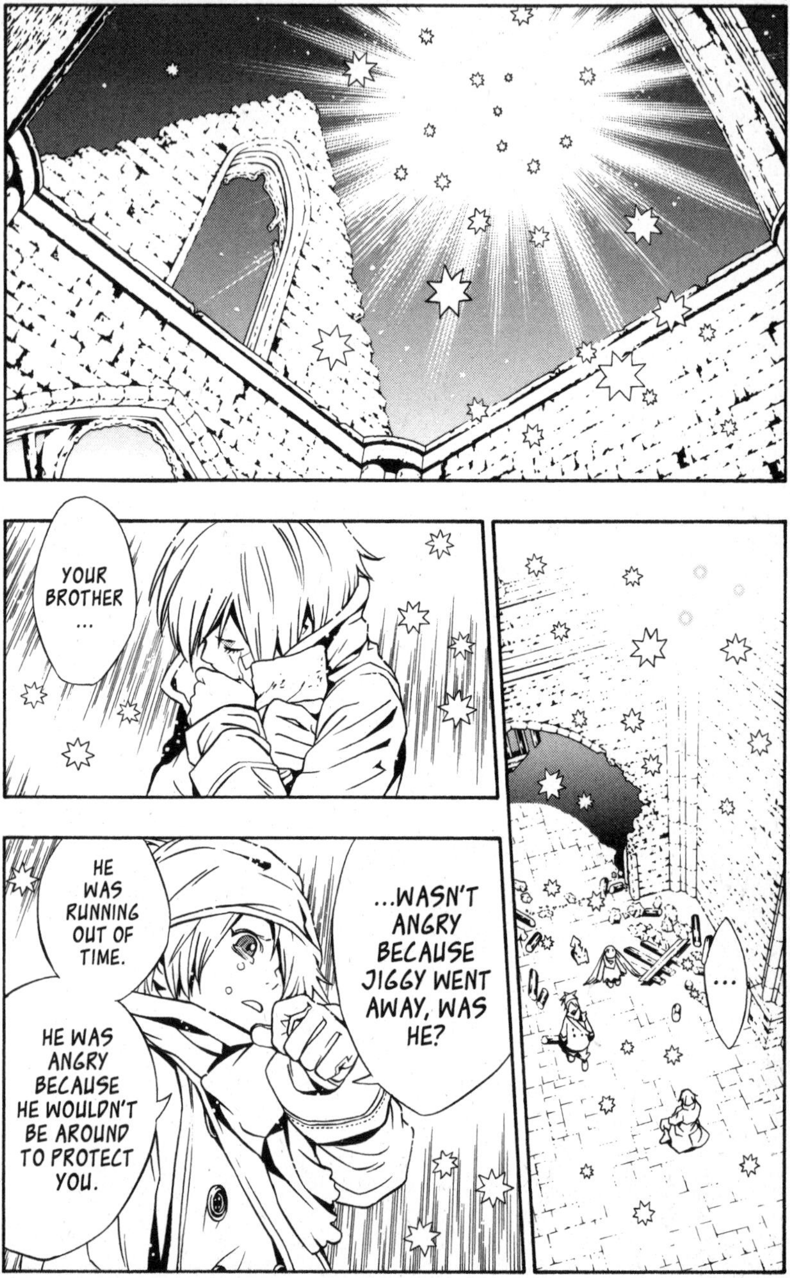
...
YOUR BROTHER ...
...WASN'T ANGRY BECAUSE JIGGY WENT AWAY, WAS HE?
HE WAS RUNNING OUT OF TIME.
HE WAS ANGRY BECAUSE HE WOULDN'T BE AROUND TO PROTECT YOU.

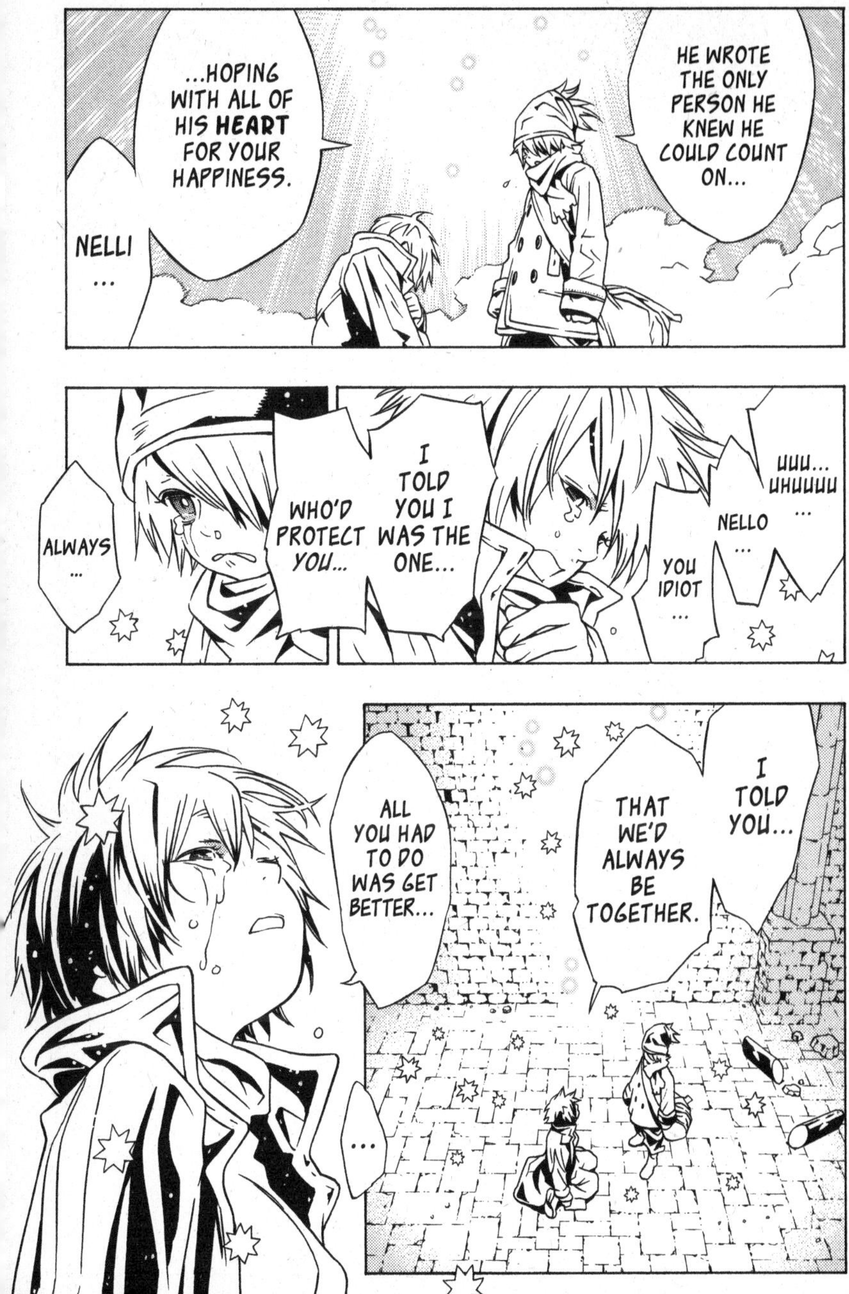
HE WROTE THE ONLY PERSON HE KNEW HE COULD COUNT ON...
...HOPING WITH ALL OF HIS **HEART** FOR YOUR HAPPINESS.
NELLI ...
UUU... UHUUUU ...
NELLO ...
YOU IDIOT ...
I TOLD YOU I WAS THE ONE...
WHO'D PROTECT *YOU*...
ALWAYS ...
I TOLD YOU...
THAT WE'D ALWAYS BE TOGETHER.
ALL YOU HAD TO DO WAS GET BETTER...
...

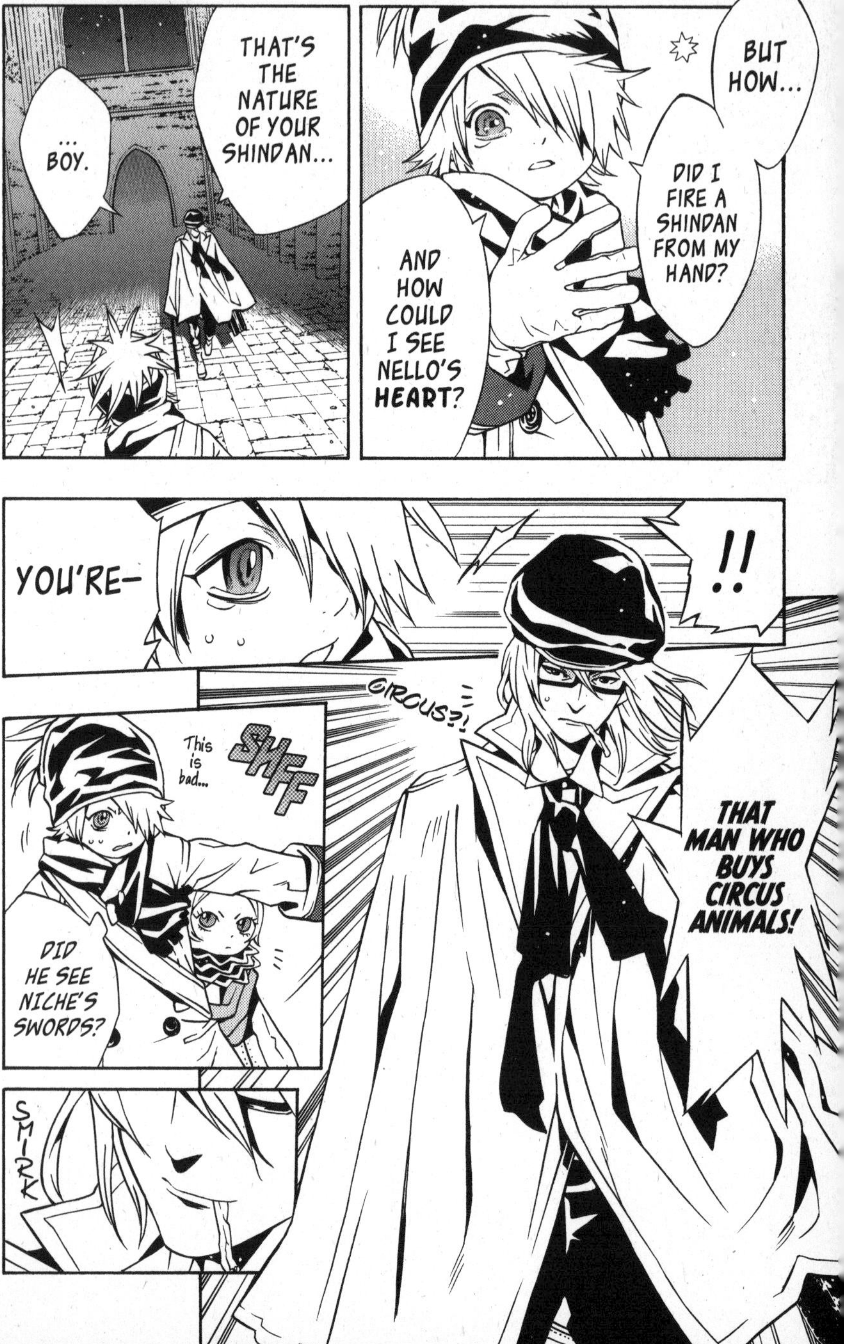
BUT HOW...
DID I FIRE A SHINDAN FROM MY HAND?
AND HOW COULD I SEE NELLO'S HEART?
THAT'S THE NATURE OF YOUR SHINDAN...
... BOY.
!!
CIRCUS?!
THAT MAN WHO BUYS CIRCUS ANIMALS!
YOU'RE—
This is bad...
SHFF
DID HE SEE NICHE'S SWORDS?
SMIRK

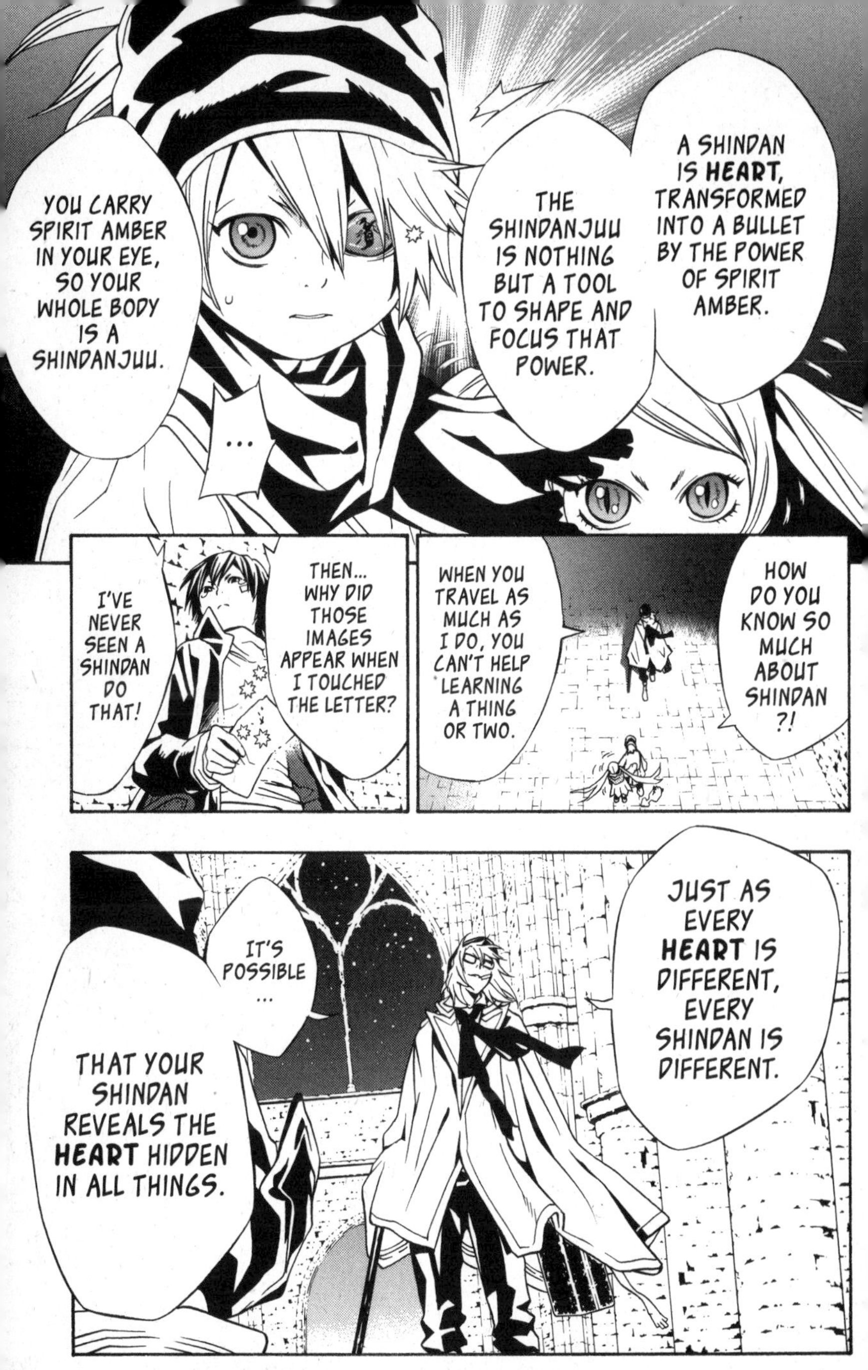
A SHINDAN IS HEART, TRANSFORMED INTO A BULLET BY THE POWER OF SPIRIT AMBER.
THE SHINDANJUU IS NOTHING BUT A TOOL TO SHAPE AND FOCUS THAT POWER.
YOU CARRY SPIRIT AMBER IN YOUR EYE, SO YOUR WHOLE BODY IS A SHINDANJUU.
...
HOW DO YOU KNOW SO MUCH ABOUT SHINDAN ?!
WHEN YOU TRAVEL AS MUCH AS I DO, YOU CAN'T HELP LEARNING A THING OR TWO.
THEN... WHY DID THOSE IMAGES APPEAR WHEN I TOUCHED THE LETTER?
I'VE NEVER SEEN A SHINDAN DO THAT!
JUST AS EVERY HEART IS DIFFERENT, EVERY SHINDAN IS DIFFERENT.
IT'S POSSIBLE ...
THAT YOUR SHINDAN REVEALS THE HEART HIDDEN IN ALL THINGS.

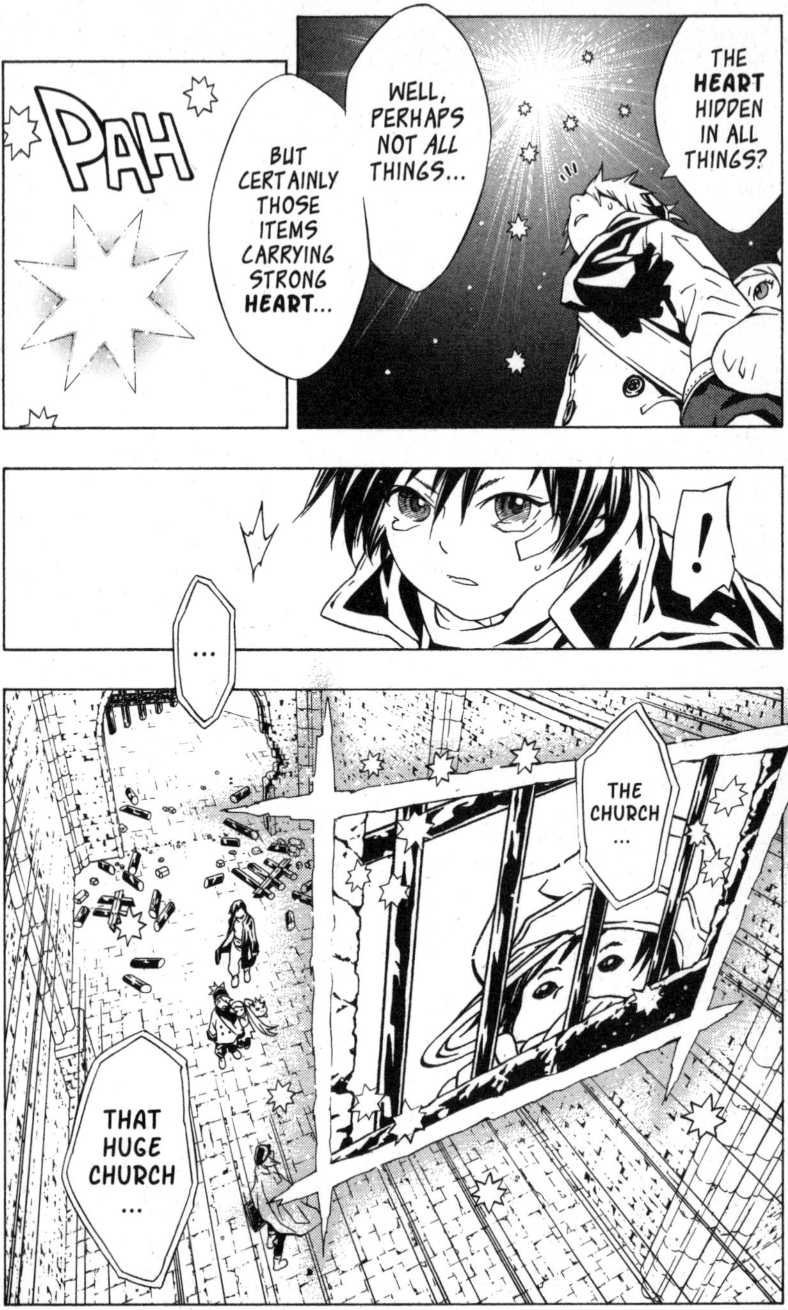
THE HEART HIDDEN IN ALL THINGS?
WELL, PERHAPS NOT ALL THINGS...
BUT CERTAINLY THOSE ITEMS CARRYING STRONG HEART...
PAH
!
...
THE CHURCH ...
THAT HUGE CHURCH ...

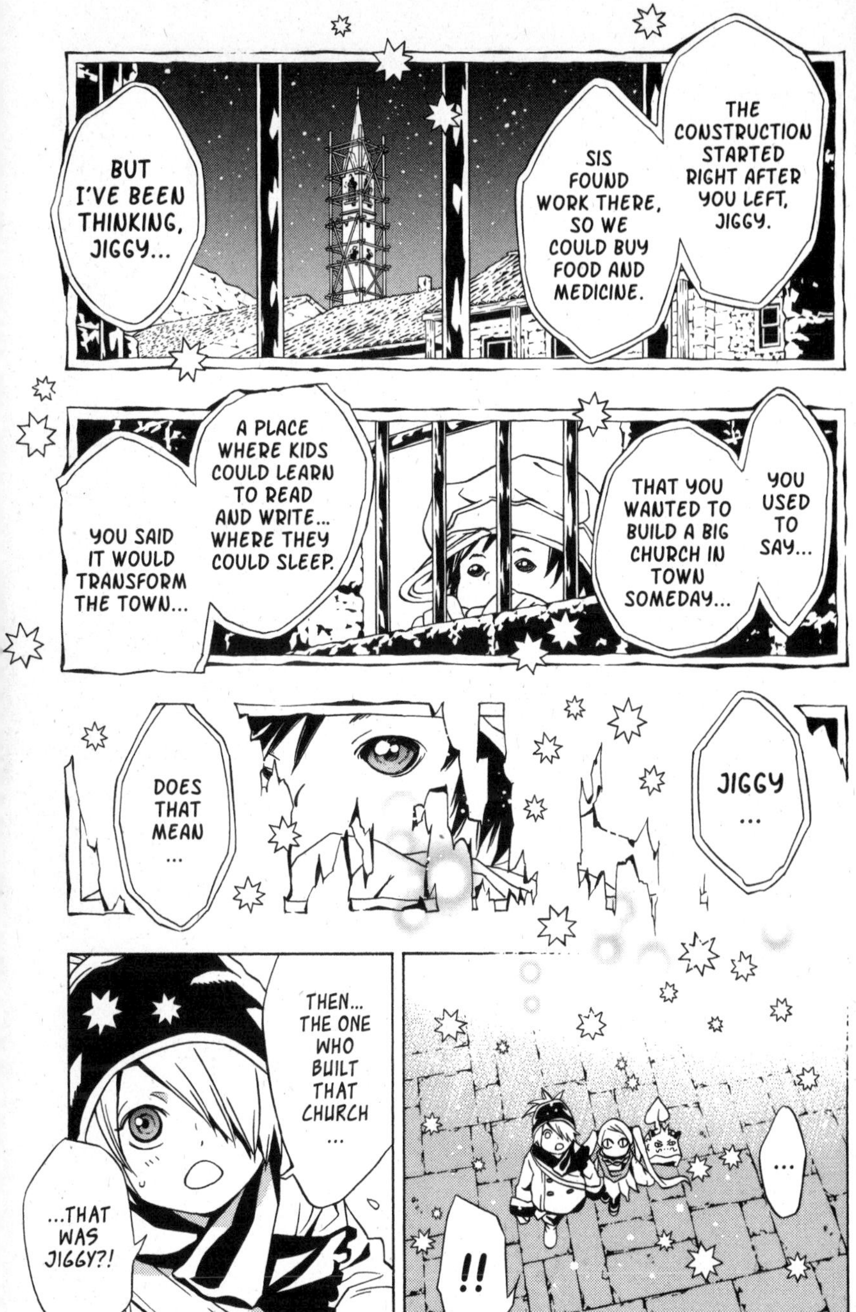
THE CONSTRUCTION STARTED RIGHT AFTER YOU LEFT, JIGGY.
SIS FOUND WORK THERE, SO WE COULD BUY FOOD AND MEDICINE.
BUT I'VE BEEN THINKING, JIGGY...
YOU USED TO SAY...
THAT YOU WANTED TO BUILD A BIG CHURCH IN TOWN SOMEDAY...
A PLACE WHERE KIDS COULD LEARN TO READ AND WRITE... WHERE THEY COULD SLEEP.
YOU SAID IT WOULD TRANSFORM THE TOWN...
JIGGY...
DOES THAT MEAN...
...
!!
THEN... THE ONE WHO BUILT THAT CHURCH...
...THAT WAS JIGGY?!

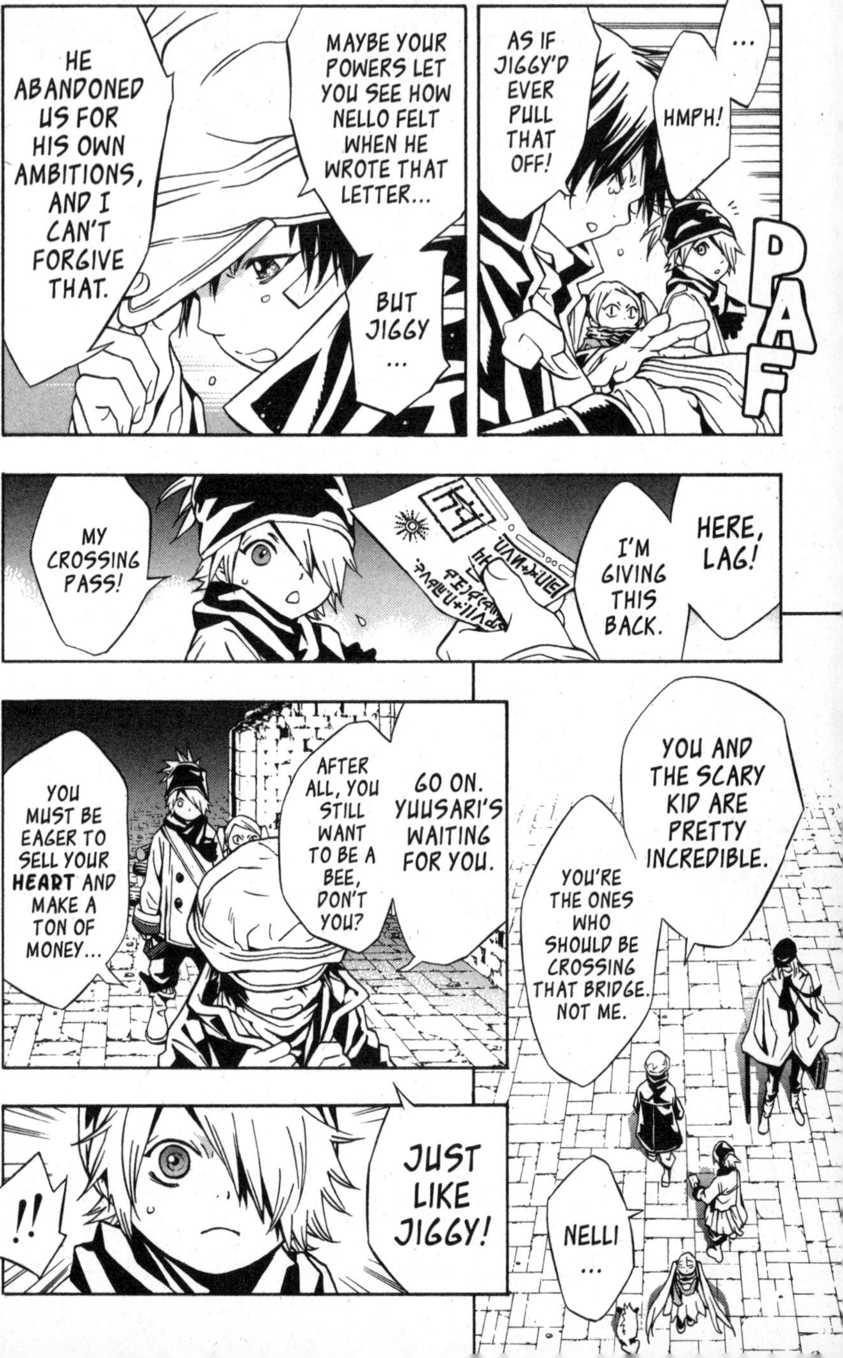
...
HMPH!
PAF
AS IF JIGGY'D EVER PULL THAT OFF!
MAYBE YOUR POWERS LET YOU SEE HOW NELLO FELT WHEN HE WROTE THAT LETTER...
BUT JIGGY ...
HE ABANDONED US FOR HIS OWN AMBITIONS, AND I CAN'T FORGIVE THAT.
HERE, LAG!
I'M GIVING THIS BACK.
MY CROSSING PASS!
YOU AND THE SCARY KID ARE PRETTY INCREDIBLE.
YOU'RE THE ONES WHO SHOULD BE CROSSING THAT BRIDGE. NOT ME.
NELLI ...
GO ON. YUUSARI'S WAITING FOR YOU.
AFTER ALL, YOU STILL WANT TO BE A BEE, DON'T YOU?
YOU MUST BE EAGER TO SELL YOUR **HEART** AND MAKE A TON OF MONEY...
JUST LIKE JIGGY!
!!

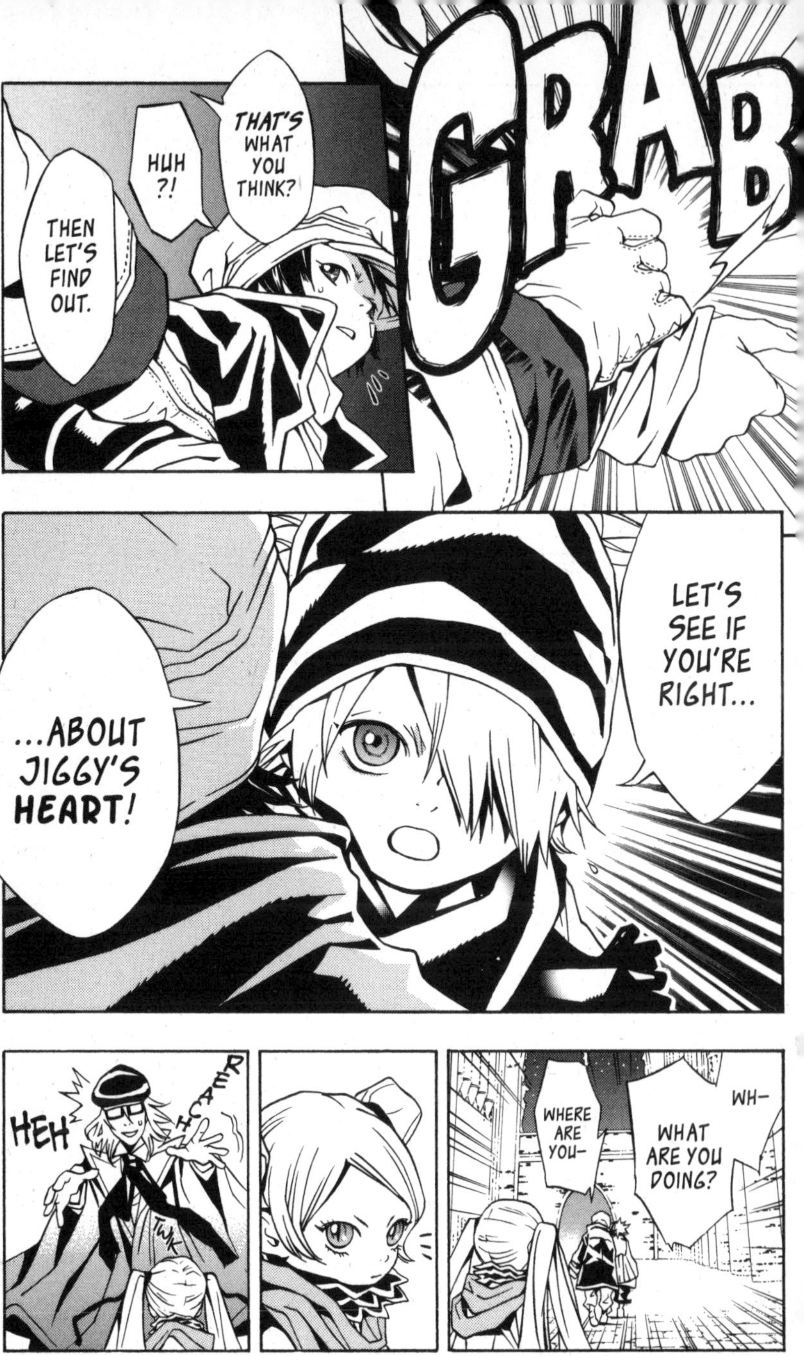
GRAB
THAT'S WHAT YOU THINK?
HUH?!
THEN LET'S FIND OUT.
LET'S SEE IF YOU'RE RIGHT...
...ABOUT JIGGY'S **HEART**!
WH-
WHAT ARE YOU DOING?
WHERE ARE YOU-
REACH
HEH
TWK

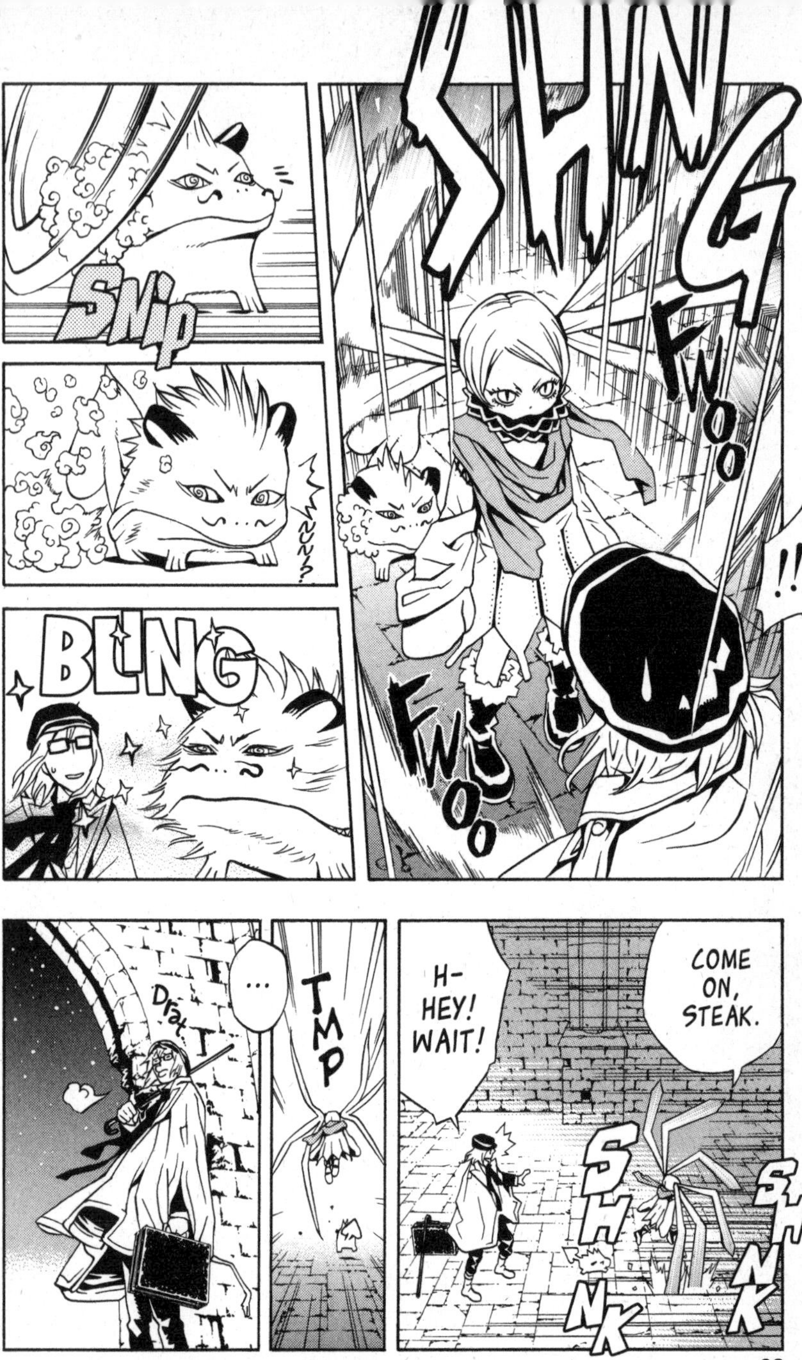
SHNG
FWOOO
!!
FWOOO
SNIP
NUN?
BLING
COME ON, STEAK.
H-HEY! WAIT!
SHNK
SHNK
...
TMP
Drat.

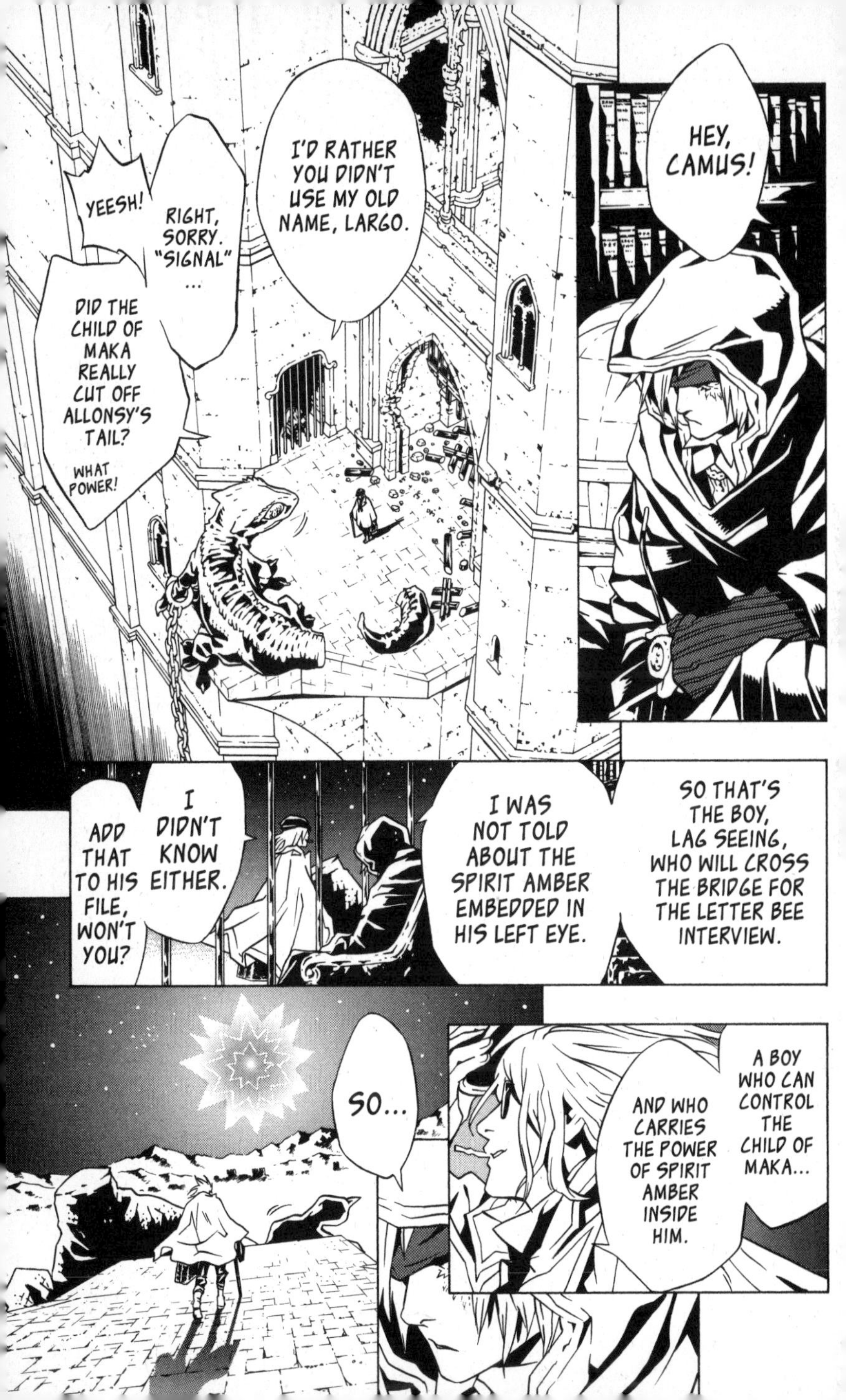
HEY, CAMUS!
I'D RATHER YOU DIDN'T USE MY OLD NAME, LARGO.
RIGHT, SORRY. "SIGNAL" ...
YEESH!
DID THE CHILD OF MAKA REALLY CUT OFF ALLONSY'S TAIL?
WHAT POWER!
SO THAT'S THE BOY, LAG SEEING, WHO WILL CROSS THE BRIDGE FOR THE LETTER BEE INTERVIEW.
I WAS NOT TOLD ABOUT THE SPIRIT AMBER EMBEDDED IN HIS LEFT EYE.
I DIDN'T KNOW EITHER.
ADD THAT TO HIS FILE, WON'T YOU?
A BOY WHO CAN CONTROL THE CHILD OF MAKA...
AND WHO CARRIES THE POWER OF SPIRIT AMBER INSIDE HIM.
SO...

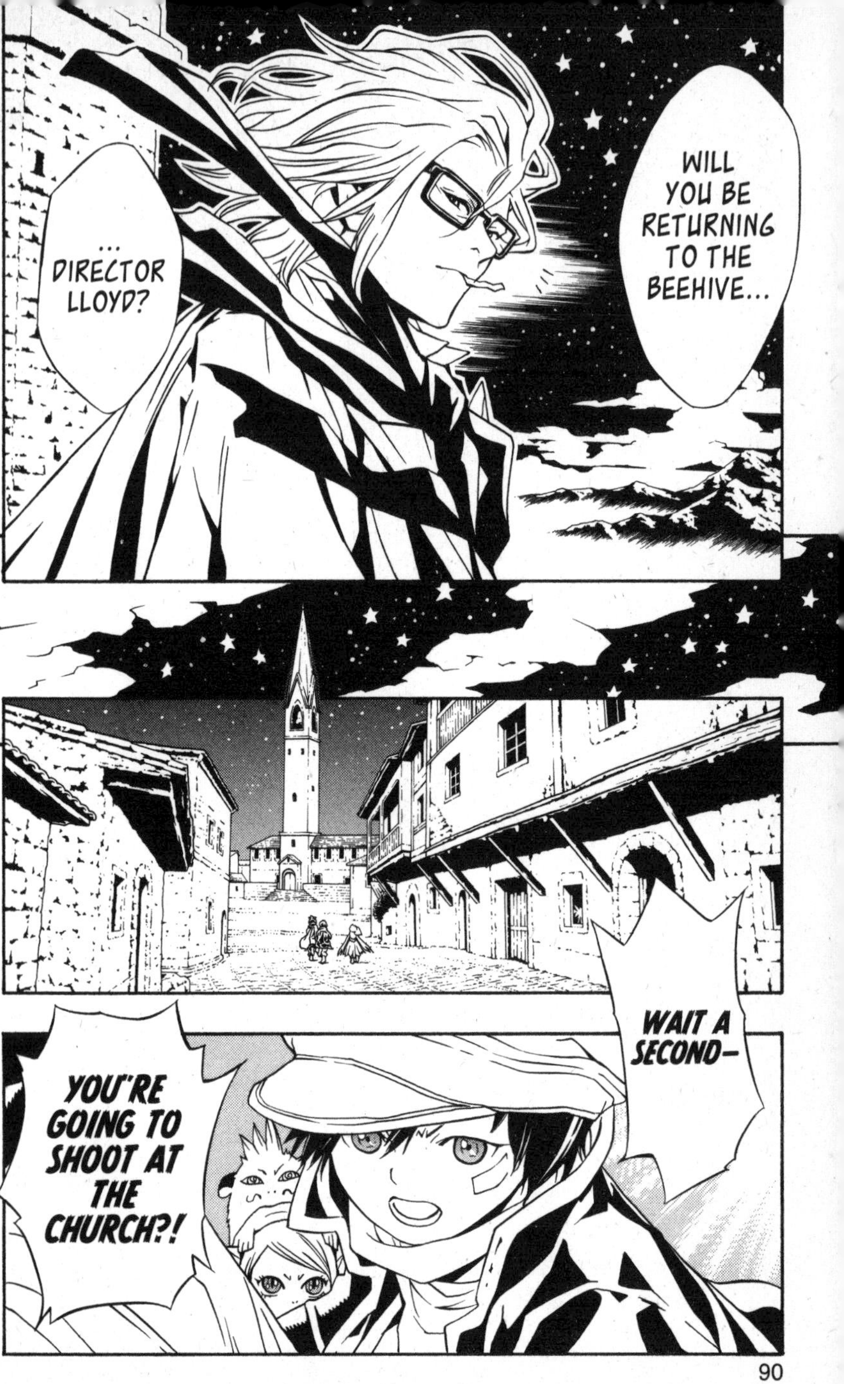
WILL YOU BE RETURNING TO THE BEEHIVE...
...DIRECTOR LLOYD?
WAIT A SECOND—
YOU'RE GOING TO SHOOT AT THE CHURCH?!

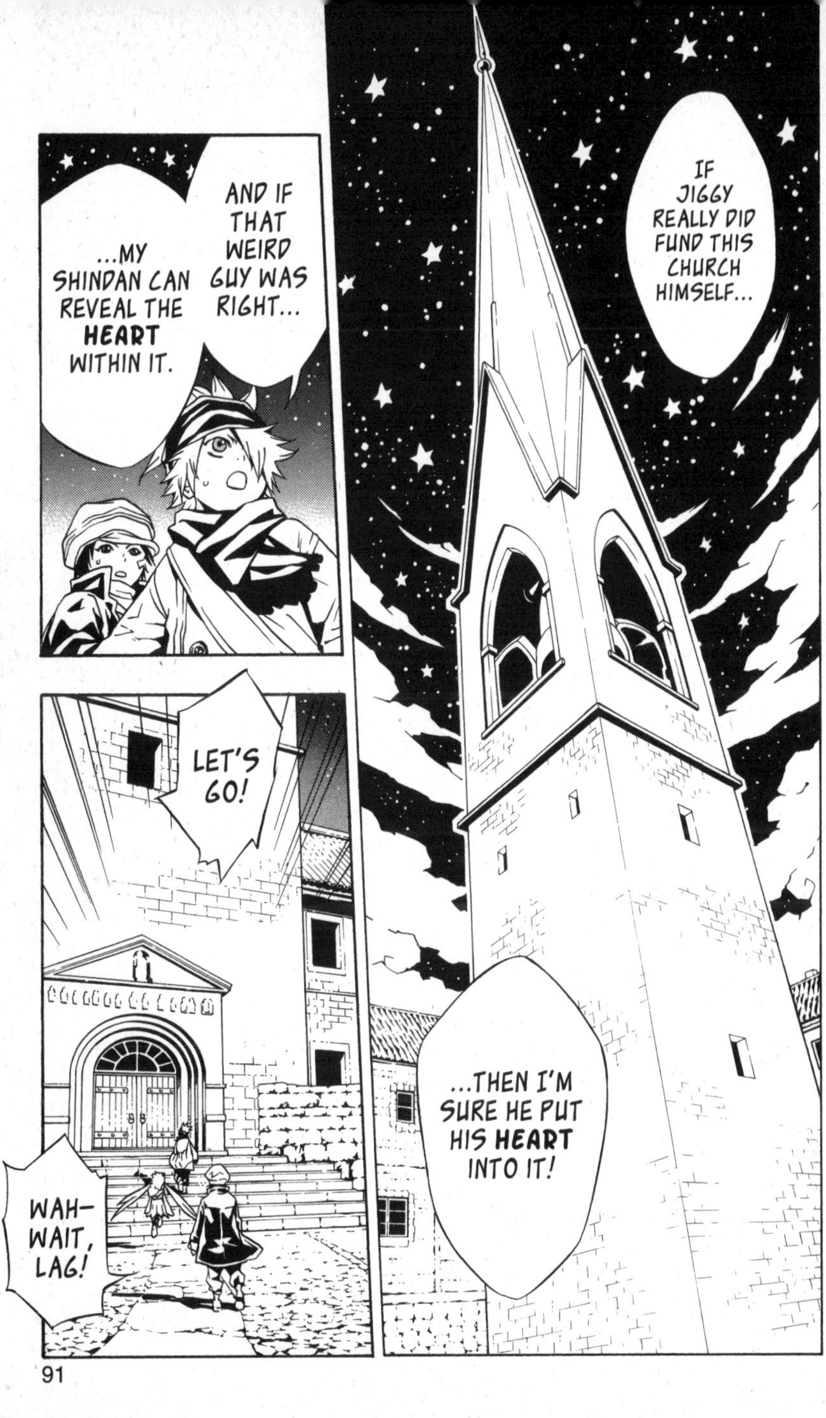
IF JIGGY REALLY DID FUND THIS CHURCH HIMSELF...
...THEN I'M SURE HE PUT HIS **HEART** INTO IT!
AND IF THAT WEIRD GUY WAS RIGHT...
...MY SHINDAN CAN REVEAL THE **HEART** WITHIN IT.
LET'S GO!
WAH-WAIT, LAG!

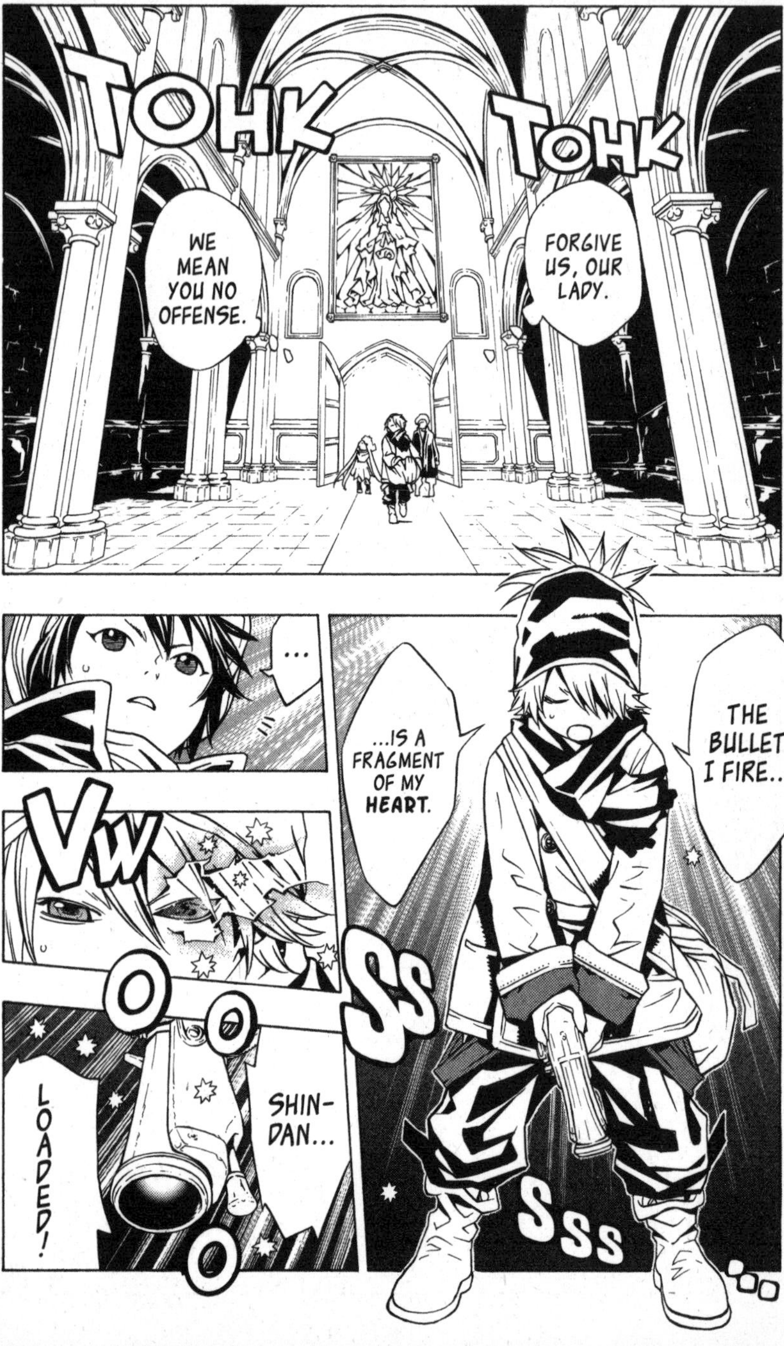
TOHK
TOHK
FORGIVE US, OUR LADY.
WE MEAN YOU NO OFFENSE.
THE BULLET I FIRE...
...IS A FRAGMENT OF MY HEART.
SSS
...
VW
OOOSS
SHIN-DAN...
LOADED!

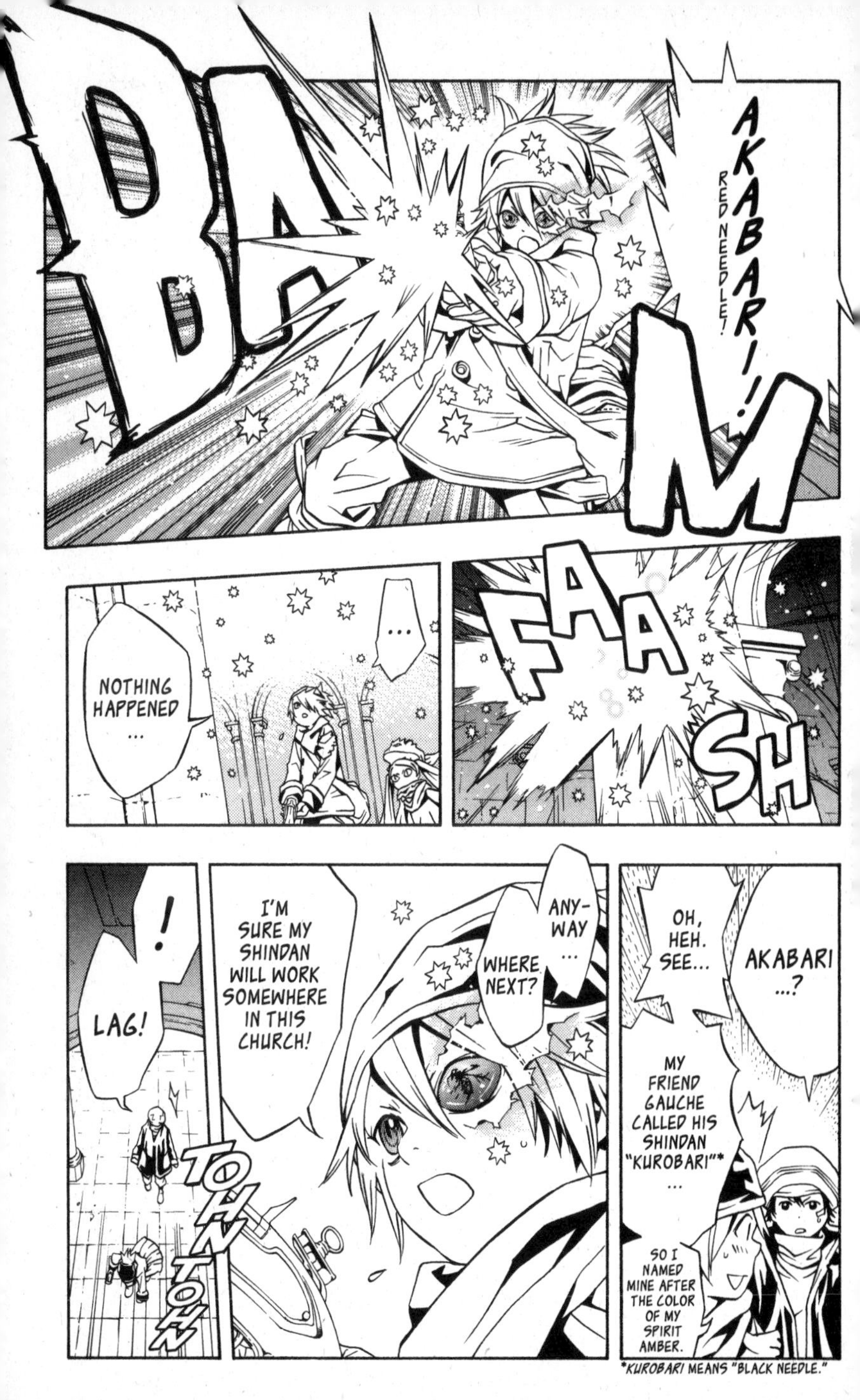
AKABARI...!
RED NEEDLE!
BAM
FAAASH
...
NOTHING HAPPENED ...
AKABARI ...?
OH, HEH. SEE...
MY FRIEND GAUCHE CALLED HIS SHINDAN "KUROBARI"* ...
SO I NAMED MINE AFTER THE COLOR OF MY SPIRIT AMBER.
ANY-WAY ...
WHERE NEXT?
I'M SURE MY SHINDAN WILL WORK SOMEWHERE IN THIS CHURCH!
!
LAG!
TOHN TOHN

*KUROBARI MEANS "BLACK NEEDLE."

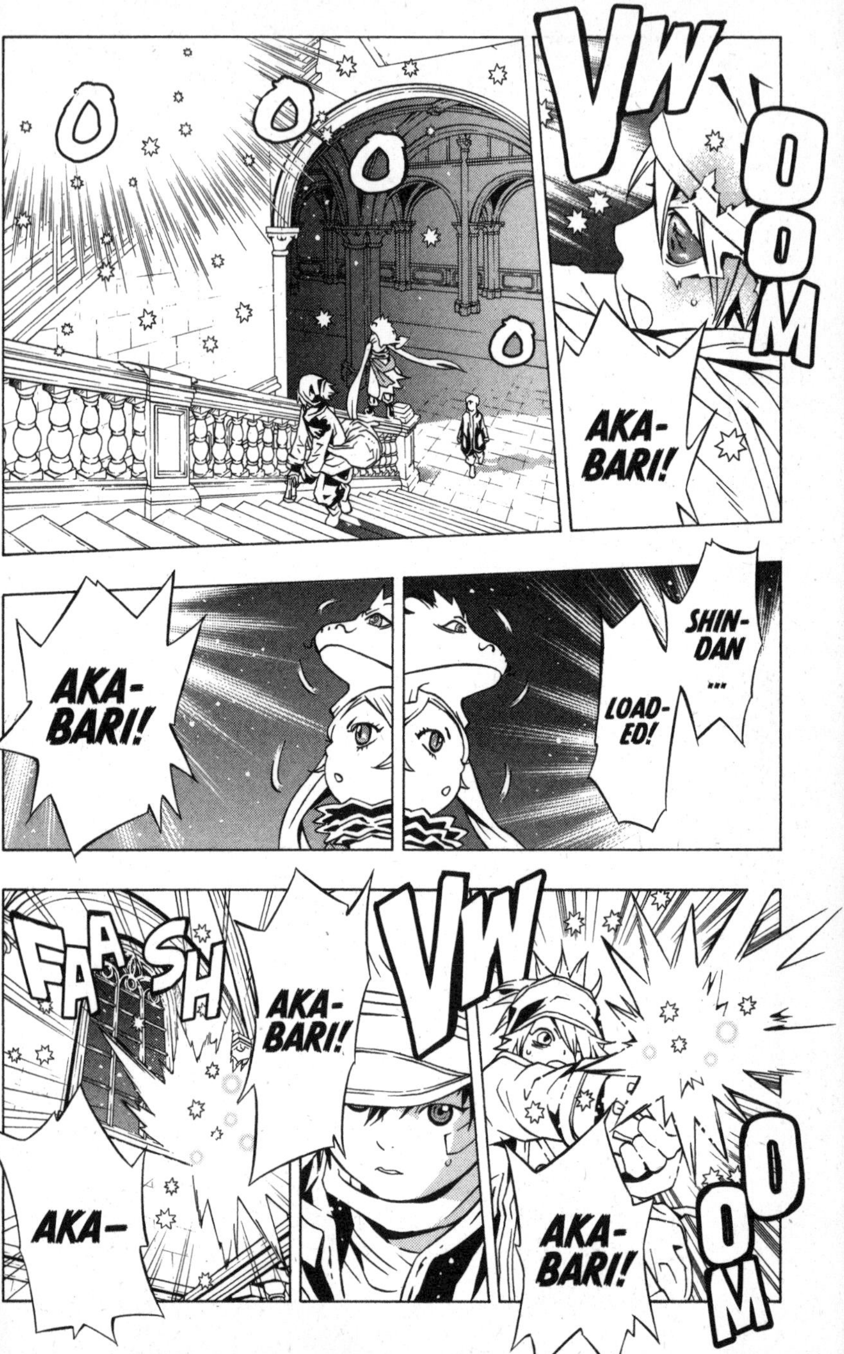
VWOOOM
AKA-BARI!
SHIN-DAN...
LOADED!
AKA-BARI!
VWOOM
AKA-BARI!
AKA-BARI!
FAASH
AKA-

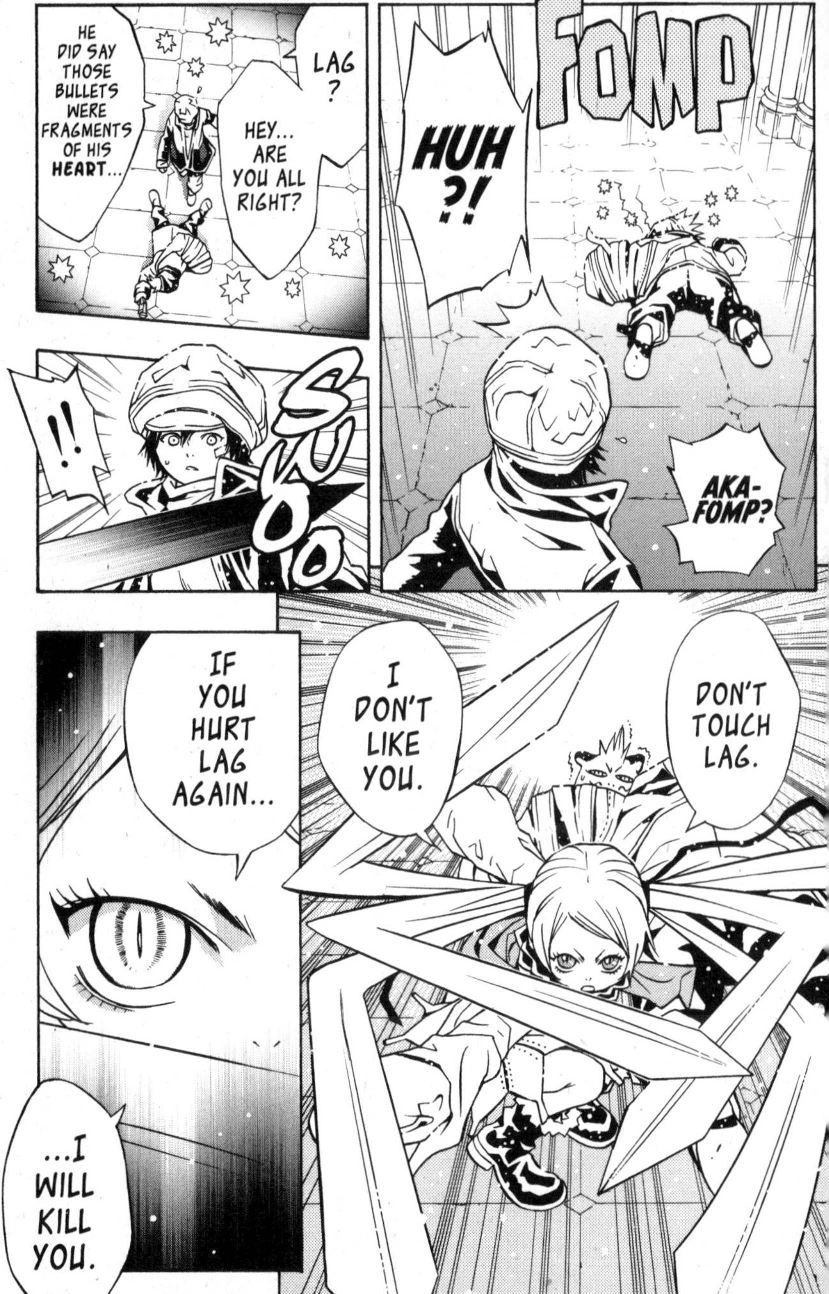
FOMP
HUH ?!
AKA-FOMP?
LAG ?
HEY... ARE YOU ALL RIGHT?
HE DID SAY THOSE BULLETS WERE FRAGMENTS OF HIS HEART...
!!
SUOO
DON'T TOUCH LAG.
I DON'T LIKE YOU.
IF YOU HURT LAG AGAIN...
...I WILL KILL YOU.

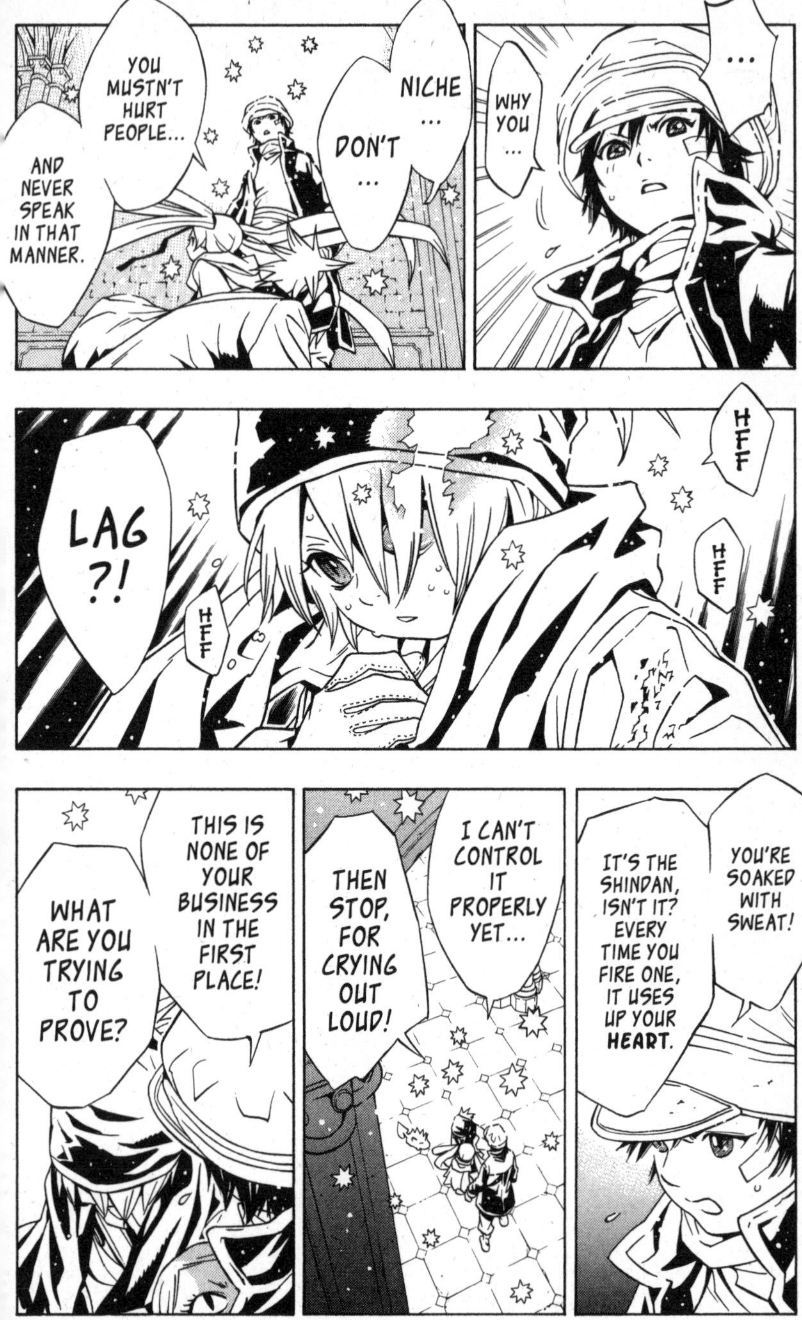
...
WHY YOU ...
NICHE ... DON'T ...
YOU MUSTN'T HURT PEOPLE...
AND NEVER SPEAK IN THAT MANNER.
HFF
HFF
LAG?!
HFF
YOU'RE SOAKED WITH SWEAT!
IT'S THE SHINDAN, ISN'T IT? EVERY TIME YOU FIRE ONE, IT USES UP YOUR **HEART**.
I CAN'T CONTROL IT PROPERLY YET...
THEN STOP, FOR CRYING OUT LOUD!
THIS IS NONE OF YOUR BUSINESS IN THE FIRST PLACE!
WHAT ARE YOU TRYING TO PROVE?

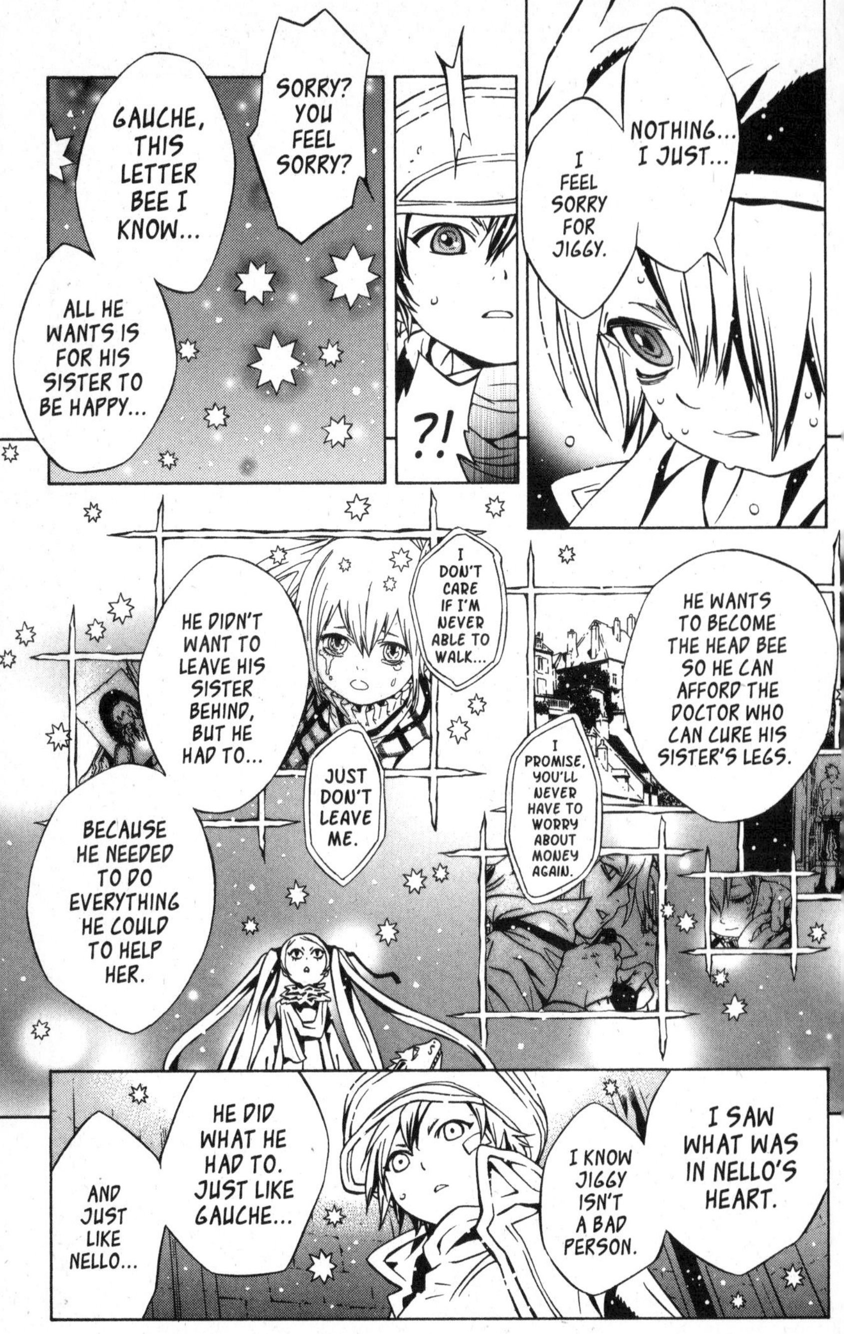
NOTHING... I JUST...
I FEEL SORRY FOR JIGGY.
?!
SORRY? YOU FEEL SORRY?
GAUCHE, THIS LETTER BEE I KNOW...
ALL HE WANTS IS FOR HIS SISTER TO BE HAPPY...
HE WANTS TO BECOME THE HEAD BEE SO HE CAN AFFORD THE DOCTOR WHO CAN CURE HIS SISTER'S LEGS.
I PROMISE, YOU'LL NEVER HAVE TO WORRY ABOUT MONEY AGAIN.
I DON'T CARE IF I'M NEVER ABLE TO WALK...
JUST DON'T LEAVE ME.
HE DIDN'T WANT TO LEAVE HIS SISTER BEHIND, BUT HE HAD TO...
BECAUSE HE NEEDED TO DO EVERYTHING HE COULD TO HELP HER.
I SAW WHAT WAS IN NELLO'S HEART.
I KNOW JIGGY ISN'T A BAD PERSON.
HE DID WHAT HE HAD TO. JUST LIKE GAUCHE...
AND JUST LIKE NELLO...

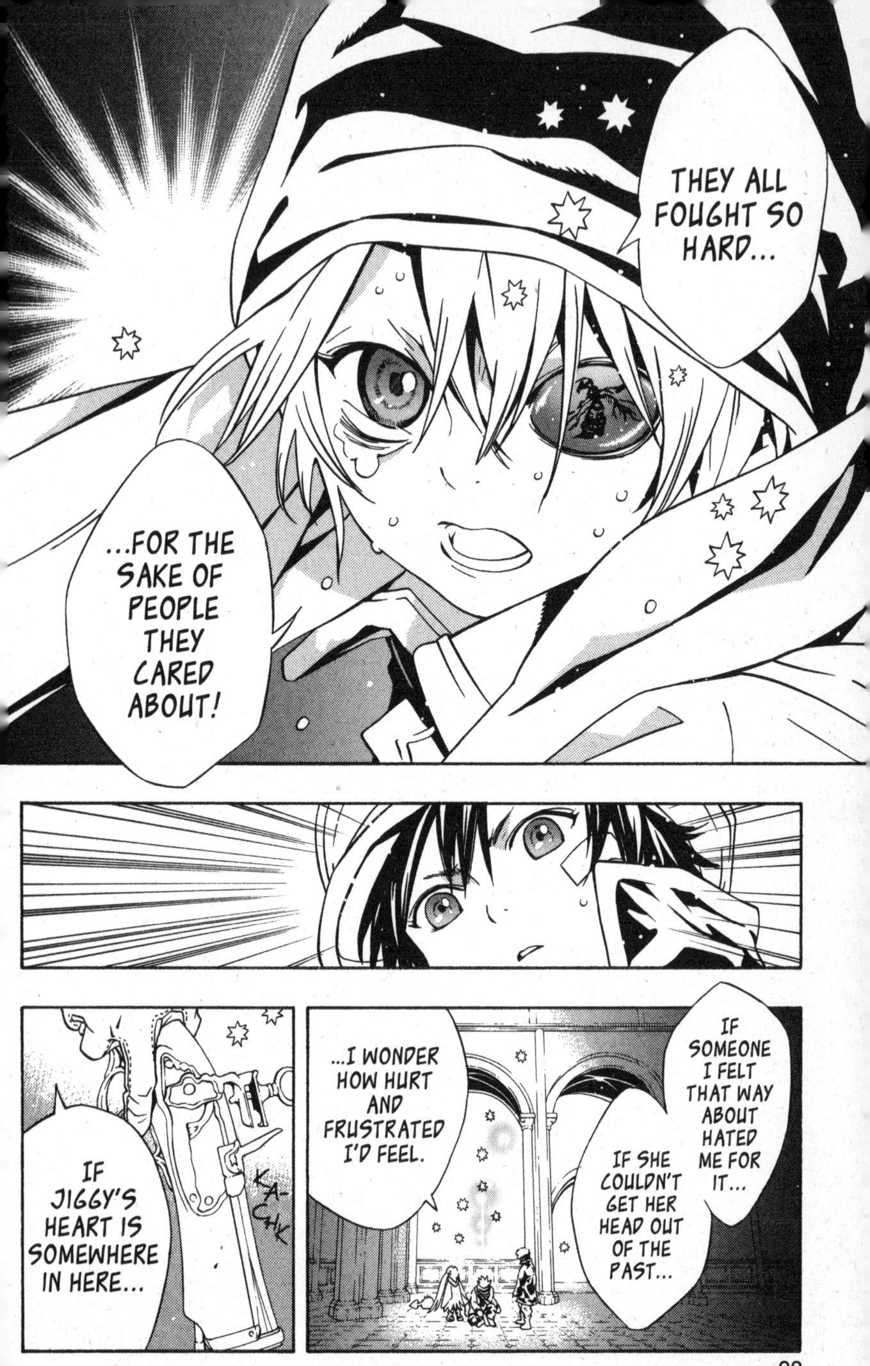
THEY ALL FOUGHT SO HARD...
...FOR THE SAKE OF PEOPLE THEY CARED ABOUT!
IF SOMEONE I FELT THAT WAY ABOUT HATED ME FOR IT...
IF SHE COULDN'T GET HER HEAD OUT OF THE PAST...
...I WONDER HOW HURT AND FRUSTRATED I'D FEEL.
KA-CHK
IF JIGGY'S HEART IS SOMEWHERE IN HERE...

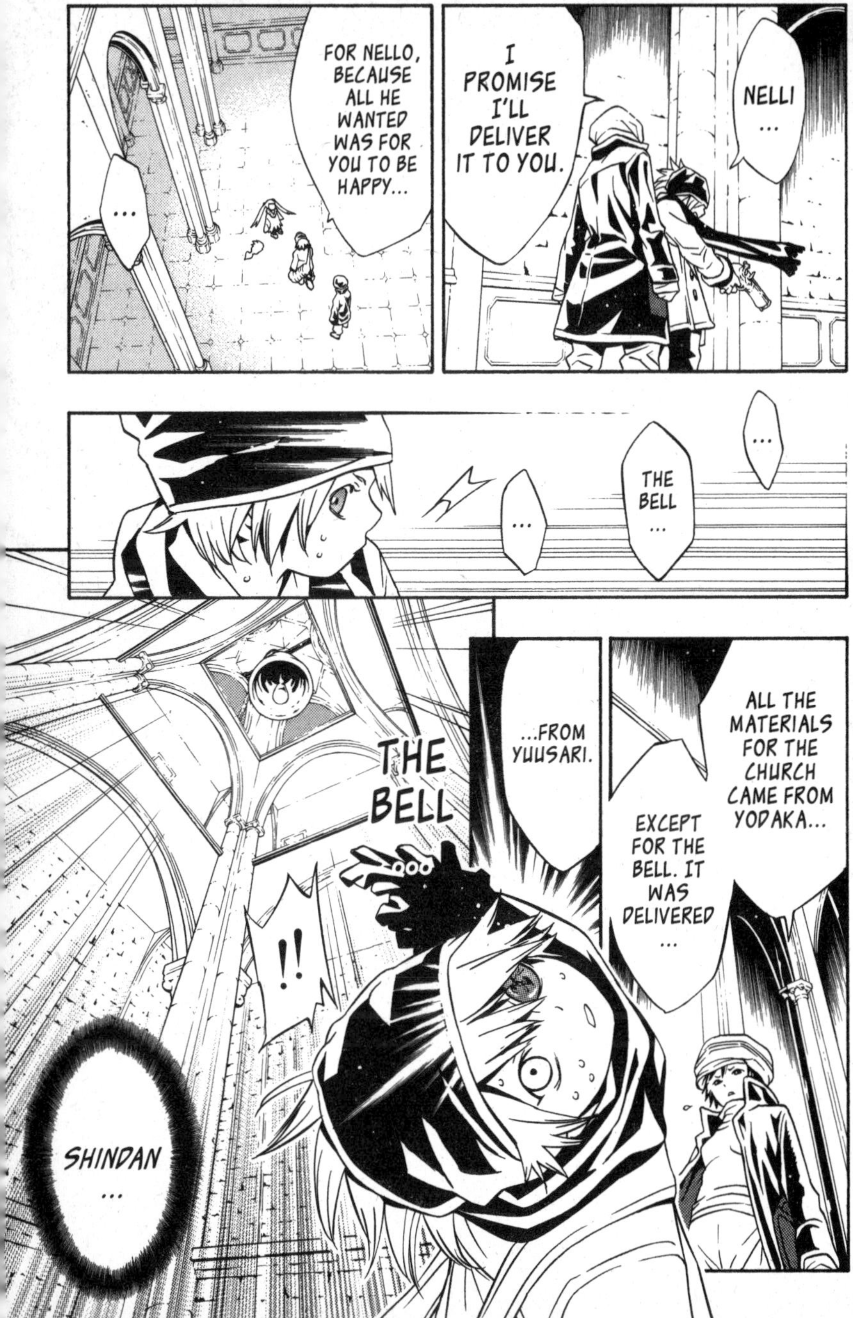
NELLI ...
I PROMISE I'LL DELIVER IT TO YOU.
FOR NELLO, BECAUSE ALL HE WANTED WAS FOR YOU TO BE HAPPY...
...
...
THE BELL ...
...
ALL THE MATERIALS FOR THE CHURCH CAME FROM YODAKA...
EXCEPT FOR THE BELL. IT WAS DELIVERED ...
...FROM YUUSARI.
THE BELL
!!
SHINDAN ...

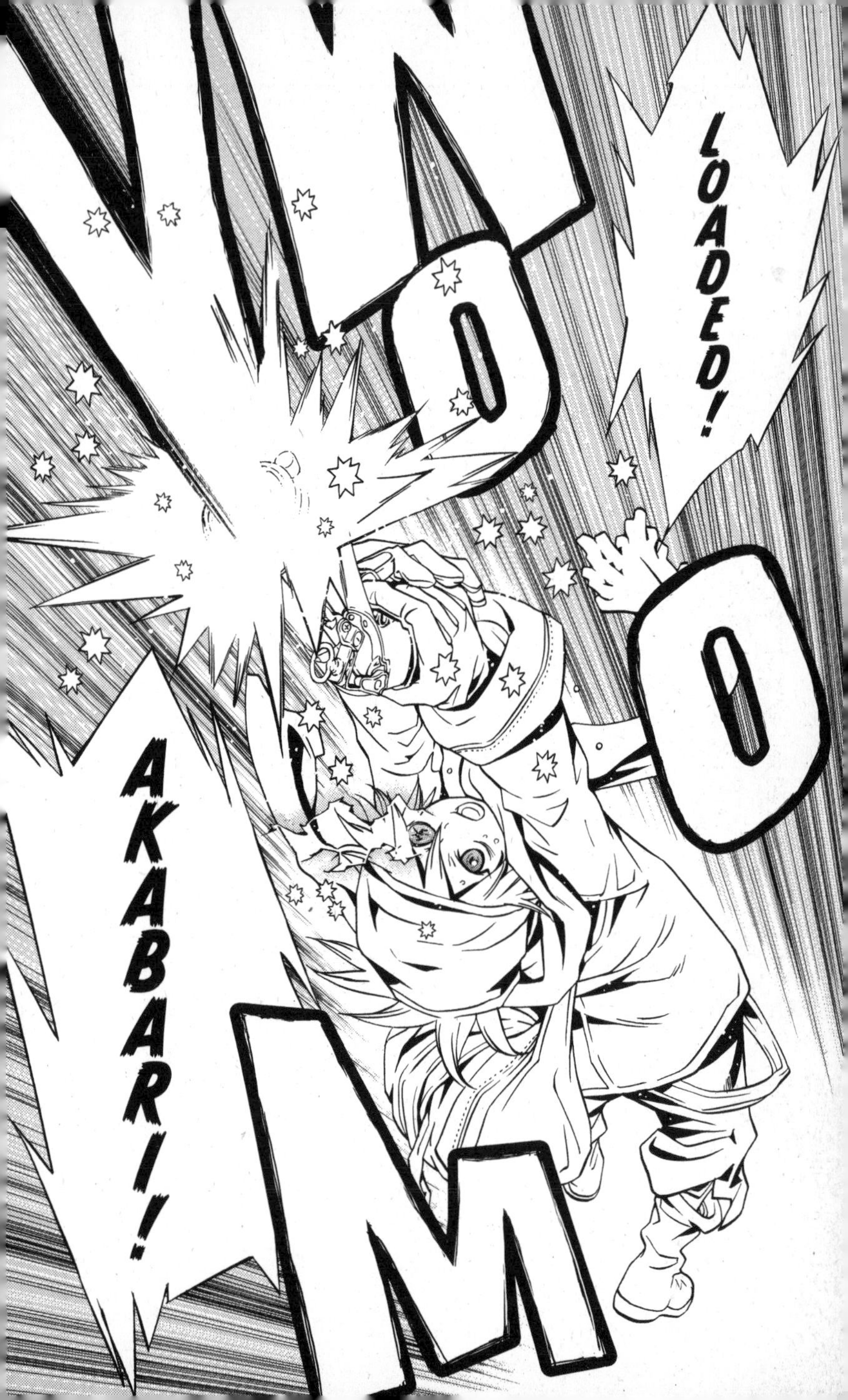
LOADED!!
AKABARI!!

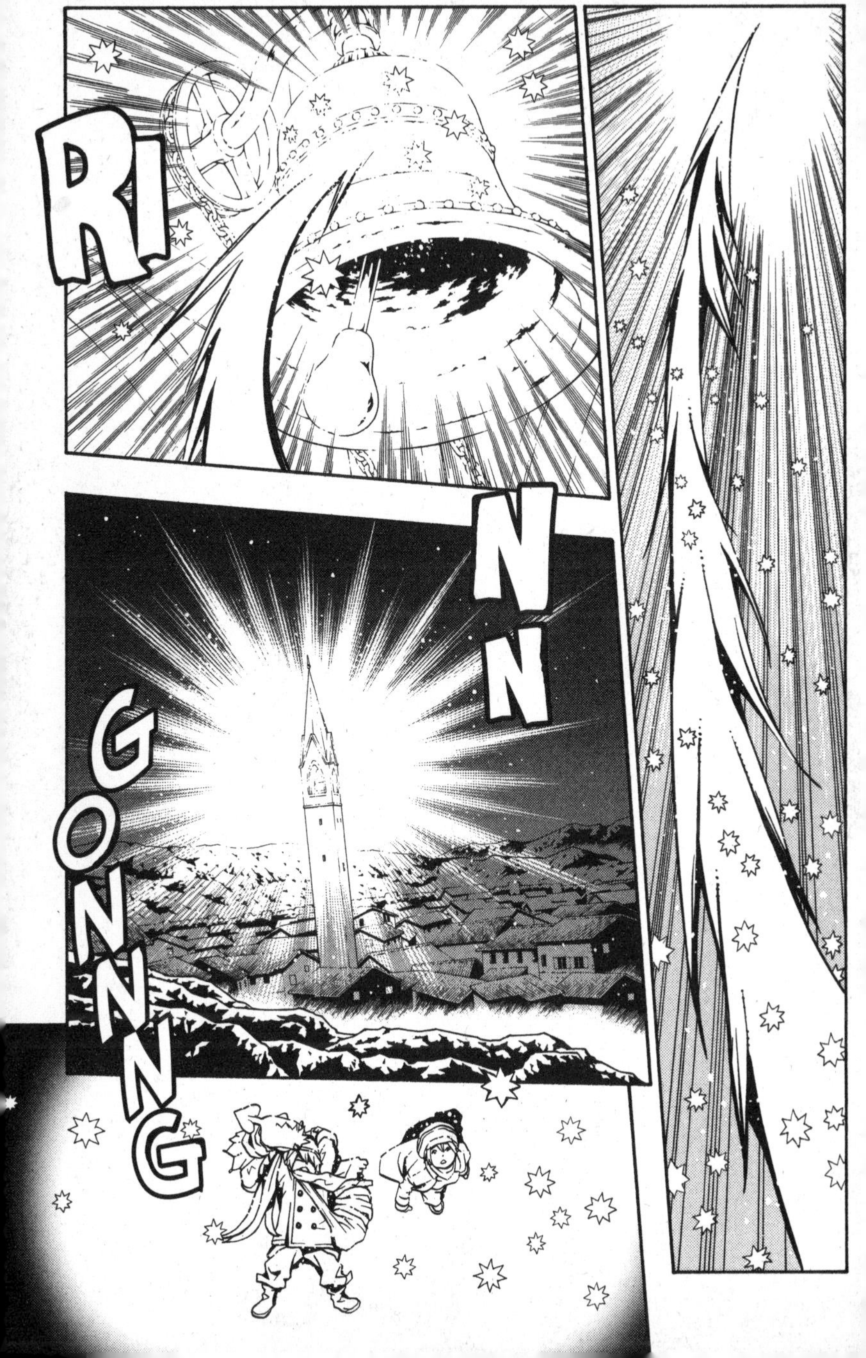
RI
NN
GONNNG

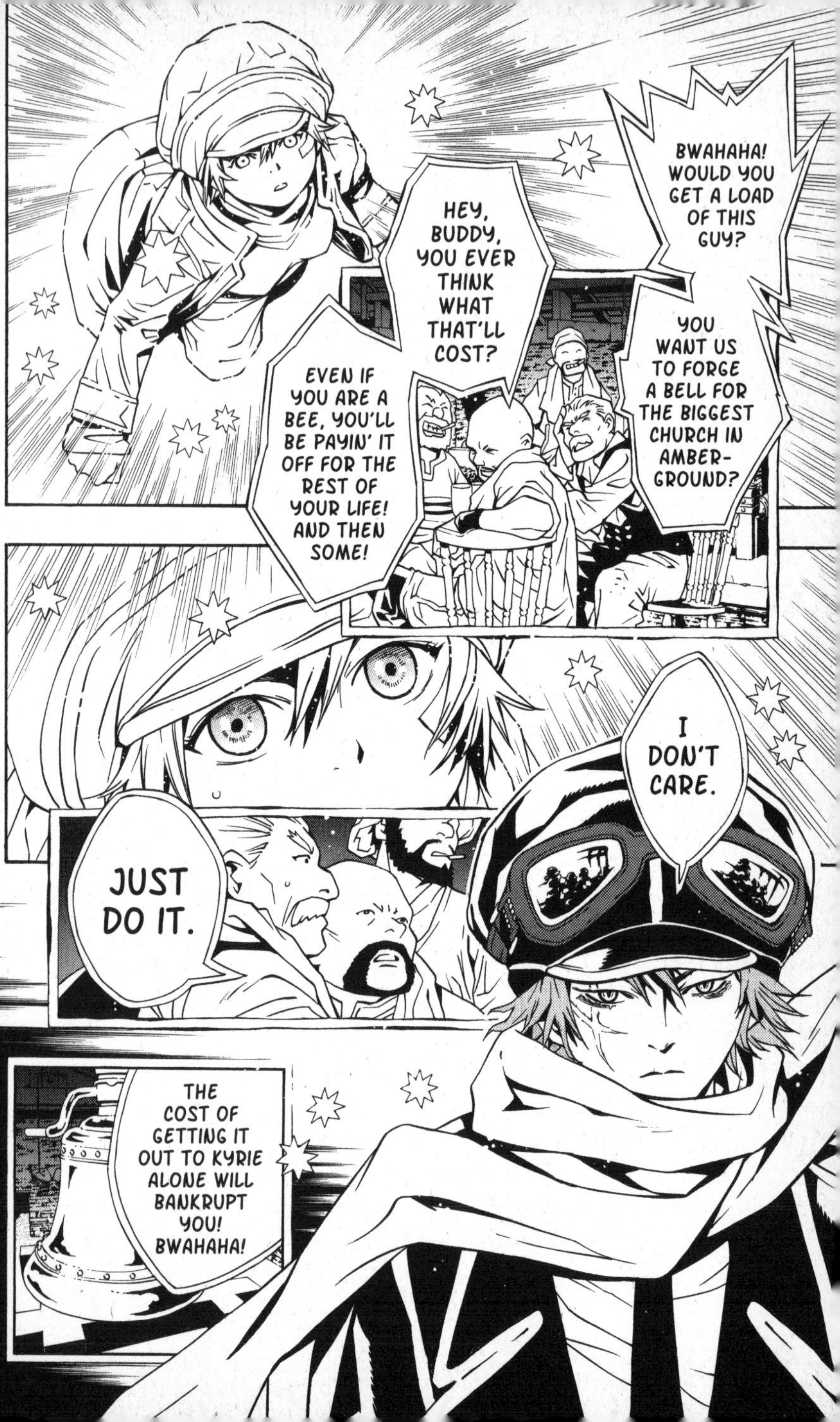
BWAHAHA! WOULD YOU GET A LOAD OF THIS GUY?
YOU WANT US TO FORGE A BELL FOR THE BIGGEST CHURCH IN AMBER-GROUND?
HEY, BUDDY, YOU EVER THINK WHAT THAT'LL COST?
EVEN IF YOU ARE A BEE, YOU'LL BE PAYIN' IT OFF FOR THE REST OF YOUR LIFE! AND THEN SOME!
I DON'T CARE.
JUST DO IT.
THE COST OF GETTING IT OUT TO KYRIE ALONE WILL BANKRUPT YOU! BWAHAHA!

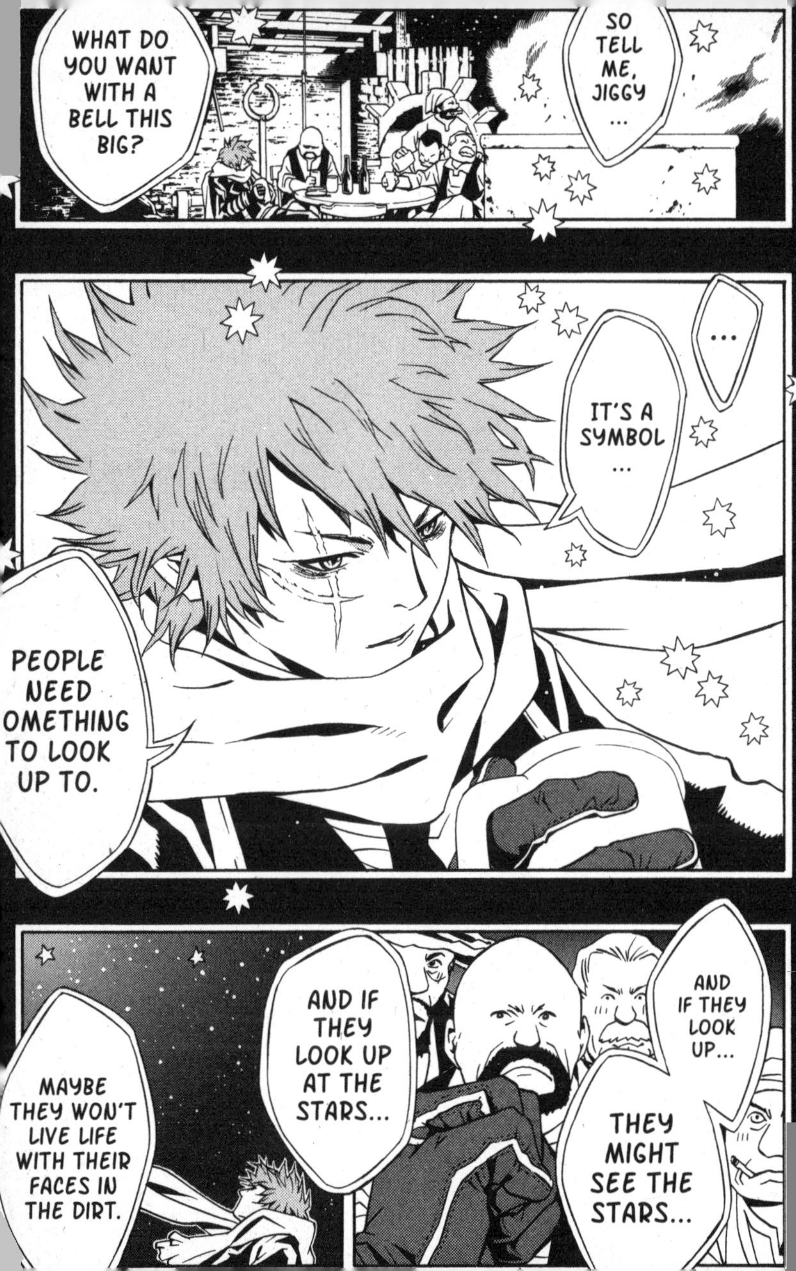
SO TELL ME, JIGGY...
WHAT DO YOU WANT WITH A BELL THIS BIG?
...
IT'S A SYMBOL...
PEOPLE NEED OMETHING TO LOOK UP TO.
AND IF THEY LOOK UP...
THEY MIGHT SEE THE STARS...
AND IF THEY LOOK UP AT THE STARS...
MAYBE THEY WON'T LIVE LIFE WITH THEIR FACES IN THE DIRT.

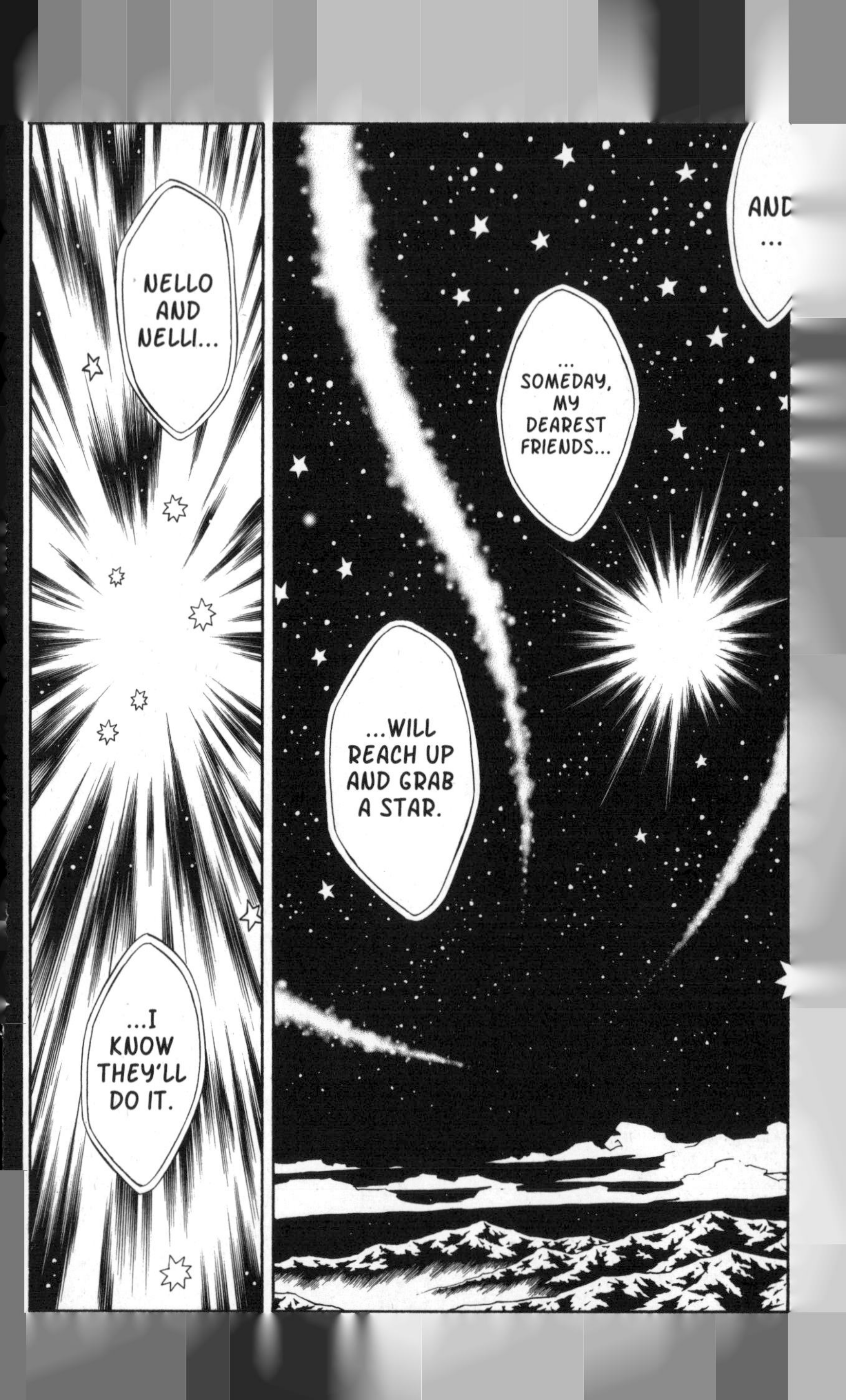
AND ...
... SOMEDAY, MY DEAREST FRIENDS...
...WILL REACH UP AND GRAB A STAR.
NELLO AND NELLI...
...I KNOW THEY'LL DO IT.

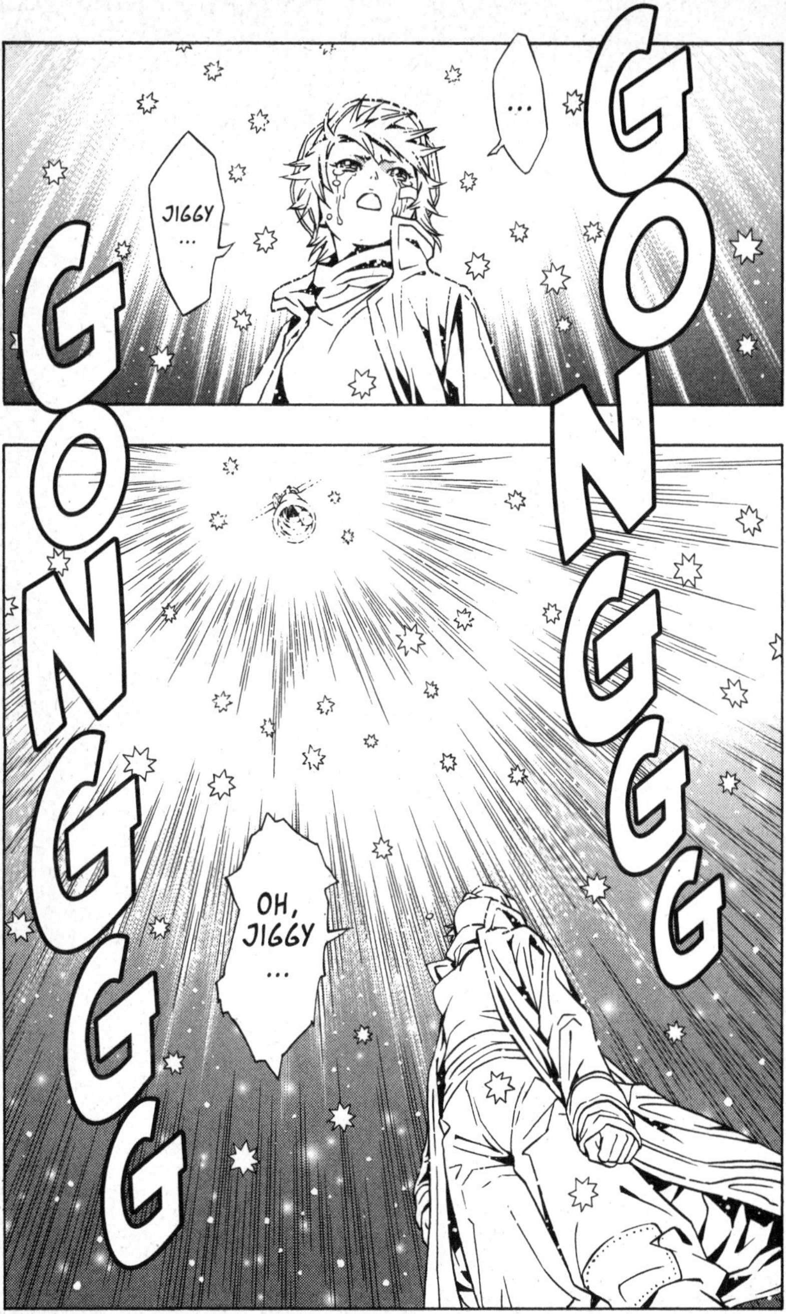
GONGGG
...
JIGGY ...
GONGGG
OH, JIGGY ...

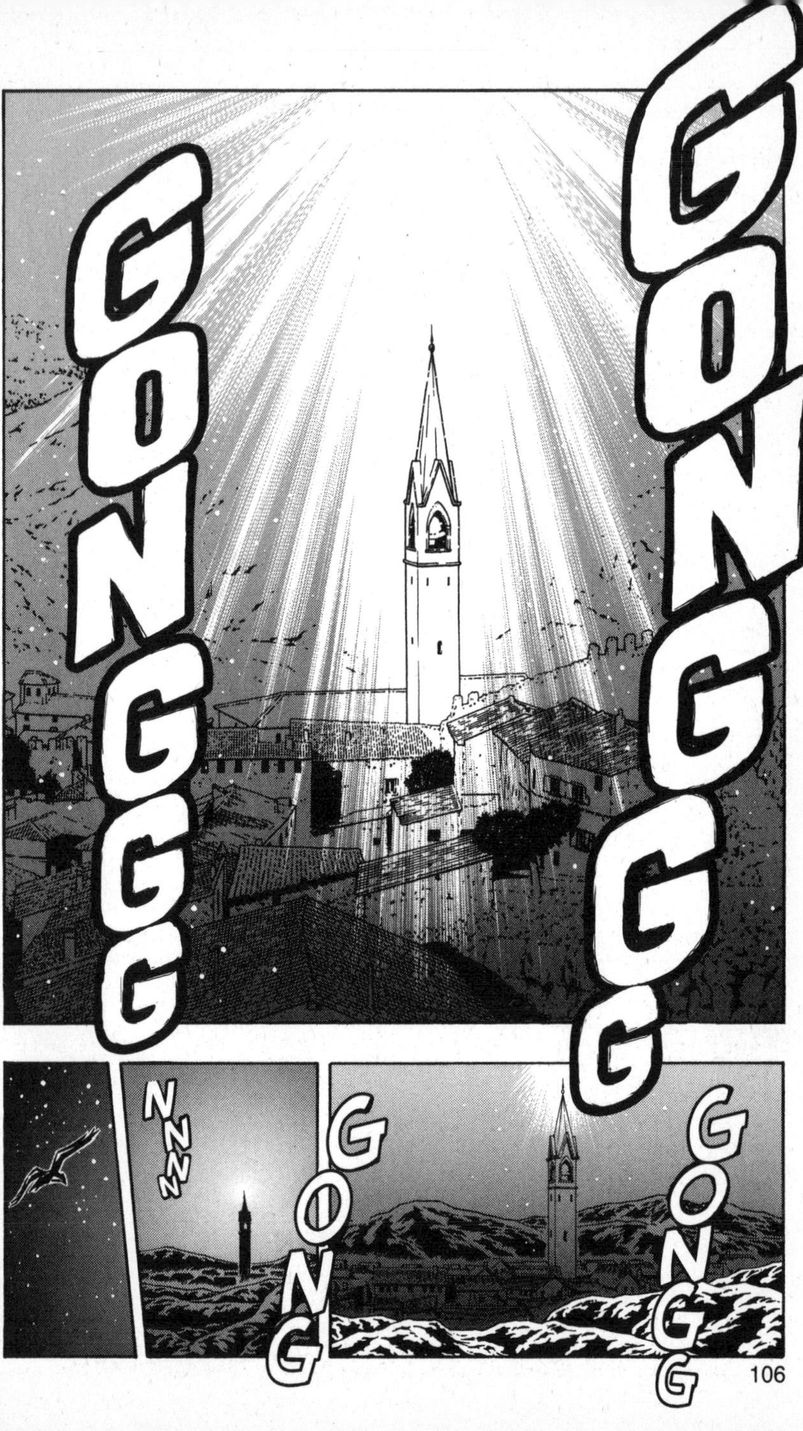
GONGGG
GONGGG
GONGG
GONG
NNNN

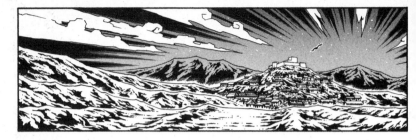

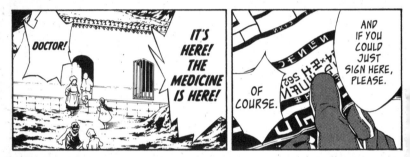

AND IF YOU COULD JUST SIGN HERE, PLEASE.
OF COURSE.
IT'S HERE! THE MEDICINE IS HERE!
DOCTOR!
OH, THANK GOOD-NESS!
DOCTOR ...
WILL HE BE ALL RIGHT?
MY LITTLE BROTHER WILL BE ALL RIGHT NOW?
THANK YOU!

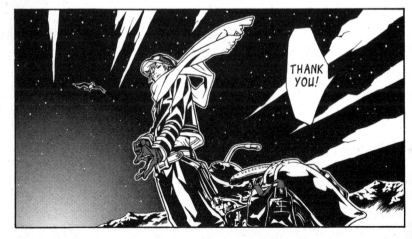

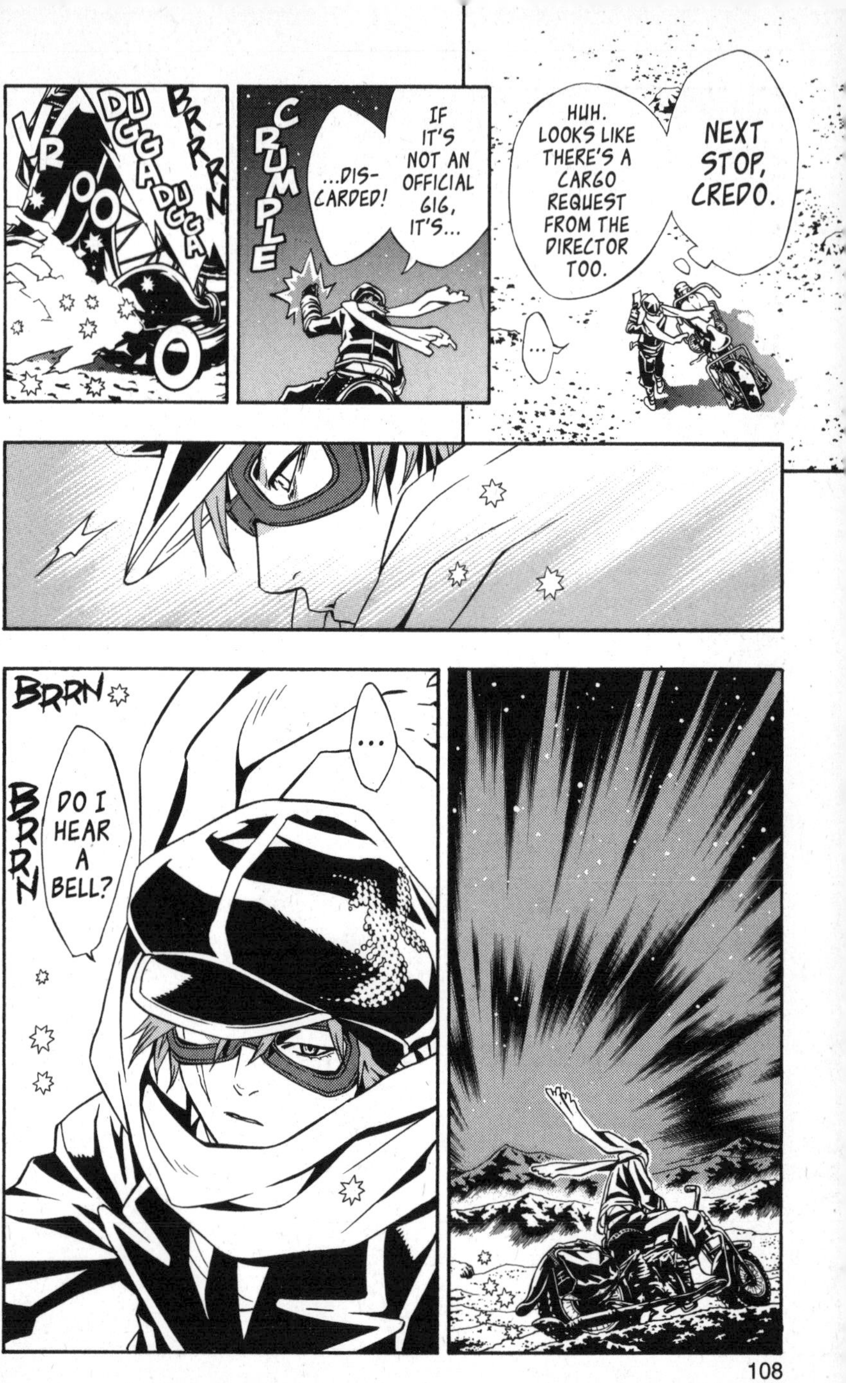
NEXT STOP, CREDO.
HUH. LOOKS LIKE THERE'S A CARGO REQUEST FROM THE DIRECTOR TOO.
...
IF IT'S NOT AN OFFICIAL GIG, IT'S...
...DIS-CARDED!
CRUMPLE
BRRRRN
DUGGADUGGA
VROOOO
...
DO I HEAR A BELL?
BRRN
BRRN

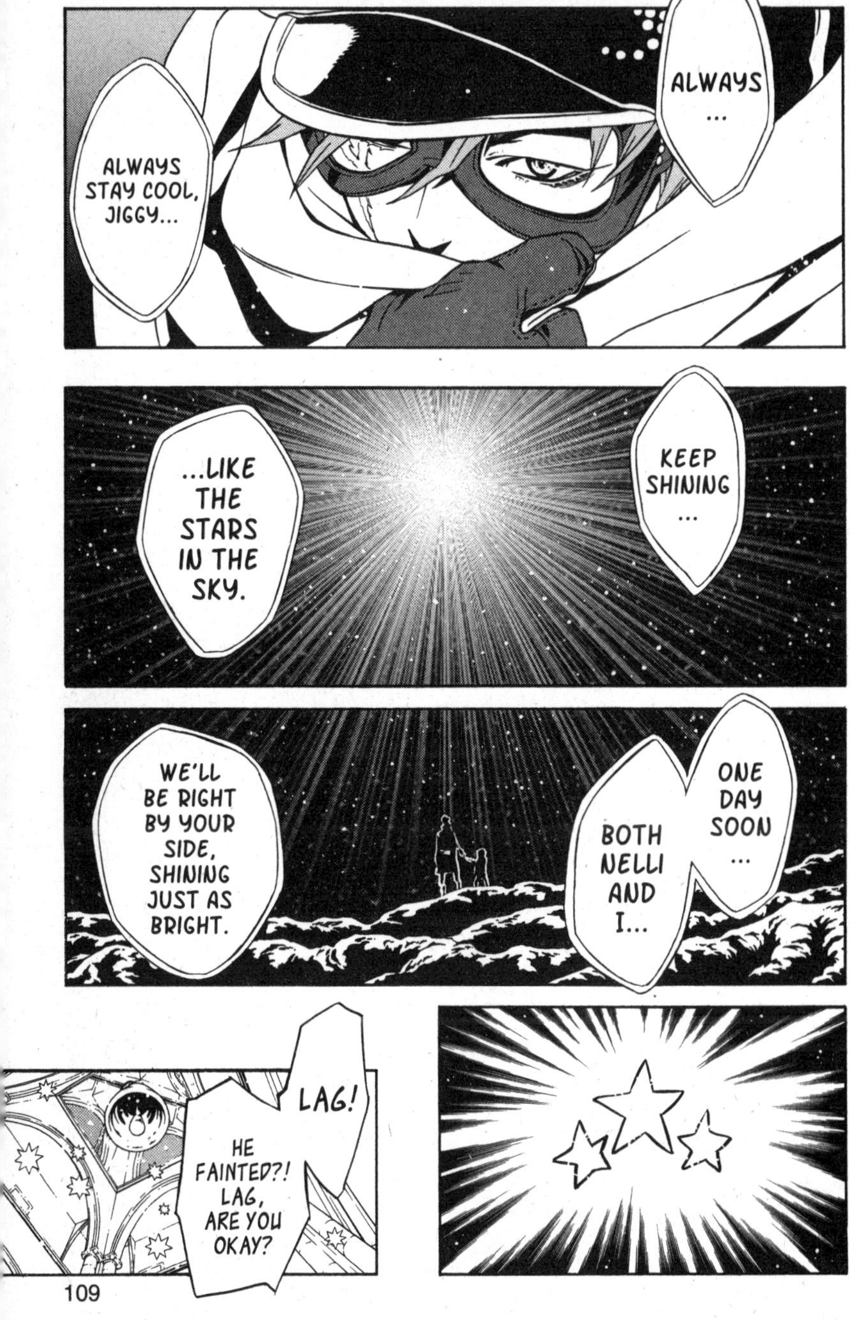
ALWAYS ...
ALWAYS STAY COOL, JIGGY...
KEEP SHINING ...
...LIKE THE STARS IN THE SKY.
ONE DAY SOON ...
BOTH NELLI AND I...
WE'LL BE RIGHT BY YOUR SIDE, SHINING JUST AS BRIGHT.
LAG!
HE FAINTED?! LAG, ARE YOU OKAY?

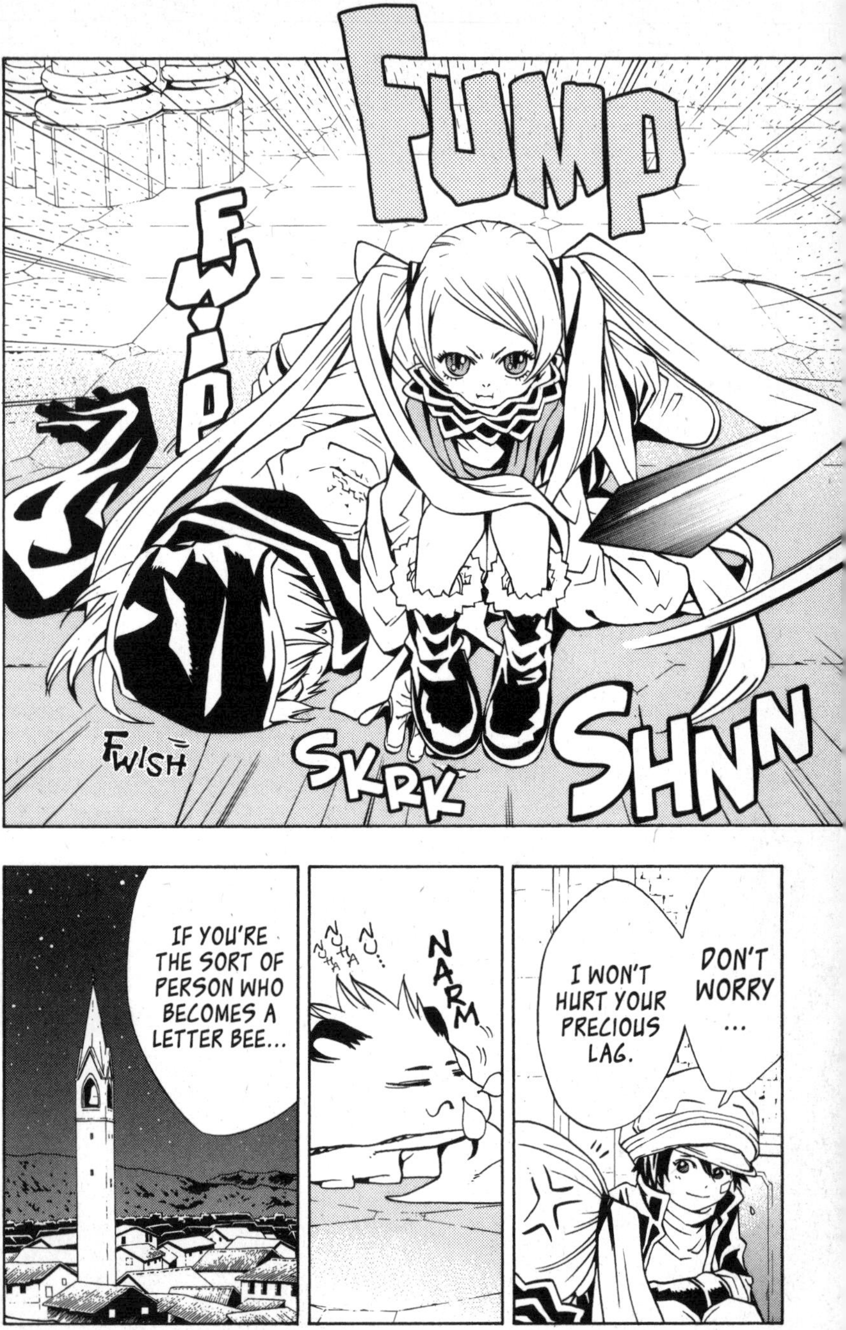
FUMP
SHNN
SKRK
FWIP
FWISH
DON'T WORRY...
I WON'T HURT YOUR PRECIOUS LAG.
NARM
IF YOU'RE THE SORT OF PERSON WHO BECOMES A LETTER BEE...

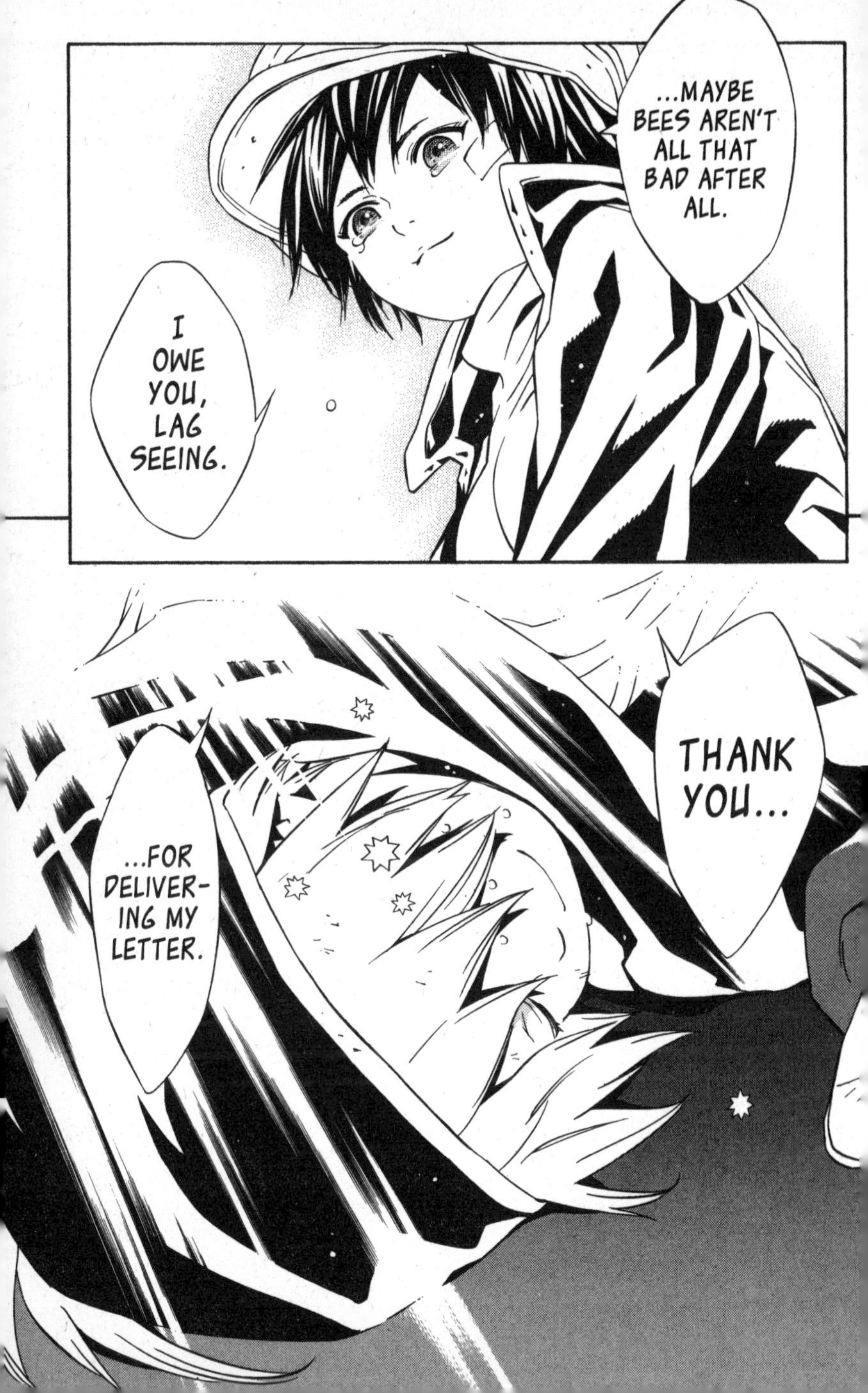
...MAYBE BEES AREN'T ALL THAT BAD AFTER ALL.
I OWE YOU, LAG SEEING.
THANK YOU...
...FOR DELIVERING MY LETTER.

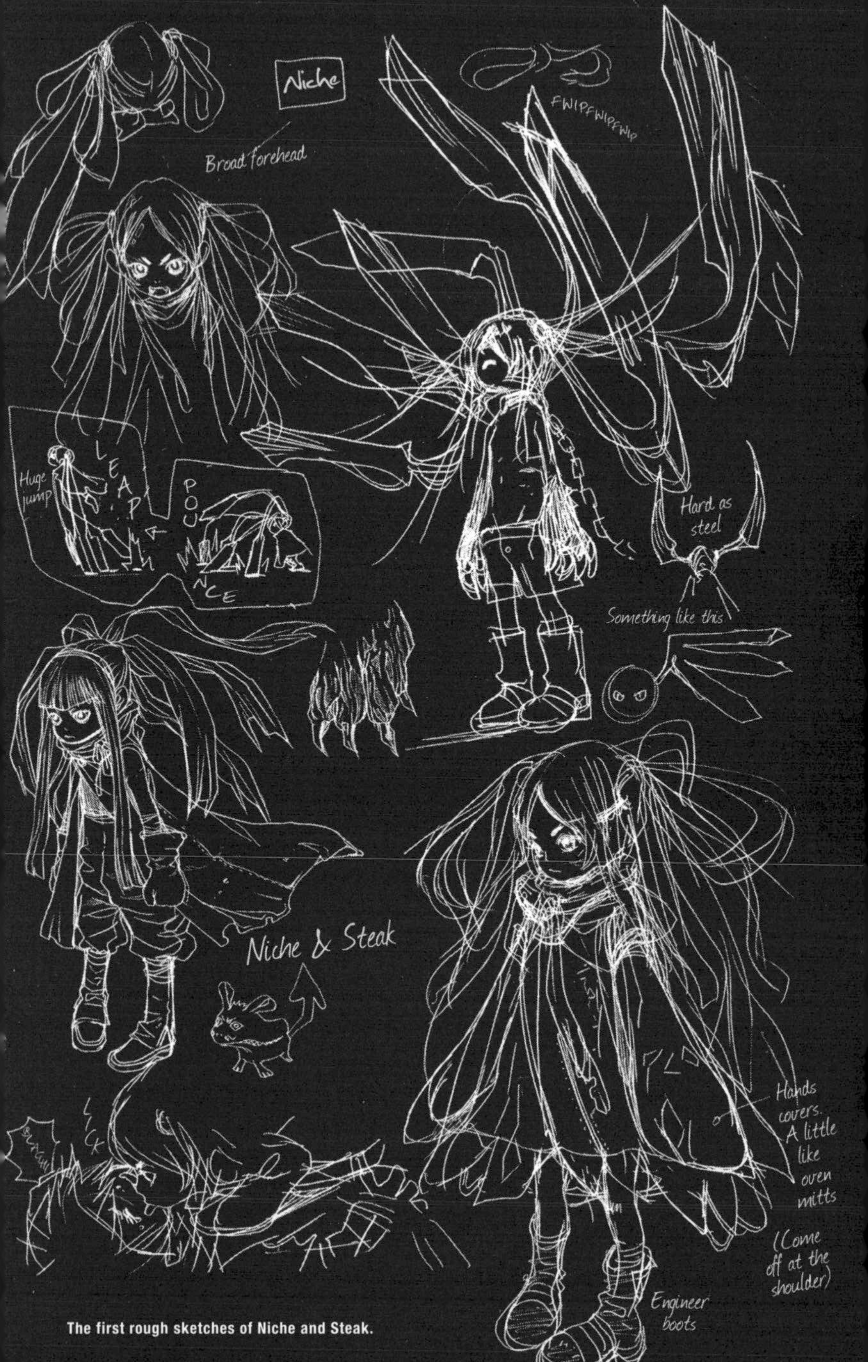
Niche
Broad forehead
FWIPFWIPFWIP
Huge jump
LEAP
POUNCE
Hard as steel
Something like this
Niche & Steak
LICK
Hands covers. A little like oven mitts
(Come off at the shoulder)
Engineer boots

The first rough sketches of Niche and Steak.

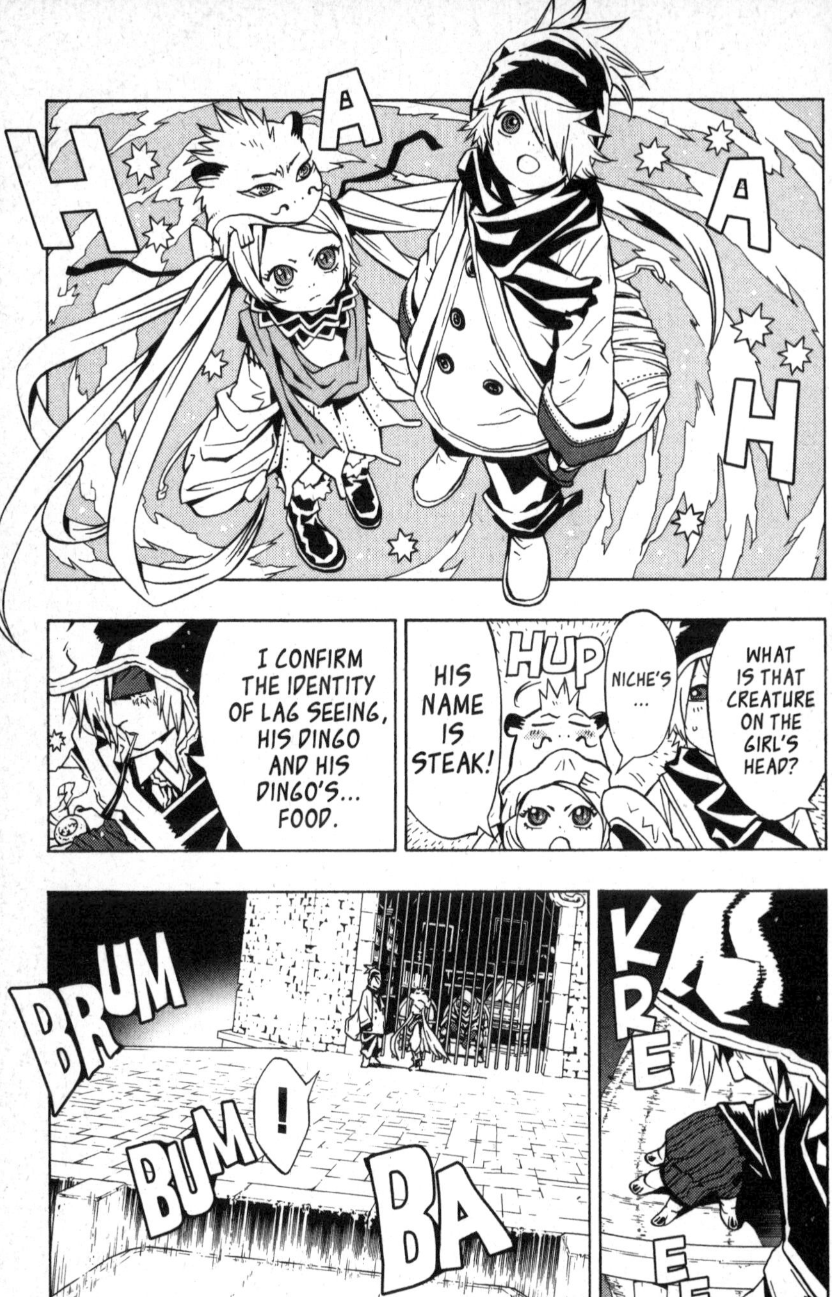
HAAH
WHAT IS THAT CREATURE ON THE GIRL'S HEAD?
NICHE'S ...
HUP
HIS NAME IS STEAK!
I CONFIRM THE IDENTITY OF LAG SEEING, HIS DINGO AND HIS DINGO'S... FOOD.
KREEEE
BRUM
BUM
!
BA

Chapter 6: Beehive, 13 Nocturne Row, Central Yuusari

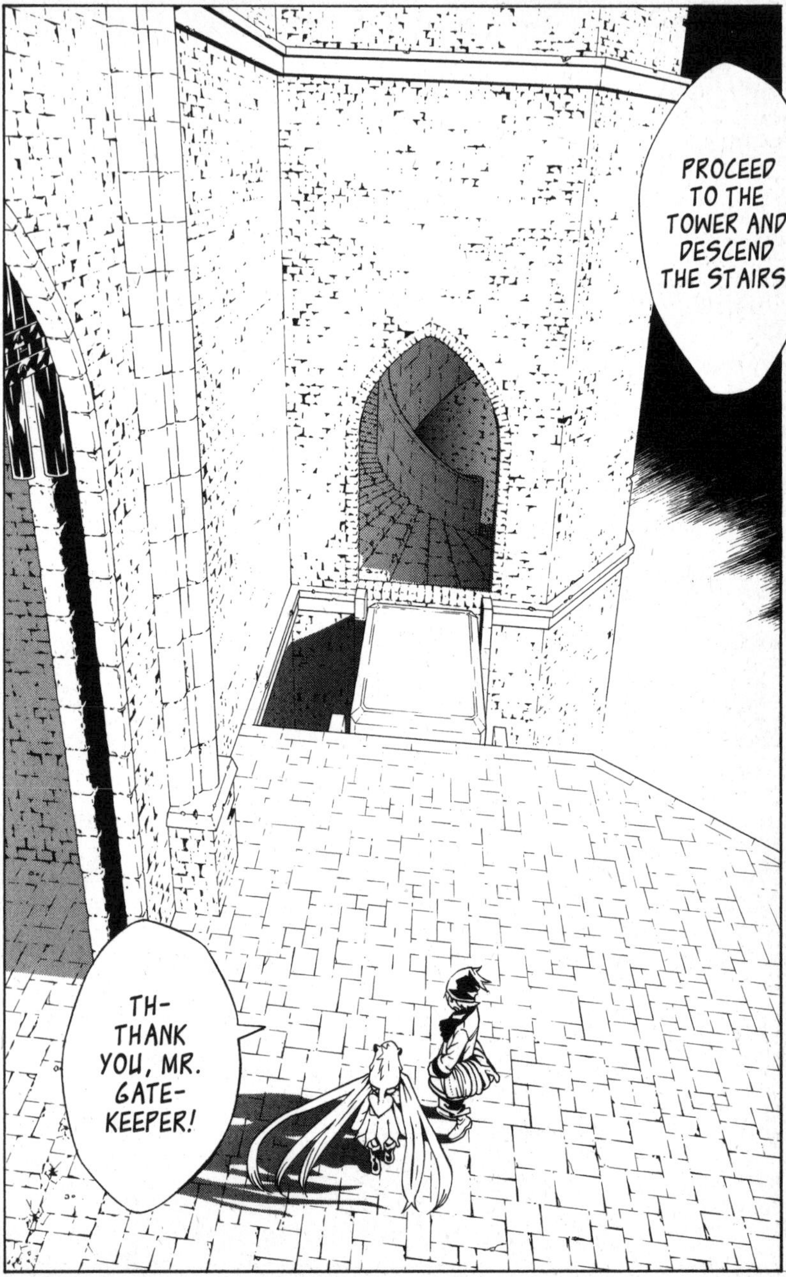
PROCEED TO THE TOWER AND DESCEND THE STAIRS.
TH- THANK YOU, MR. GATE-KEEPER!

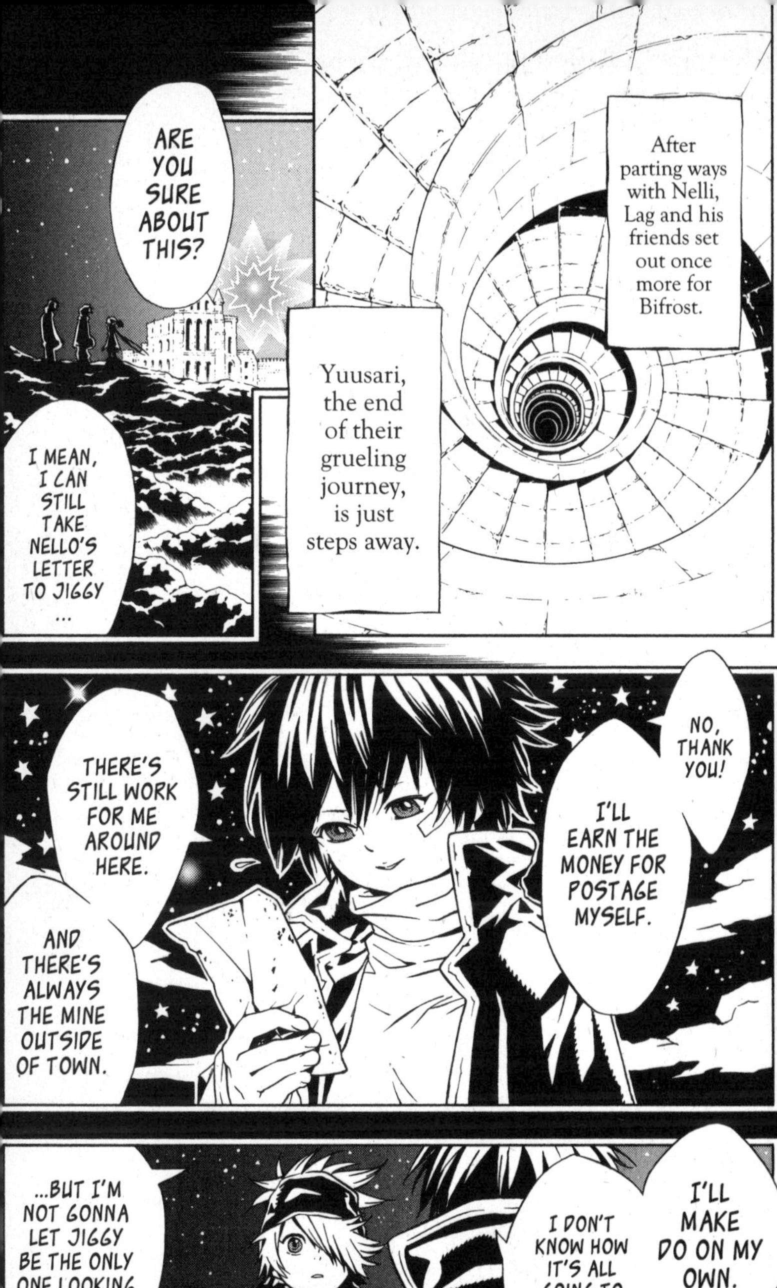
After parting ways with Nelli, Lag and his friends set out once more for Bifrost.
Yuusari, the end of their grueling journey, is just steps away.
ARE YOU SURE ABOUT THIS?
I MEAN, I CAN STILL TAKE NELLO'S LETTER TO JIGGY...
NO, THANK YOU!
I'LL EARN THE MONEY FOR POSTAGE MYSELF.
THERE'S STILL WORK FOR ME AROUND HERE.
AND THERE'S ALWAYS THE MINE OUTSIDE OF TOWN.
I'LL MAKE DO ON MY OWN.
I DON'T KNOW HOW IT'S ALL GOING TO WORK OUT...
...BUT I'M NOT GONNA LET JIGGY BE THE ONLY ONE LOOKING ALL COOL.

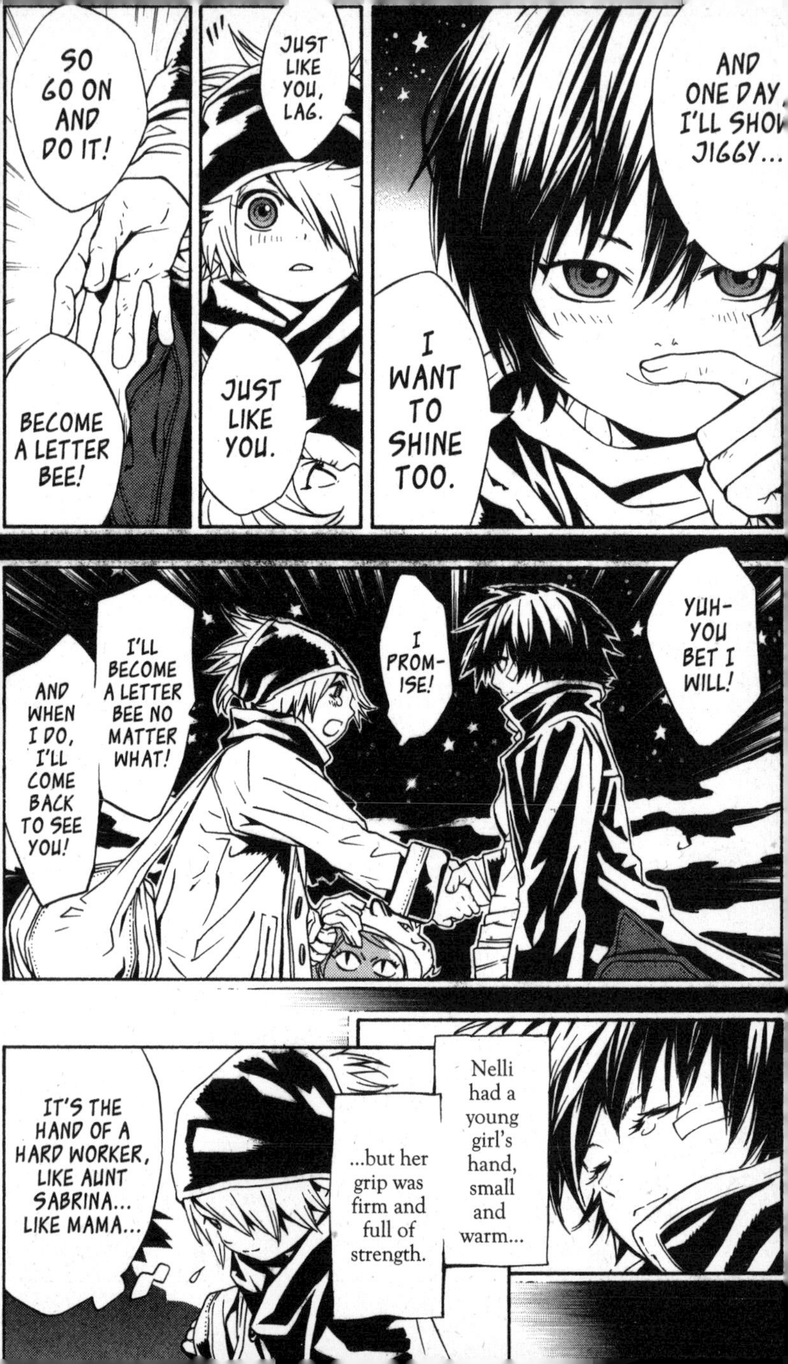
AND ONE DAY, I'LL SHOW JIGGY...
I WANT TO SHINE TOO.
JUST LIKE YOU, LAG.
JUST LIKE YOU.
SO GO ON AND DO IT!
BECOME A LETTER BEE!
YUH-YOU BET I WILL!
I PROMISE!
I'LL BECOME A LETTER BEE NO MATTER WHAT!
AND WHEN I DO, I'LL COME BACK TO SEE YOU!
Nelli had a young girl's hand, small and warm...
...but her grip was firm and full of strength.
IT'S THE HAND OF A HARD WORKER, LIKE AUNT SABRINA... LIKE MAMA...

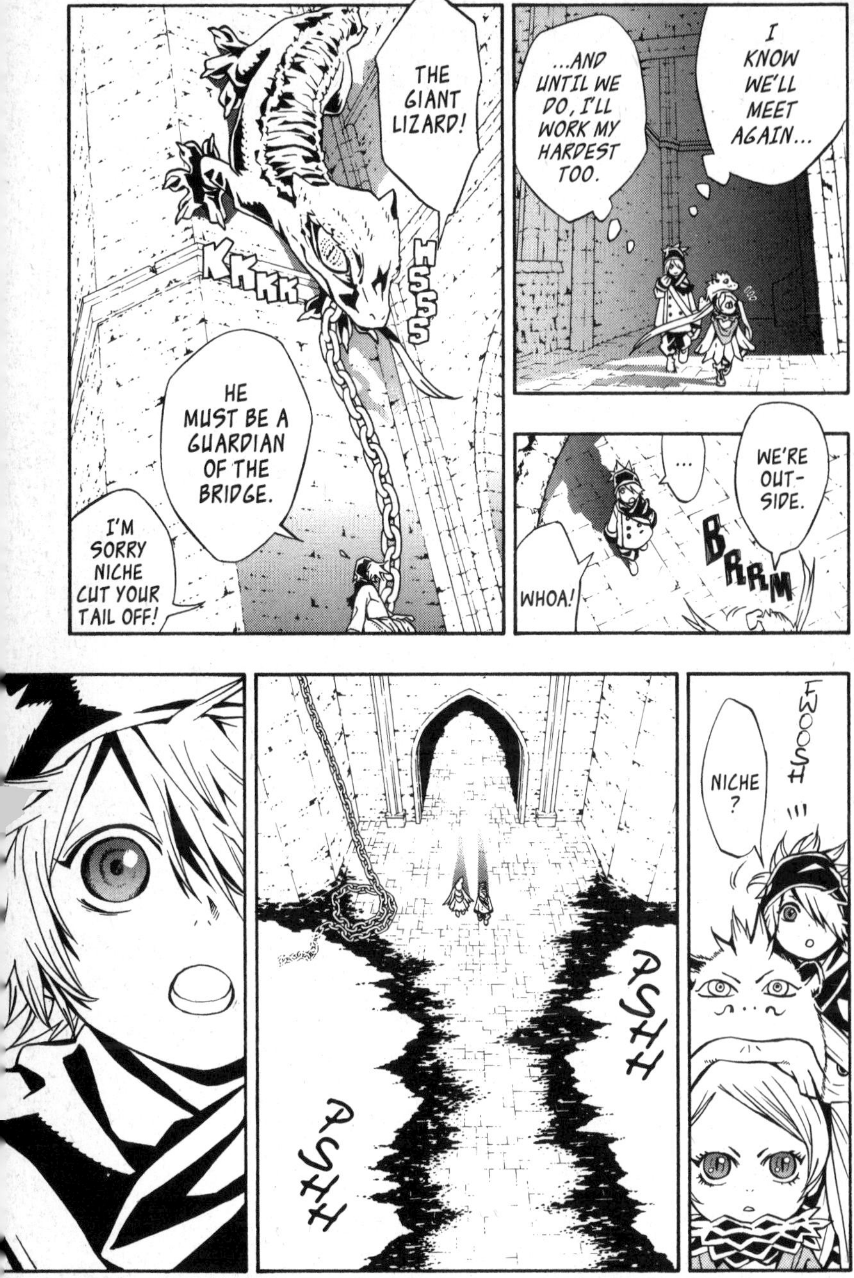

I KNOW WE'LL MEET AGAIN...
...AND UNTIL WE DO, I'LL WORK MY HARDEST TOO.
WE'RE OUT-SIDE.
...
BRRM
WHOA!
THE GIANT LIZARD!
HSSS
KKKK
HE MUST BE A GUARDIAN OF THE BRIDGE.
I'M SORRY NICHE CUT YOUR TAIL OFF!
FWOOSH
NICHE?
!!!
RSHH
RSHH

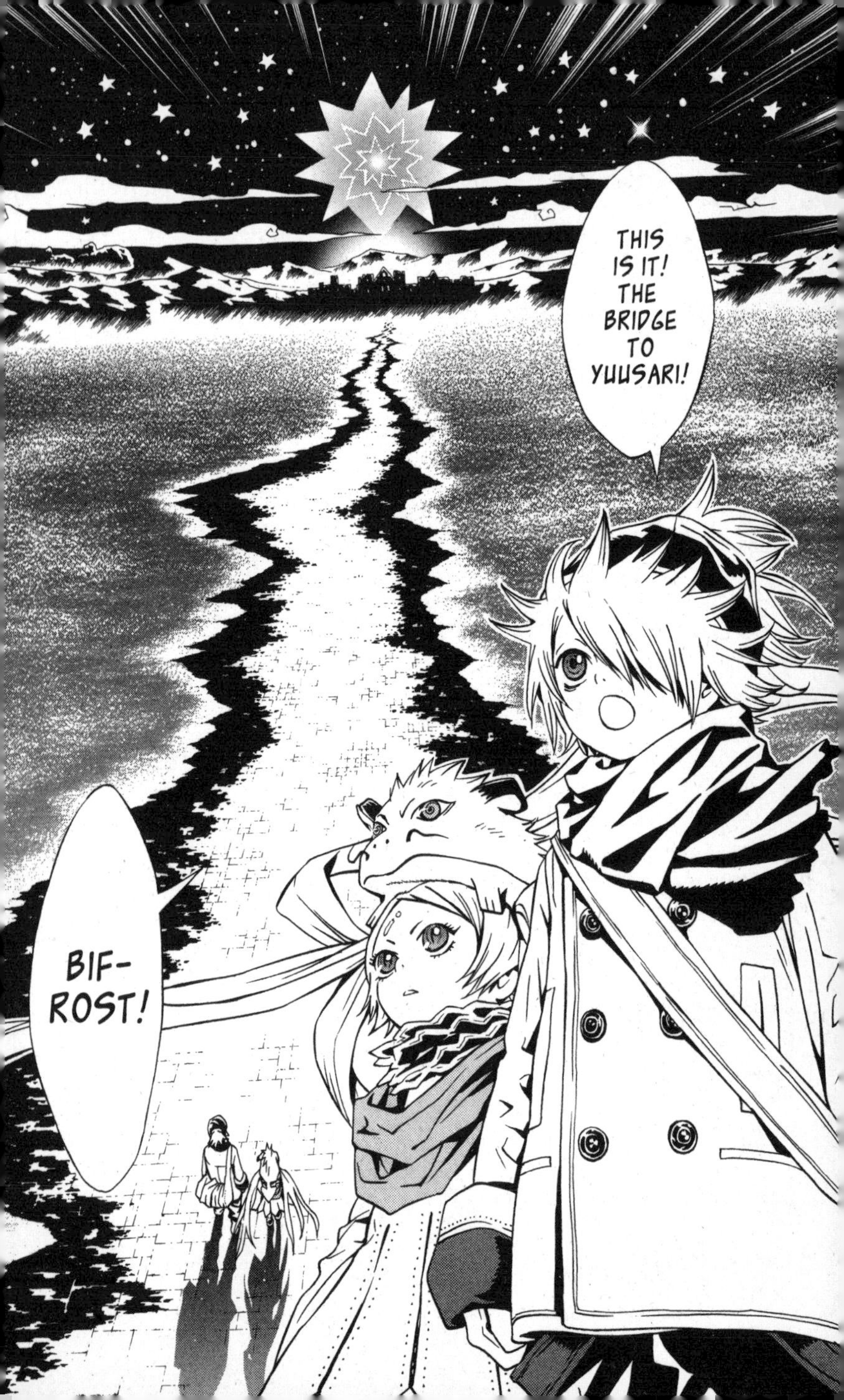
THIS IS IT! THE BRIDGE TO YUUSARI!
BIF-ROST!

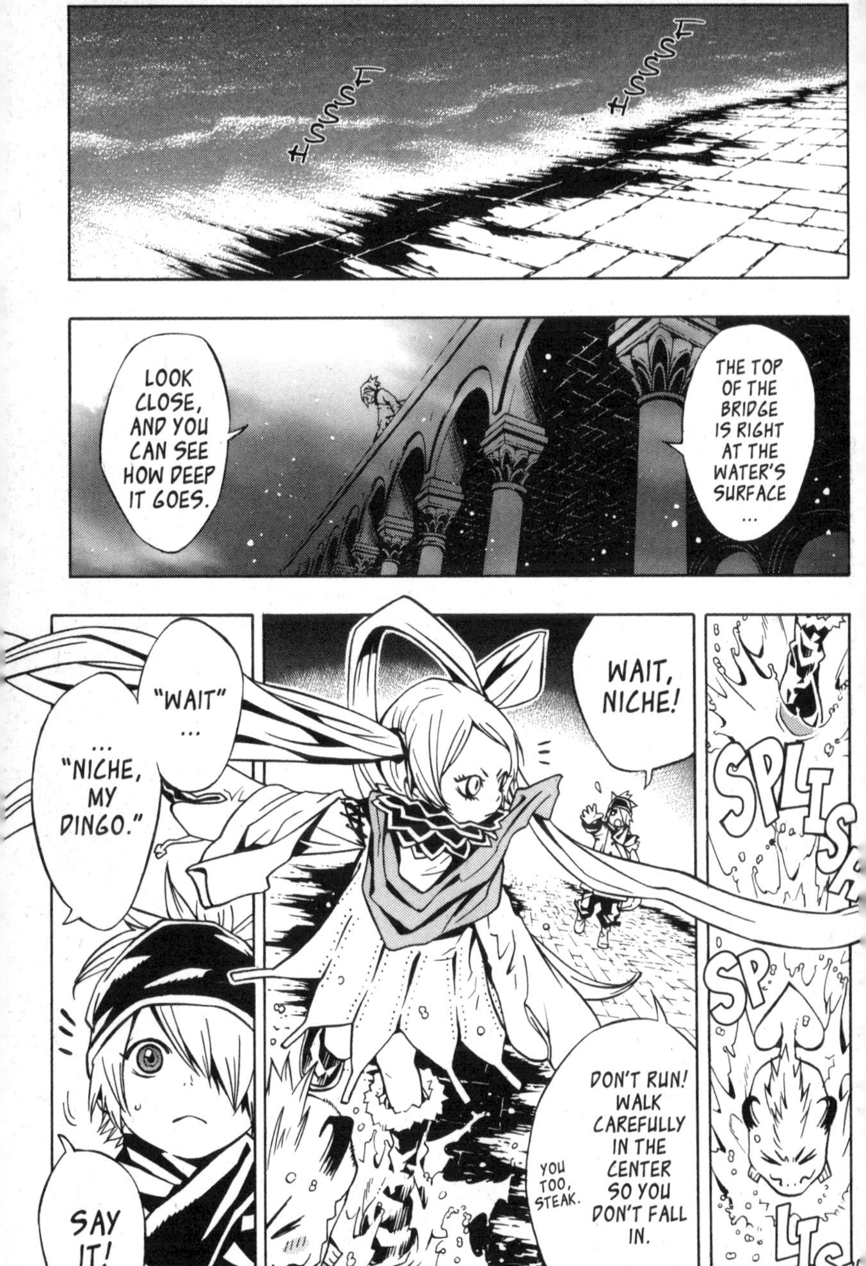
HSSSF
HSSSF
THE TOP OF THE BRIDGE IS RIGHT AT THE WATER'S SURFACE ...
LOOK CLOSE, AND YOU CAN SEE HOW DEEP IT GOES.
SPLISH
SP
LISH
WAIT, NICHE!
DON'T RUN! WALK CAREFULLY IN THE CENTER SO YOU DON'T FALL IN.
YOU TOO, STEAK.
"WAIT" ...
... "NICHE, MY DINGO."
SAY IT!

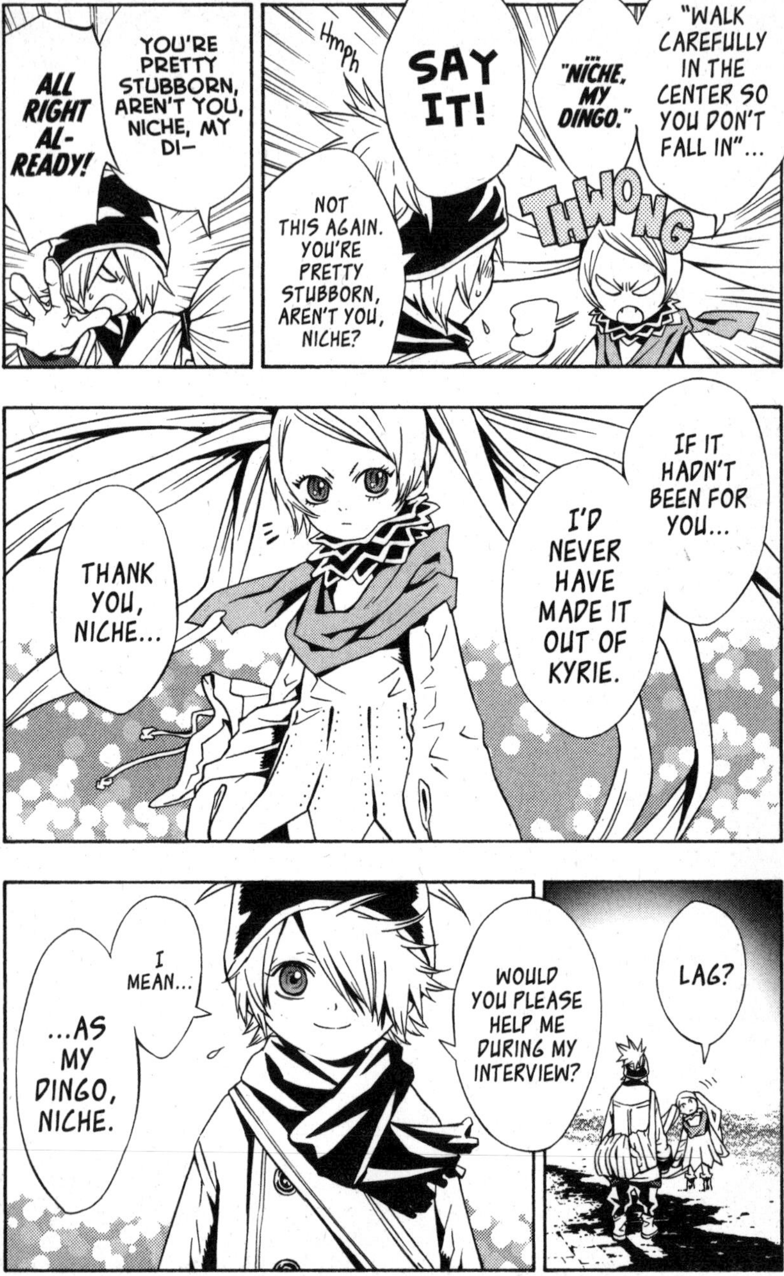
"WALK CAREFULLY IN THE CENTER SO YOU DON'T FALL IN"...
..."NICHE, MY DINGO."
THWONG
SAY IT!
Hmph
NOT THIS AGAIN. YOU'RE PRETTY STUBBORN, AREN'T YOU, NICHE?
YOU'RE PRETTY STUBBORN, AREN'T YOU, NICHE, MY DI–
ALL RIGHT AL-READY!
IF IT HADN'T BEEN FOR YOU...
I'D NEVER HAVE MADE IT OUT OF KYRIE.
THANK YOU, NICHE...
LAG?
WOULD YOU PLEASE HELP ME DURING MY INTERVIEW?
I MEAN...
...AS MY DINGO, NICHE.

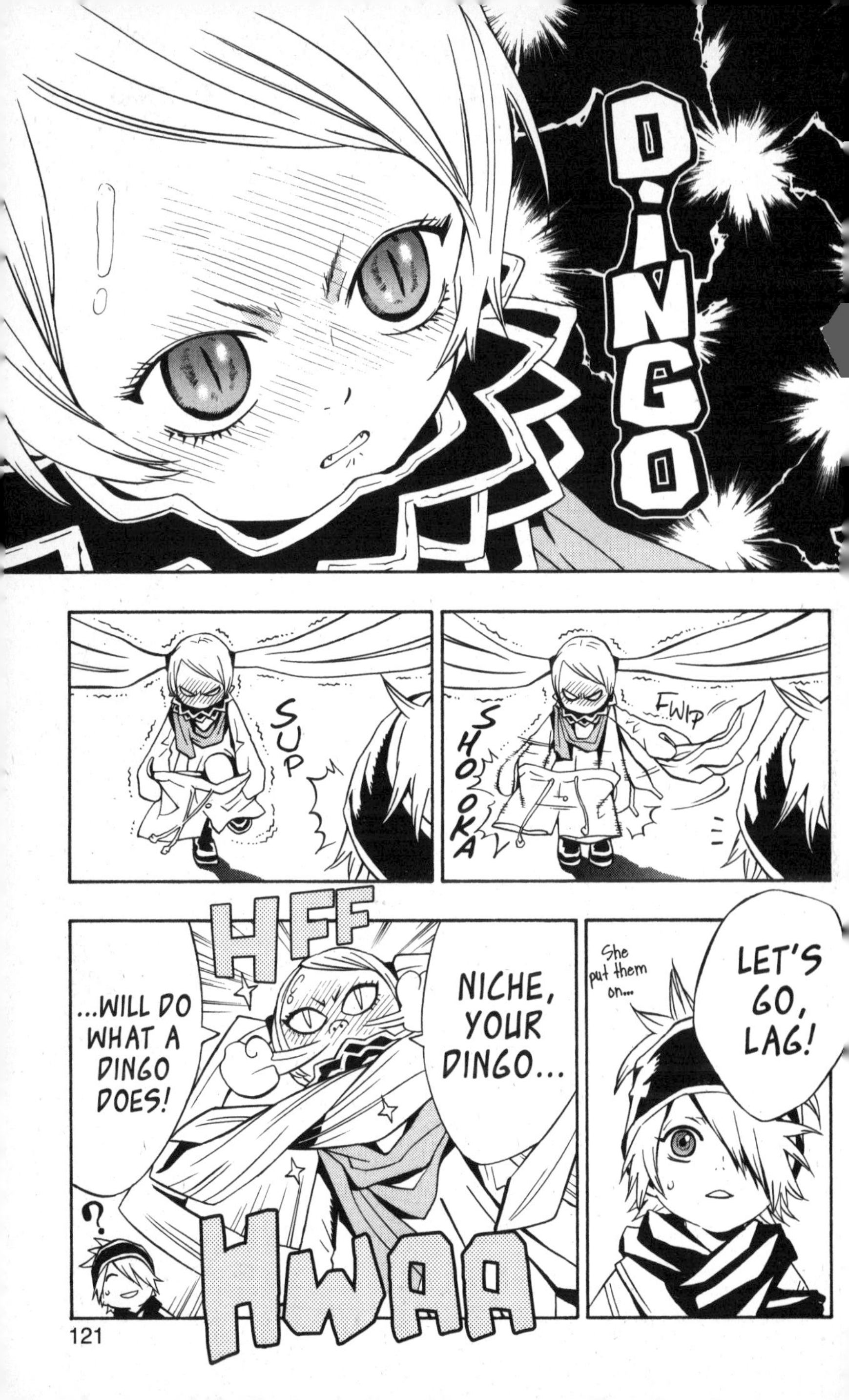
DINGO
SHOOKA
FWIP
SUP
LET'S GO, LAG!
She put them on...
HFF
NICHE, YOUR DINGO...
...WILL DO WHAT A DINGO DOES!
?
HWAA

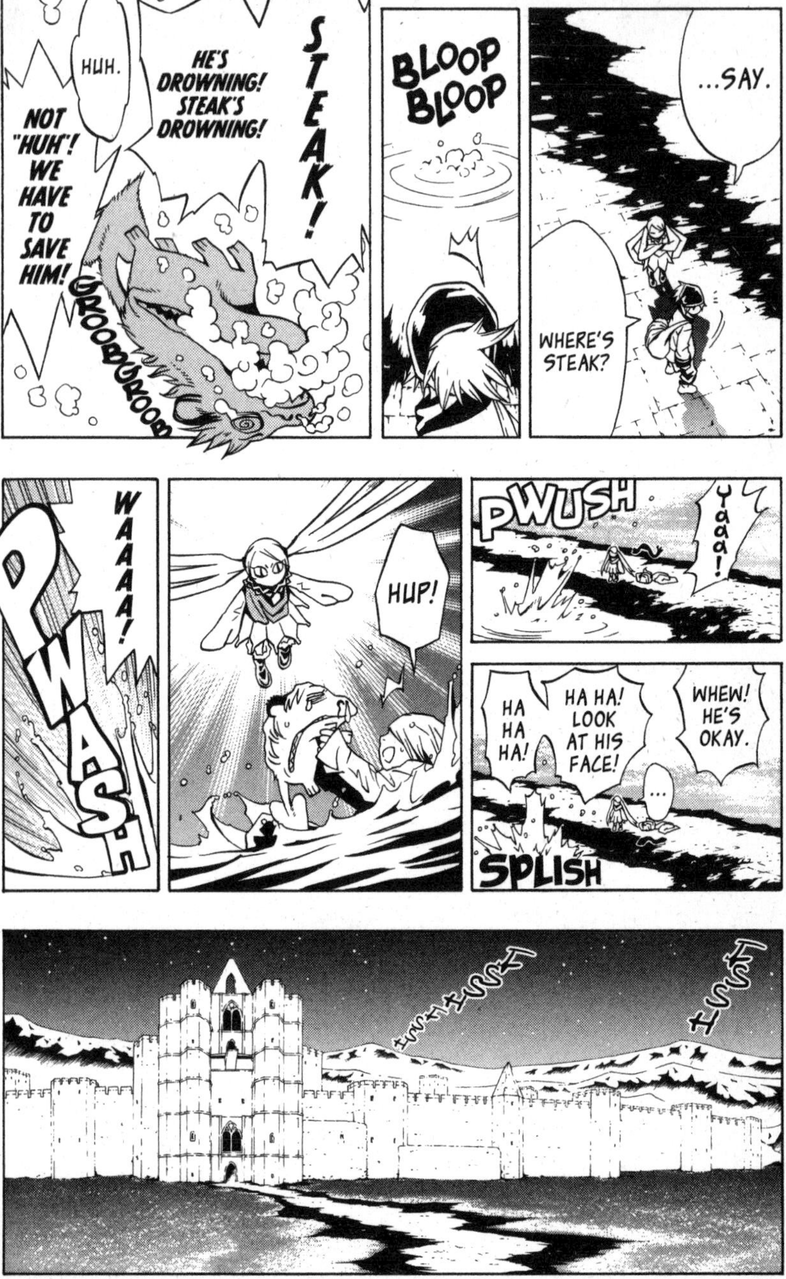
...SAY.
WHERE'S STEAK?
BLOOP BLOOP
STEAK!
HE'S DROWNING! STEAK'S DROWNING!
HUH.
NOT "HUH"! WE HAVE TO SAVE HIM!
GROOBGROOB
PWUSH
Yaaa!
WHEW! HE'S OKAY.
HA HA! LOOK AT HIS FACE!
HA HA HA!
...
SPLISH
HUP!
WAAAAA!
PWASH

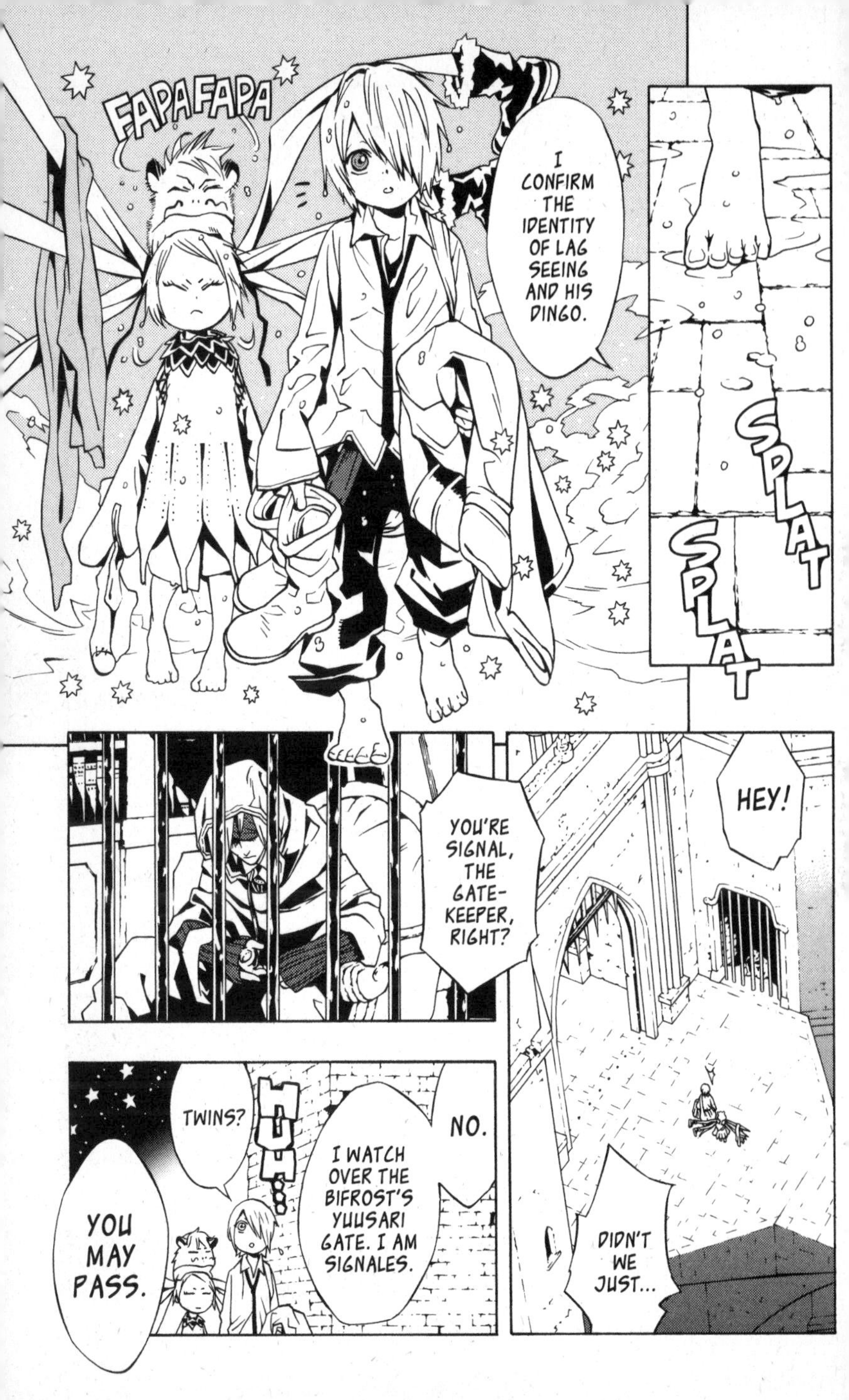
SPLAT
SPLAT
FAPAFAPA
I CONFIRM THE IDENTITY OF LAG SEEING AND HIS DINGO.
HEY!
DIDN'T WE JUST...
YOU'RE SIGNAL, THE GATE-KEEPER, RIGHT?
NO.
I WATCH OVER THE BIFROST'S YUUSARI GATE. I AM SIGNALES.
HUH???
TWINS?
YOU MAY PASS.

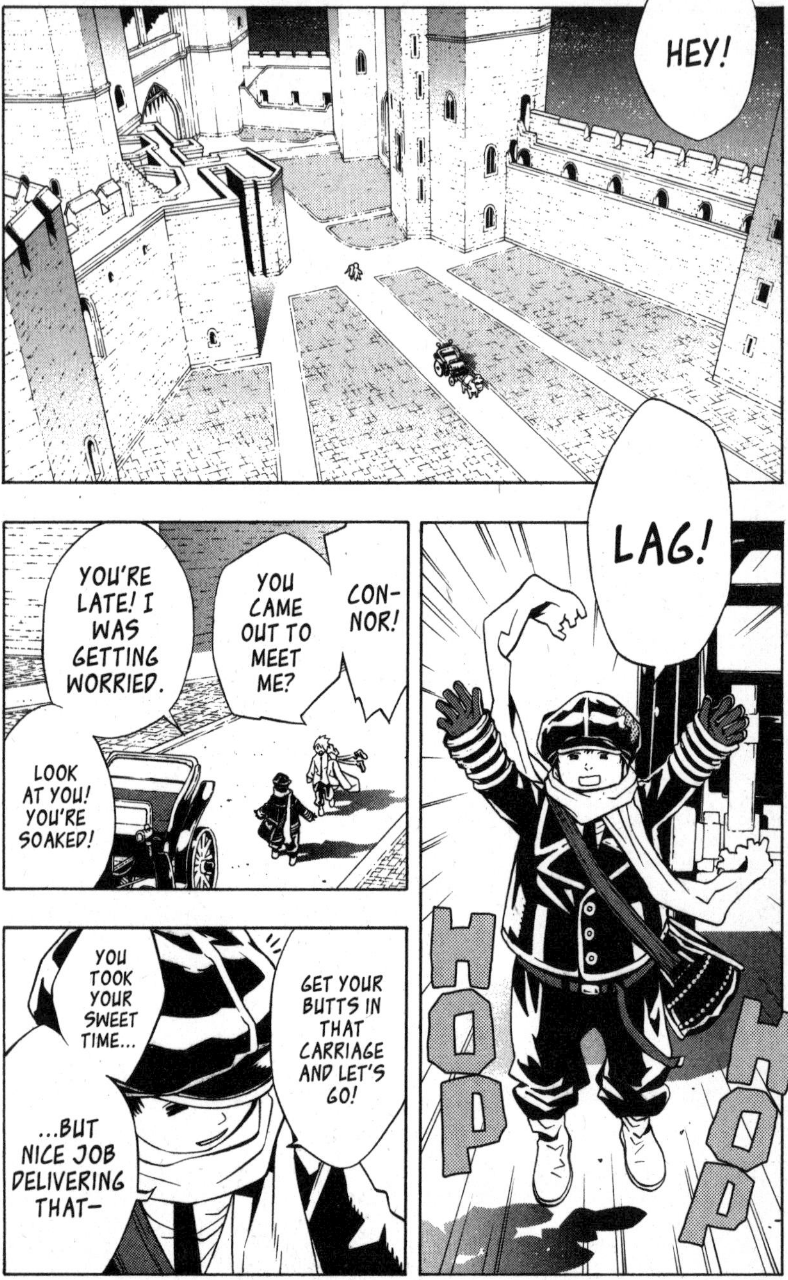
HEY!
LAG!
HOP HOP
CON-NOR!
YOU CAME OUT TO MEET ME?
YOU'RE LATE! I WAS GETTING WORRIED.
LOOK AT YOU! YOU'RE SOAKED!
GET YOUR BUTTS IN THAT CARRIAGE AND LET'S GO!
YOU TOOK YOUR SWEET TIME...
...BUT NICE JOB DELIVERING THAT—

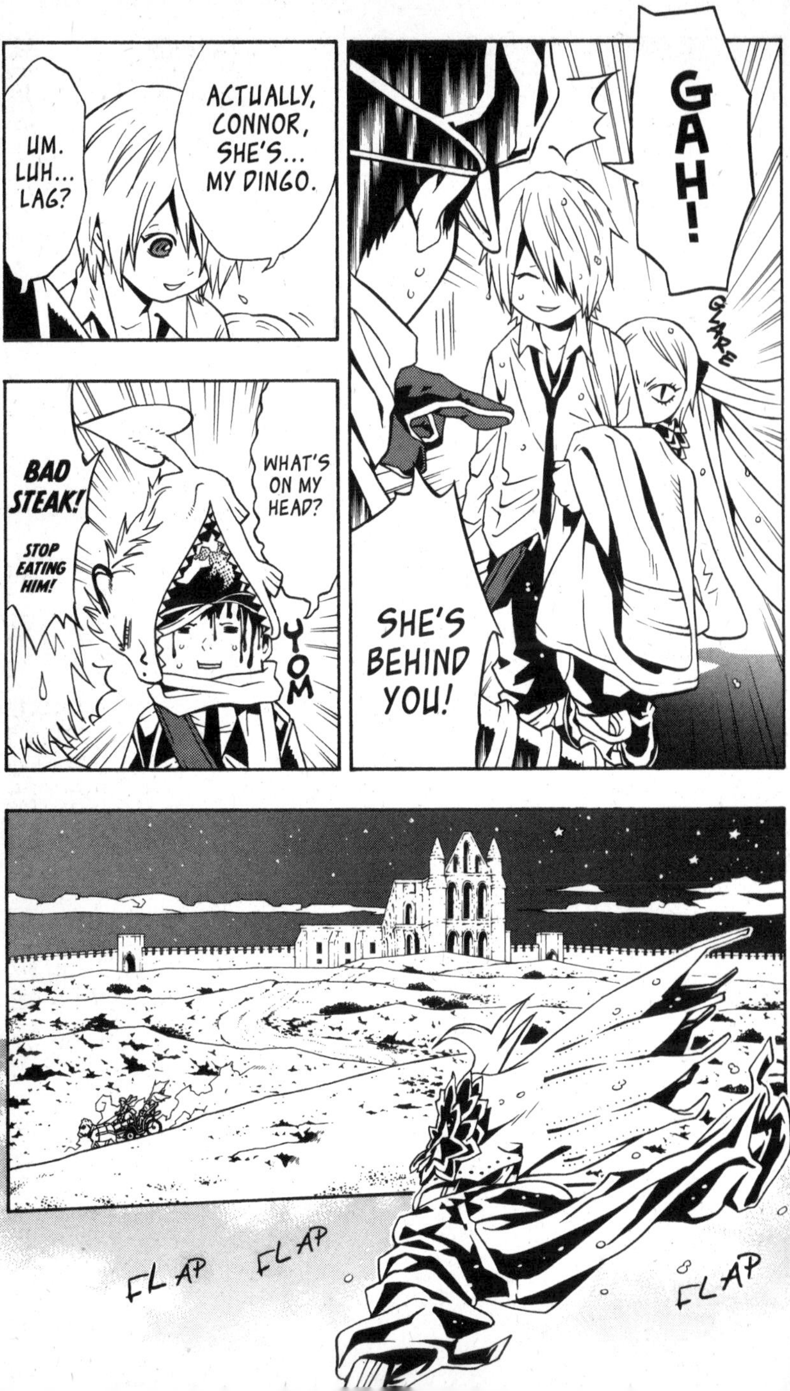
GAH!
GLARE
SHE'S BEHIND YOU!
UM. LUH... LAG?
ACTUALLY, CONNOR, SHE'S... MY DINGO.
WHAT'S ON MY HEAD?
BAD STEAK!
STOP EATING HIM!
YOM
FLAP
FLAP
FLAP

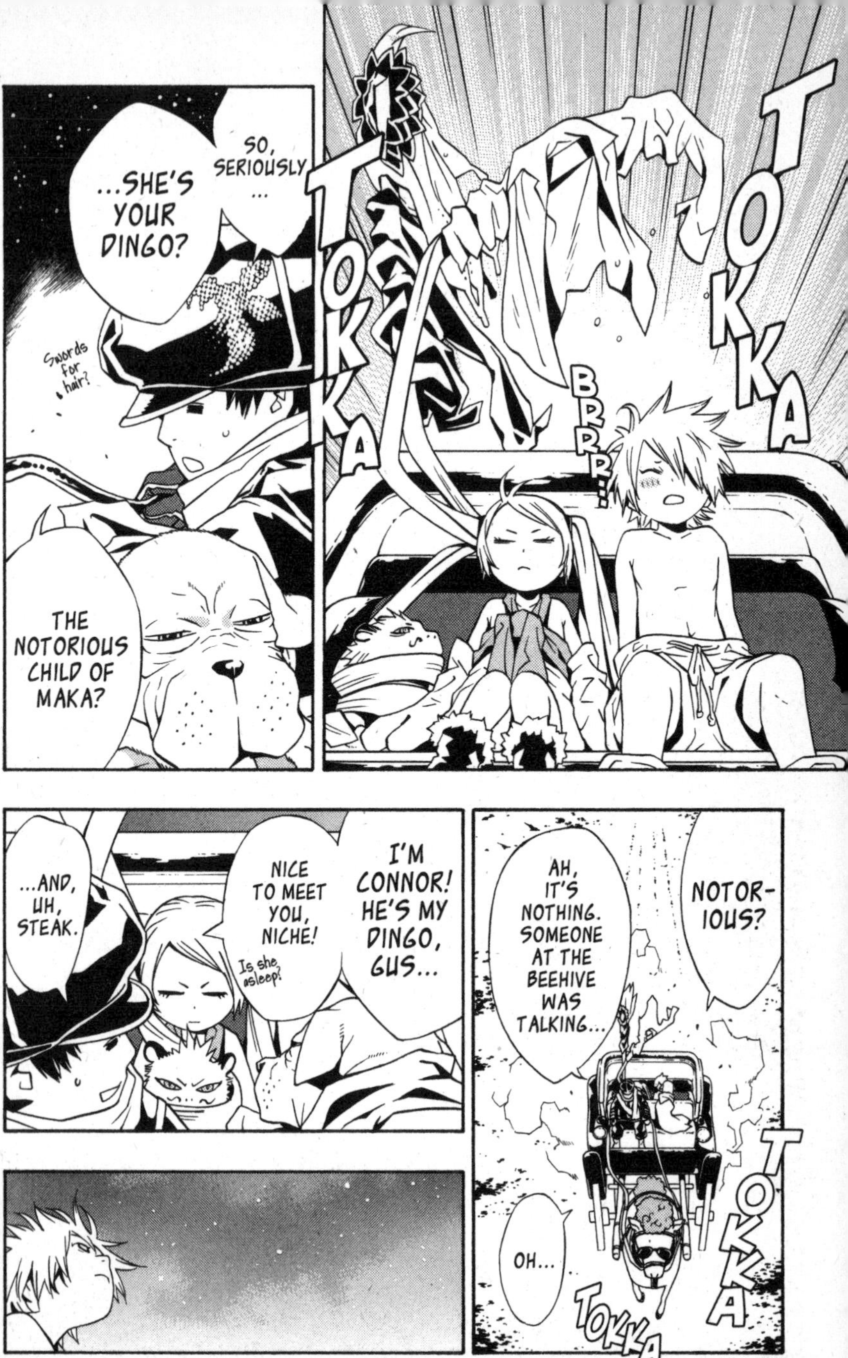
TOKKA
BRRR...
TOKKA
SO, SERIOUSLY...
...SHE'S YOUR DINGO?
Swords for hair?
THE NOTORIOUS CHILD OF MAKA?
NOTOR-IOUS?
AH, IT'S NOTHING. SOMEONE AT THE BEEHIVE WAS TALKING...
OH...
TOKKA
TOKKA
I'M CONNOR! HE'S MY DINGO, GUS...
NICE TO MEET YOU, NICHE!
Is she asleep?
...AND, UH, STEAK.

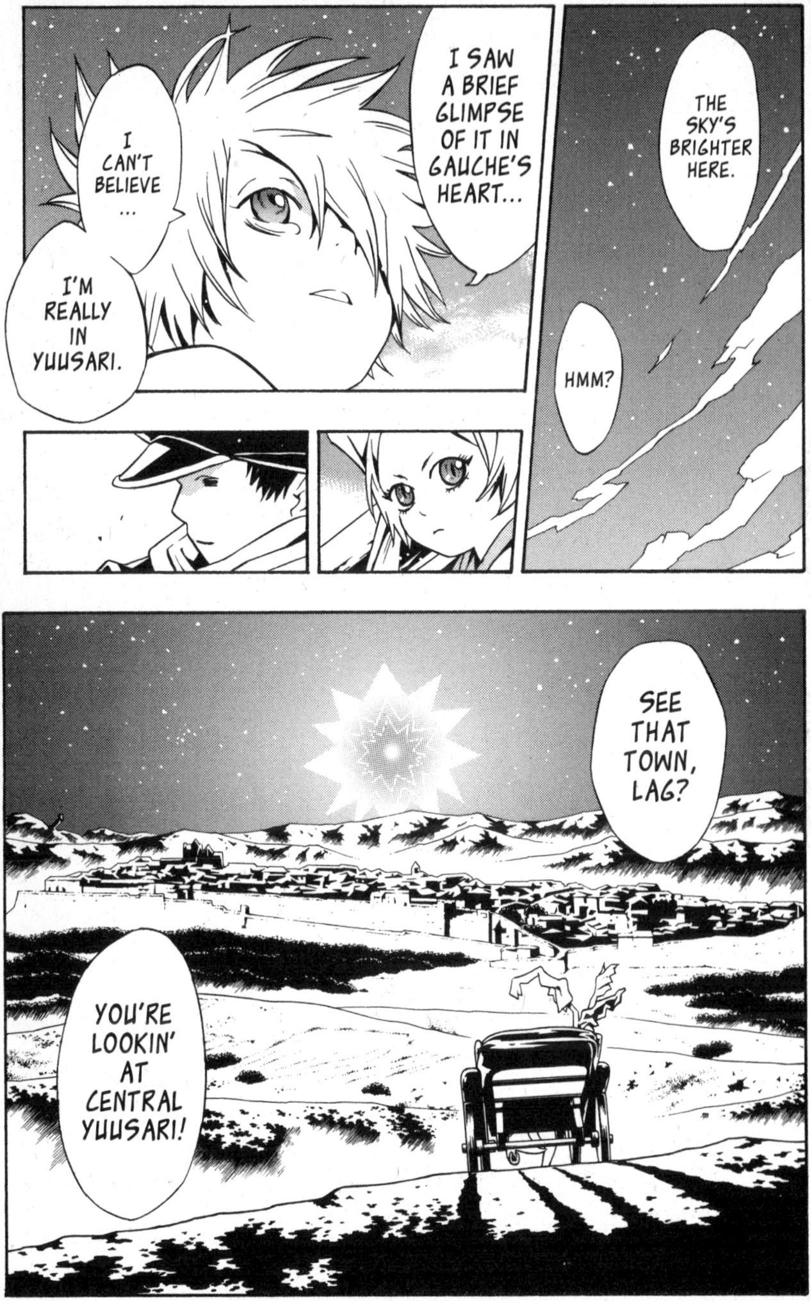
THE SKY'S BRIGHTER HERE.
HMM?
I SAW A BRIEF GLIMPSE OF IT IN GAUCHE'S HEART...
I CAN'T BELIEVE ...
I'M REALLY IN YUUSARI.
SEE THAT TOWN, LAG?
YOU'RE LOOKIN' AT CENTRAL YUUSARI!

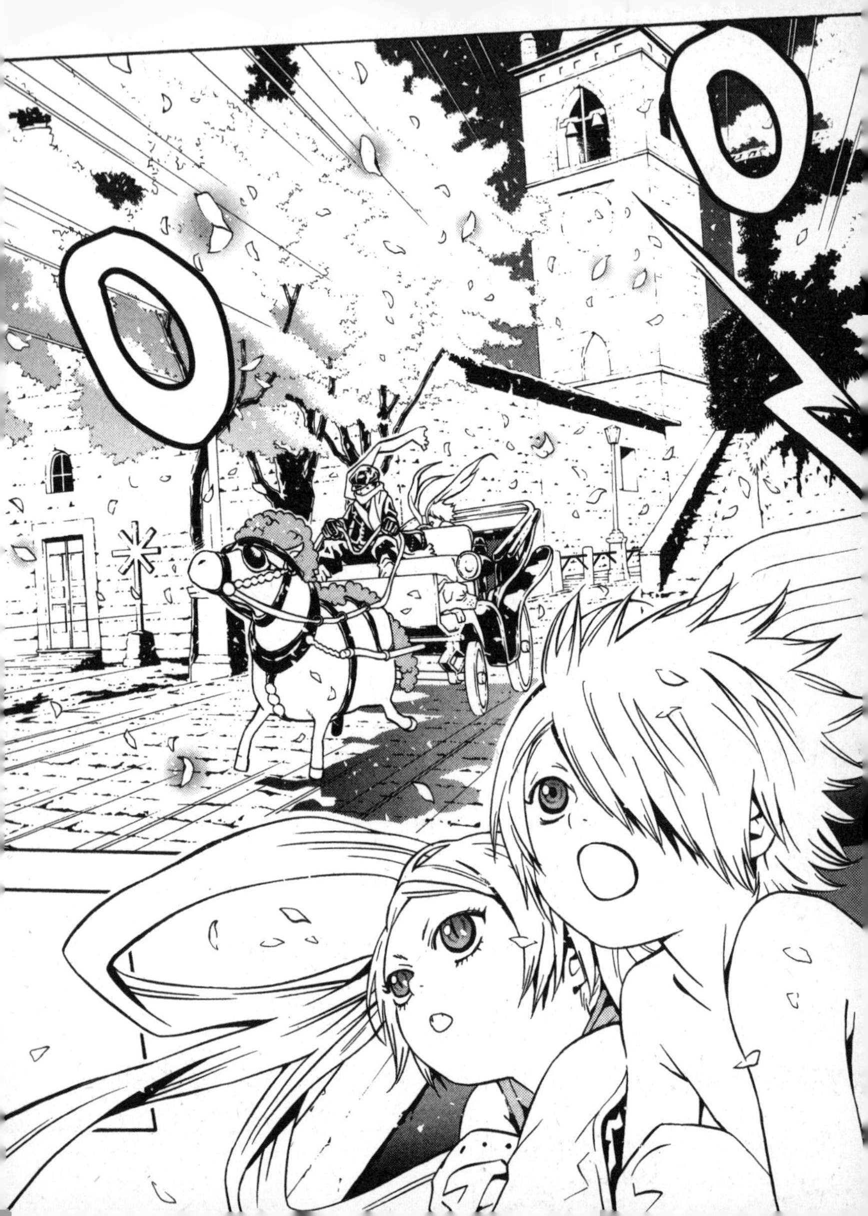

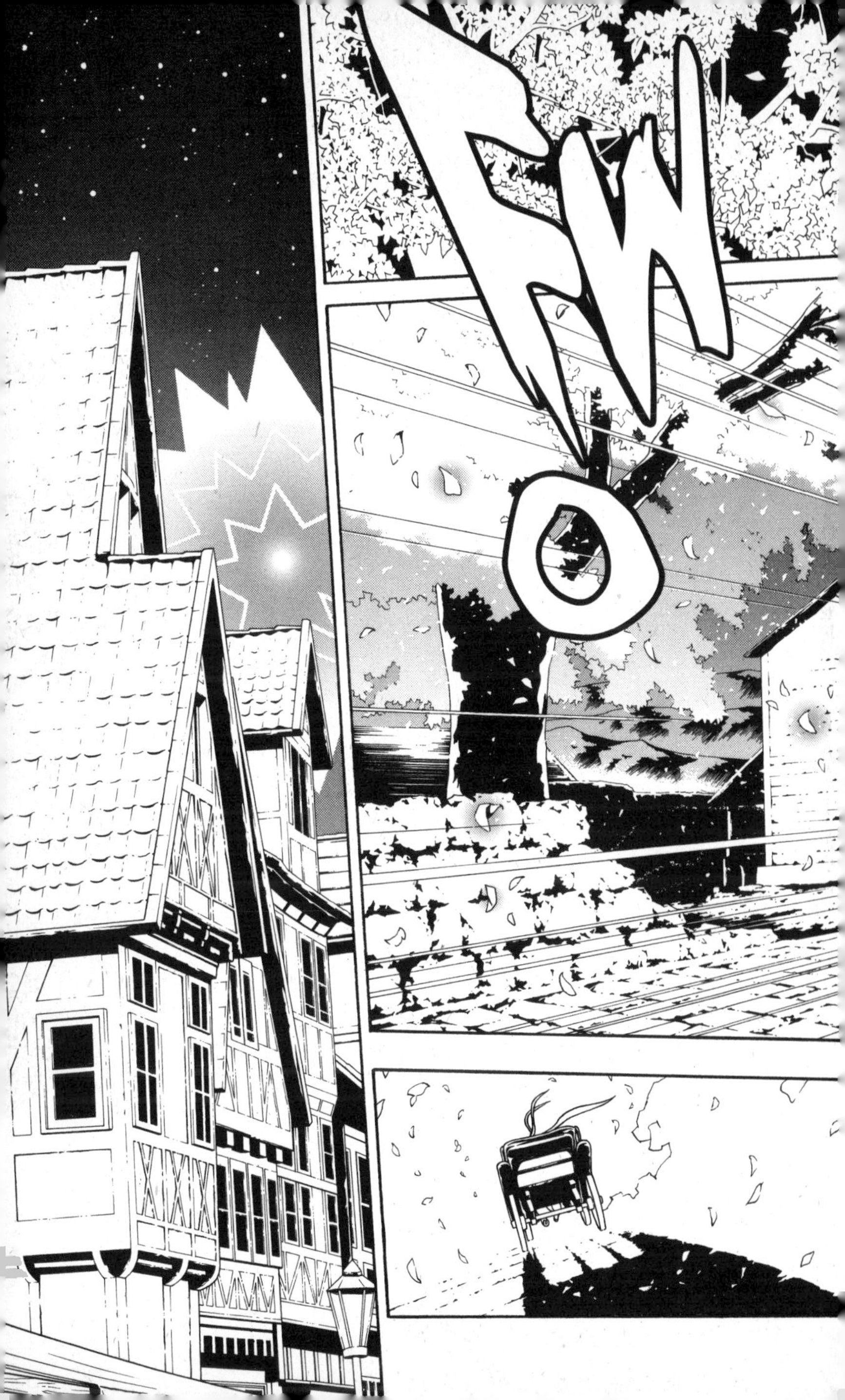
FWO

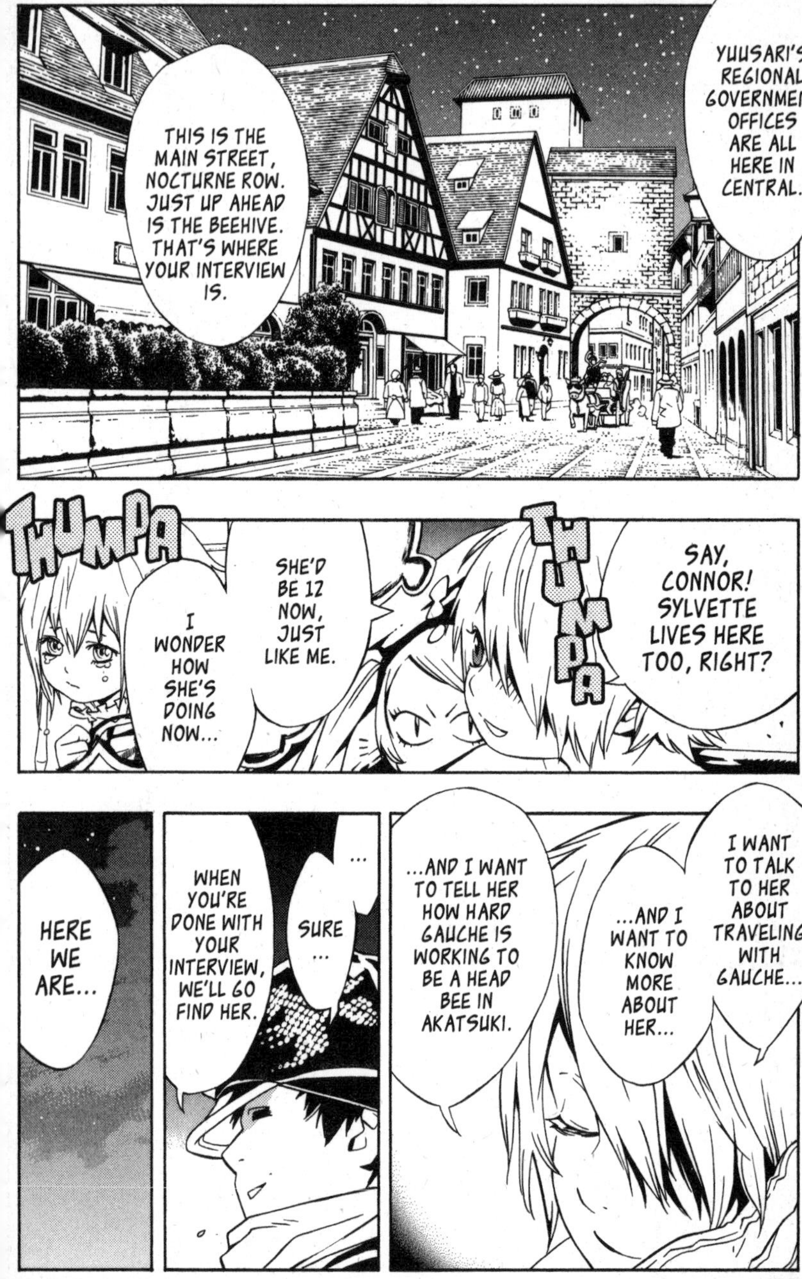
YUUSARI'S REGIONAL GOVERNMENT OFFICES ARE ALL HERE IN CENTRAL.
THIS IS THE MAIN STREET, NOCTURNE ROW. JUST UP AHEAD IS THE BEEHIVE. THAT'S WHERE YOUR INTERVIEW IS.
THUMPA
SAY, CONNOR! SYLVETTE LIVES HERE TOO, RIGHT?
SHE'D BE 12 NOW, JUST LIKE ME.
I WONDER HOW SHE'S DOING NOW...
THUMPA
I WANT TO TALK TO HER ABOUT TRAVELING WITH GAUCHE...
...AND I WANT TO KNOW MORE ABOUT HER...
...AND I WANT TO TELL HER HOW HARD GAUCHE IS WORKING TO BE A HEAD BEE IN AKATSUKI.
...
SURE...
WHEN YOU'RE DONE WITH YOUR INTERVIEW, WE'LL GO FIND HER.
HERE WE ARE...

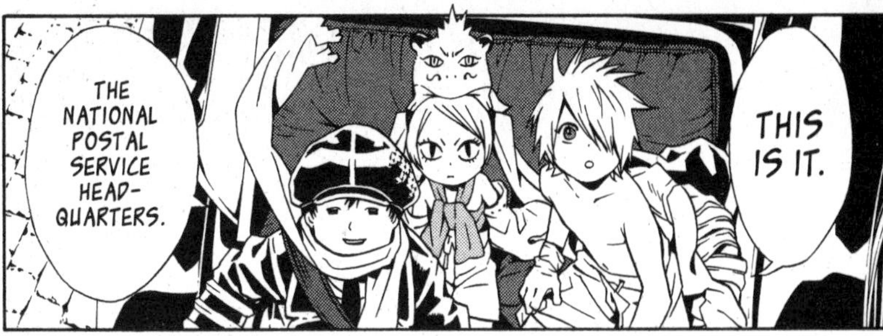
THIS IS IT.
THE NATIONAL POSTAL SERVICE HEAD-QUARTERS.

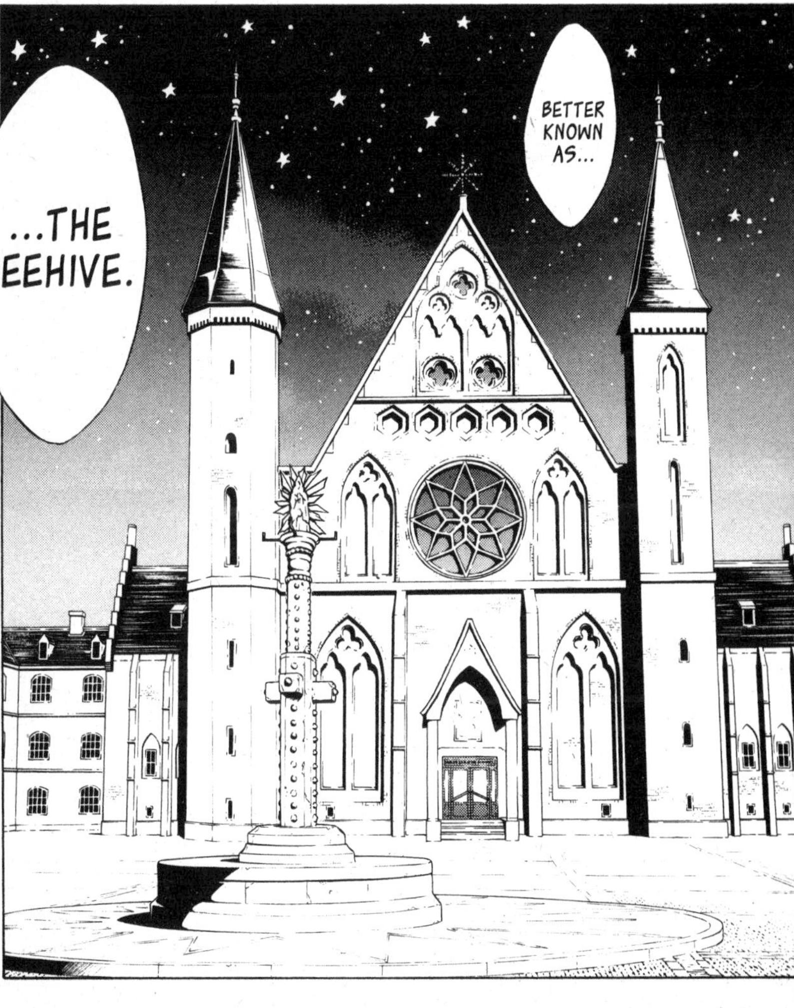
BETTER KNOWN AS...
...THE BEEHIVE.

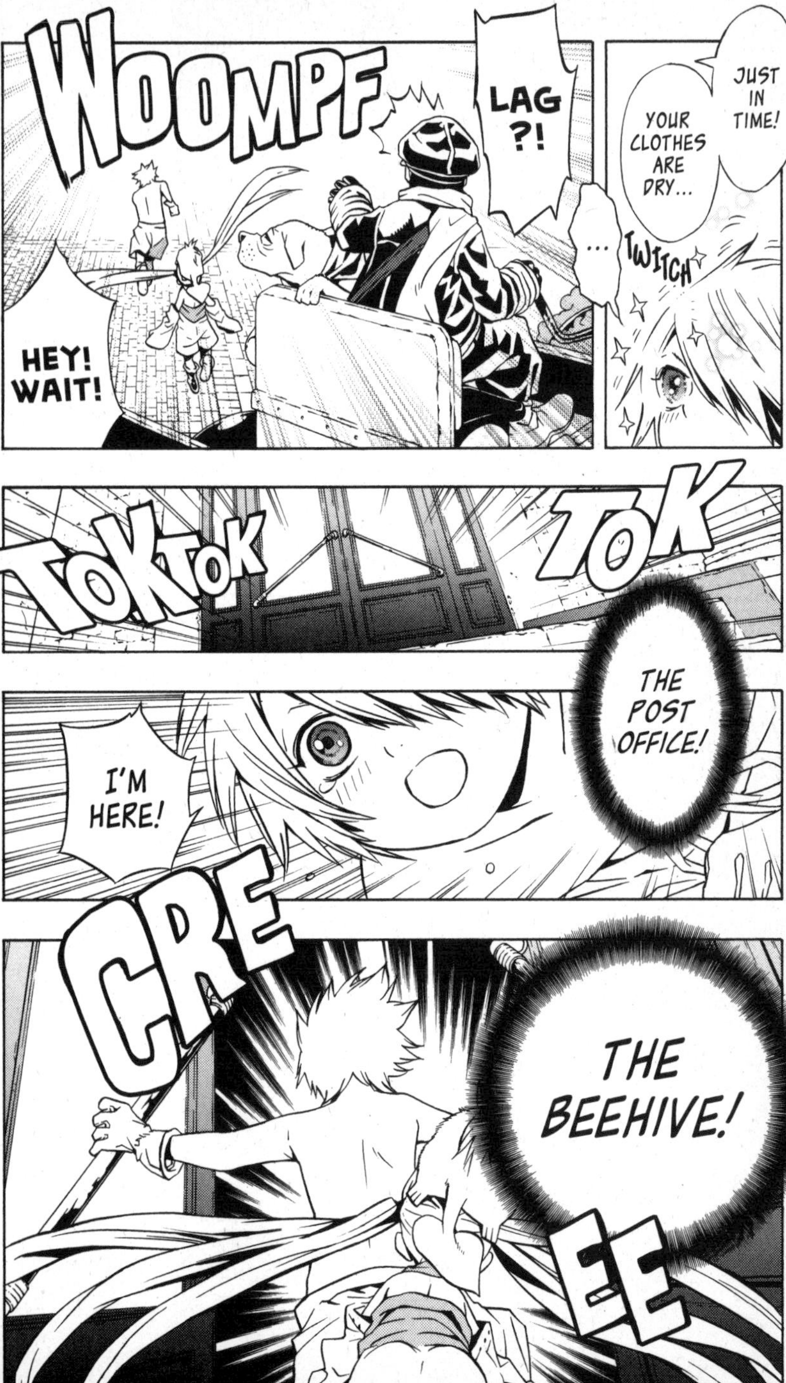

JUST IN TIME!
YOUR CLOTHES ARE DRY...
...
TWITCH
LAG ?!
WOOMPF
HEY! WAIT!
TOK
TOKTOK
THE POST OFFICE!
I'M HERE!
CRE
THE BEEHIVE!
EE

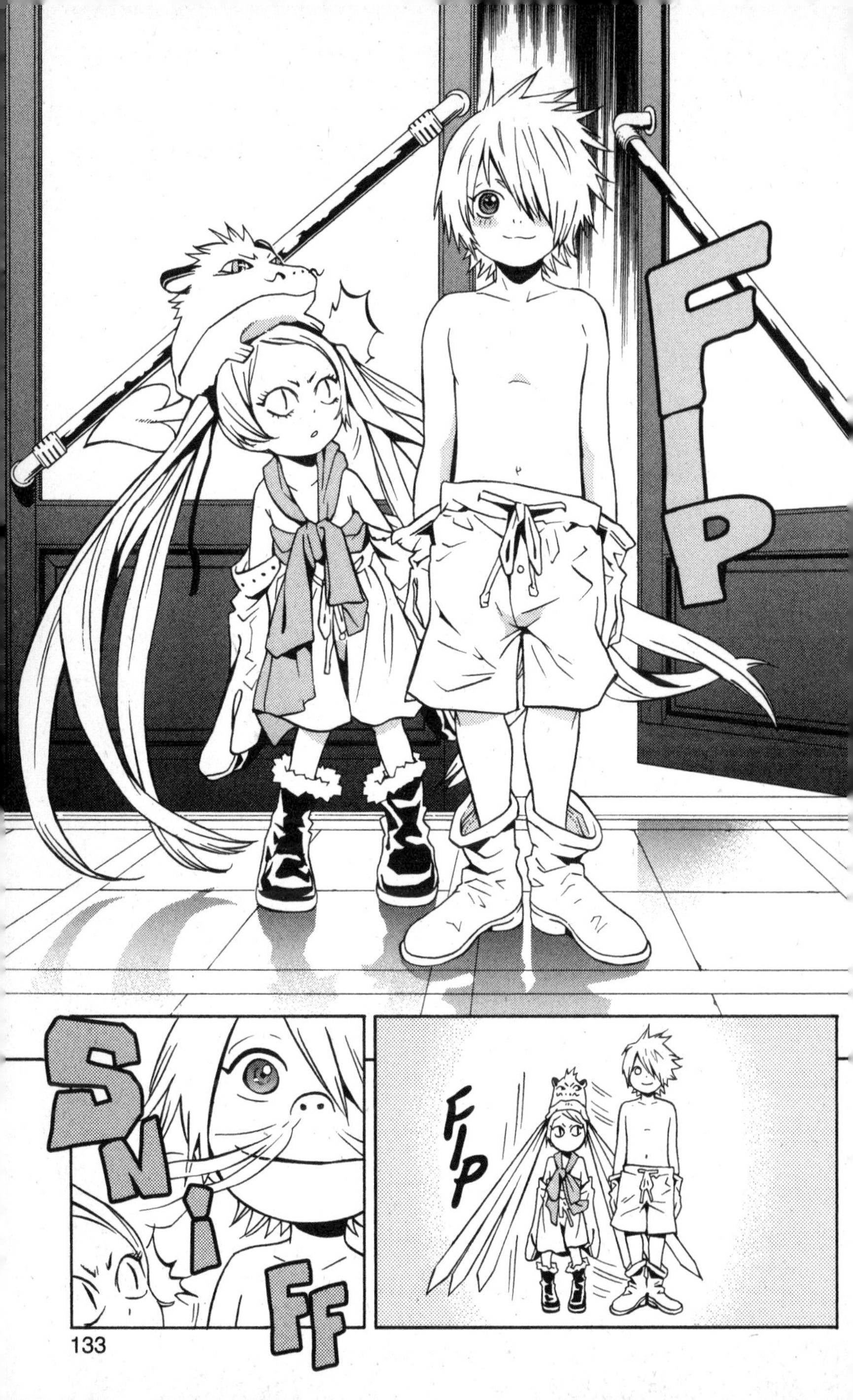
FIP
SNIFF
FIP

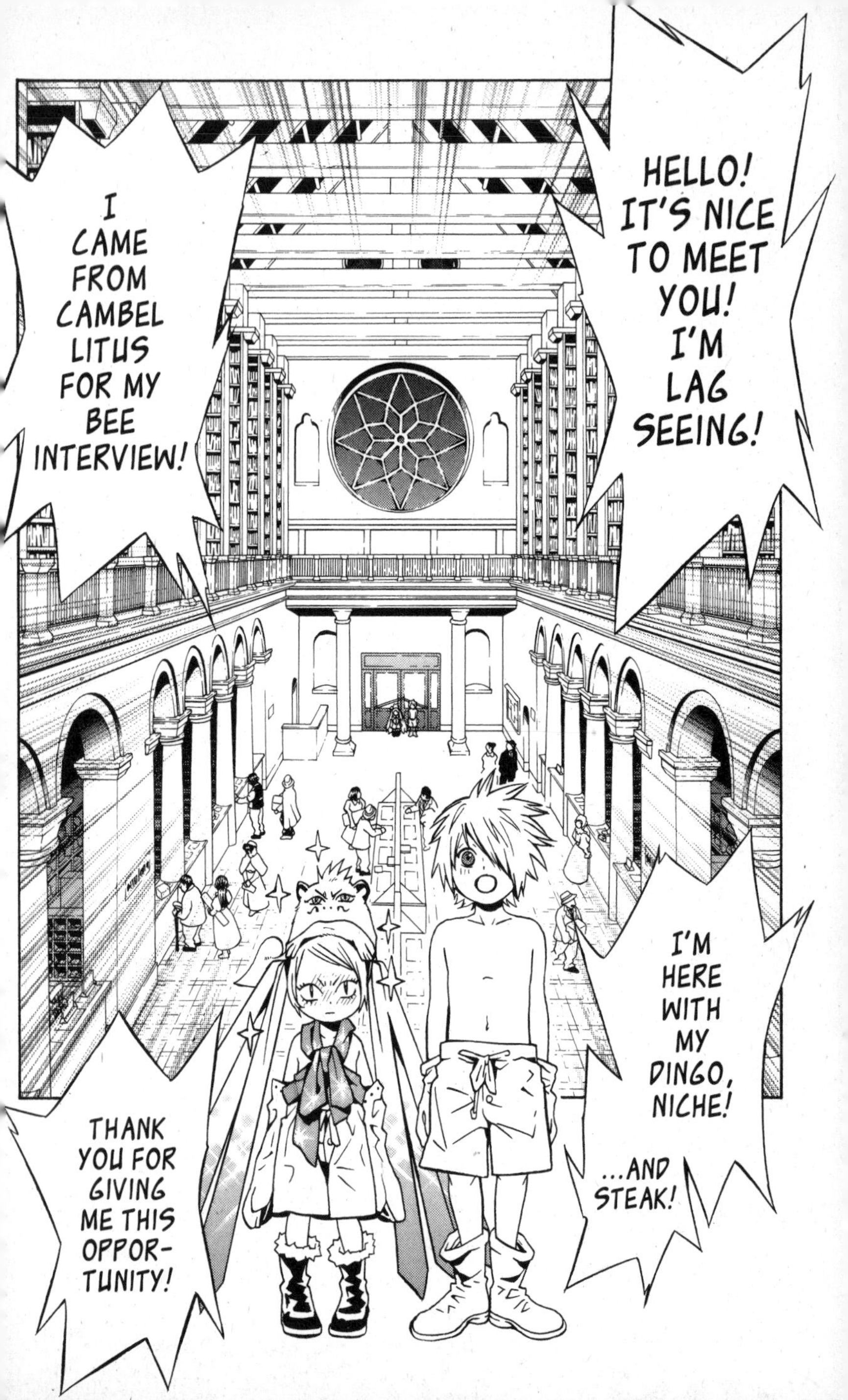
HELLO! IT'S NICE TO MEET YOU! I'M LAG SEEING!
I CAME FROM CAMBEL LITUS FOR MY BEE INTERVIEW!
I'M HERE WITH MY DINGO, NICHE!
...AND STEAK!
THANK YOU FOR GIVING ME THIS OPPOR-TUNITY!

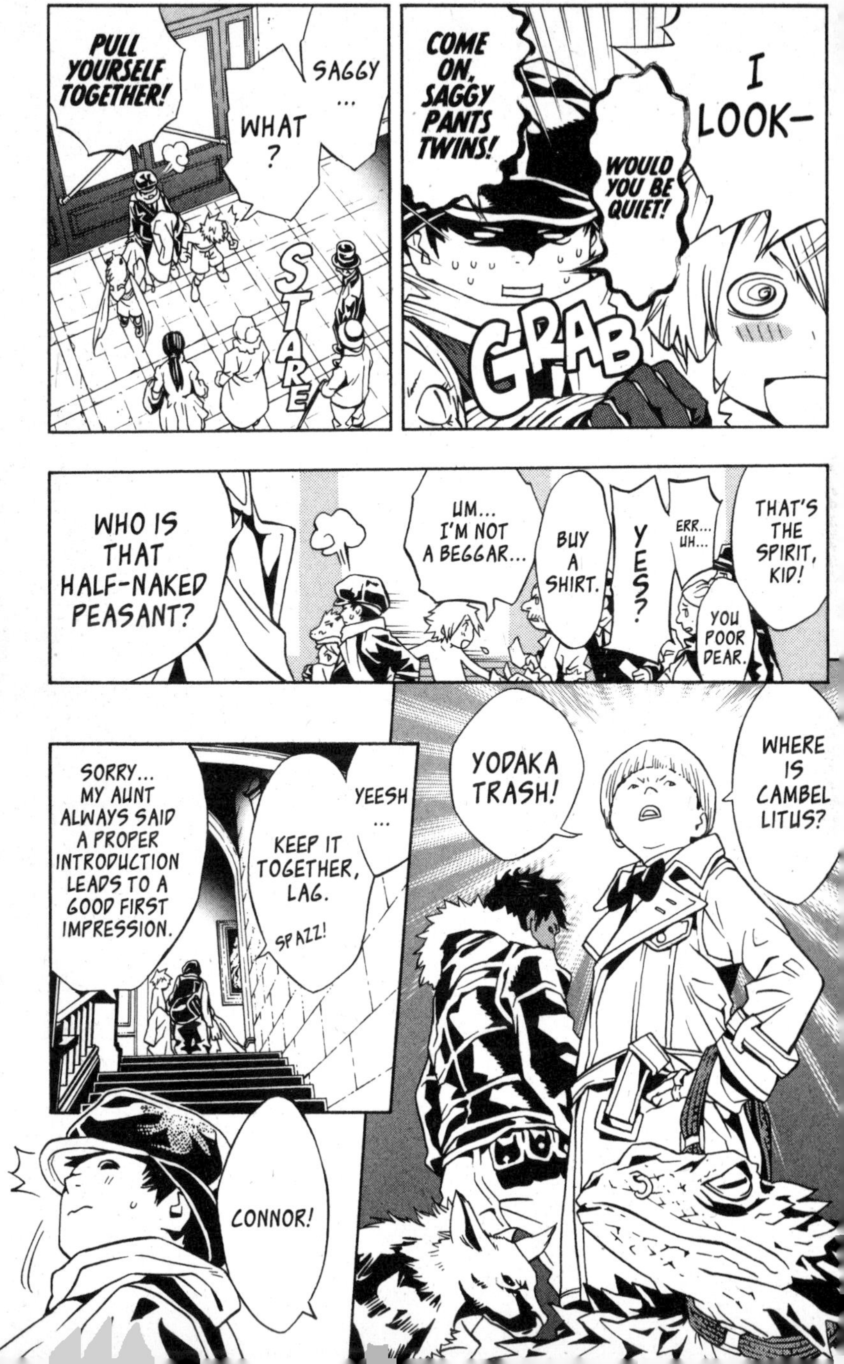
I LOOK—
COME ON, SAGGY PANTS TWINS!
WOULD YOU BE QUIET!
GRAB
SAGGY ...
WHAT ?
PULL YOURSELF TOGETHER!
STARE
THAT'S THE SPIRIT, KID!
YOU POOR DEAR.
ERR... UH...
YES?
BUY A SHIRT.
UM... I'M NOT A BEGGAR...
WHO IS THAT HALF-NAKED PEASANT?
WHERE IS CAMBEL LITUS?
YODAKA TRASH!
YEESH ...
KEEP IT TOGETHER, LAG.
SPAZZ!
SORRY... MY AUNT ALWAYS SAID A PROPER INTRODUCTION LEADS TO A GOOD FIRST IMPRESSION.
CONNOR!

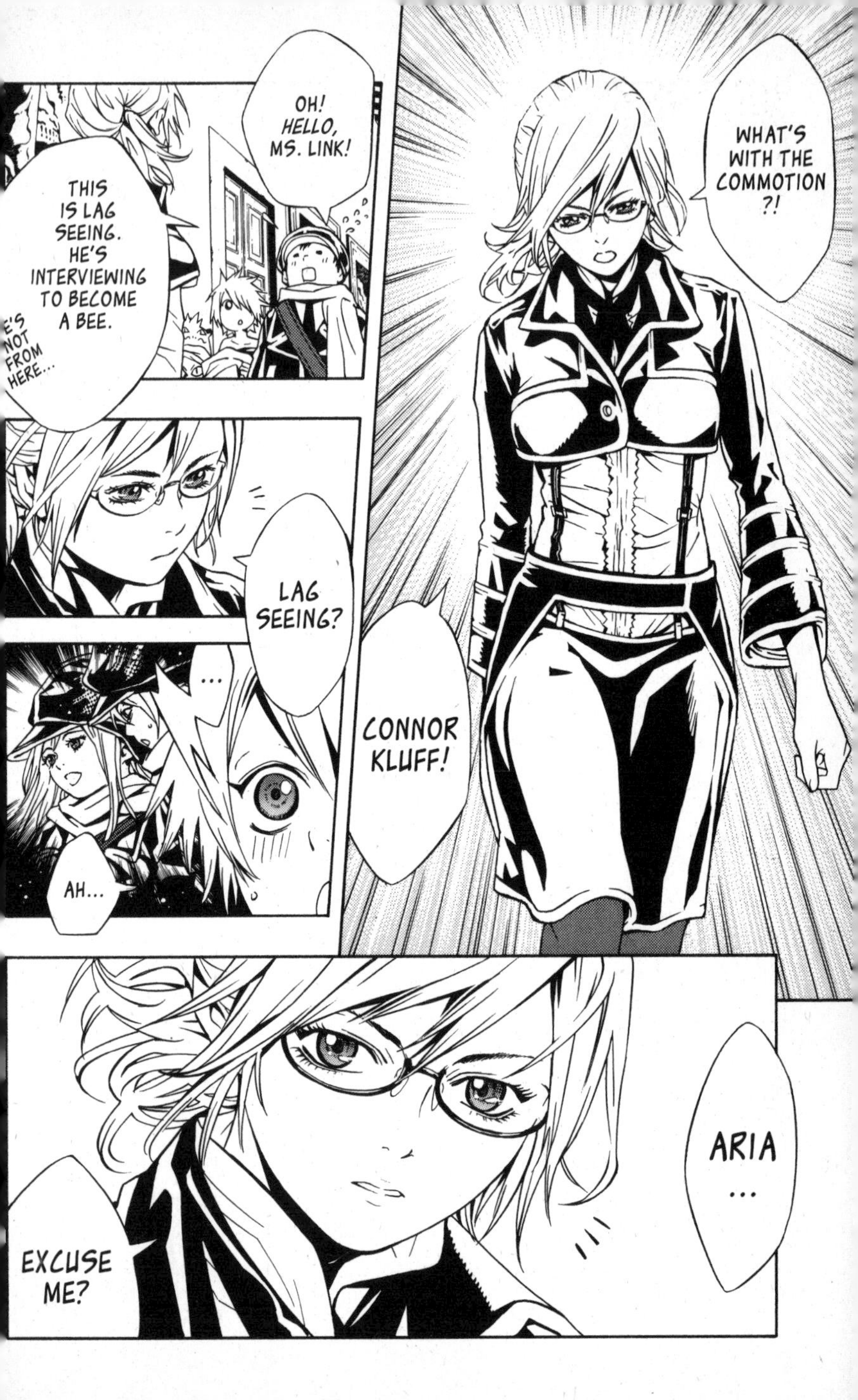
WHAT'S WITH THE COMMOTION ?!
OH! HELLO, MS. LINK!
THIS IS LAG SEEING. HE'S INTERVIEWING TO BECOME A BEE.
E'S NOT FROM HERE...
LAG SEEING?
...
CONNOR KLUFF!
AH...
ARIA ...
EXCUSE ME?

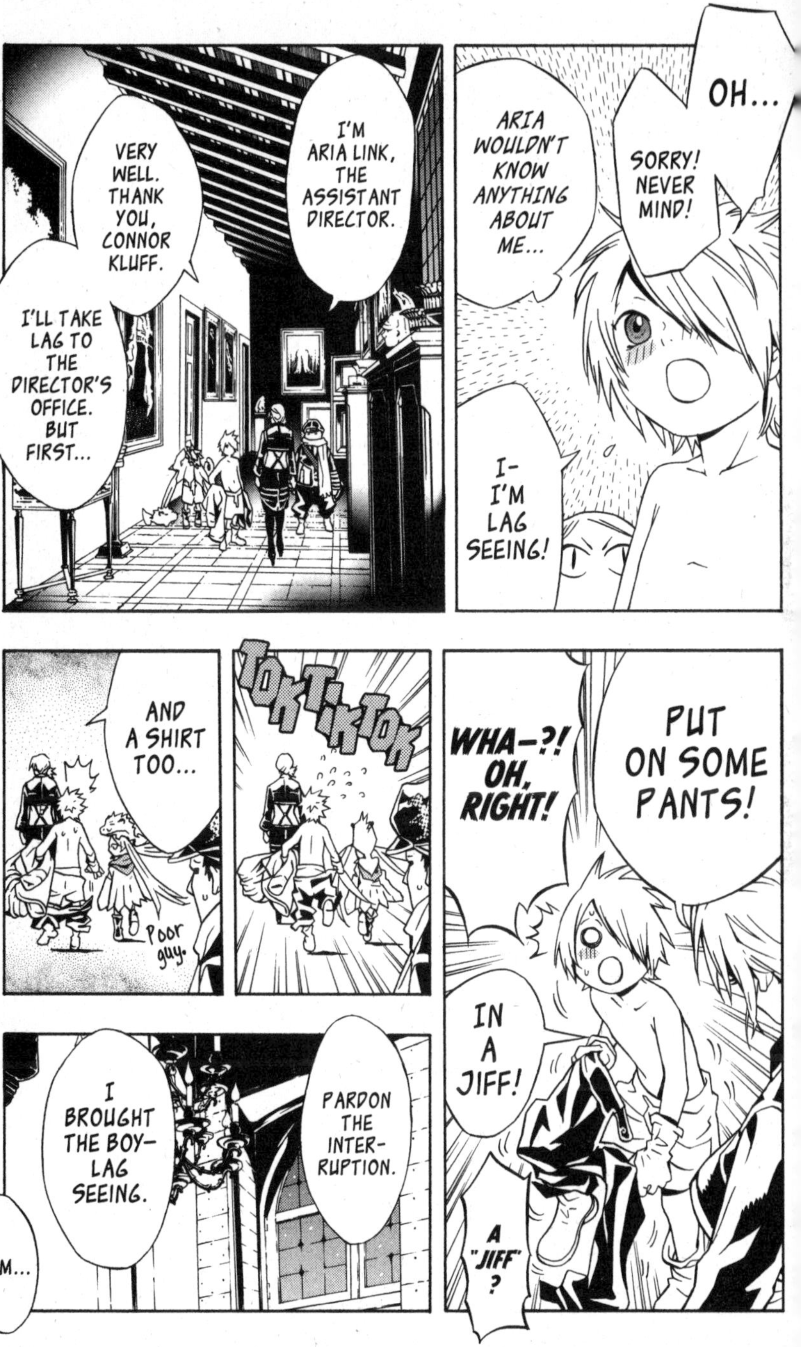
OH...
SORRY! NEVER MIND!
ARIA WOULDN'T KNOW ANYTHING ABOUT ME...
I- I'M LAG SEEING!
I'M ARIA LINK, THE ASSISTANT DIRECTOR.
VERY WELL. THANK YOU, CONNOR KLUFF.
I'LL TAKE LAG TO THE DIRECTOR'S OFFICE. BUT FIRST...
PUT ON SOME PANTS!
WHA-?! OH, RIGHT!
IN A JIFF!
A "JIFF"?
TOKTIKTOK
AND A SHIRT TOO...
Poor guy.
PARDON THE INTER-RUPTION.
I BROUGHT THE BOY-LAG SEEING.
HMM...

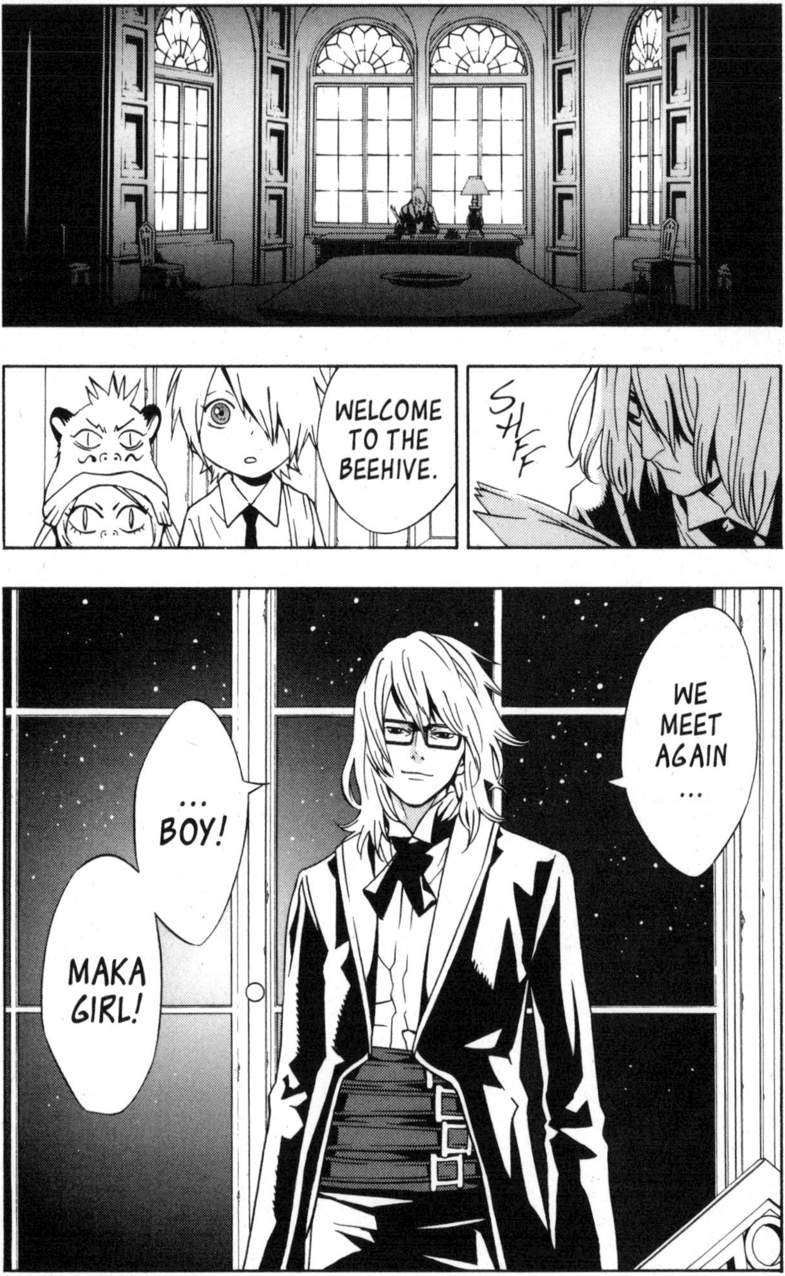
SHFF
WELCOME TO THE BEEHIVE.
WE MEET AGAIN ...
... BOY!
MAKA GIRL!

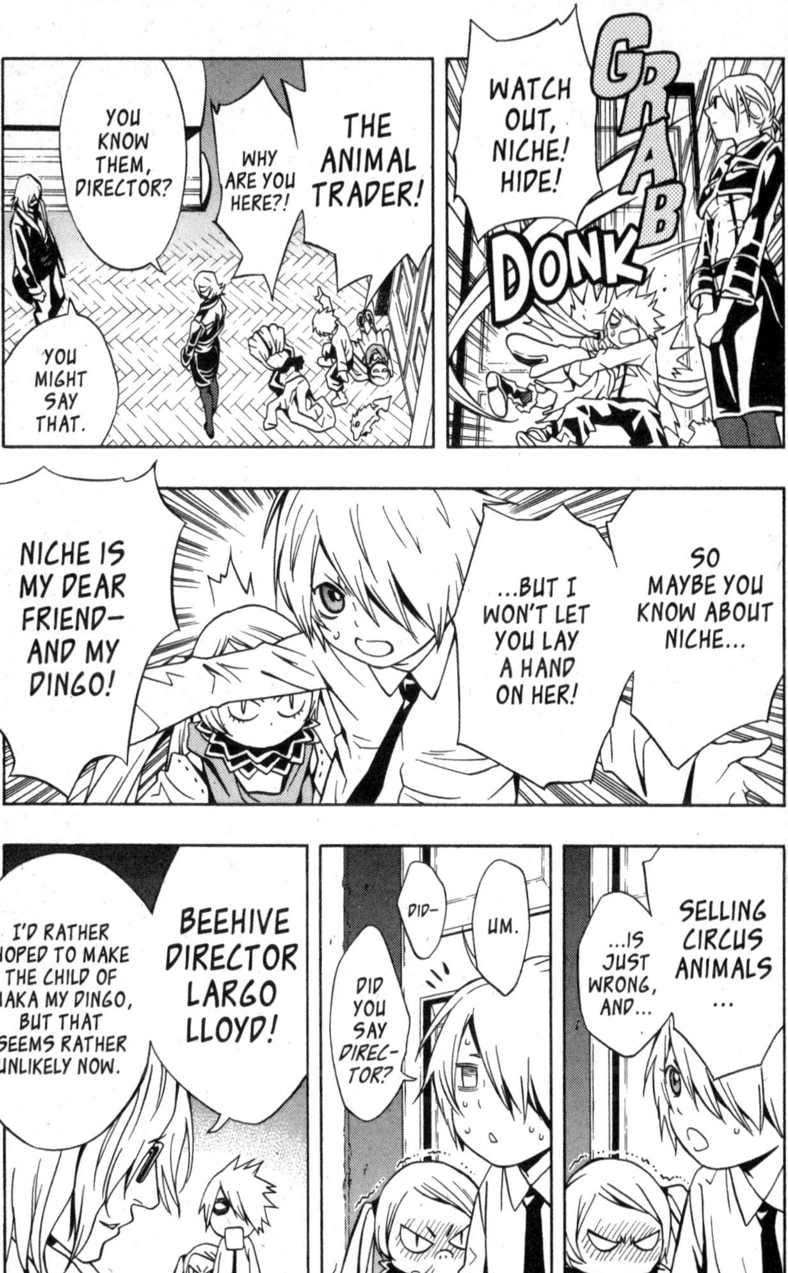
GRAB
WATCH OUT, NICHE! HIDE!
DONK
THE ANIMAL TRADER!
WHY ARE YOU HERE?!
YOU KNOW THEM, DIRECTOR?
YOU MIGHT SAY THAT.
SO MAYBE YOU KNOW ABOUT NICHE...
...BUT I WON'T LET YOU LAY A HAND ON HER!
NICHE IS MY DEAR FRIEND—AND MY DINGO!
SELLING CIRCUS ANIMALS ...
...IS JUST WRONG, AND...
UM.
DID—
DID YOU SAY DIREC-TOR?
BEEHIVE DIRECTOR LARGO LLOYD!
I'D RATHER HOPED TO MAKE THE CHILD OF MAKA MY DINGO, BUT THAT SEEMS RATHER UNLIKELY NOW.

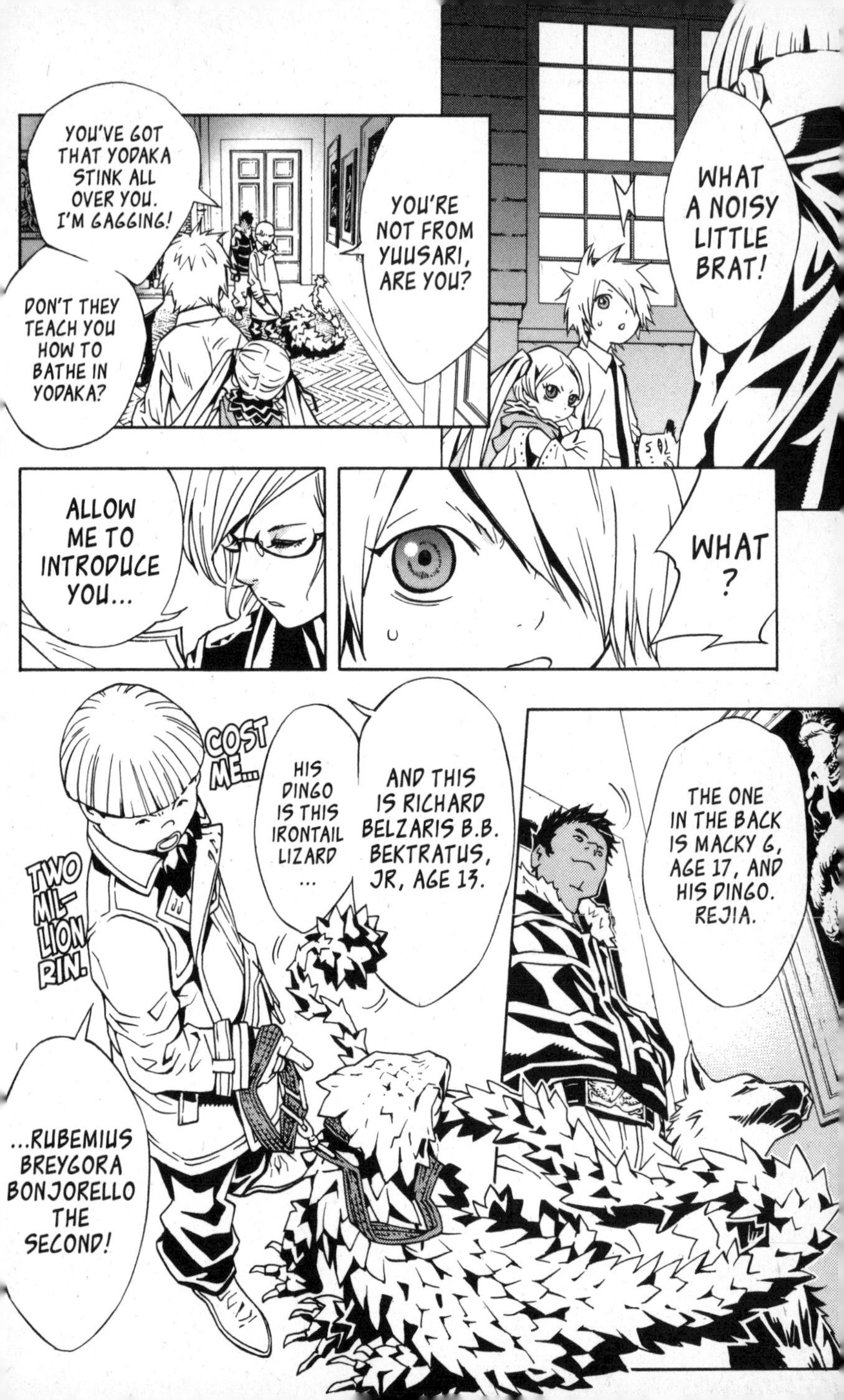
WHAT A NOISY LITTLE BRAT!
YOU'RE NOT FROM YUUSARI, ARE YOU?
YOU'VE GOT THAT YODAKA STINK ALL OVER YOU. I'M GAGGING!
DON'T THEY TEACH YOU HOW TO BATHE IN YODAKA?
WHAT ?
ALLOW ME TO INTRODUCE YOU...
THE ONE IN THE BACK IS MACKY 6, AGE 17, AND HIS DINGO. REJIA.
AND THIS IS RICHARD BELZARIS B.B. BEKTRATUS, JR, AGE 13.
HIS DINGO IS THIS IRONTAIL LIZARD ...
COST ME...
TWO MILLION RIN.
...RUBEMIUS BREYGORA BONJORELLO THE SECOND!

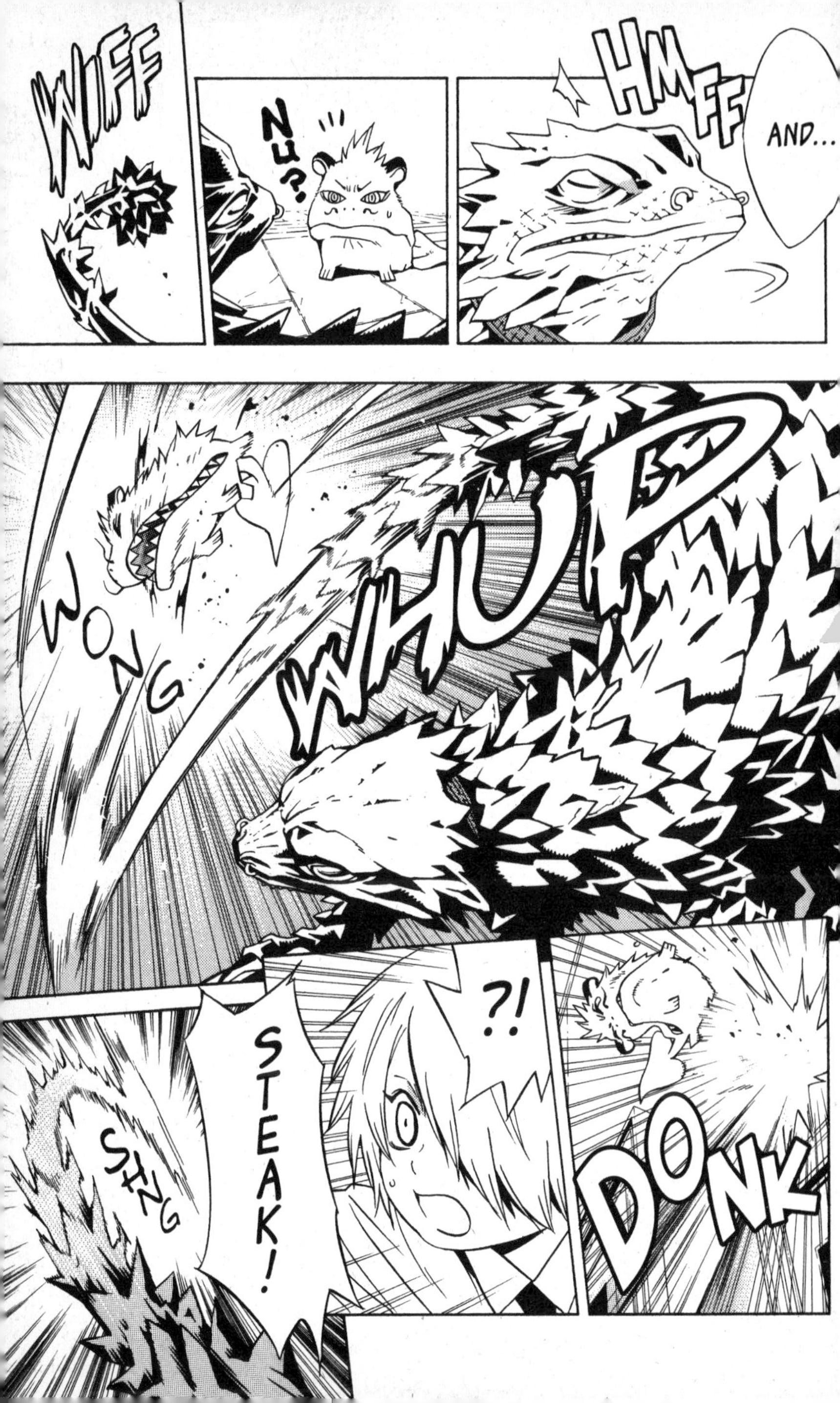
AND...
HMFF
NU?
WIFF
WHUP
WONG...
DONK
?!
STEAK!
SHNG

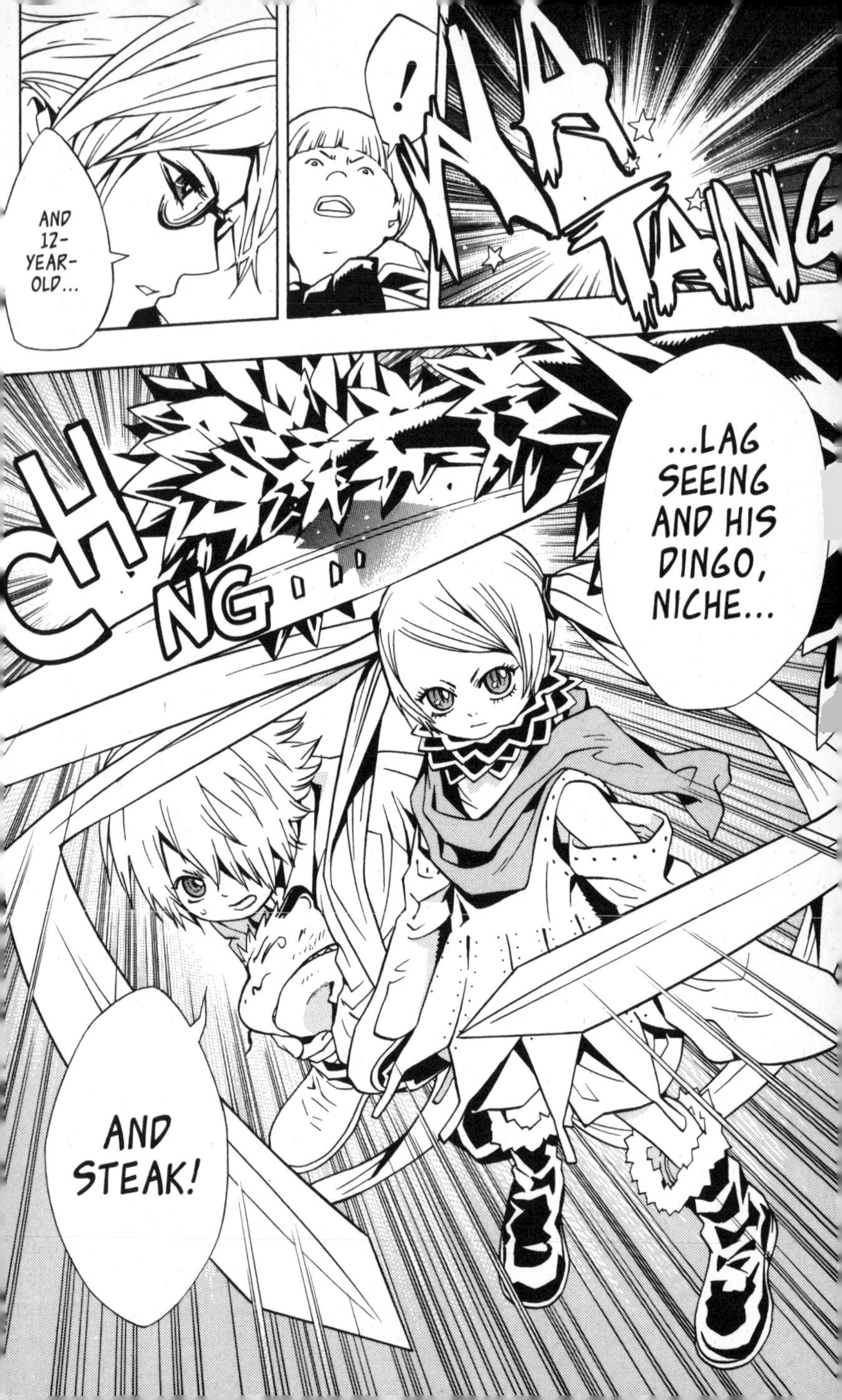
TANG
!
AND 12-YEAR-OLD...
...LAG SEEING AND HIS DINGO, NICHE...
CHING...
AND STEAK!

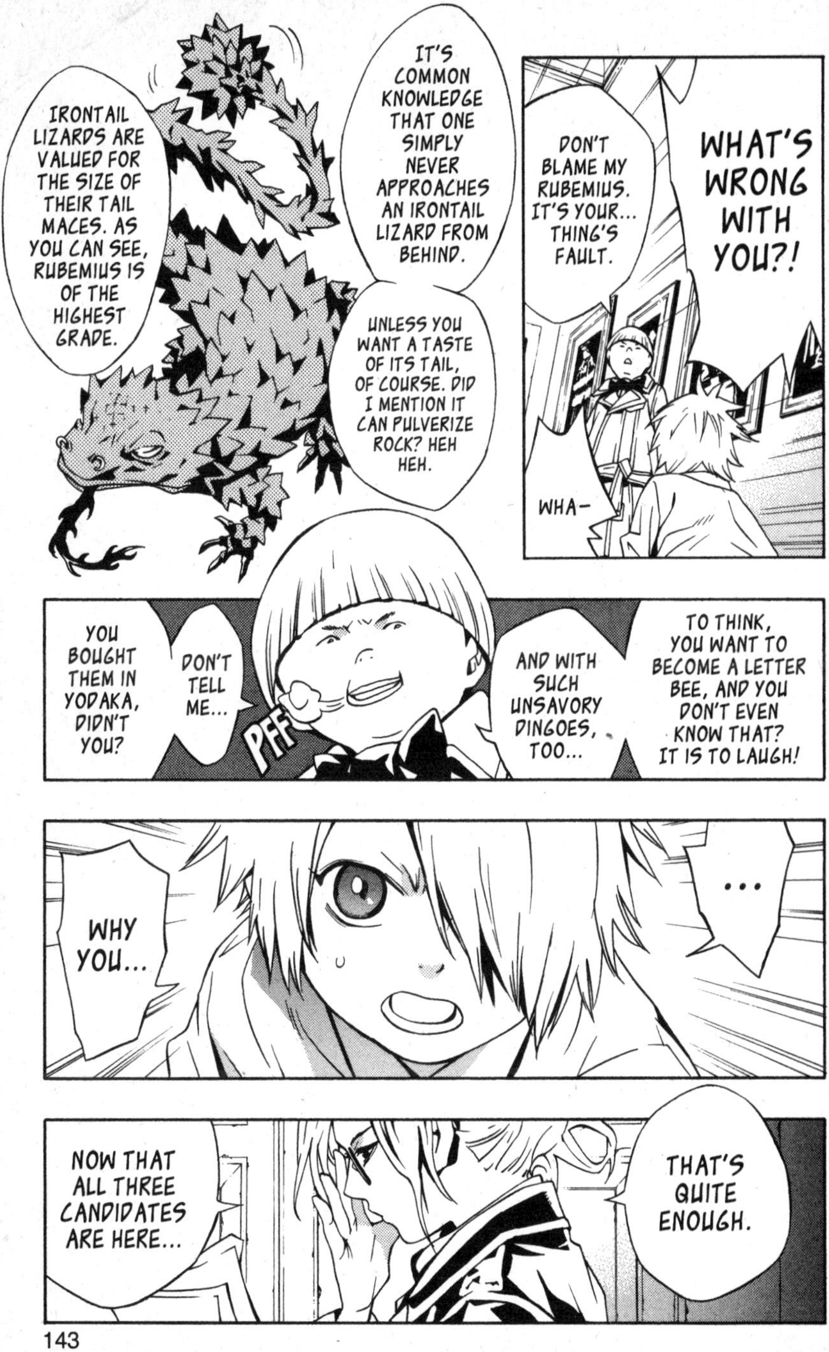
WHAT'S WRONG WITH YOU?!
DON'T BLAME MY RUBEMIUS. IT'S YOUR... THING'S FAULT.
WHA-
IT'S COMMON KNOWLEDGE THAT ONE SIMPLY NEVER APPROACHES AN IRONTAIL LIZARD FROM BEHIND.
UNLESS YOU WANT A TASTE OF ITS TAIL, OF COURSE. DID I MENTION IT CAN PULVERIZE ROCK? HEH HEH.
IRONTAIL LIZARDS ARE VALUED FOR THE SIZE OF THEIR TAIL MACES. AS YOU CAN SEE, RUBEMIUS IS OF THE HIGHEST GRADE.
TO THINK, YOU WANT TO BECOME A LETTER BEE, AND YOU DON'T EVEN KNOW THAT? IT IS TO LAUGH!
AND WITH SUCH UNSAVORY DINGOES, TOO...
PFF
DON'T TELL ME...
YOU BOUGHT THEM IN YODAKA, DIDN'T YOU?
...
WHY YOU...
THAT'S QUITE ENOUGH.
NOW THAT ALL THREE CANDIDATES ARE HERE...

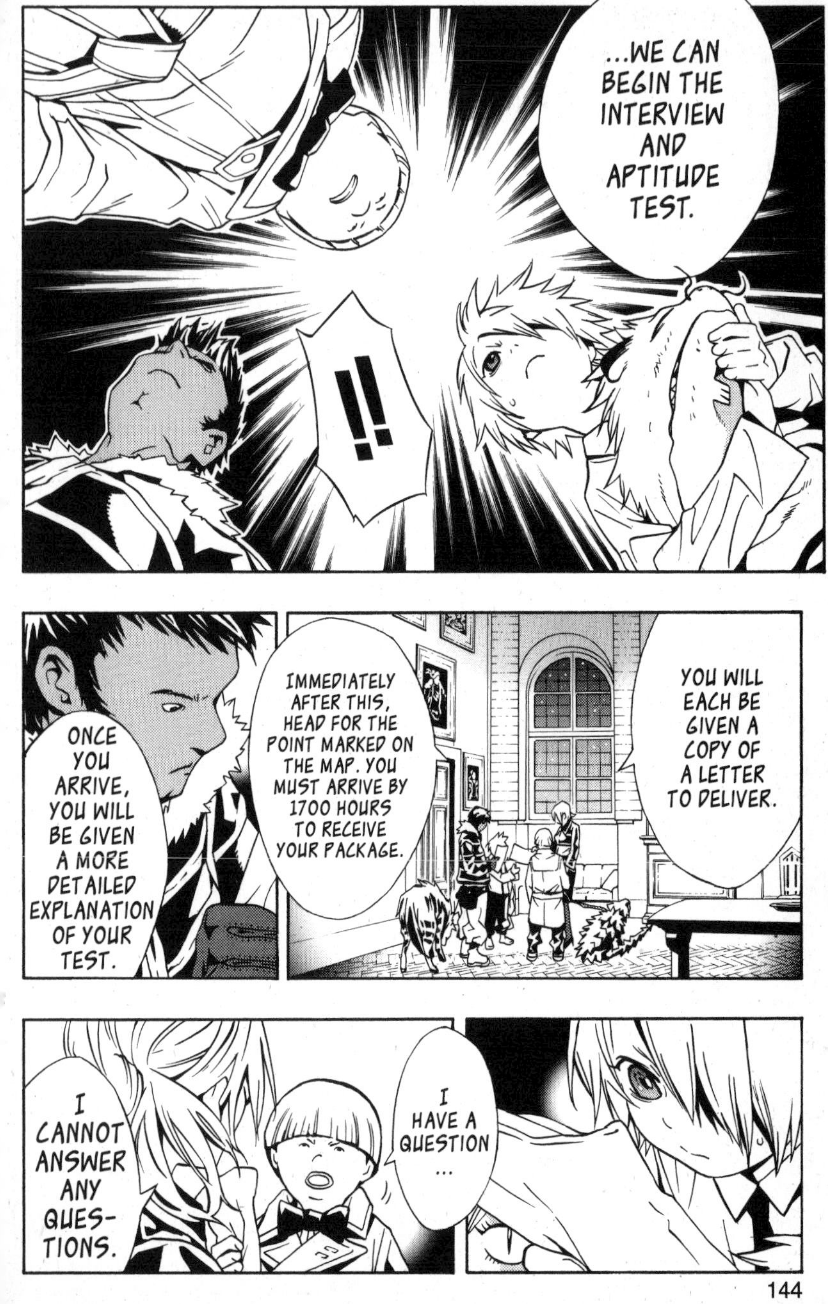
...WE CAN BEGIN THE INTERVIEW AND APTITUDE TEST.
!!
YOU WILL EACH BE GIVEN A COPY OF A LETTER TO DELIVER.
IMMEDIATELY AFTER THIS, HEAD FOR THE POINT MARKED ON THE MAP. YOU MUST ARRIVE BY 1700 HOURS TO RECEIVE YOUR PACKAGE.
ONCE YOU ARRIVE, YOU WILL BE GIVEN A MORE DETAILED EXPLANATION OF YOUR TEST.
I HAVE A QUESTION ...
I CANNOT ANSWER ANY QUES-TIONS.

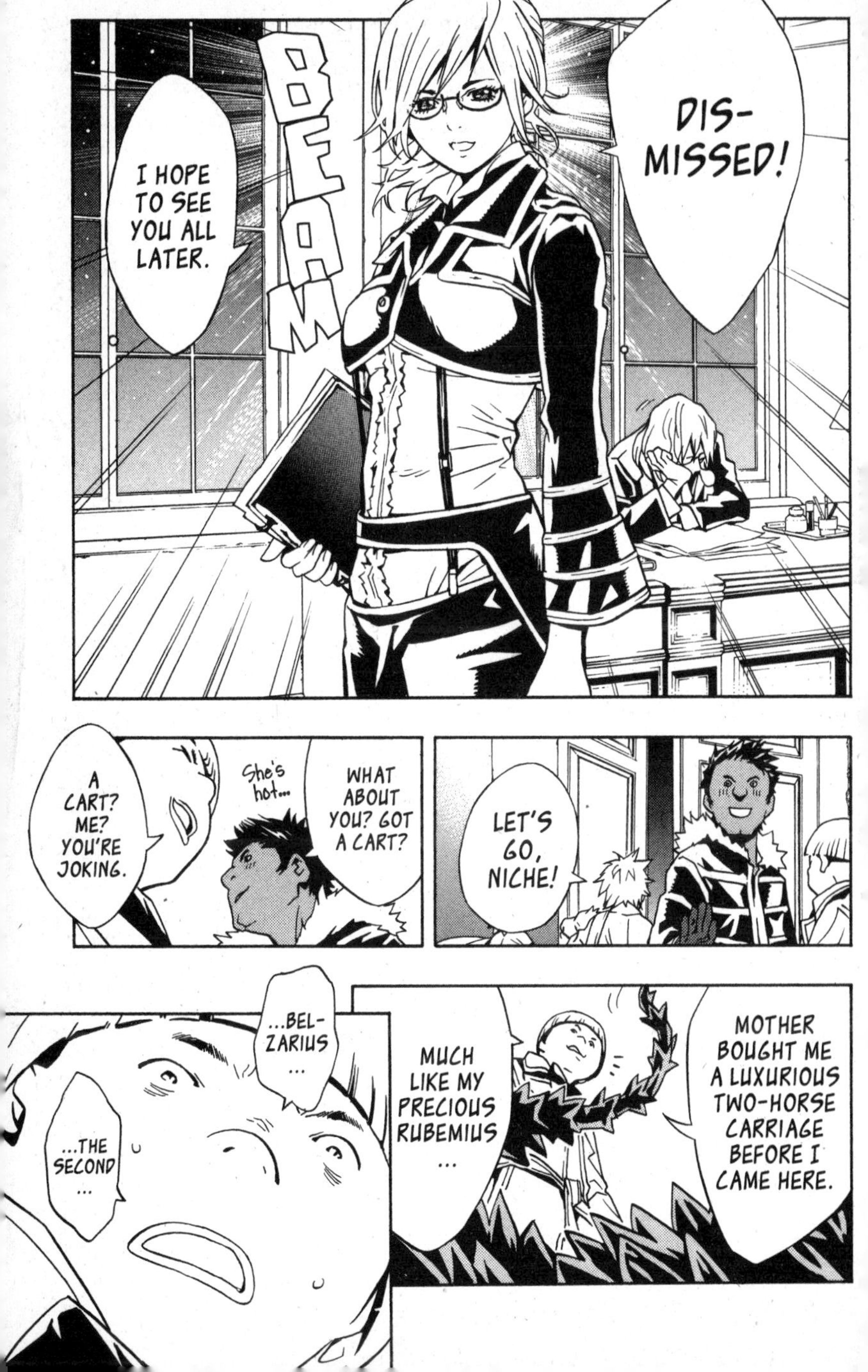
DIS-MISSED!
BEAM
I HOPE TO SEE YOU ALL LATER.
LET'S GO, NICHE!
WHAT ABOUT YOU? GOT A CART?
She's hot...
A CART? ME? YOU'RE JOKING.
MOTHER BOUGHT ME A LUXURIOUS TWO-HORSE CARRIAGE BEFORE I CAME HERE.
MUCH LIKE MY PRECIOUS RUBEMIUS ...
...BEL-ZARIUS ...
...THE SECOND ...

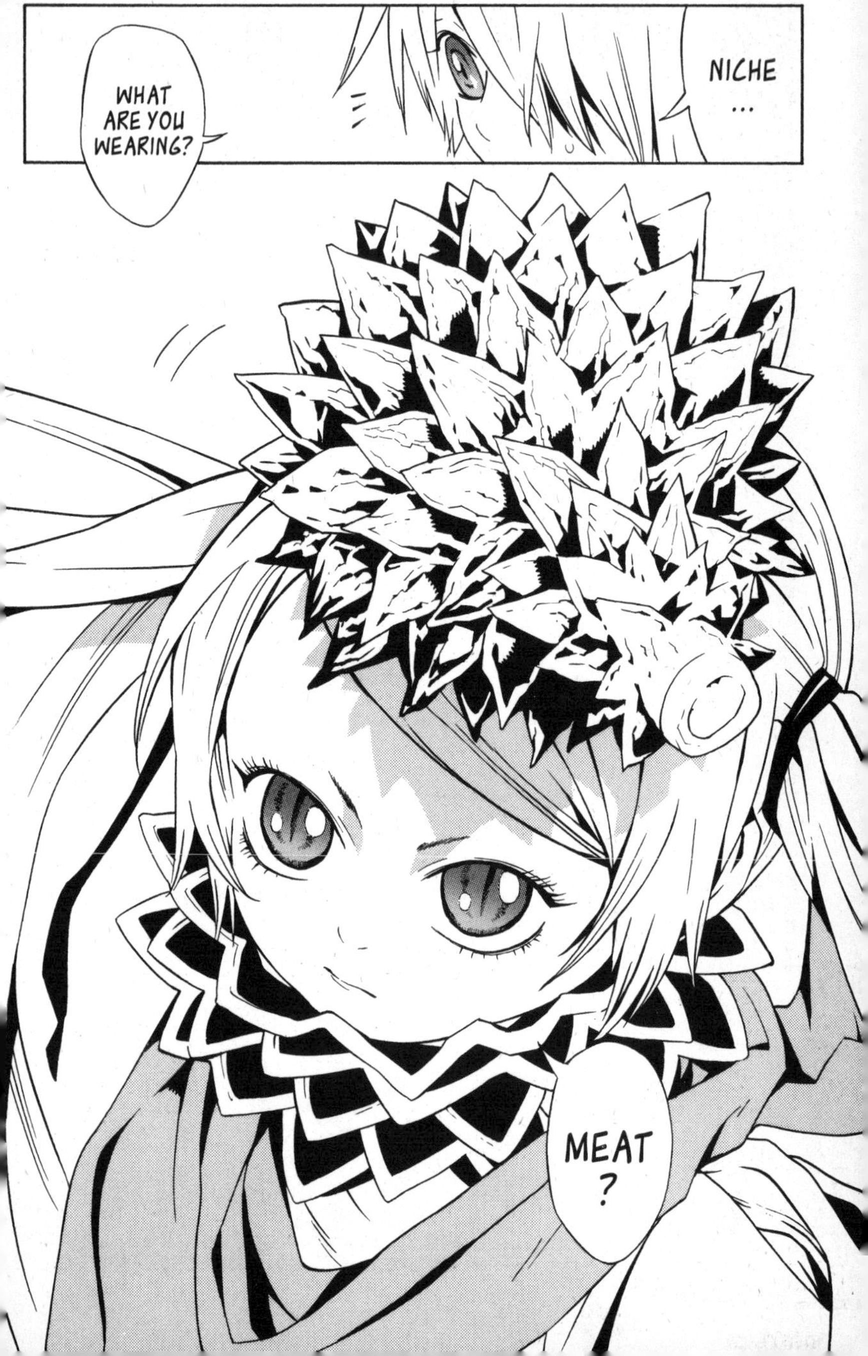
NICHE ...
WHAT ARE YOU WEARING?
MEAT ?

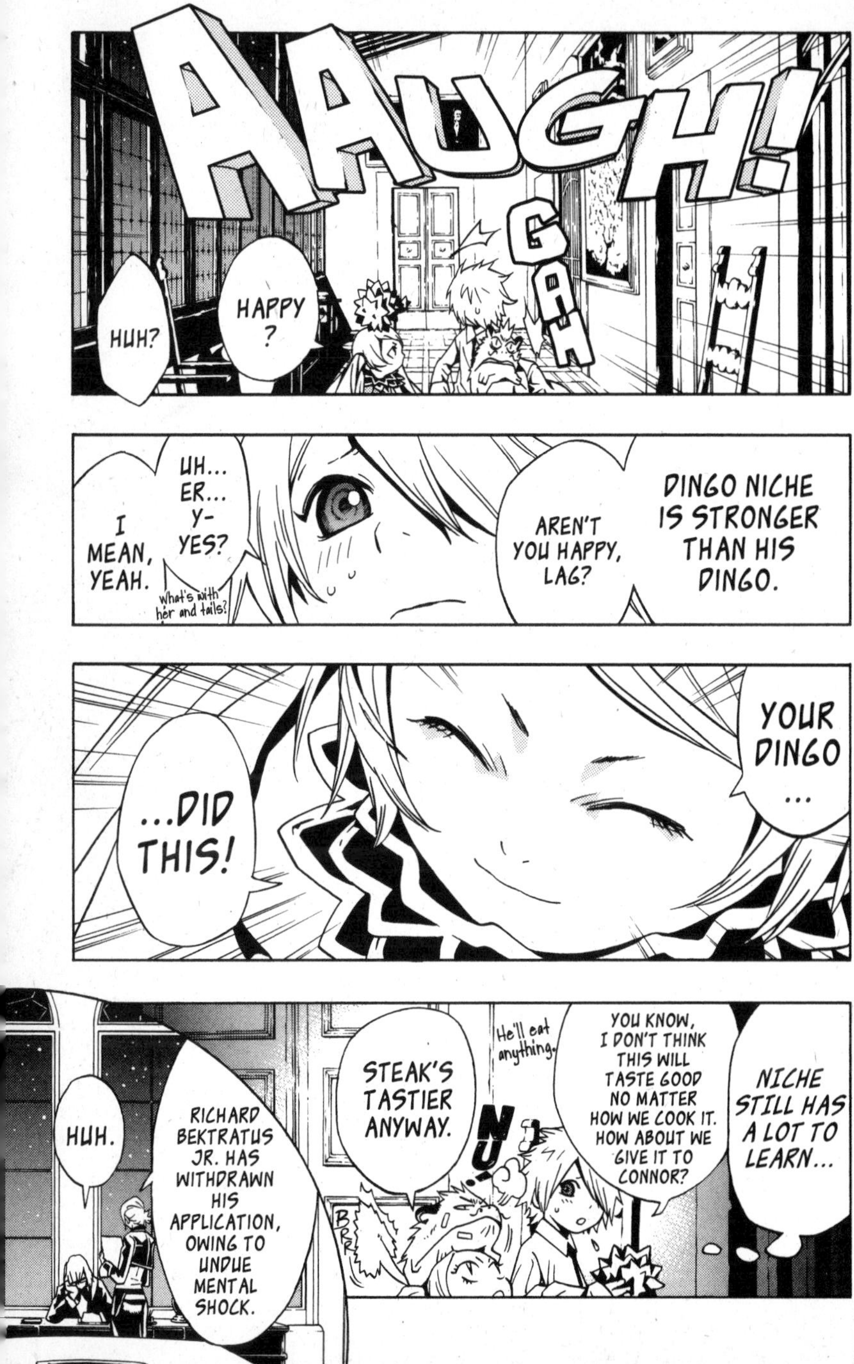
AAUGH!
GAAH
HAPPY ?
HUH?
DINGO NICHE IS STRONGER THAN HIS DINGO.
AREN'T YOU HAPPY, LAG?
UH... ER... Y- YES?
I MEAN, YEAH.
What's with her and tails?
YOUR DINGO ...
...DID THIS!
NICHE STILL HAS A LOT TO LEARN...
YOU KNOW, I DON'T THINK THIS WILL TASTE GOOD NO MATTER HOW WE COOK IT. HOW ABOUT WE GIVE IT TO CONNOR?
He'll eat anything.
NU!
STEAK'S TASTIER ANYWAY.
BRR
RICHARD BEKTRATUS JR. HAS WITHDRAWN HIS APPLICATION, OWING TO UNDUE MENTAL SHOCK.
HUH.

Connor Kluff コナー・クリフ

Connor means "wolf lover" or "wolf kin" in Gaelic.

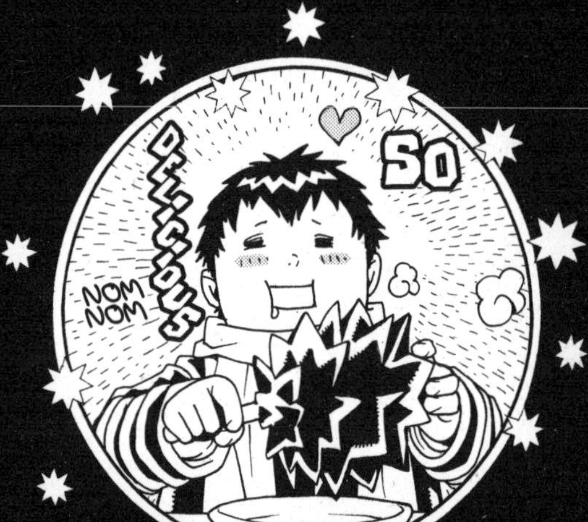
SO
DELICIOUS
NOM NOM

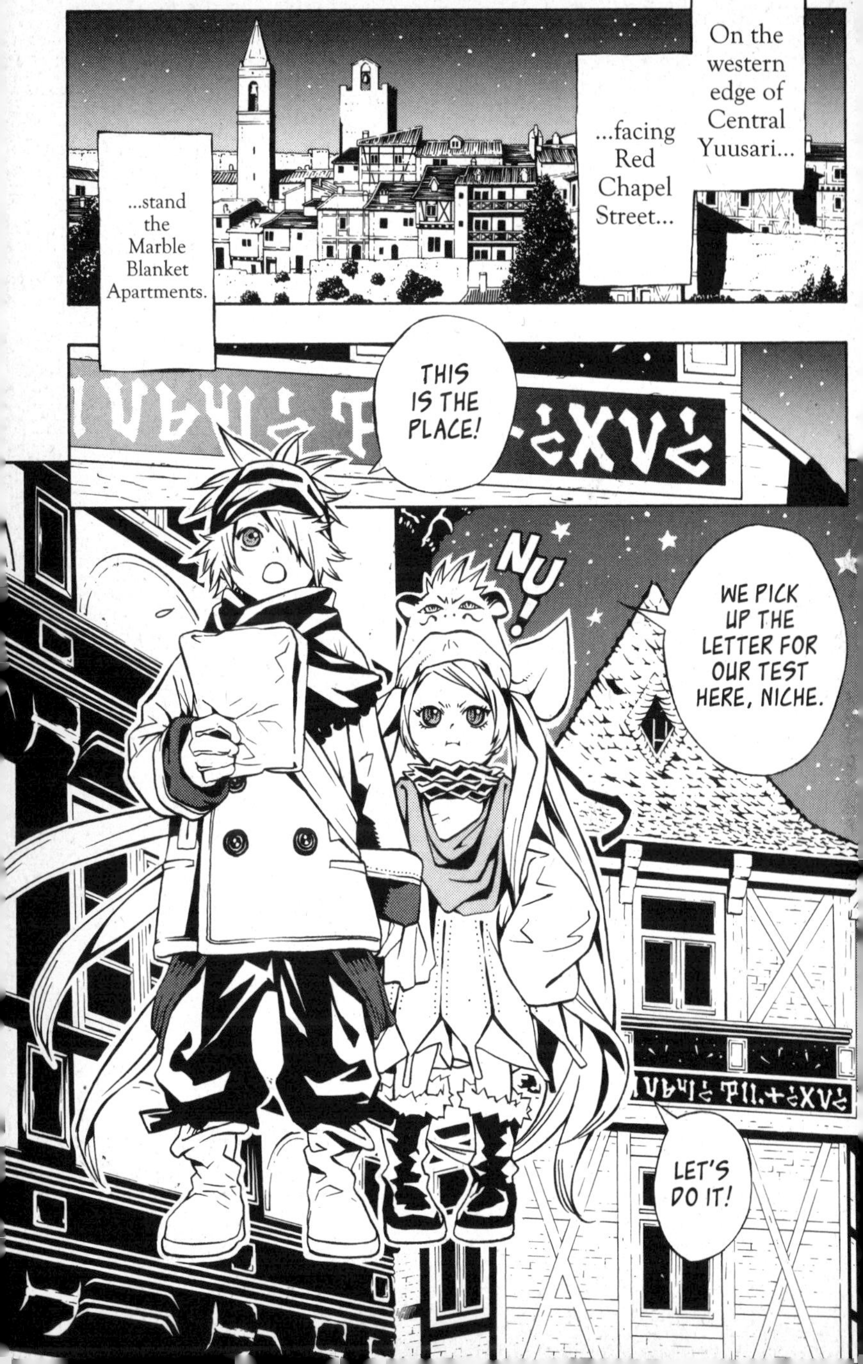

On the western edge of Central Yuusari...
...facing Red Chapel Street...
...stand the Marble Blanket Apartments.
THIS IS THE PLACE!
WE PICK UP THE LETTER FOR OUR TEST HERE, NICHE.
NU!
LET'S DO IT!

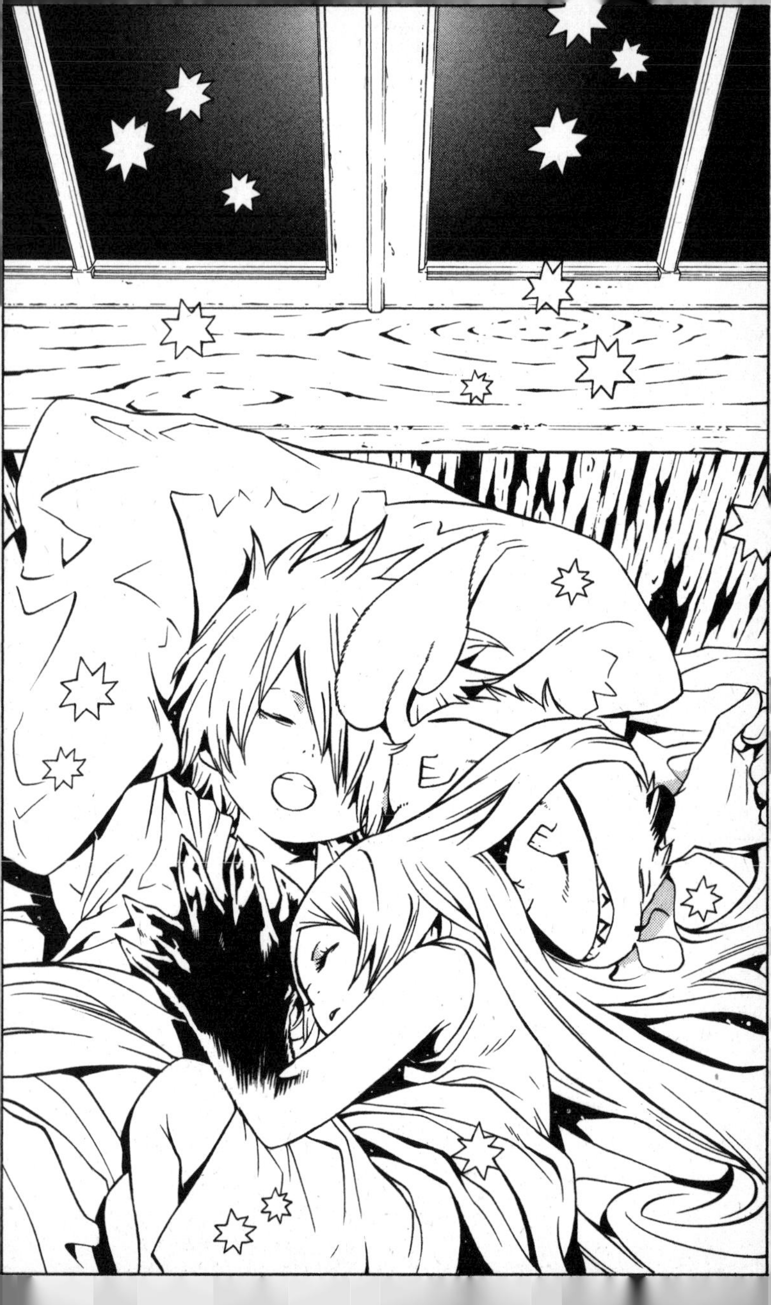

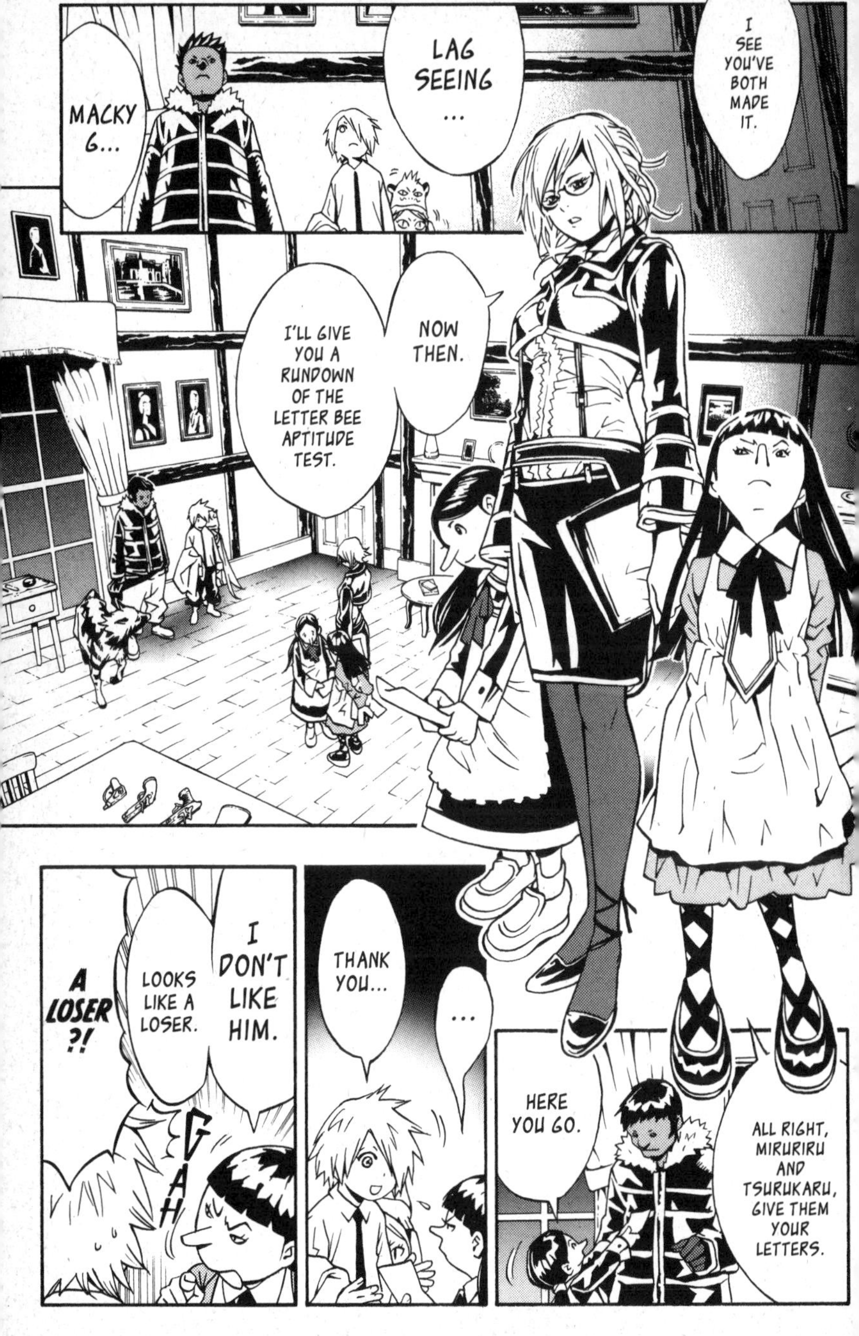
I SEE YOU'VE BOTH MADE IT.
LAG SEEING...
MACKY G...
NOW THEN.
I'LL GIVE YOU A RUNDOWN OF THE LETTER BEE APTITUDE TEST.
ALL RIGHT, MIRURIRU AND TSURUKARU, GIVE THEM YOUR LETTERS.
HERE YOU GO.
...
THANK YOU...
I DON'T LIKE HIM.
LOOKS LIKE A LOSER.
A LOSER?!
GAH

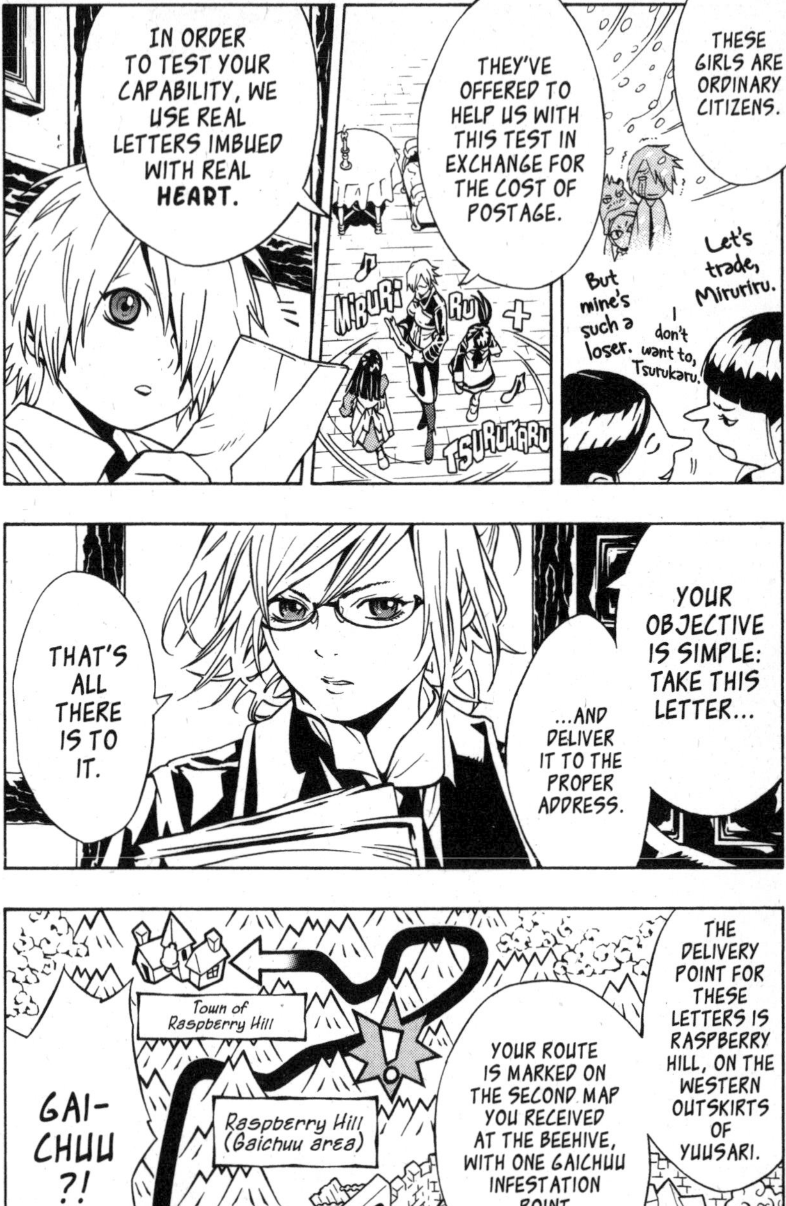

THESE GIRLS ARE ORDINARY CITIZENS.
Let's trade, Miruriru.
I don't want to, Tsurukaru.
But mine's such a loser.
THEY'VE OFFERED TO HELP US WITH THIS TEST IN EXCHANGE FOR THE COST OF POSTAGE.
MIRURIRU
TSURUKARU
IN ORDER TO TEST YOUR CAPABILITY, WE USE REAL LETTERS IMBUED WITH REAL **HEART**.
YOUR OBJECTIVE IS SIMPLE: TAKE THIS LETTER...
...AND DELIVER IT TO THE PROPER ADDRESS.
THAT'S ALL THERE IS TO IT.
THE DELIVERY POINT FOR THESE LETTERS IS RASPBERRY HILL, ON THE WESTERN OUTSKIRTS OF YUUSARI.
YOUR ROUTE IS MARKED ON THE SECOND MAP YOU RECEIVED AT THE BEEHIVE, WITH ONE GAICHUU INFESTATION POINT HIGHLIGHTED.
Town of Raspberry Hill
Raspberry Hill (Gaichuu area)
Central Yuusari – West
GAI-CHUU?!

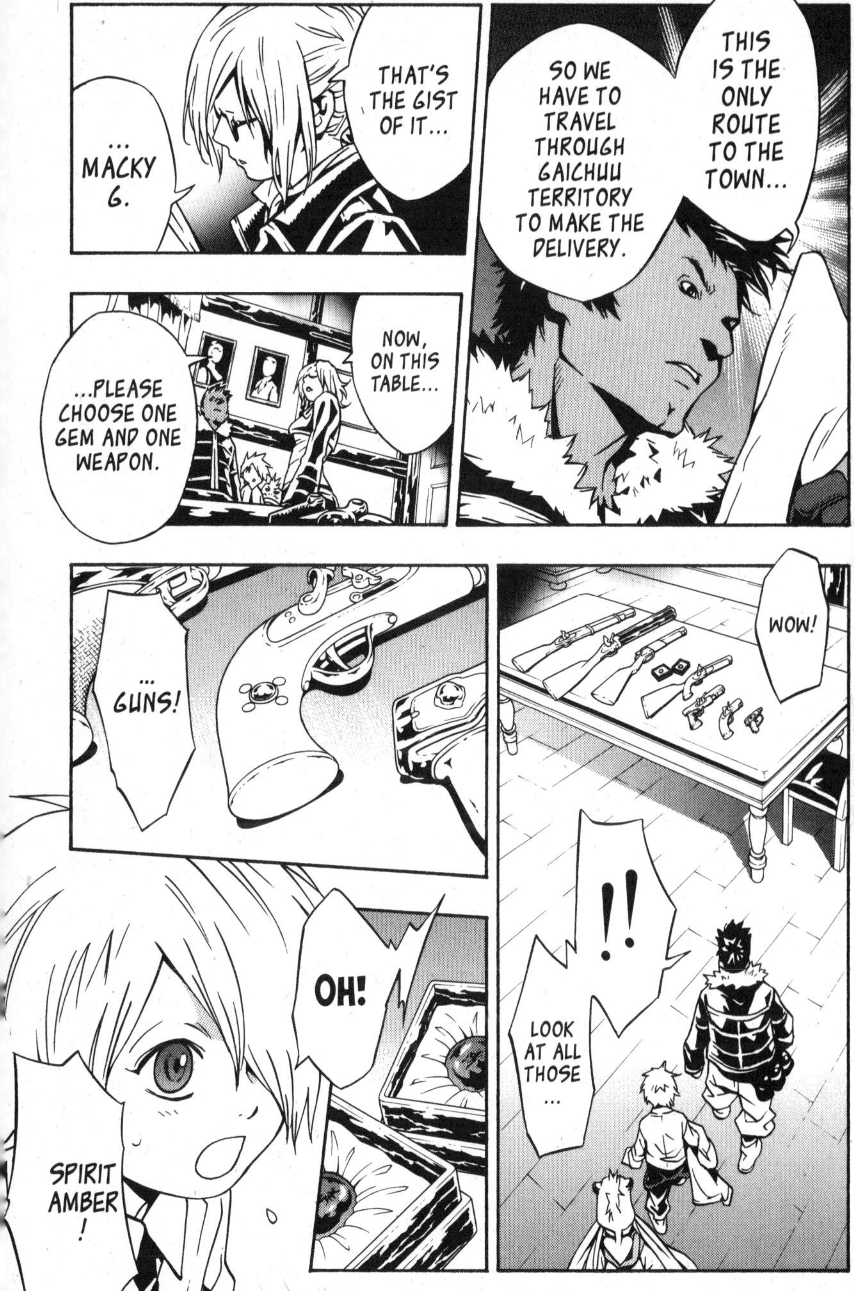
THIS IS THE ONLY ROUTE TO THE TOWN...
SO WE HAVE TO TRAVEL THROUGH GAICHUU TERRITORY TO MAKE THE DELIVERY.
THAT'S THE GIST OF IT...
... MACKY G.
NOW, ON THIS TABLE...
...PLEASE CHOOSE ONE GEM AND ONE WEAPON.
WOW!
!!
LOOK AT ALL THOSE ...
... GUNS!
OH!
SPIRIT AMBER!

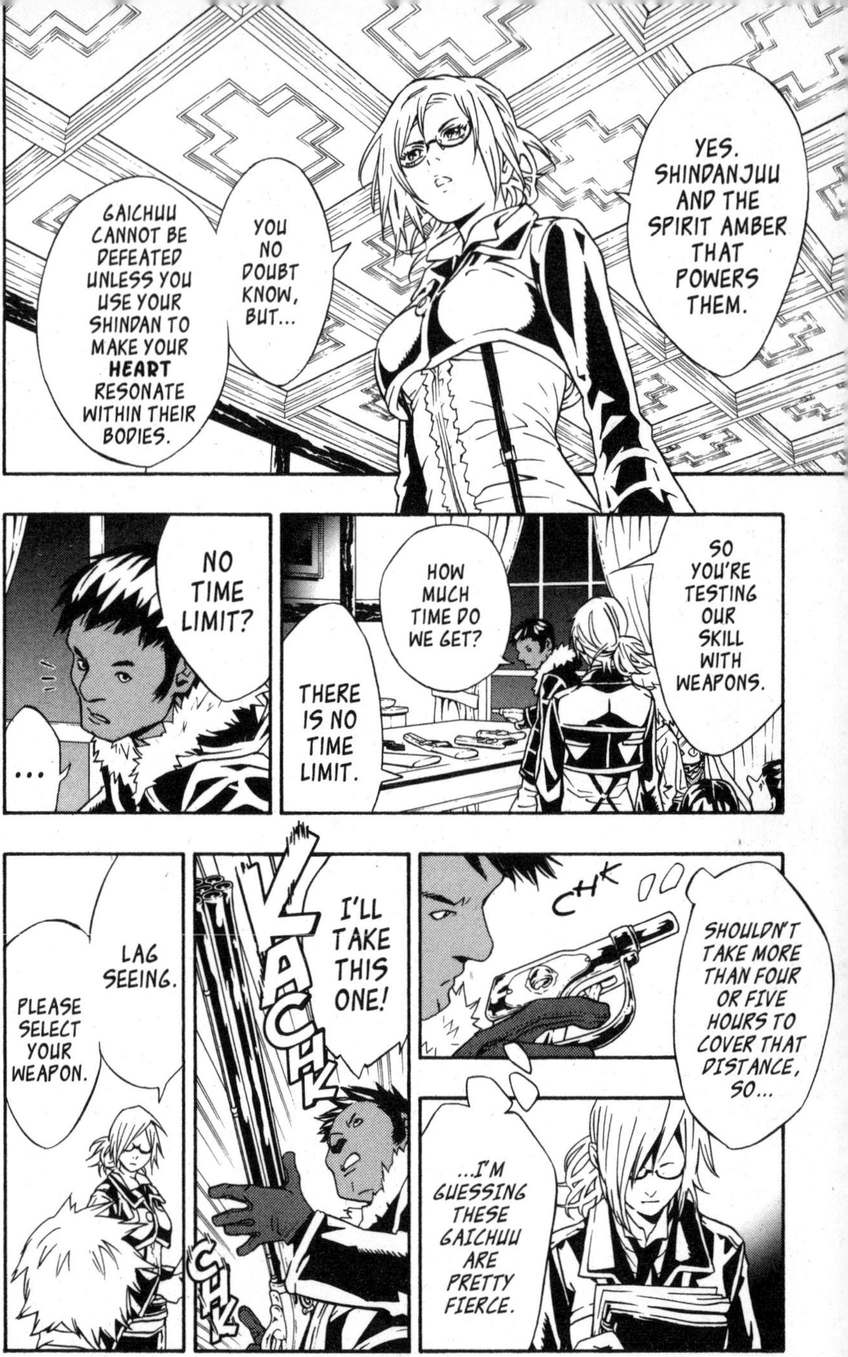
YES. SHINDANJUU AND THE SPIRIT AMBER THAT POWERS THEM.
YOU NO DOUBT KNOW, BUT...
GAICHUU CANNOT BE DEFEATED UNLESS YOU USE YOUR SHINDAN TO MAKE YOUR **HEART** RESONATE WITHIN THEIR BODIES.
SO YOU'RE TESTING OUR SKILL WITH WEAPONS.
HOW MUCH TIME DO WE GET?
THERE IS NO TIME LIMIT.
NO TIME LIMIT?
...
CHK
SHOULDN'T TAKE MORE THAN FOUR OR FIVE HOURS TO COVER THAT DISTANCE, SO...
...I'M GUESSING THESE GAICHUU ARE PRETTY FIERCE.
VLACHUK
I'LL TAKE THIS ONE!
CHK
LAG SEEING.
PLEASE SELECT YOUR WEAPON.

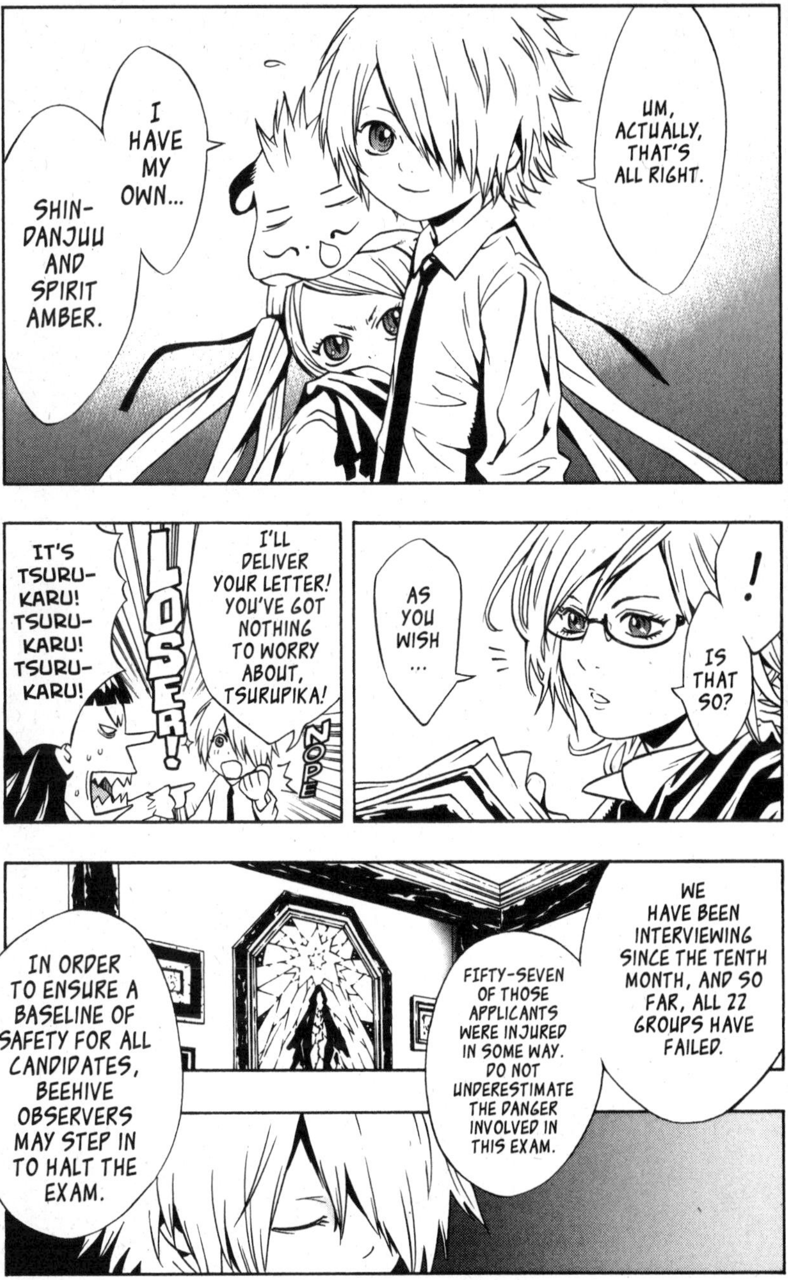
UM, ACTUALLY, THAT'S ALL RIGHT.
I HAVE MY OWN...
SHIN-DANJUU AND SPIRIT AMBER.
!
IS THAT SO?
AS YOU WISH...
I'LL DELIVER YOUR LETTER! YOU'VE GOT NOTHING TO WORRY ABOUT, TSURUPIKA!
NOPE
LOSER!
IT'S TSURU-KARU! TSURU-KARU! TSURU-KARU!
WE HAVE BEEN INTERVIEWING SINCE THE TENTH MONTH, AND SO FAR, ALL 22 GROUPS HAVE FAILED.
FIFTY-SEVEN OF THOSE APPLICANTS WERE INJURED IN SOME WAY. DO NOT UNDERESTIMATE THE DANGER INVOLVED IN THIS EXAM.
IN ORDER TO ENSURE A BASELINE OF SAFETY FOR ALL CANDIDATES, BEEHIVE OBSERVERS MAY STEP IN TO HALT THE EXAM.

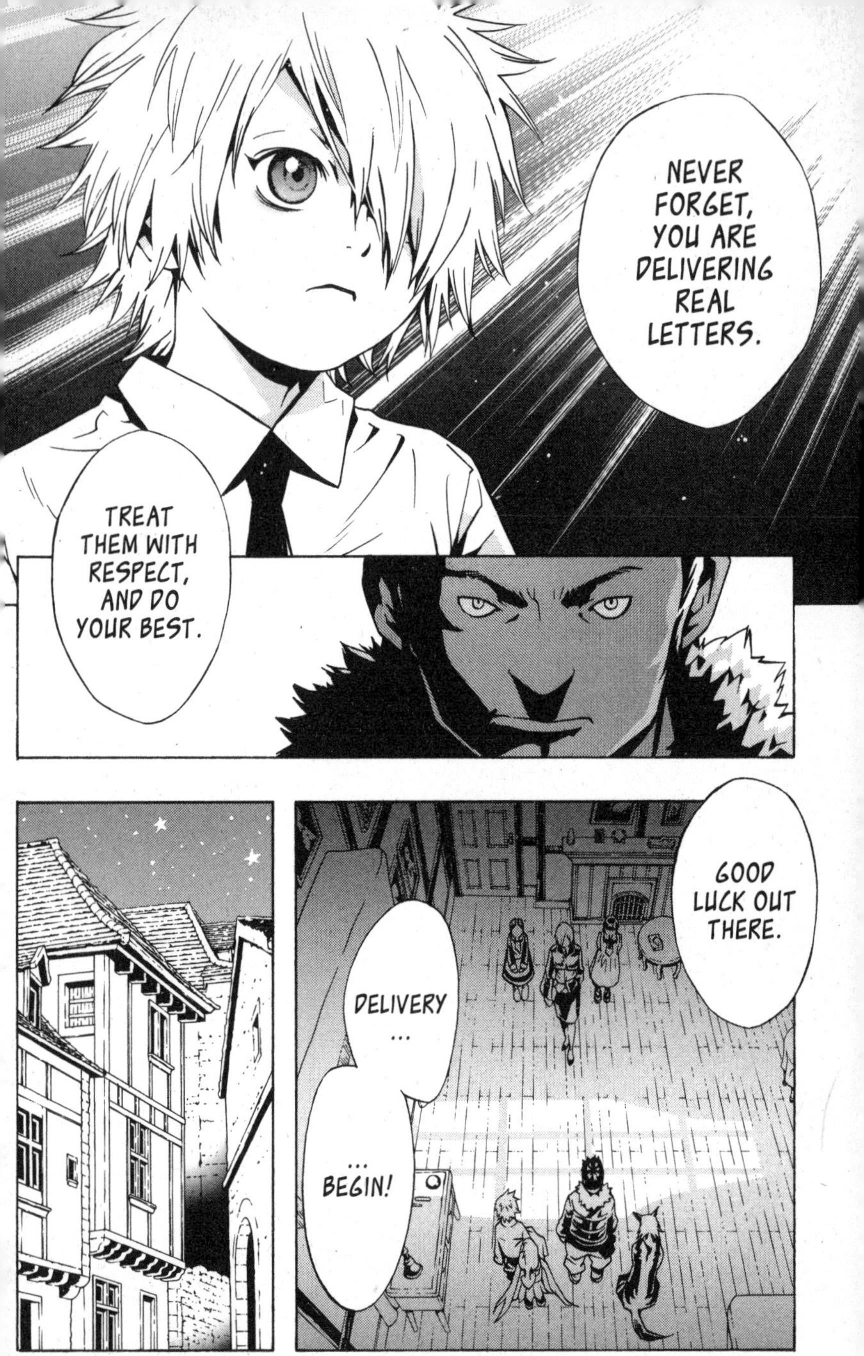
NEVER FORGET, YOU ARE DELIVERING REAL LETTERS.
TREAT THEM WITH RESPECT, AND DO YOUR BEST.
GOOD LUCK OUT THERE.
DELIVERY ...
... BEGIN!

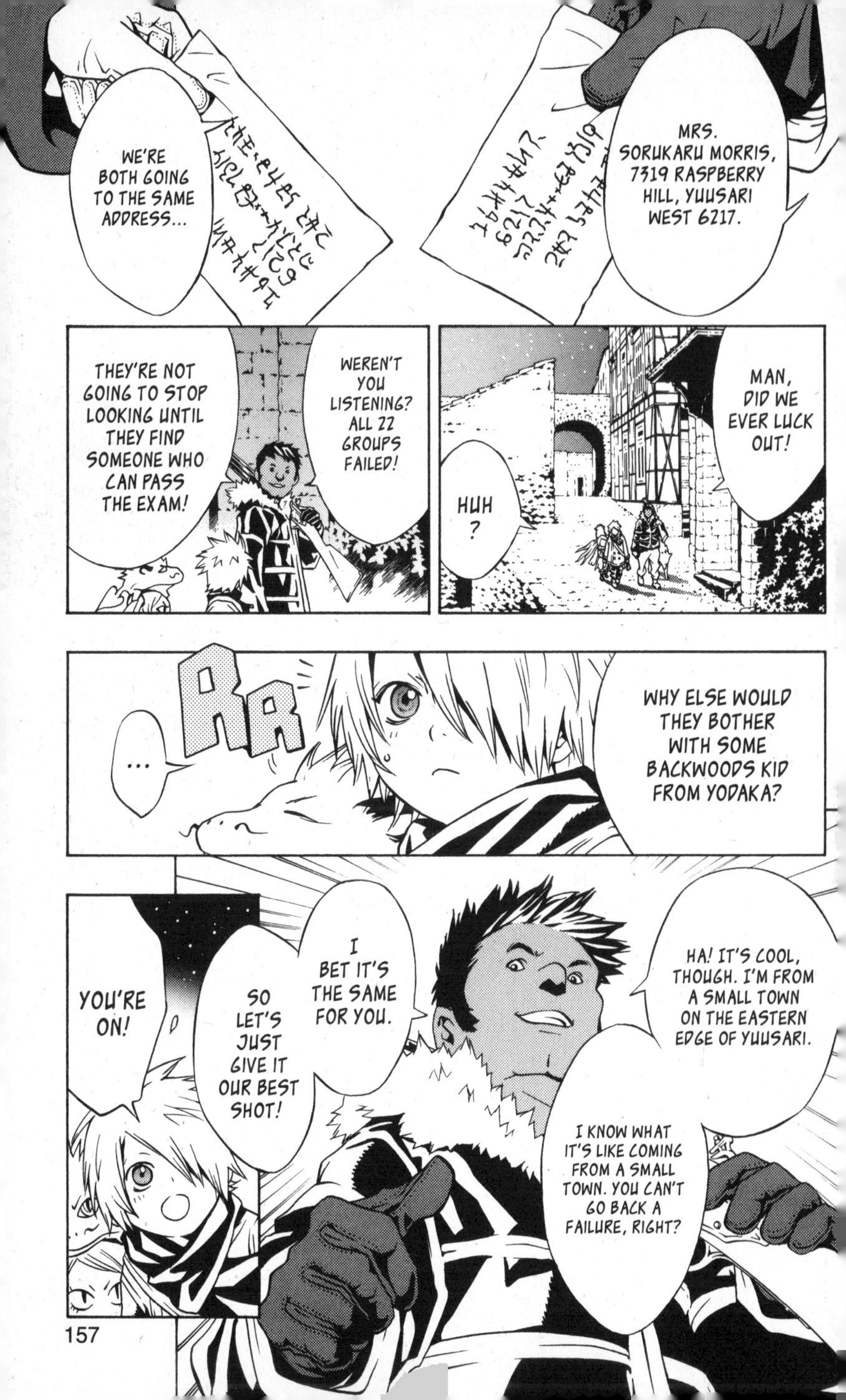
MRS. SORUKARU MORRIS, 7319 RASPBERRY HILL, YUUSARI WEST 6217.
WE'RE BOTH GOING TO THE SAME ADDRESS...
MAN, DID WE EVER LUCK OUT!
HUH?
WEREN'T YOU LISTENING? ALL 22 GROUPS FAILED!
THEY'RE NOT GOING TO STOP LOOKING UNTIL THEY FIND SOMEONE WHO CAN PASS THE EXAM!
WHY ELSE WOULD THEY BOTHER WITH SOME BACKWOODS KID FROM YODAKA?
RR
...
HA! IT'S COOL, THOUGH. I'M FROM A SMALL TOWN ON THE EASTERN EDGE OF YUUSARI.
I KNOW WHAT IT'S LIKE COMING FROM A SMALL TOWN. YOU CAN'T GO BACK A FAILURE, RIGHT?
I BET IT'S THE SAME FOR YOU.
SO LET'S JUST GIVE IT OUR BEST SHOT!
YOU'RE ON!

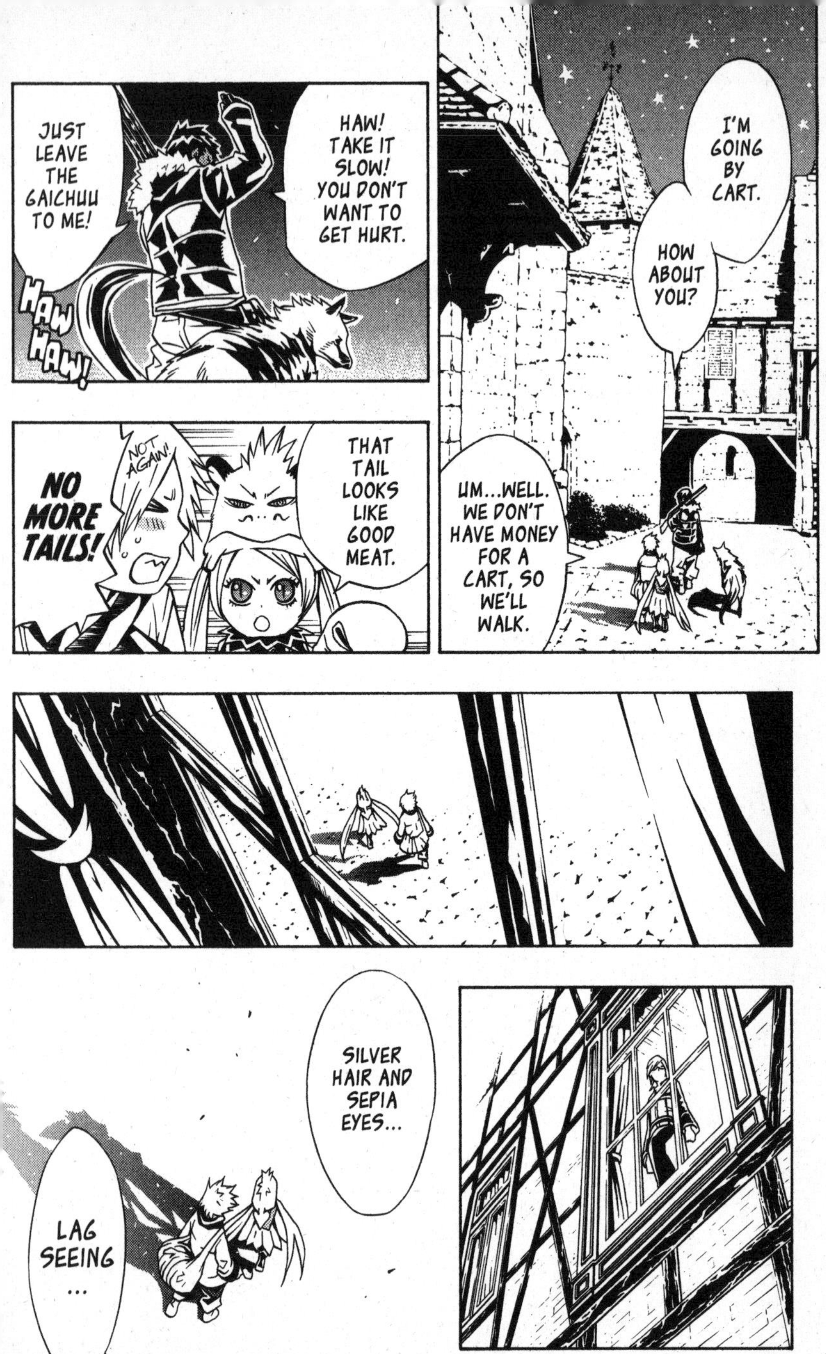
I'M GOING BY CART.
HOW ABOUT YOU?
UM...WELL. WE DON'T HAVE MONEY FOR A CART, SO WE'LL WALK.
HAW! TAKE IT SLOW! YOU DON'T WANT TO GET HURT.
JUST LEAVE THE GAICHUU TO ME!
HAW HAW!
THAT TAIL LOOKS LIKE GOOD MEAT.
NOT AGAIN!
NO MORE TAILS!
SILVER HAIR AND SEPIA EYES...
LAG SEEING ...

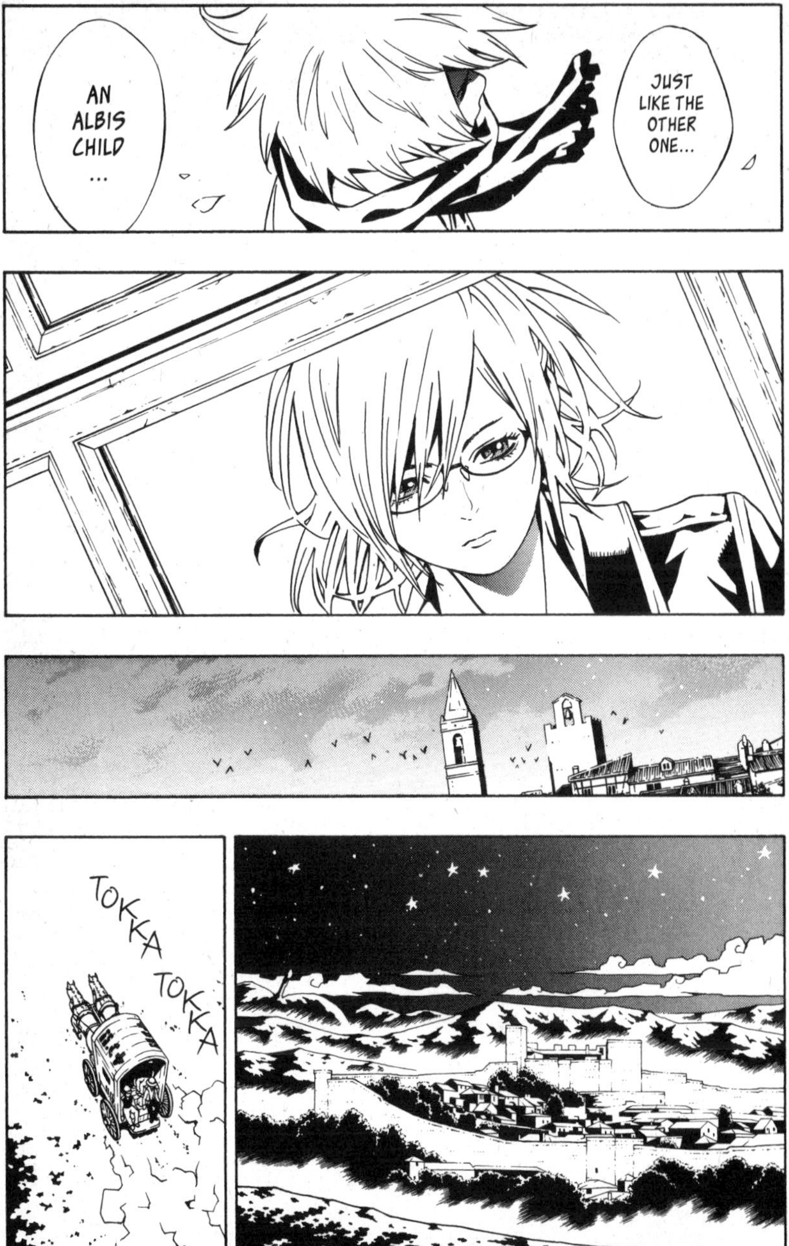
JUST LIKE THE OTHER ONE...
AN ALBIS CHILD ...
TOKKA TOKKA

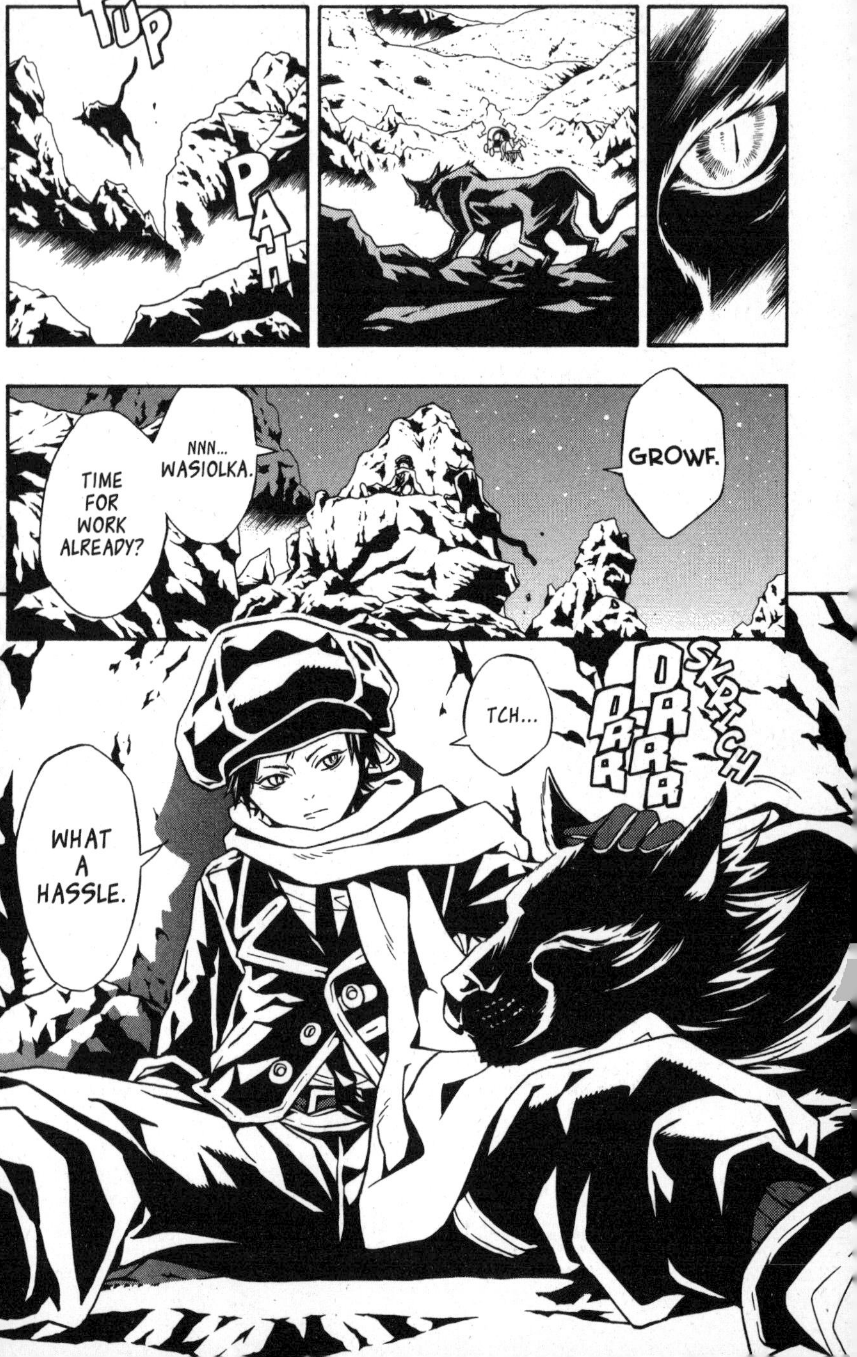
TUP
PAH
GROWF.
NNN... WASIOLKA.
TIME FOR WORK ALREADY?
SKRICH
DRRR
DRRR
TCH...
WHAT A HASSLE.

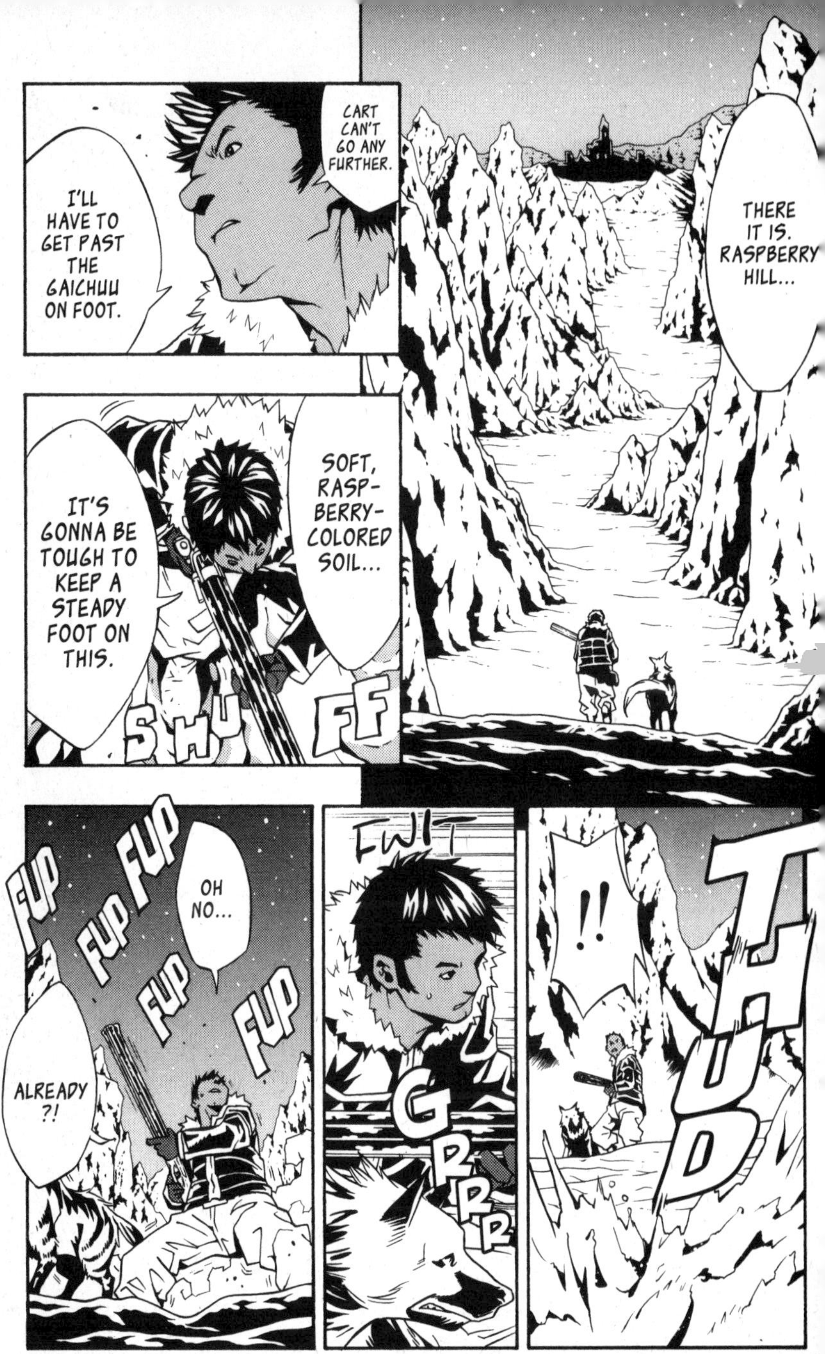
THERE IT IS. RASPBERRY HILL...
CART CAN'T GO ANY FURTHER.
I'LL HAVE TO GET PAST THE GAICHUU ON FOOT.
SOFT, RASP-BERRY-COLORED SOIL...
IT'S GONNA BE TOUGH TO KEEP A STEADY FOOT ON THIS.
SHUFF
THUD
!!
FWIT
GRRR
FUP FUP FUP FUP FUP
OH NO...
ALREADY?!

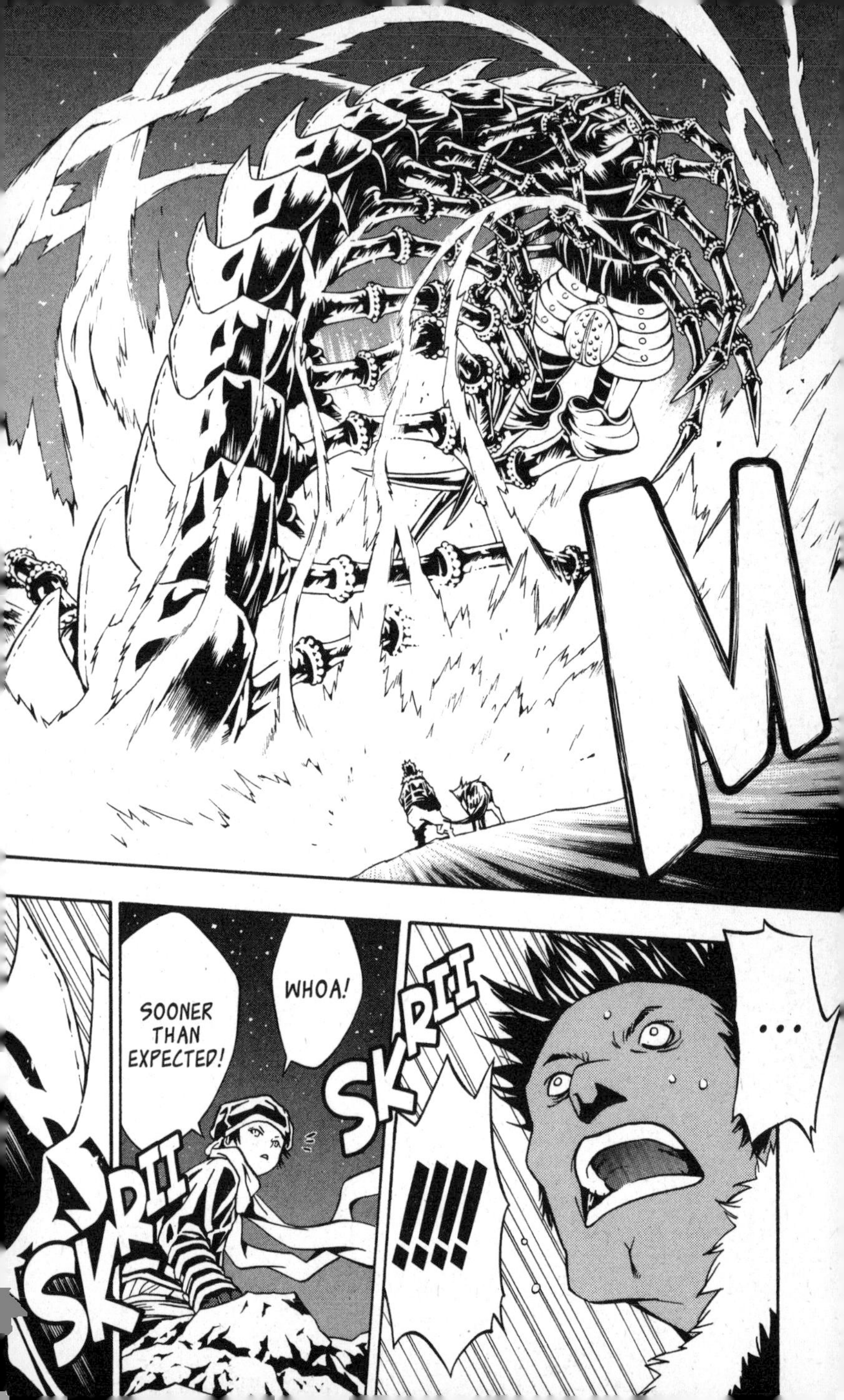
M
...
!!!!!
SKRII
WHOA!
SOONER THAN EXPECTED!
SKRII

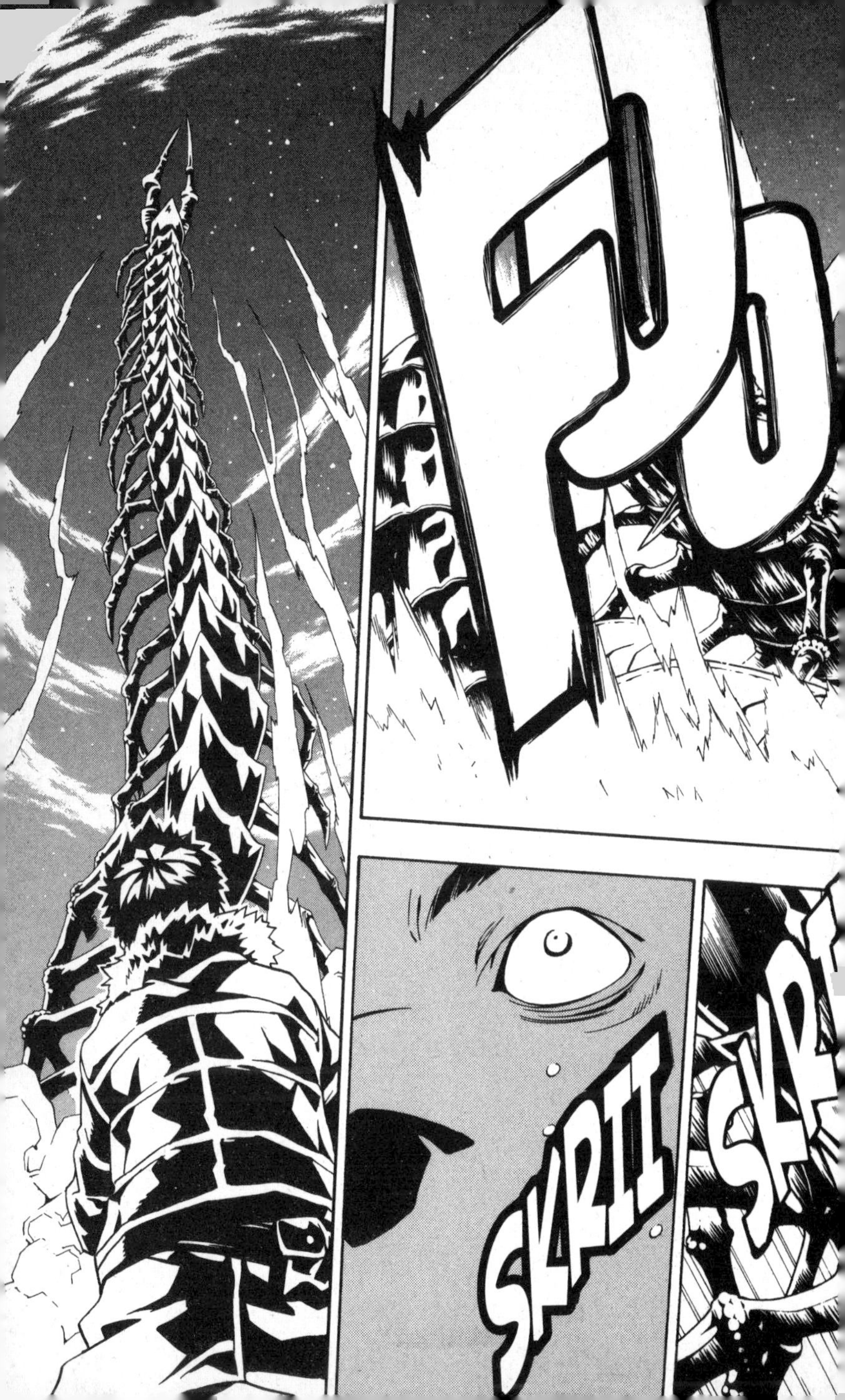
SKR
SKRII

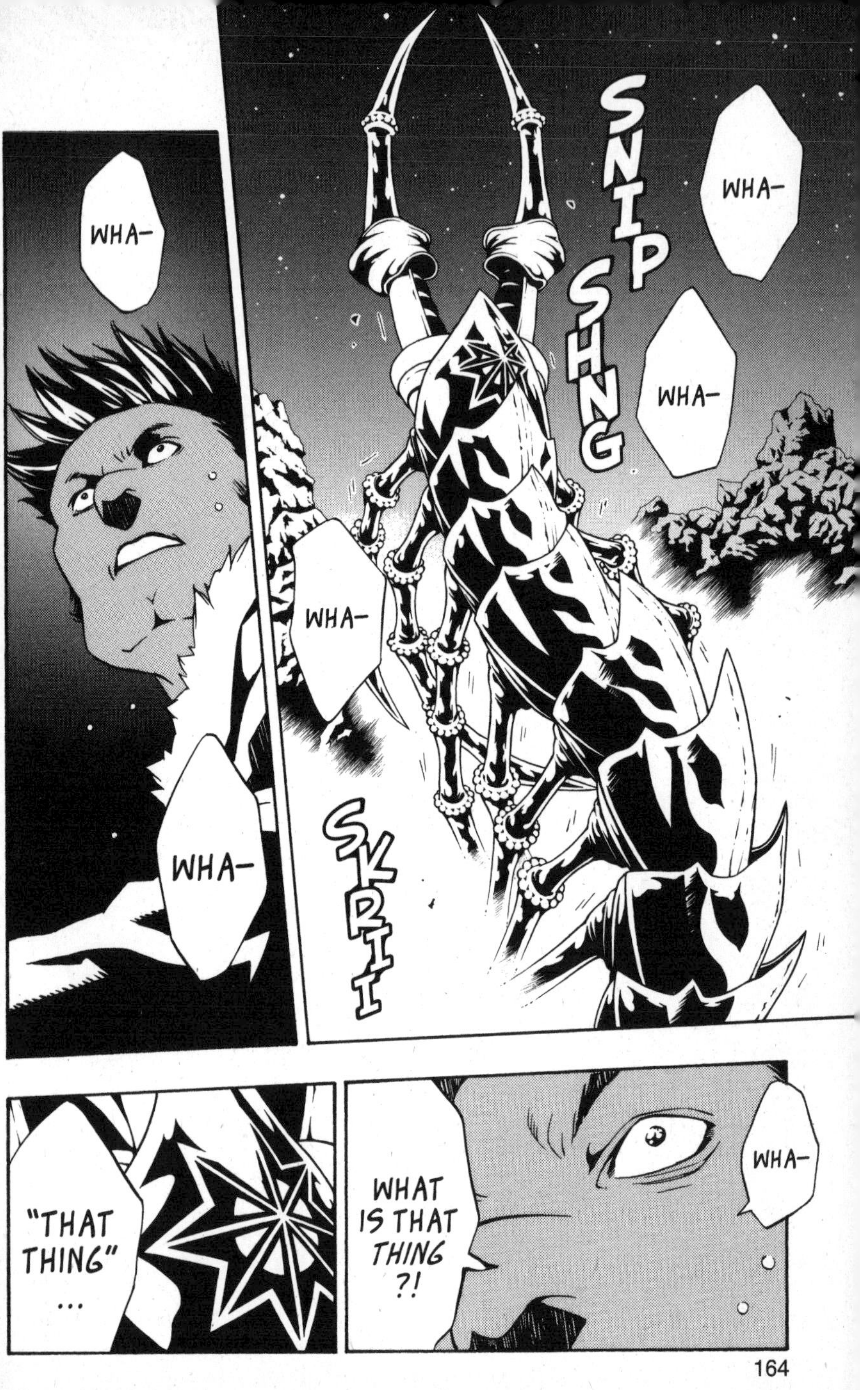
WHA-
SNIP
SHNG
WHA-
WHA-
SKRII
WHA-
WHA-
WHA-
WHAT IS THAT THING ?!
"THAT THING" ...

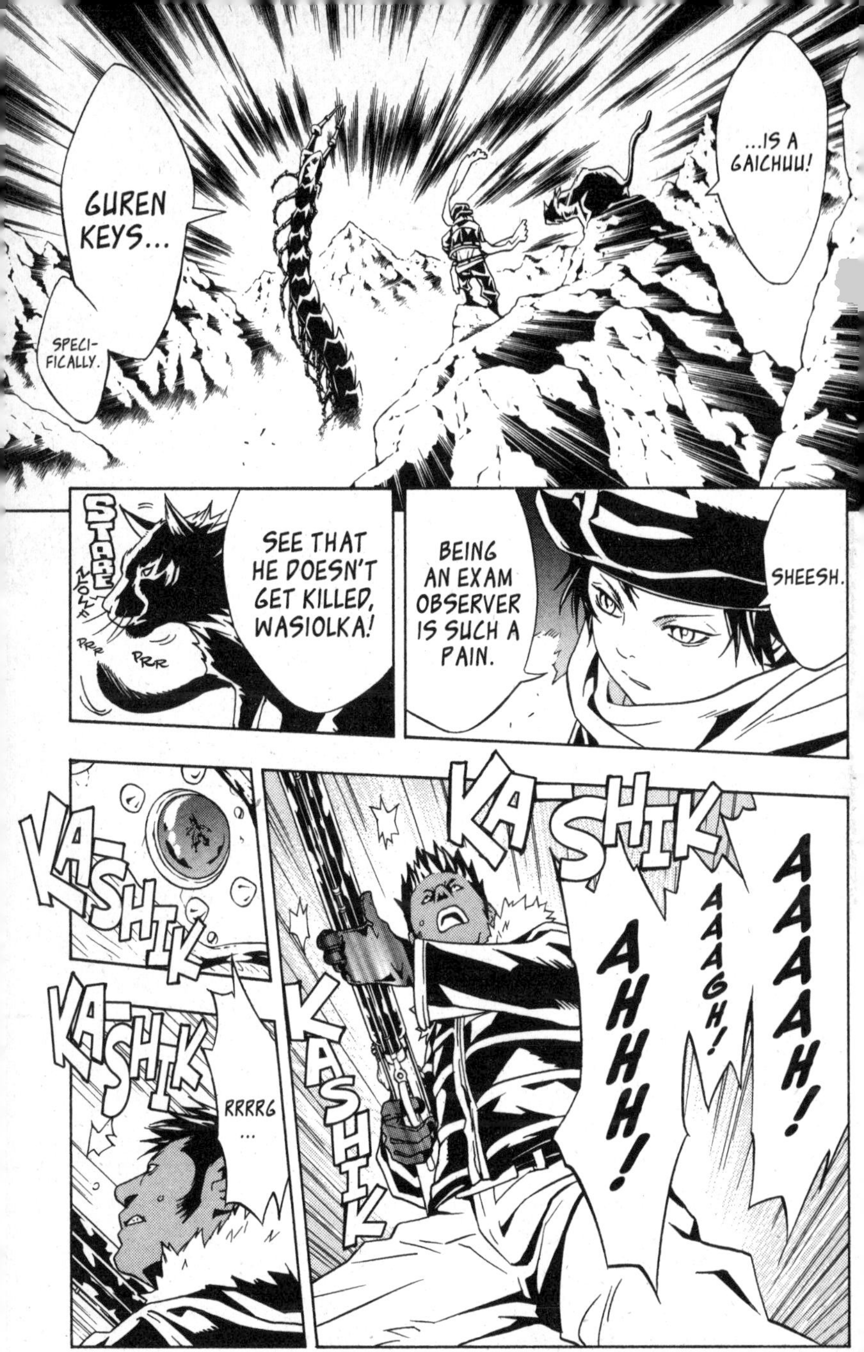
...IS A GAICHUU!
GUREN KEYS...
SPECIFICALLY.
SHEESH.
BEING AN EXAM OBSERVER IS SUCH A PAIN.
SEE THAT HE DOESN'T GET KILLED, WASIOLKA!
STARE
MOWF
PRR
PRR
KA-SHIK
AAAAAH!
AAAAGH!
AHHHH!
KASHIK
KA-SHIK
KA-SHIK
RRRRG ...

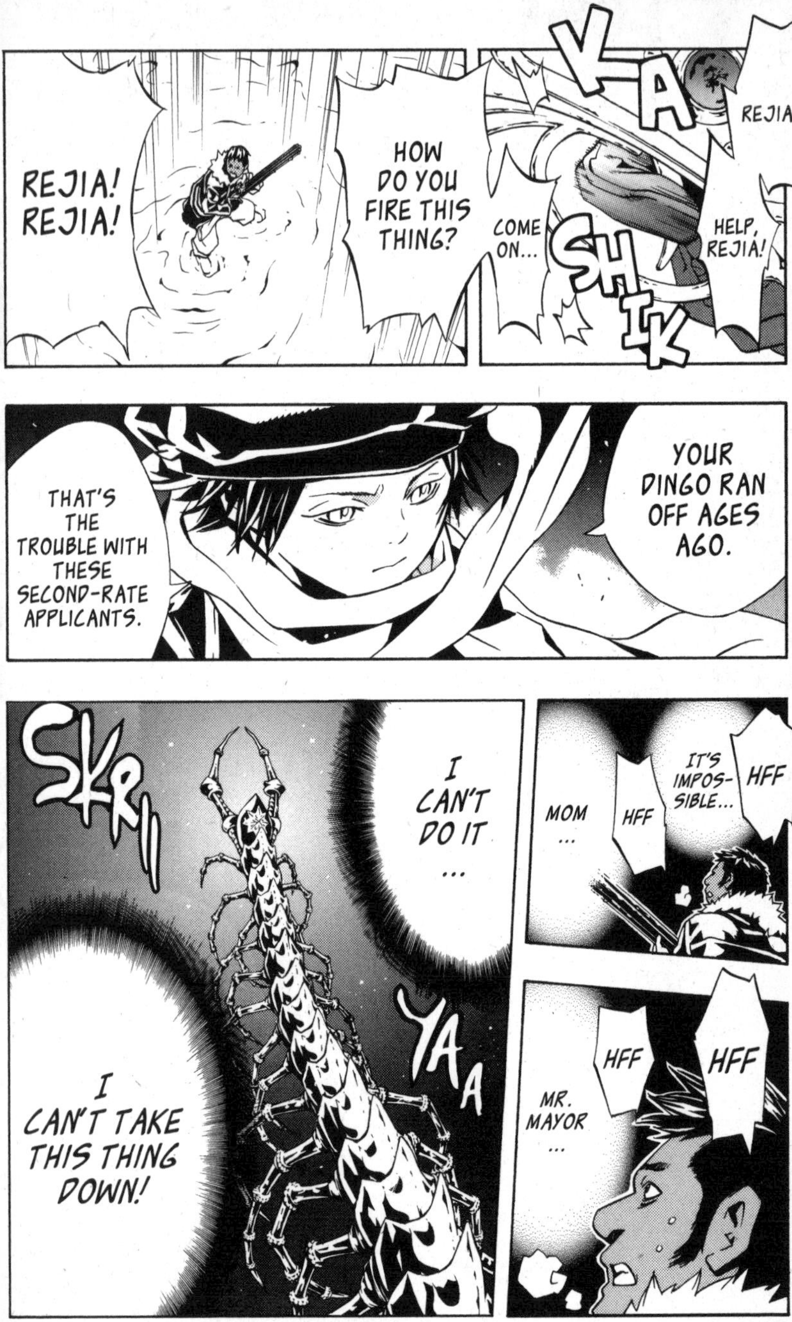
KA
REJIA!
HELP, REJIA!
COME ON...
SHIK
HOW DO YOU FIRE THIS THING?
REJIA! REJIA!
YOUR DINGO RAN OFF AGES AGO.
THAT'S THE TROUBLE WITH THESE SECOND-RATE APPLICANTS.
HFF
IT'S IMPOSSIBLE...
HFF
MOM...
HFF
HFF
MR. MAYOR...
I CAN'T DO IT...
SKRII
YAAA
I CAN'T TAKE THIS THING DOWN!

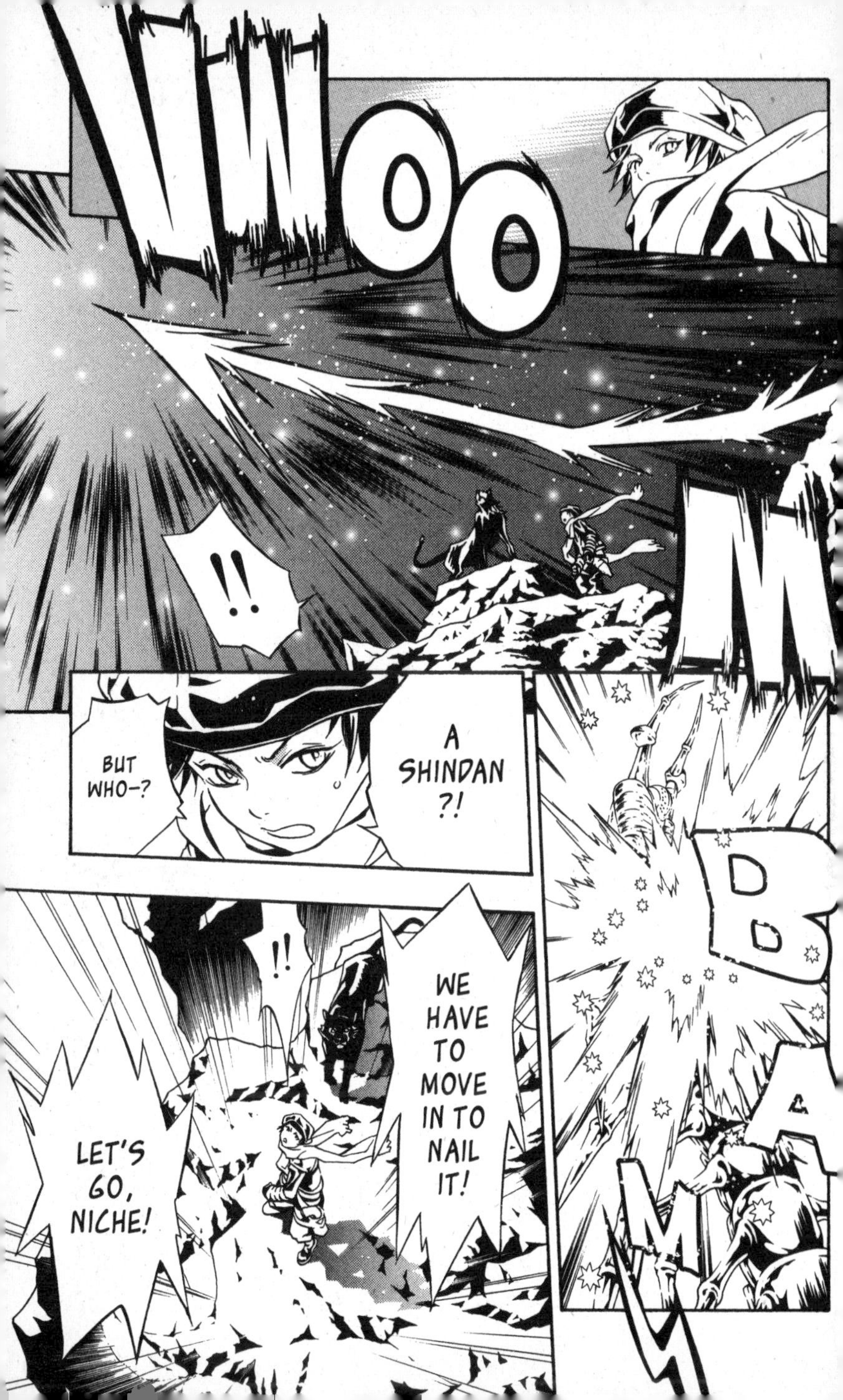
WHOOM
!!
BAM
A SHINDAN ?!
BUT WHO-?
!!
WE HAVE TO MOVE IN TO NAIL IT!
LET'S GO, NICHE!

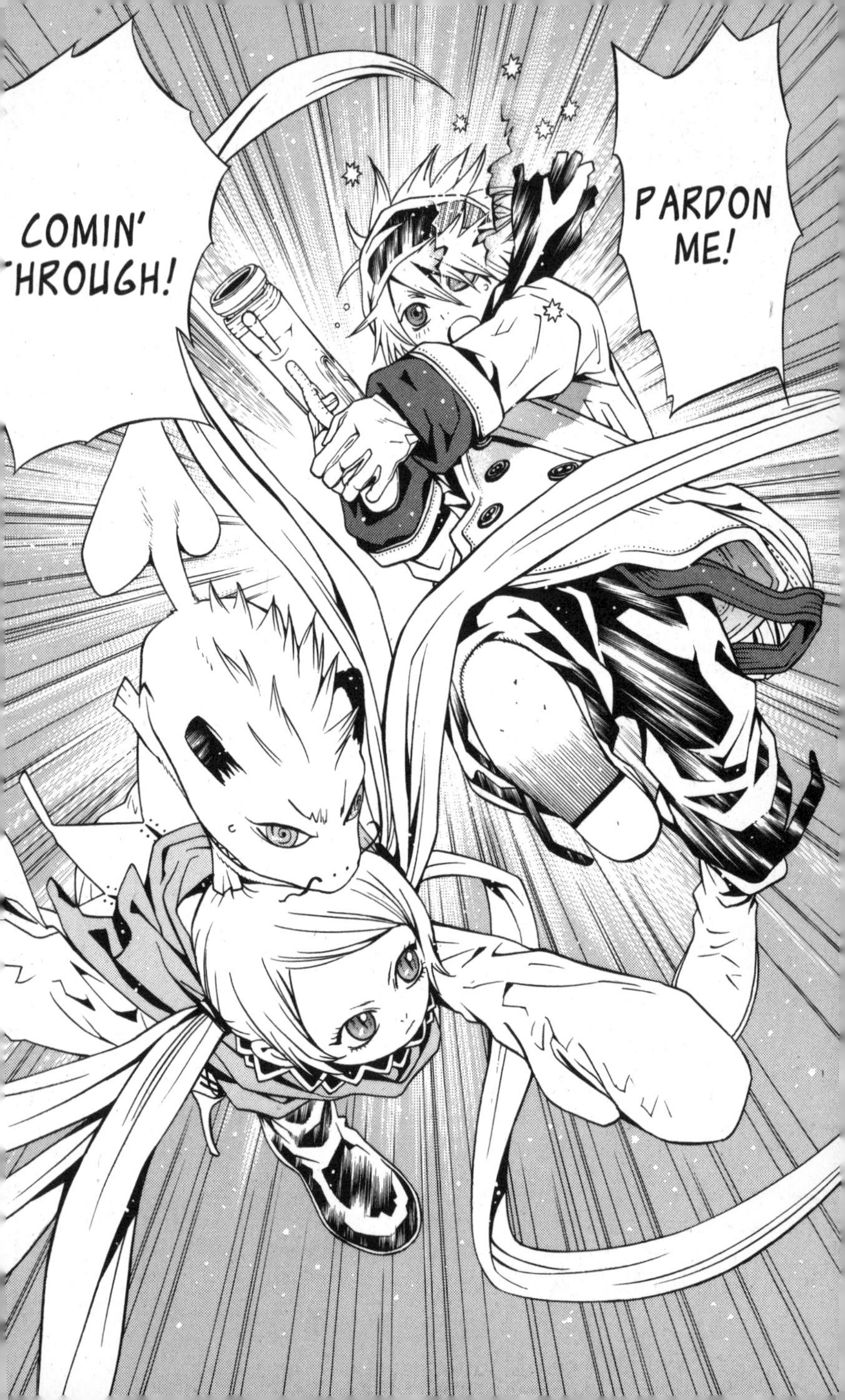
PARDON ME!
COMIN' THROUGH!

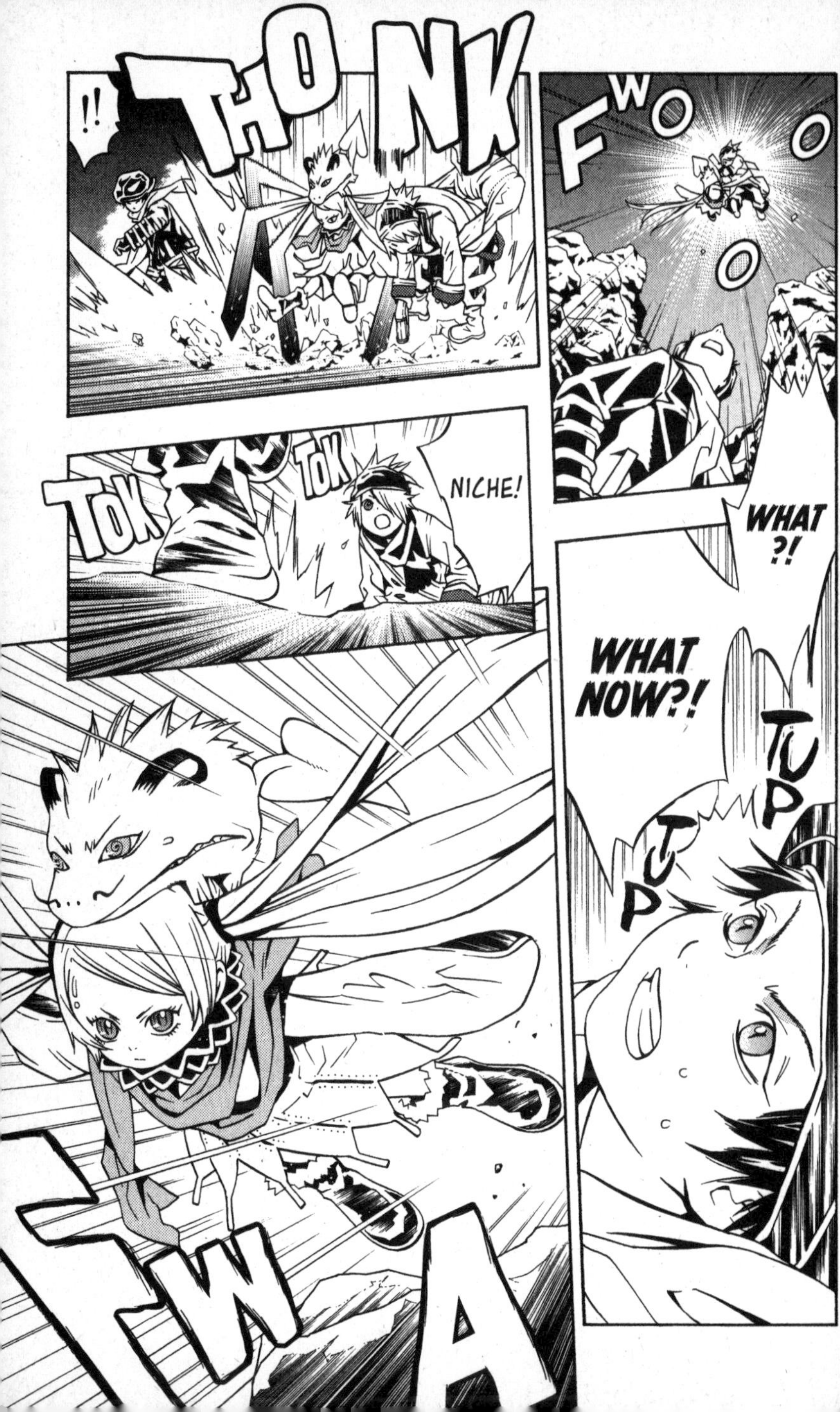
FWOOOO
THONK
!!
NICHE!
TOK
TOK
WHAT?!
WHAT NOW?!
TUP
TUP
TUP
TWA

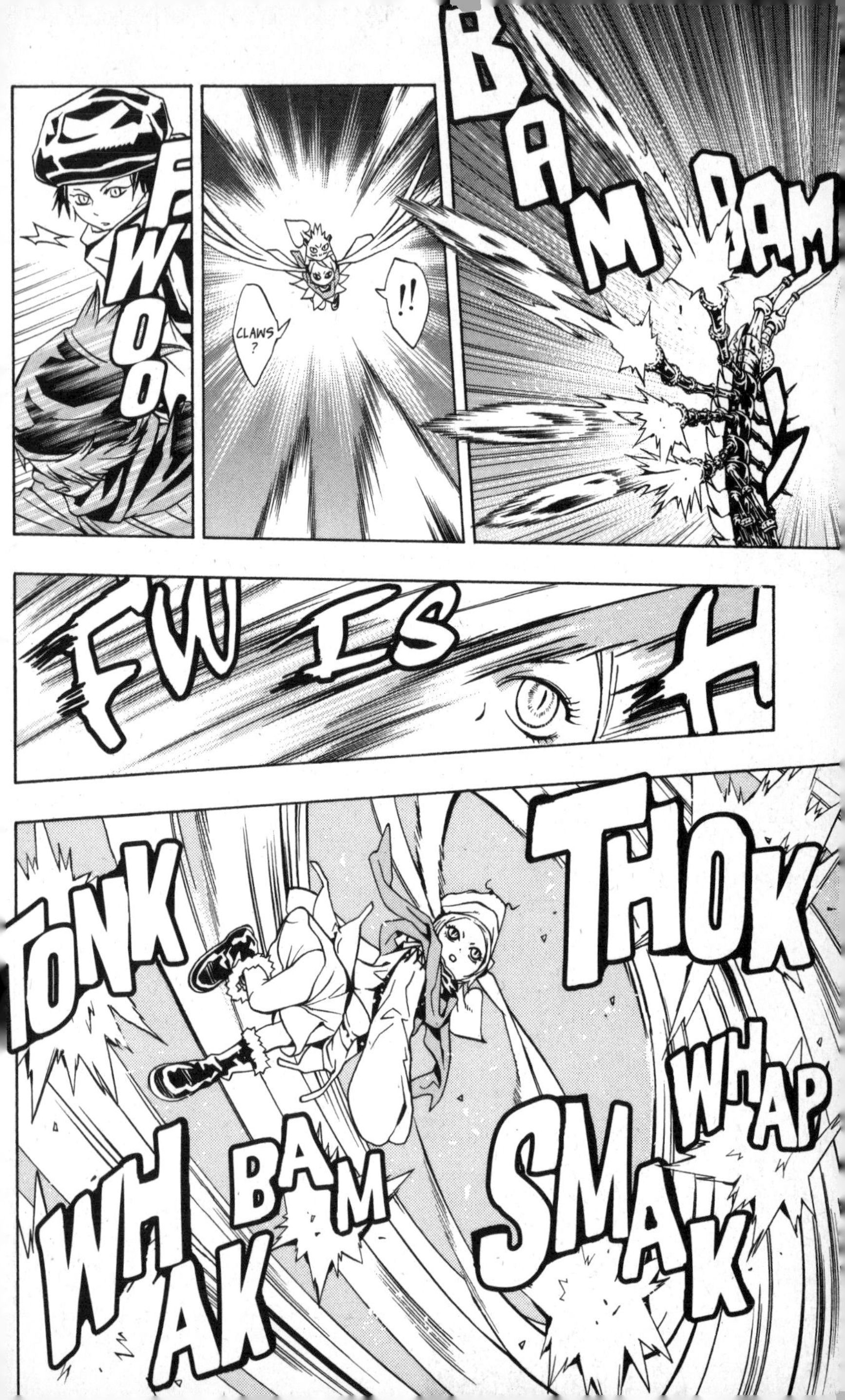
BAM
BAM
!!
CLAWS?
FWOOO
FWISH
THOK
TONK
WHAP
SMAK
BAM
WHAK

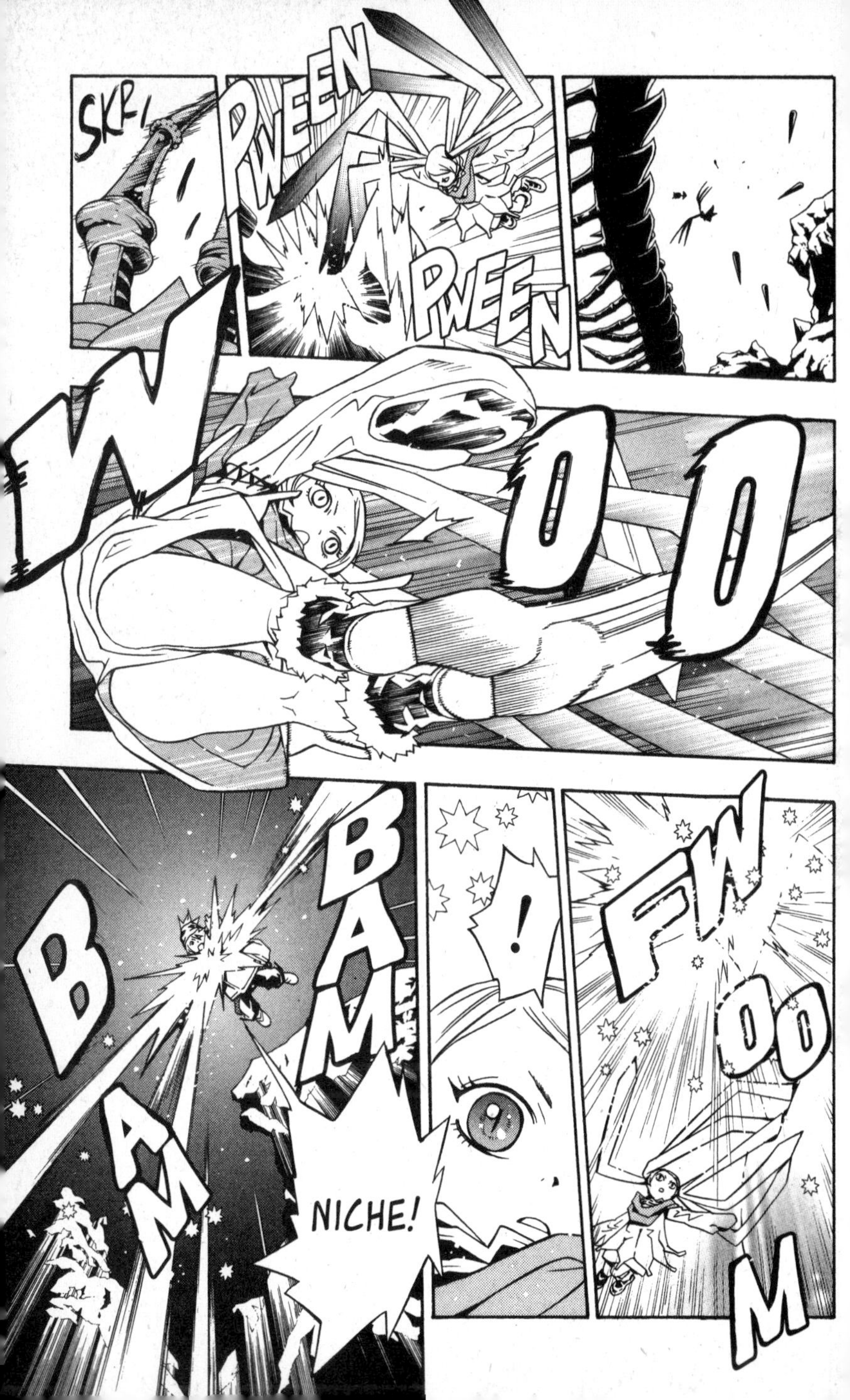

PWEEN
PWEEN
SKRI
WOO
FWOOM
!
BAM
BAM
NICHE!

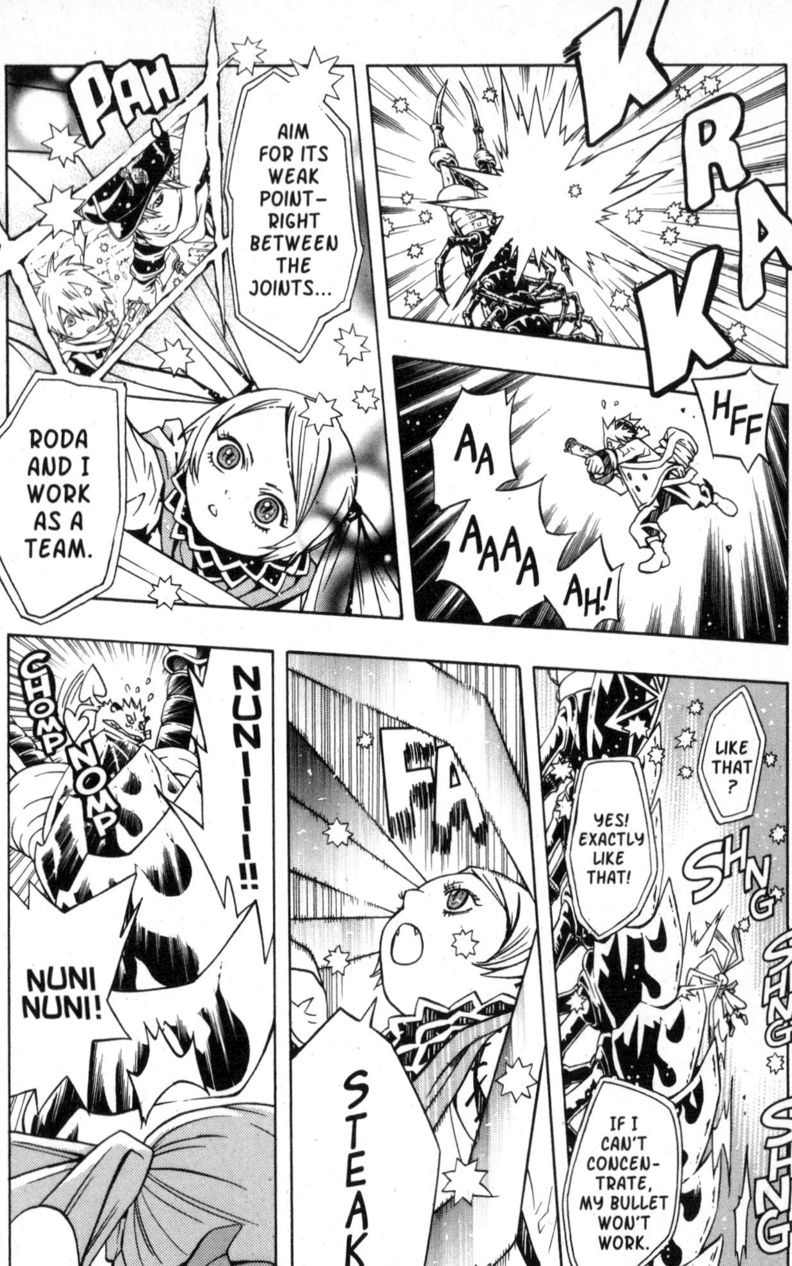
KRAKA
HFF
AAAAAAH!
PAH
AIM FOR ITS WEAK POINT- RIGHT BETWEEN THE JOINTS...
RODA AND I WORK AS A TEAM.
LIKE THAT?
YES! EXACTLY LIKE THAT!
SHNG
SHNG
SHNG
IF I CAN'T CONCEN- TRATE, MY BULLET WON'T WORK.
FA
STEAK!
NUNIIIIII!!
CHOMP NOMP
NUNI NUNI!
YES!

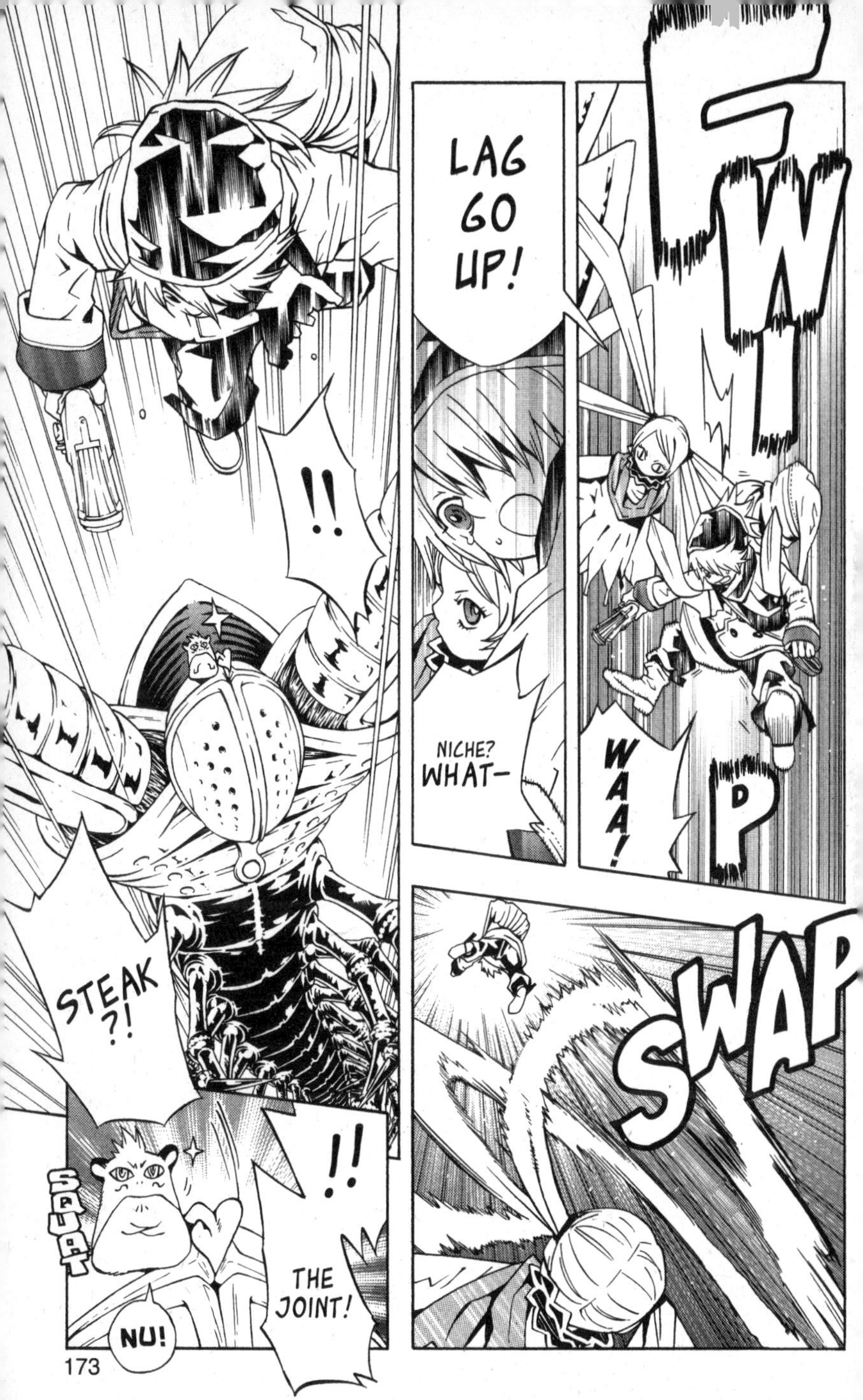
FWIP
WAA!
LAG GO UP!
NICHE? WHAT-
SWAP
!!
STEAK?!
!!
THE JOINT!
SQUAT
NU!

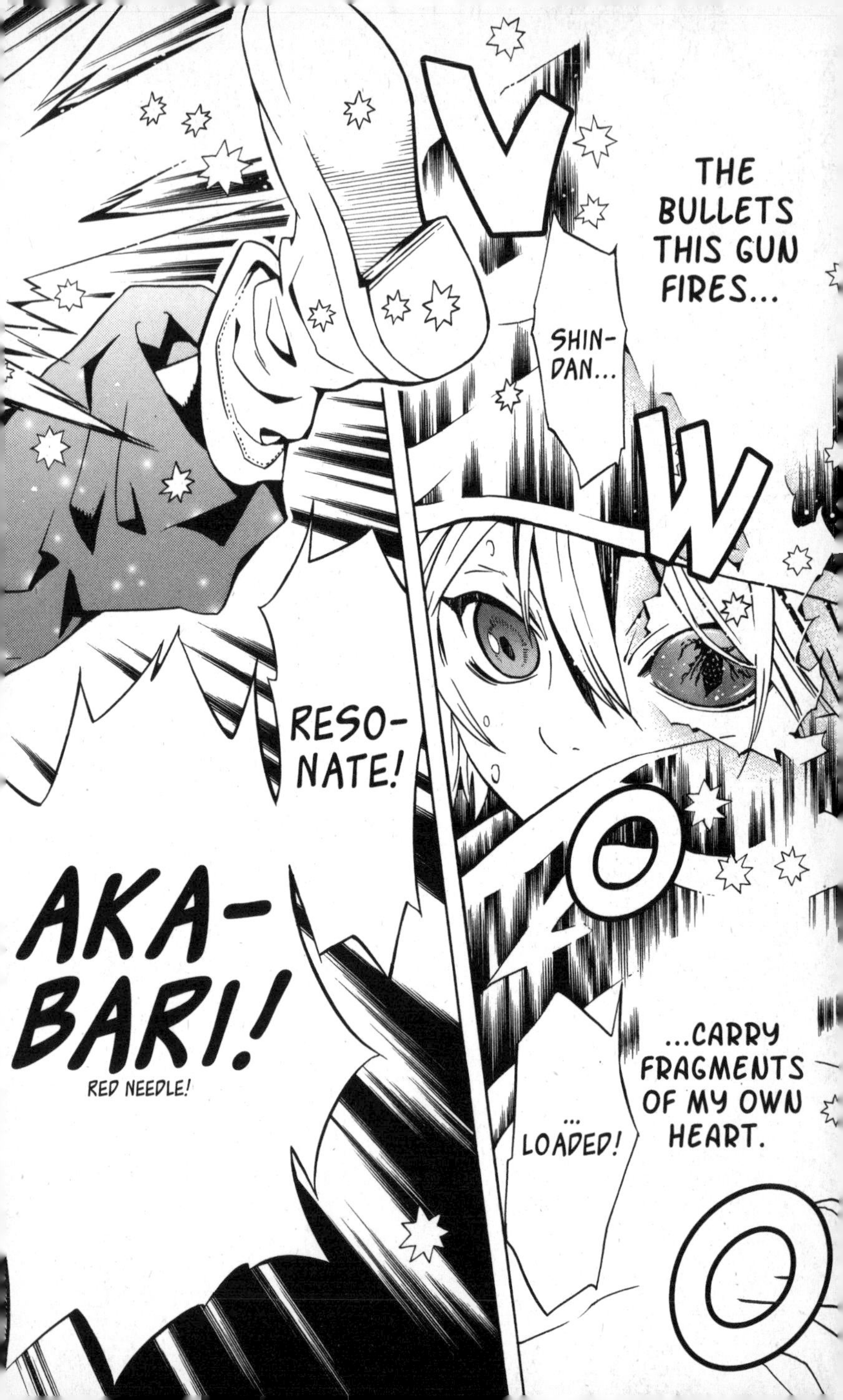
THE BULLETS THIS GUN FIRES...
SHIN-DAN...
VWOO
...CARRY FRAGMENTS OF MY OWN HEART.
...LOADED!
RESO-NATE!
AKA-BARI!
RED NEEDLE!

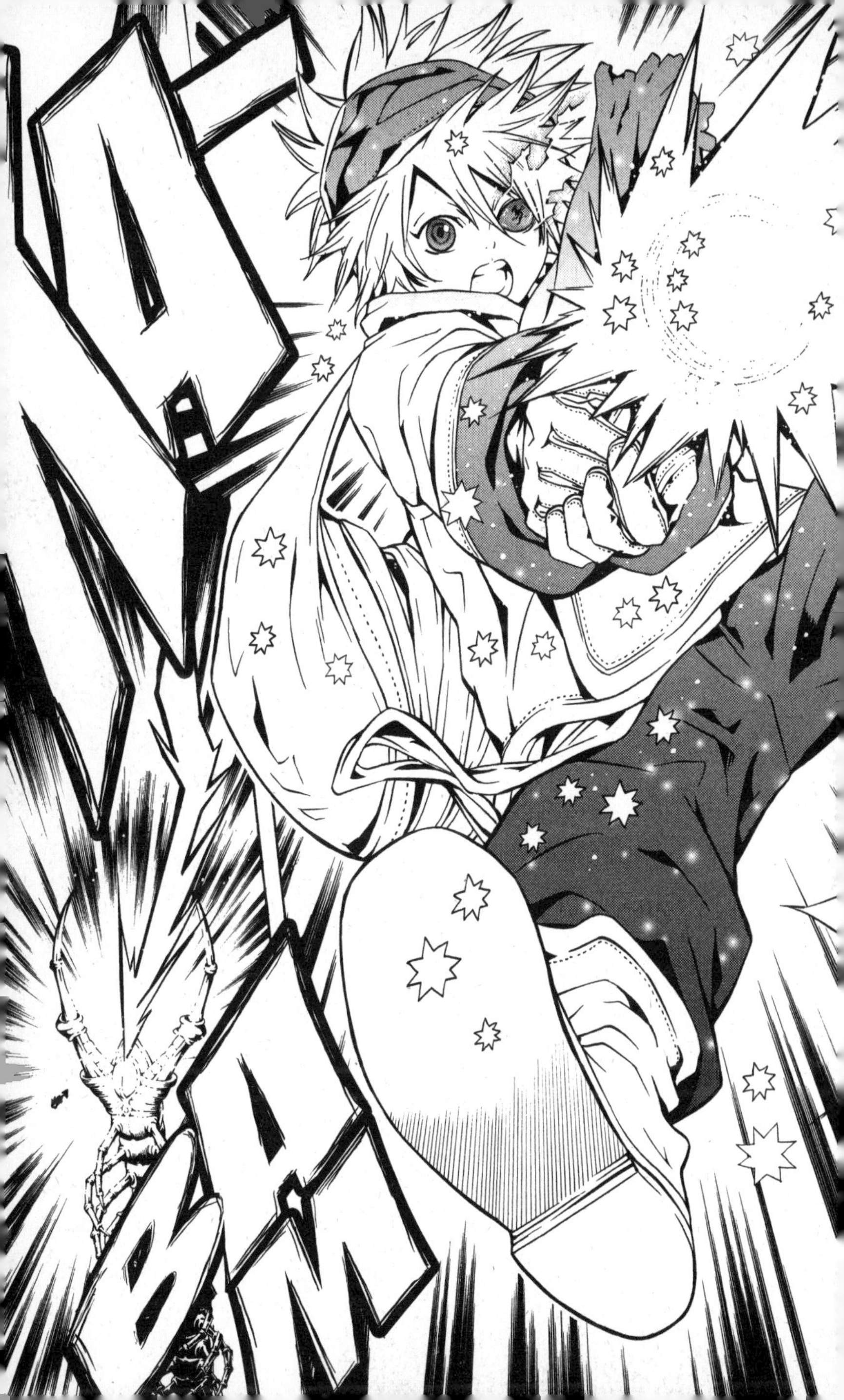
BAM

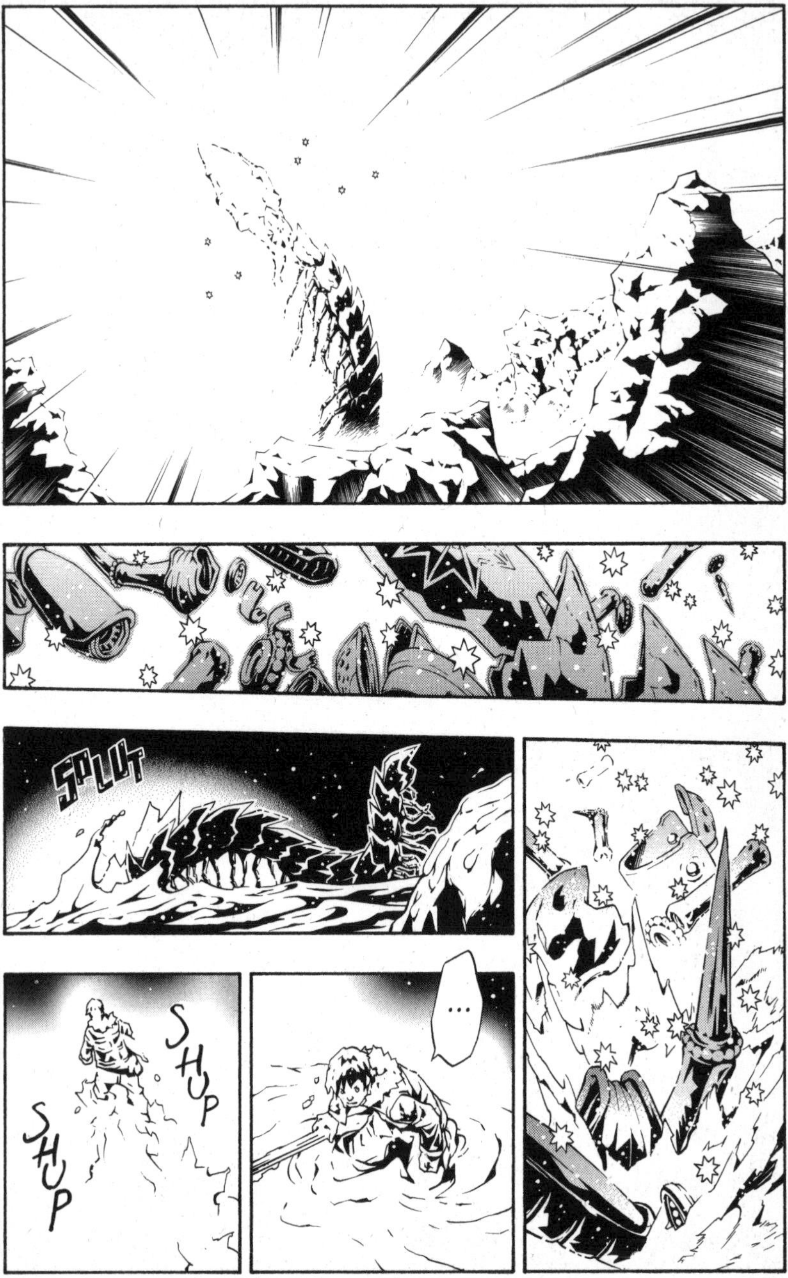
SPLUT
...
SHUP
SHUP

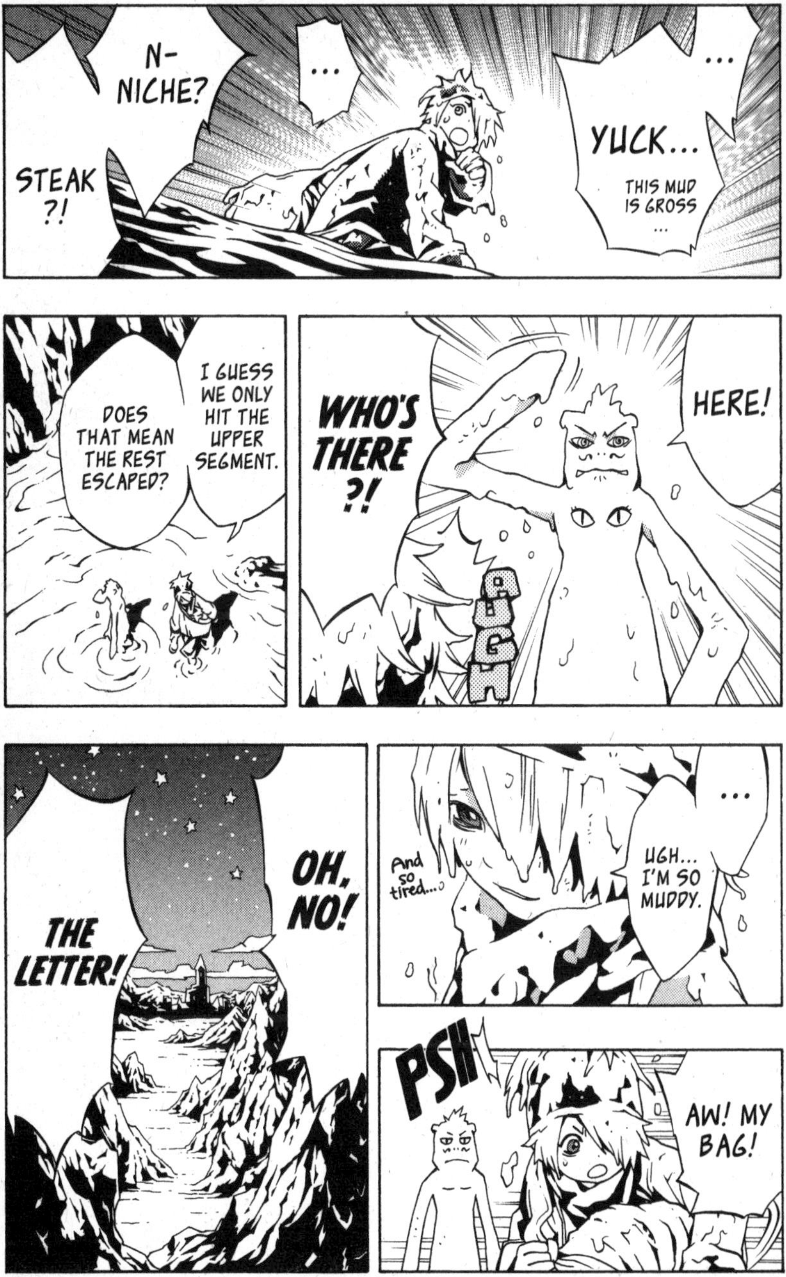
...
YUCK...
THIS MUD IS GROSS ...
...
N- NICHE?
STEAK ?!
HERE!
WHO'S THERE ?!
AUGH
I GUESS WE ONLY HIT THE UPPER SEGMENT.
DOES THAT MEAN THE REST ESCAPED?
...
UGH... I'M SO MUDDY.
And so tired...
AW! MY BAG!
PSH
OH, NO!
THE LETTER!

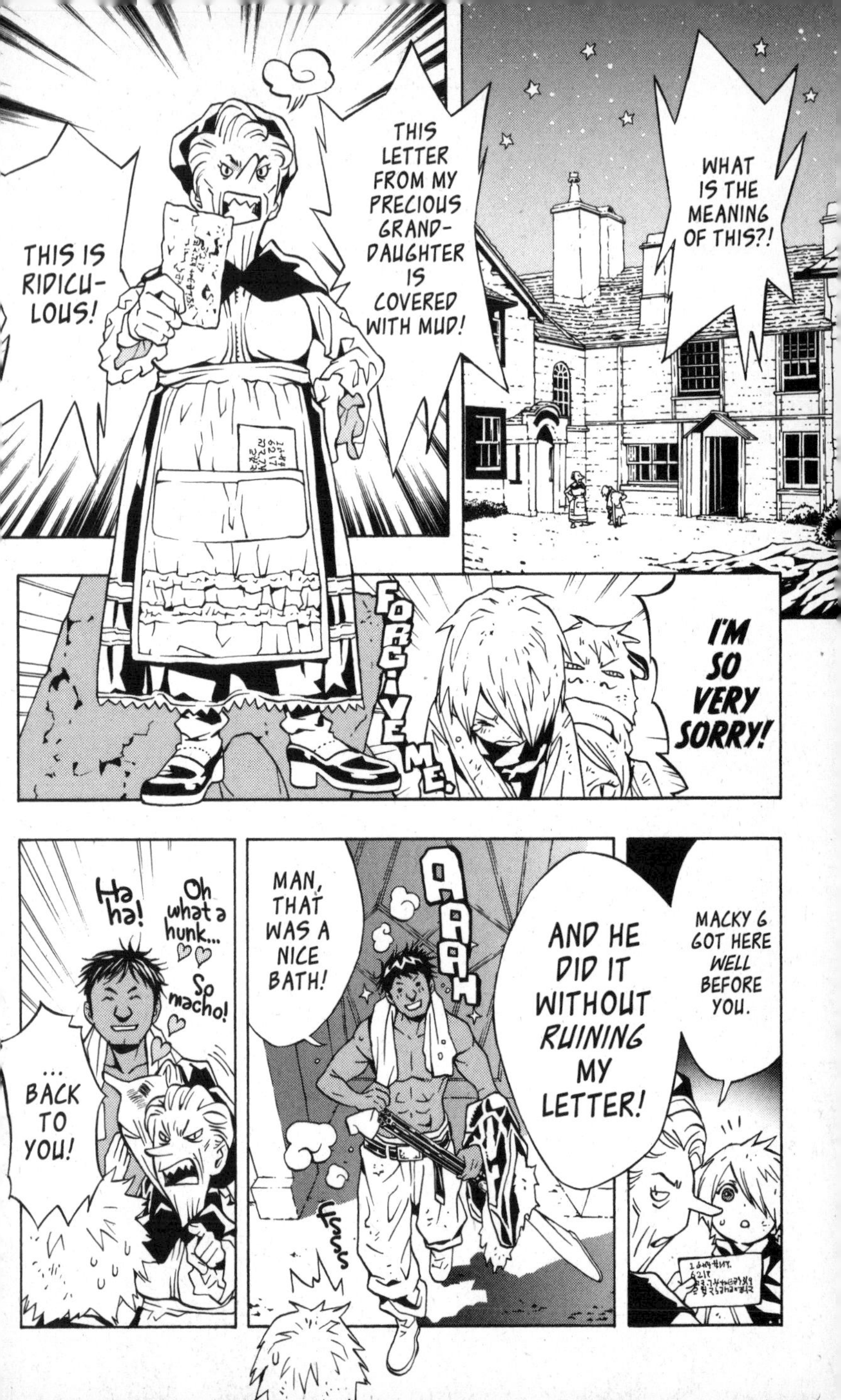
WHAT IS THE MEANING OF THIS?!
THIS LETTER FROM MY PRECIOUS GRAND-DAUGHTER IS COVERED WITH MUD!
THIS IS RIDICU-LOUS!
I'M SO VERY SORRY!
FORGIVEME.
MACKY 6 GOT HERE WELL BEFORE YOU.
AND HE DID IT WITHOUT RUINING MY LETTER!
AAAAH
MAN, THAT WAS A NICE BATH!
Oh what a hunk...
So macho!
Ha ha!
... BACK TO YOU!

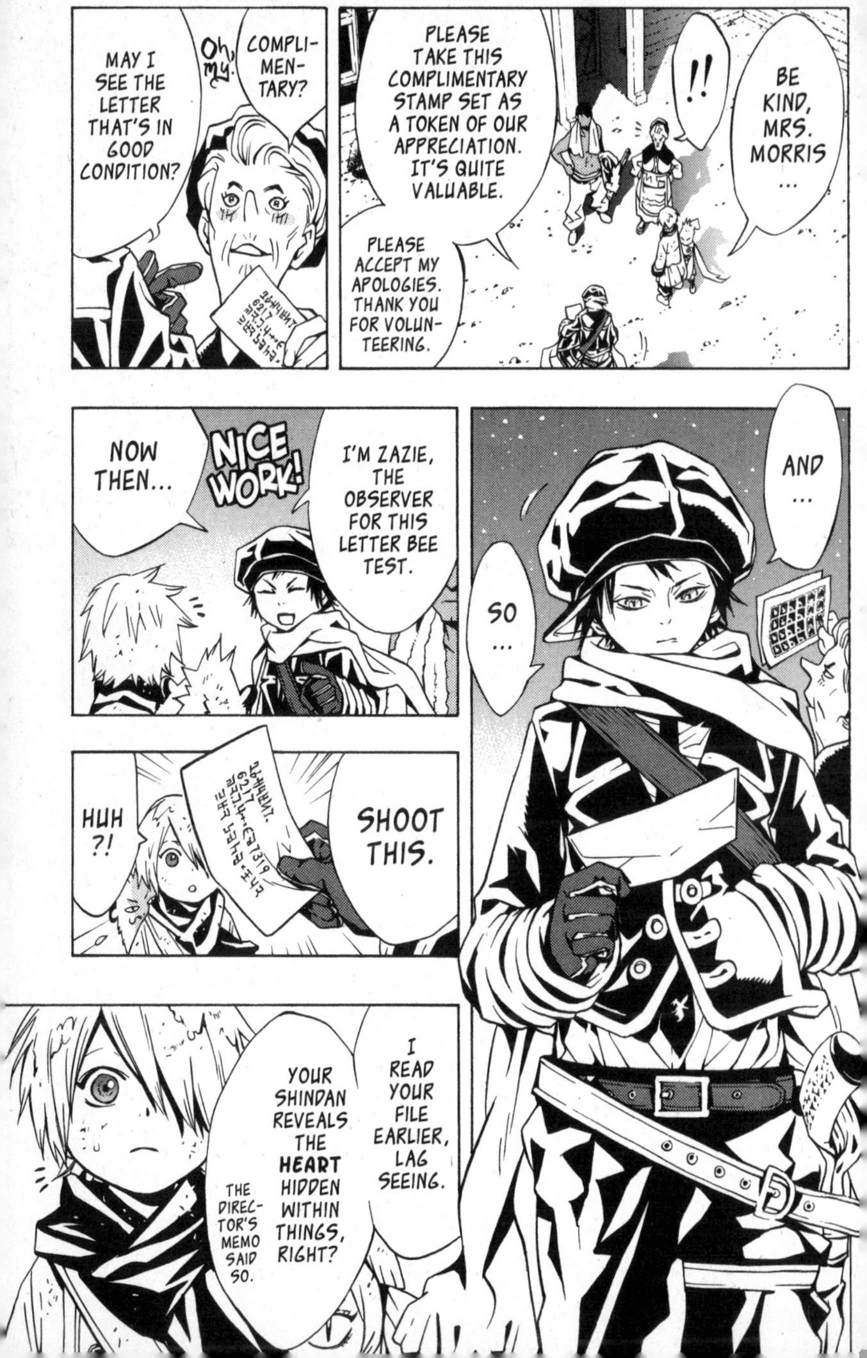
BE KIND, MRS. MORRIS...
!!
PLEASE TAKE THIS COMPLIMENTARY STAMP SET AS A TOKEN OF OUR APPRECIATION. IT'S QUITE VALUABLE.
PLEASE ACCEPT MY APOLOGIES. THANK YOU FOR VOLUNTEERING.
COMPLIMENTARY?
Oh, my.
MAY I SEE THE LETTER THAT'S IN GOOD CONDITION?
AND...
SO...
I'M ZAZIE, THE OBSERVER FOR THIS LETTER BEE TEST.
NICE WORK!
NOW THEN...
SHOOT THIS.
HUH?!
I READ YOUR FILE EARLIER, LAG SEEING.
YOUR SHINDAN REVEALS THE HEART HIDDEN WITHIN THINGS, RIGHT?
THE DIRECTOR'S MEMO SAID SO.

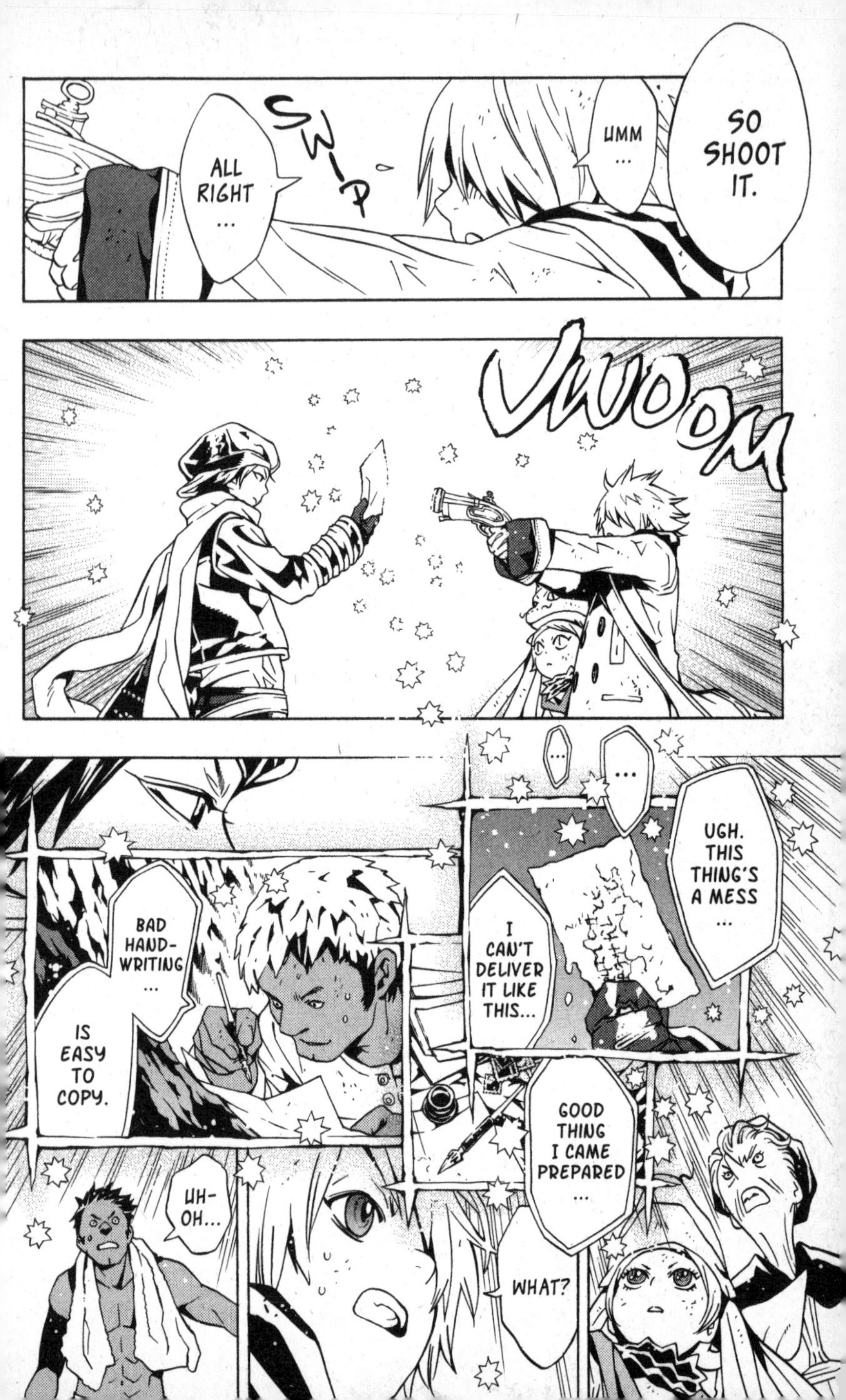
SO SHOOT IT.
UMM...
SWIP
ALL RIGHT...
JWOOM
...
...
UGH. THIS THING'S A MESS...
I CAN'T DELIVER IT LIKE THIS...
BAD HAND-WRITING...
IS EASY TO COPY.
GOOD THING I CAME PREPARED...
WHAT?
UH-OH...

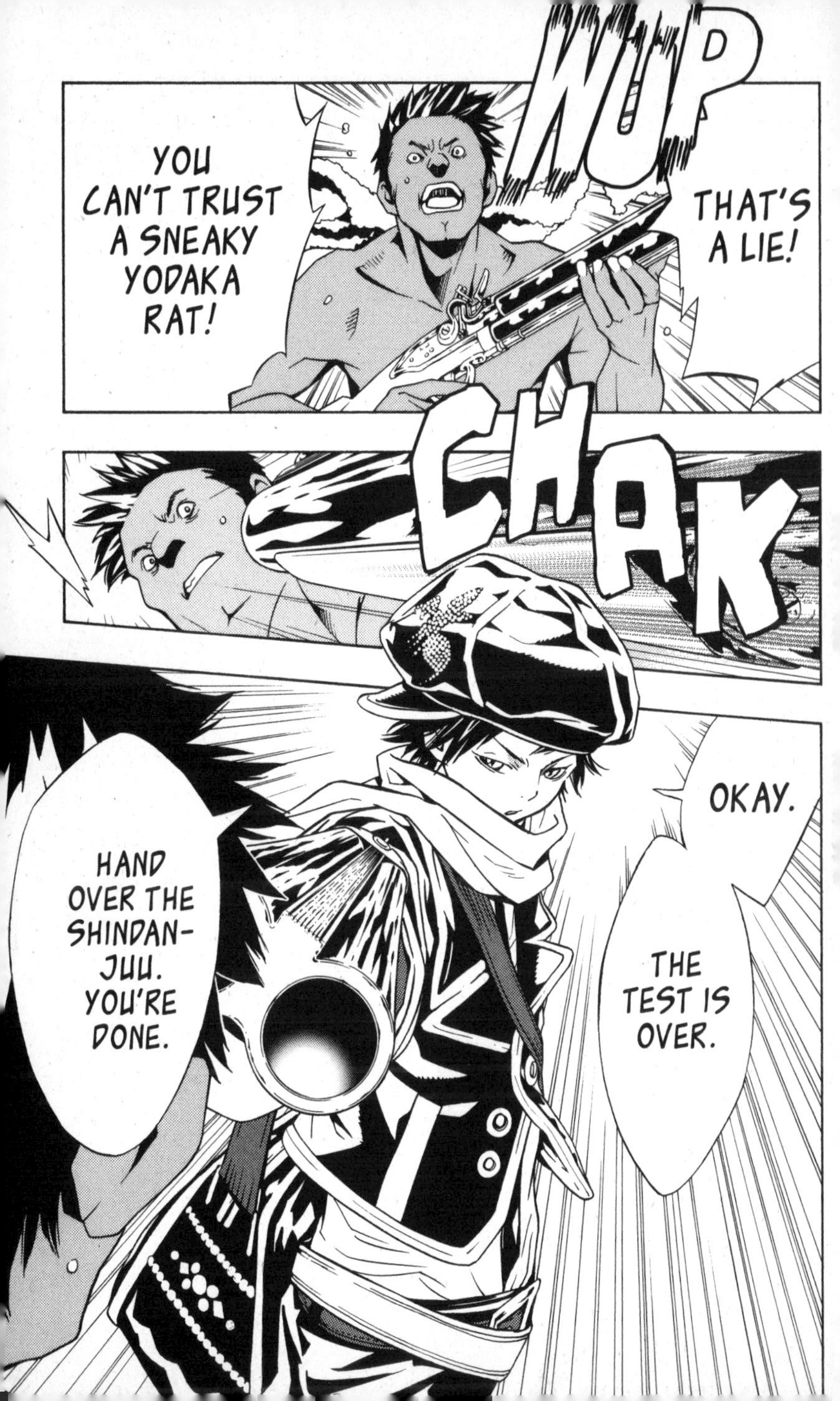
NUP
THAT'S A LIE!
YOU CAN'T TRUST A SNEAKY YODAKA RAT!
CHAK
OKAY.
THE TEST IS OVER.
HAND OVER THE SHINDAN-JUU. YOU'RE DONE.

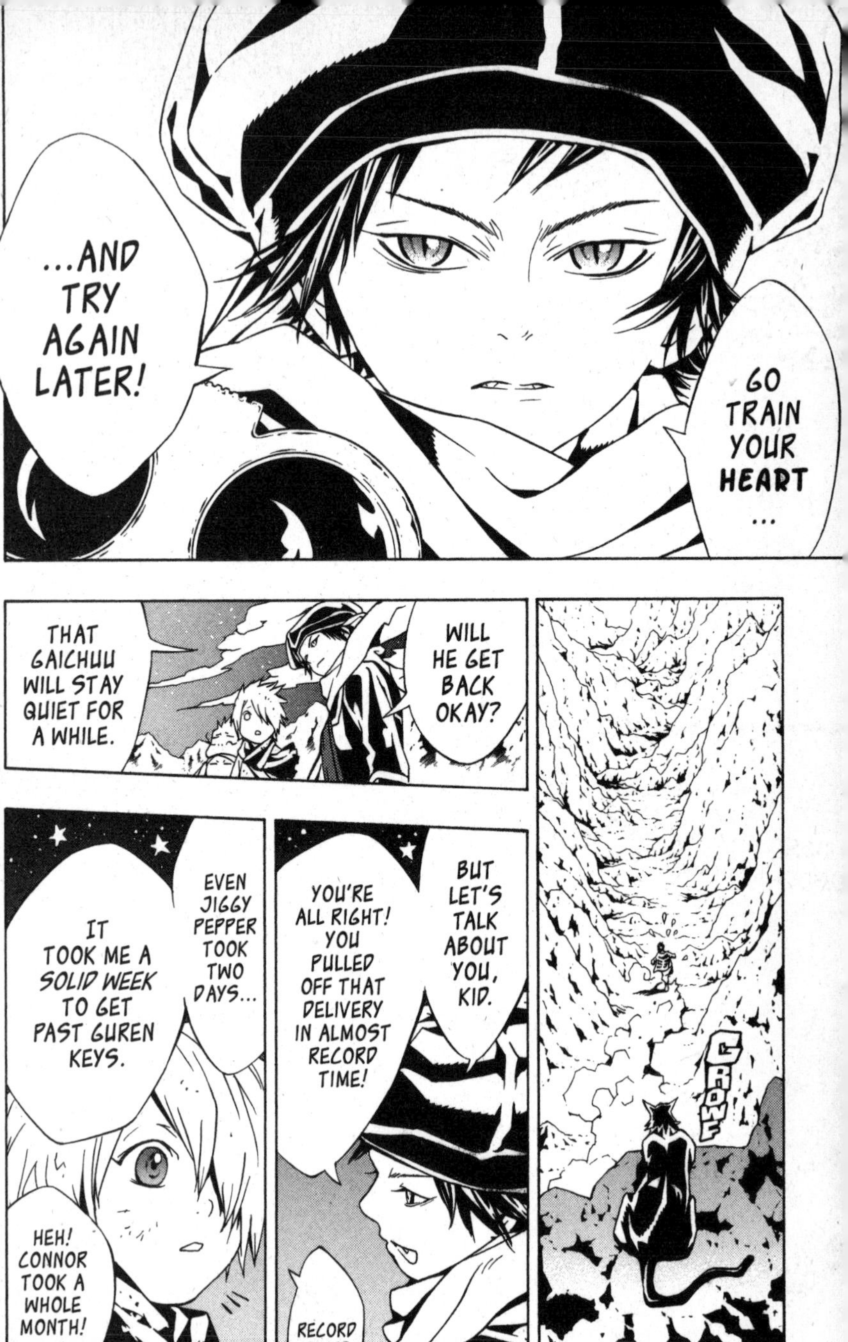
GO TRAIN YOUR HEART...
...AND TRY AGAIN LATER!
GROWF
WILL HE GET BACK OKAY?
THAT GAICHUU WILL STAY QUIET FOR A WHILE.
BUT LET'S TALK ABOUT YOU, KID.
YOU'RE ALL RIGHT! YOU PULLED OFF THAT DELIVERY IN ALMOST RECORD TIME!
RECORD TIME?
EVEN JIGGY PEPPER TOOK TWO DAYS...
IT TOOK ME A *SOLID WEEK* TO GET PAST GUREN KEYS.
HEH! CONNOR TOOK A WHOLE MONTH!

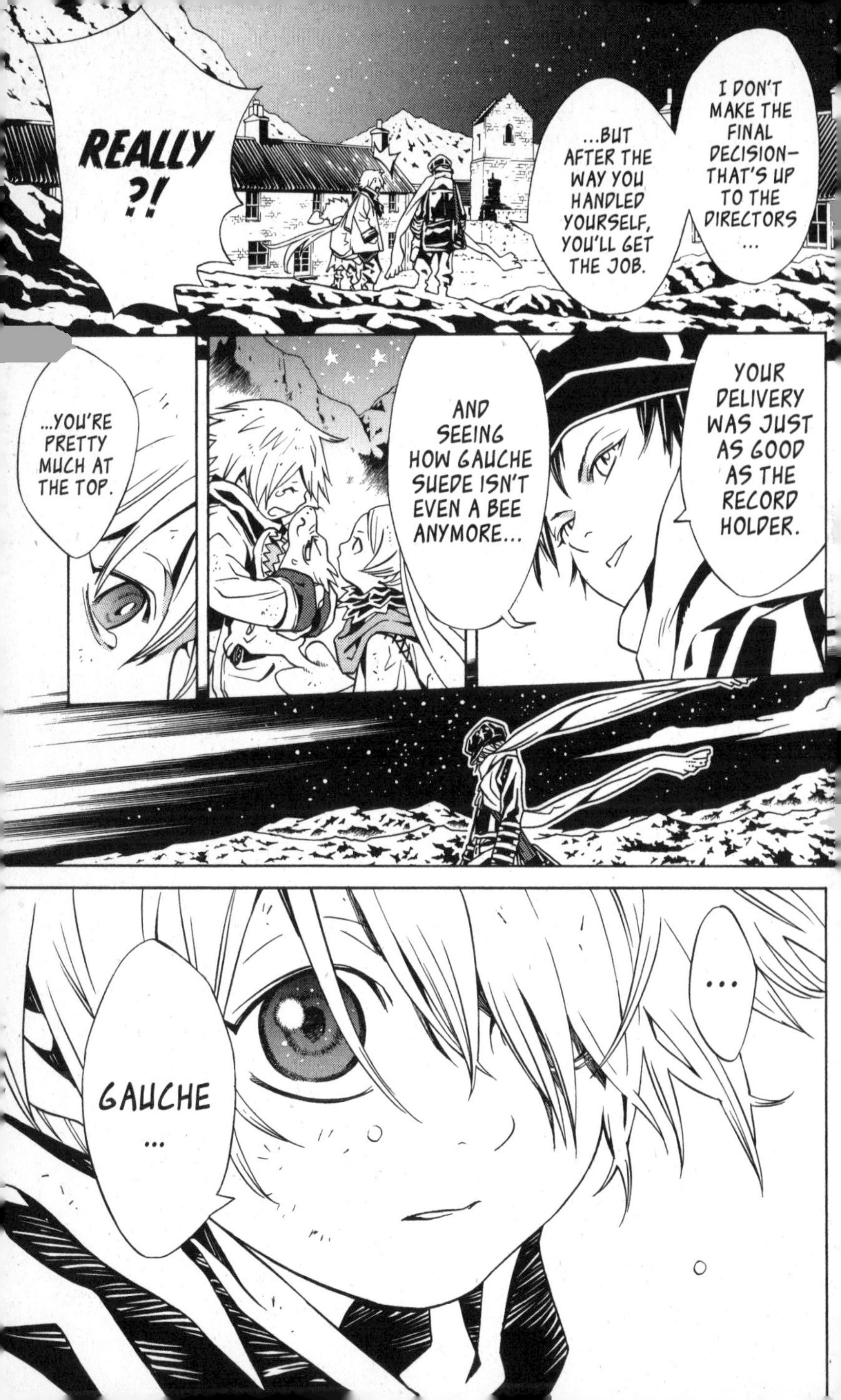
I DON'T MAKE THE FINAL DECISION—THAT'S UP TO THE DIRECTORS ...
...BUT AFTER THE WAY YOU HANDLED YOURSELF, YOU'LL GET THE JOB.
REALLY ?!
YOUR DELIVERY WAS JUST AS GOOD AS THE RECORD HOLDER.
AND SEEING HOW GAUCHE SUEDE ISN'T EVEN A BEE ANYMORE...
...YOU'RE PRETTY MUCH AT THE TOP.
...
GAUCHE ...

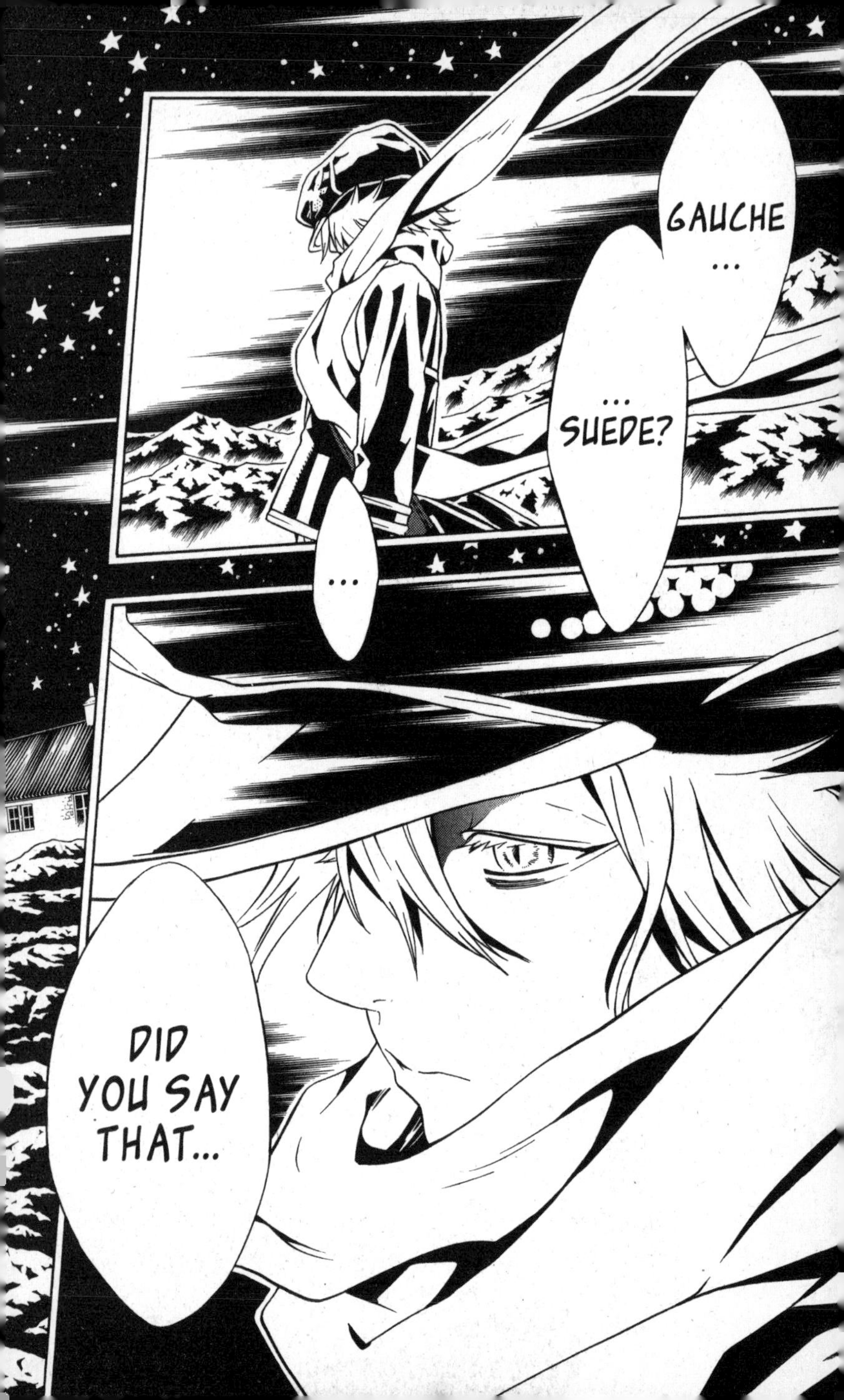
GAUCHE ...
... SUEDE?
...
DID YOU SAY THAT...

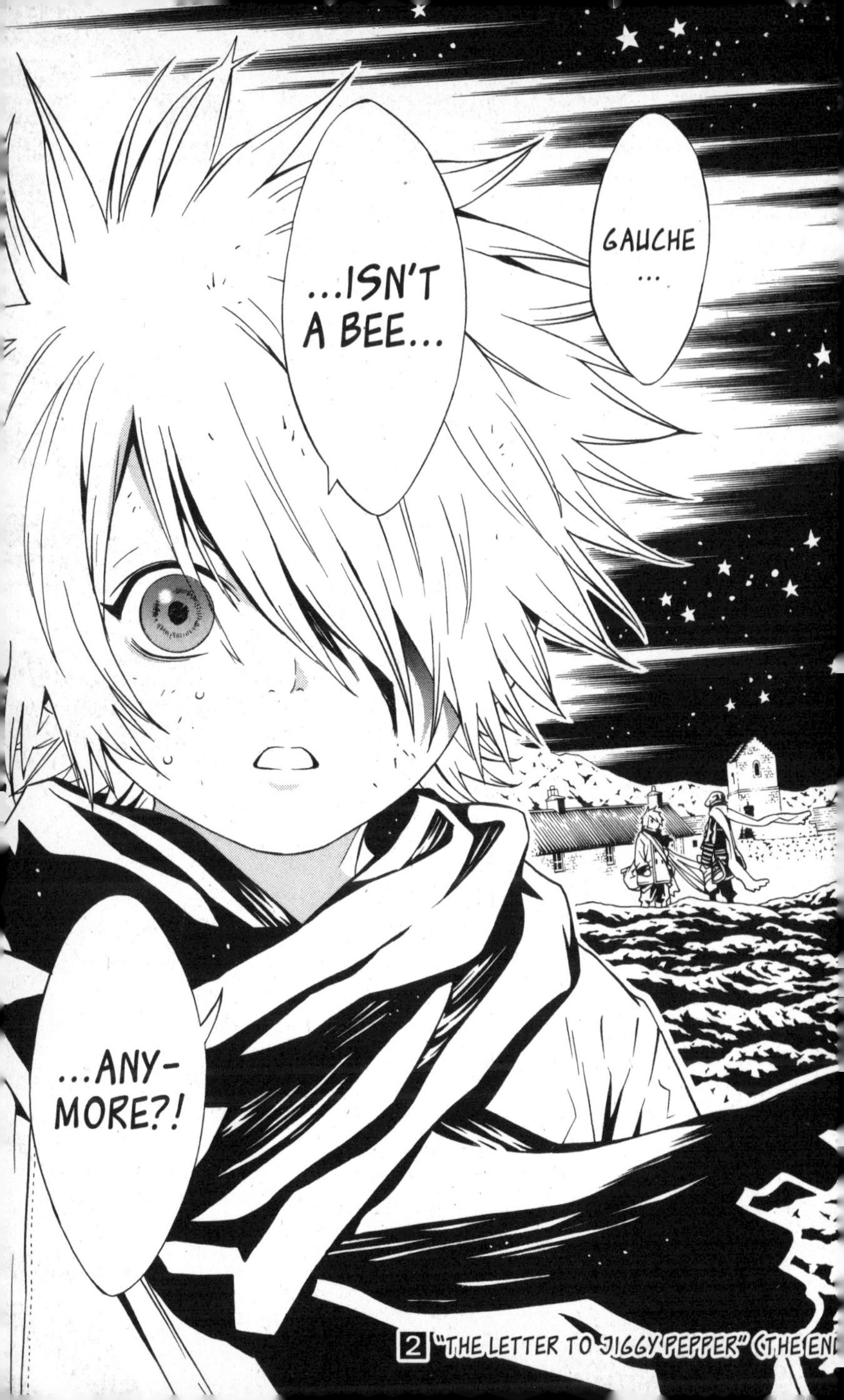
GAUCHE...
...ISN'T A BEE...
...ANY-MORE?!
2 "THE LETTER TO JIGGY PEPPER" (THE END

Dr. Thunderland's Reference Desk

I am Dr. Thunderland, presumably. "Presumably?" you say?

Well, I've yet to make a proper appearance in the series,
and I'm beginning to get a bad feeling about this.

But no! I must have faith. I'm sure that, soon enough, I shall
be a regular, like Gauche Suede. Oh, you must believe! Everyone
out there in the galaxy, grant me just a bit of your strength!

Now then, I work at the Beehive in Yuusari, spending my days researching
all manner of things. Presumably. For this lesson, I'd like to review
the information I've compiled about this world and its circumstances.

Not in any particular order, mind you. It's all such a bother, really.
Such a bother. I mean, I'm not even in this series. Yet.

■ THE TOWN OF KYRIE

Kyrie comes from Greek, meaning pity or compassion. It also appears in the first chorus of the Ordinary of the Mass: "*Kyrie eleison*," meaning "Lord, have mercy."

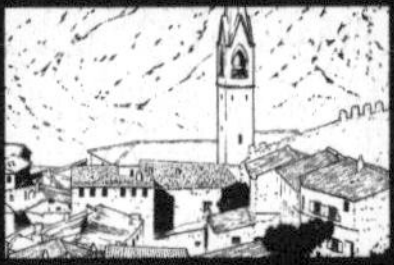

■ BIFROST

This bridge connects Yodaka to Yuusari. Very few people qualify to cross this bridge. A Crossing Pass is required to do so, and the government thoroughly investigates every applicant. The gatekeeper twins, Signal and Signales, use Spirit Amber in their pipes to produce a peculiar smoke that verifies the identities of the crossers. I wonder how they do it. And how long have they been the gatekeepers? They seem to have some former connection to the Director. Or maybe not.

nb: In Norse mythology, Bifrost is the rainbow bridge that links the human world with the realm of the gods. If you cross it, your wishes will come true.

nb: Bifrost's guardian Allonsy is named after the French expression *allons-y*, meaning "let's go."

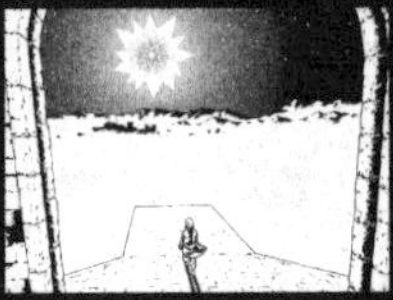

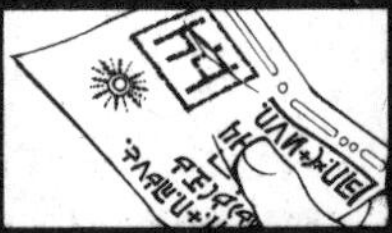

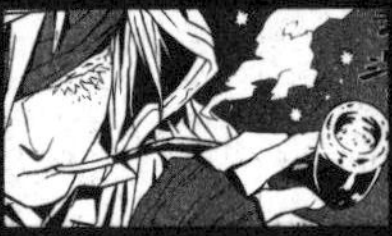

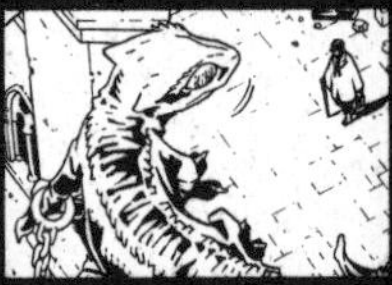

■ EXPRESS DELIVERY BEE

Just like in the formation of a Shindan, Jiggy Pepper uses the power of the Spirit Amber to catalyze his *heart* into fuel to power his steel horse. He is the only Express Delivery Bee. The drain on his *heart* must be incredible! He built his endurance in Kyrie, where he grew up an orphan. His perseverance and resilience gave him a rugged manliness that belies his age. Jiggy is essential to the Beehive because of his high-speed deliveries. His dingo, the bird of prey Harry, can convey messages by air. Harry also helps Jiggy navigate. Jiggy's so cool. Reminds me of a young me, really.

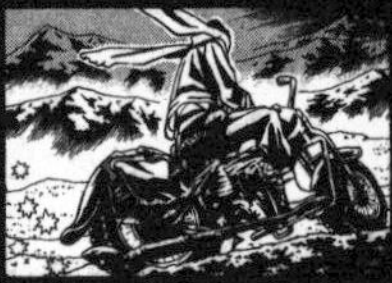

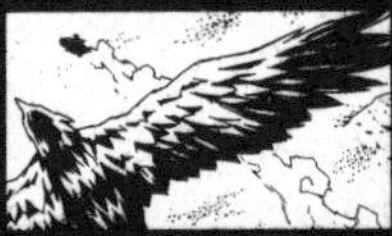

■ THE EMPRESS: ORGANIZED RELIGION

Amberground is ruled by the Empress, who "inherited the blood of gods." She is the most exalted figure in this region, the highest member of the church. You could say she embodies the religion itself. Icons of the Empress appear in churches and classrooms. I'll talk more about the Empress in the future.

■ CENTRAL YUUSARI

A large walled town that is the heart of Yuusari, even though it is actually quite close to Yodaka.

■ NOCTURNE ROW

The main street in Central Yuusari. You can find many craftsmen here, from cartographers to blacksmiths, as well as the bakery/arms dealership, Sinners. The curious cigarette that Director Lloyd chews on but never seems to light comes from the Pink Elephant Pharmacy. You can find anything you want on Nocturne Row.

■ BEEHIVE, 13 NOCTURNE ROW

Facing Nocturne Row, this is the only post office serving both Yuusari and Yodaka. It's the main headquarters for the Letter Bees. Many civil servants work here, as do I, presumably. This facility stores most of the equipment common to Letter Bees.

As you saw from Nelli's difficulties sending her little brother's letter, the postage rates here are prohibitively high. It's not unreasonable—Letter Bees risk their lives to make deliveries. The rate jacks up as soon as you hit the Bifrost Bridge. The delivery distance and cargo weight also affect the price. [continued on page 190]

When Gauche Suede delivered Lag Seeing from Coza Bel to Cambel Litus at the western tip of Yodaka, that was unbelievably expensive. I wonder who paid *that* postage. There are a few private postal services, but they add their own service fees, so whether you're sending a letter or signing for one, the Beehive is the most affordable way to go.

■ RASPBERRY HILL
True to its name, Raspberry Hill is both sweet and sour. The soil has a nasty taste. There must be another way back to town. Either that, or that old woman is stronger than any Gaichuu along the way.

nb: Macky G's name comes from McKay shoes, one of the early specimens of machine-produced footwear sold during the U.S. Civil War. They were vulnerable to rain and didn't hold up for long-distance walking.

Route Map

Finally, I'm including a map created by the lovely people at the Lonely Goatherd Map Station in Central Yuusari.

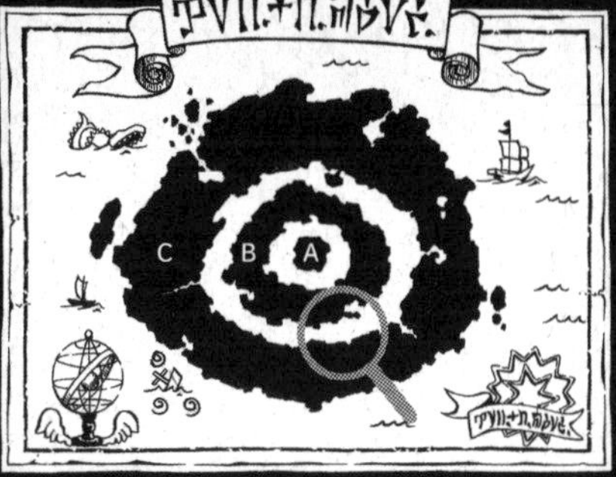
C
B
A

A: Akatsuki B: Yuusari C: Yodaka

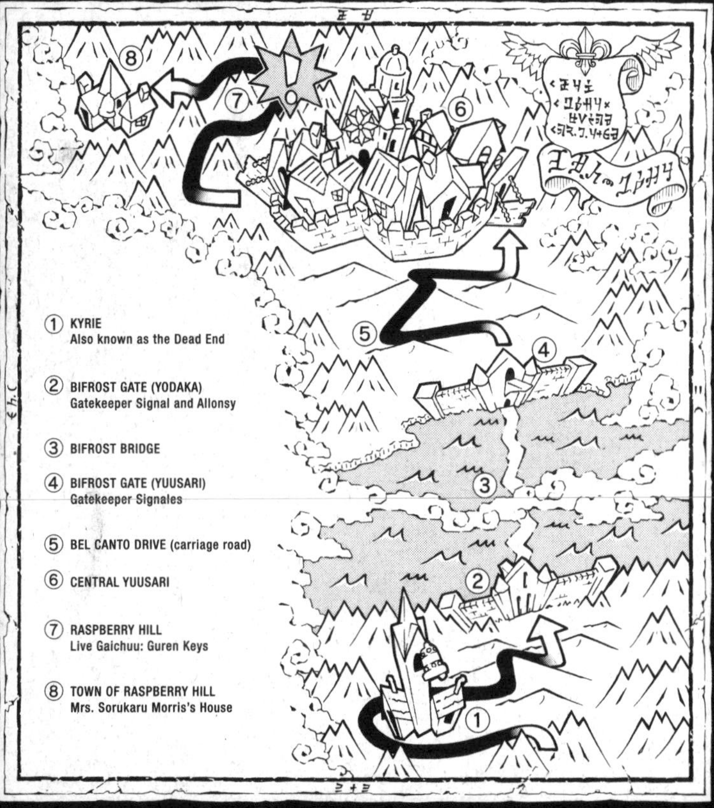
① KYRIE
Also known as the Dead End
② BIFROST GATE (YODAKA)
Gatekeeper Signal and Allonsy
③ BIFROST BRIDGE
④ BIFROST GATE (YUUSARI)
Gatekeeper Signales
⑤ BEL CANTO DRIVE (carriage road)
⑥ CENTRAL YUUSARI
⑦ RASPBERRY HILL
Live Gaichuu: Guren Keys
⑧ TOWN OF RASPBERRY HILL
Mrs. Sorukaru Morris's House

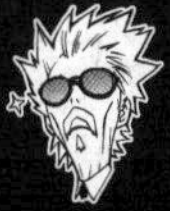

How was this lesson? Not tedious? Is anyone actually reading all of this? And while I'm at it, am...ahem...am I ever going to make an appearance? Hm? Yes?

Volume 2

SHONEN JUMP Manga Edition
This manga contains material that was originally published in English in
SHONEN JUMP #79–83.

Story and Art by Hiroyuki Asada

English Adaptation/Rich Amtower
Translation/JN Productions
Touch-up and Lettering/Annaliese Christman
Design/Frances O. Liddell
Editor/Daniel Gillespie

VP, Production/Alvin Lu
VP, Sales & Product Marketing/Gonzalo Ferreyra
VP, Creative/Linda Espinosa
Publisher/Hyoe Narita

Published by VIZ Media, LLC
P.O. Box 77010
San Francisco, CA 94107

10 9 8 7 6 5 4 3 2 1
First printing, March 2010

www.viz.com

www.shonenjump.com

In the next volume...

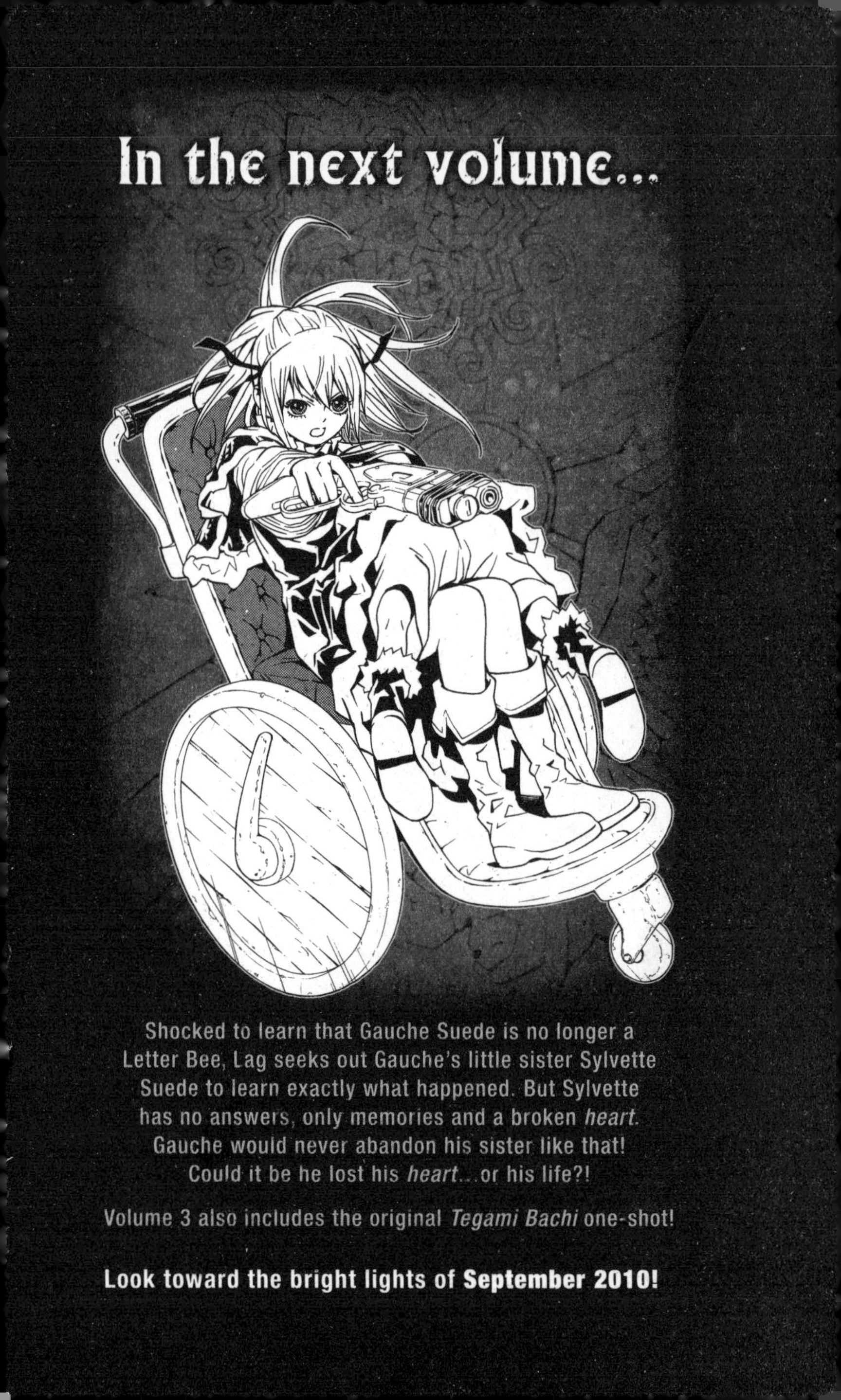

Shocked to learn that Gauche Suede is no longer a Letter Bee, Lag seeks out Gauche's little sister Sylvette Suede to learn exactly what happened. But Sylvette has no answers, only memories and a broken *heart*. Gauche would never abandon his sister like that! Could it be he lost his *heart*...or his life?!

Volume 3 also includes the original *Tegami Bachi* one-shot!

Look toward the bright lights of September 2010!